D0893705

When Wall Street
Met Main Street

WHEN WALL STREET MET MAIN STREET

The Quest for an Investors' Democracy

JULIA C. OTT

HARVARD UNIVERSITY PRESS
Cambridge, Massachusetts
London, England
2011

Library of Congress Cataloging-in-Publication Data

Ott, Julia C., 1974-
When Wall Street met Main Street : the quest for an investors' democracy /
Julia C. Ott.
p. cm.
Includes bibliographical references and index.
ISBN 978-0-674-05065-5 (alk. paper)
1. New York Stock Exchange—History.
2. Securities industry—United States—History.
3. Securities—United States—History.
4. Wall Street (New York, N.Y.)—History.
I. Title.
HG4572.O87   2011
332.64'273—dc22   2010047293

For Richard Vermillion
and our girls

Contents

The Quest for an
Investors' Democracy

O N the afternoon of December 30, 1899, the members of the New York Stock Exchange assembled on the trading floor to revel in their notoriety. Amidst yuletide greenery, incandescent lights, and showers of confetti, the Seventh Regiment band struck a lively tune. "Two colored pugilists" disguised as a bull and a bear traded blows in a makeshift ring. When the bull scored a knockout, NYSE members boisterously debated whether the bear had thrown the fight. Frenzy erupted as confetti, bonbons, and red rubber balls rained down from the gallery. Brokers lobbed the balls at the heads of bald brethren. Hapless traders found themselves hooded, "hands seized from behind," as colleagues "buffeted" them about the floor. The bedlam only abated when former Rough Rider Charles Knoblauch auctioned a "bull, a bear, and a lamb, and as is usually the case when they are dealt with by brokers, the lamb was turned away as worthless." Some prankster had already removed his tail. (His fate could have been worse. In the next year's Christmas festivities, balloons fashioned from bladders and labeled "The Fatted Calf" were snatched by members "who proceeded to kill them in the most approved style"). The bear fetched $100, the bull, $200. Carousing then concluded with "a cakewalk."[1]

As those who owned seats on the nation's leading securities exchange fell in line for their "grotesque march," they scarcely could have imagined that the lambs—outsider investors of modest means—soon would have their day. Like most Americans at century's turn, the assembled traders and brokers

understood the stock market as suitable only for those persons with substantial means. Cherishing independent producers and production, most
Americans believed that bond- or stockholders warranted little consideration in economic theory or policy. Between 1900 and 1934, however, first
economic theorists and reformers, next policy makers and the wartime state,
then corporations, and finally financial institutions identified the small investor as an object of serious concern. Whereas less than 1 percent of the
population owned stocks or bonds at the time of the brokers' bash, approximately one-third of the population (34 million Americans) purchased some
form of federal bond during World War I. Roughly one-quarter of U.S.
households (an estimated 8 million) owned shares in a publicly traded corporation by 1929.[2] In the three decades following the frolic on the floor, securities investment traveled from the margin to the mainstream of economic
and political life in the United States—where it would remain. At the close
of the next century, the majority of U.S. households owned corporate
stock.[3] Neoliberal economic theory—entrenched within both political
parties—recommends that government take a hands-off approach to the
economy, espouses the maximization of shareholder value as the key aim
of corporate and government policy, and champions financial markets as
the optimal mechanism for allocating economic resources and risk.[4] The
financial calamities that began in 2007 failed to discredit these assertions
and only strengthened the tendency to regard stock prices as real-time in-
dicators of corporate and national economic performance.

This remarkable turnaround in Americans' involvement with and perceptions of financial securities and markets could not have been foreseen
by members of the Exchange or by members of the public observing from
the gallery as the nineteenth century faded into history. Since the founding
of the Republic, Americans for the most part had viewed financial securities,
the individuals who traded bonds and stocks, and the private associations
(like the NYSE) that administered securities exchanges as antithetical to
their most cherished economic ideals, political values, and savings practices. Popular economic thought held that economic value derived from
diligent labor and steadfast thrift—qualities utterly absent in the scuffle of
the stock exchanges' trading floors. American political culture identified
ownership and control of real property as the foundation of a citizen's
virtue and independence, of his investment in the nation. Bonds, stocks,
and the malefactors who traded them seemed to imperil this ideal of proprietary democracy. The lure of speculative riches subverted the ethic of
work and thrift; it diverted capital from productive pursuits. Financial
securities appeared to be related only indirectly to the way in which the
vast majority of individuals and firms saved or raised money. Even so,

stocks and bonds facilitated the massive turn-of-the-century corporate mergers that seemingly threatened to replace independent proprietors with hordes of unskilled, propertyless wage-laborers. Accordingly, throughout the nineteenth century, reformers of all stripes—from Jeffersonians and Jacksonians to Populists, anti-monopolists, socialists, and organized labor—denounced the Exchange as the tool of unaccountable, dishonest, rapacious elites.

In their New Year's revel, Stock Exchange members symbolically conceded the charges levied against them. Outrageous bids offered for worthless toys affirmed the perception that stock and bond prices bore scarce relation to intrinsic economic value. The bout of brutes verified that contests between "bulls" (those traders who schemed to drive prices up) and "bears" (those who conspired to drive prices down) in fact drove oscillations in securities prices. The music of the Seventh Regiment, manned by the sons of the wealthiest New Yorkers, marked the financial securities markets as an elite province. Indeed, as members cast the mangled lamb from their auction, they acknowledged that those few NYSE firms that offered brokerage service to outsiders of modest means both cheated and disdained those sorry dupes. With their closing cakewalk, the brokers recapitulated countless representations of the securities markets. Bulls, bears, and sometimes lambs chased one another in an endless, futile round. Stock and bond prices rose. Stock and bond prices fell. However furious these fluctuations, they contributed little to productive enterprise and signified nothing to the vast majority of Americans.[5]

By 1934, practices and perceptions on the part of both Stock Exchange members and the public had changed dramatically, and permanently. Looking back on the Great Bull Market of the late 1920s, financial journalist Alexander Noyes recollected that demand for corporate stocks had known "neither geographical nor social bounds," while any "expression of disapproval or skepticism" about the stock market provoked accusations that the critic "was trying to discredit or stop American prosperity." The securities of publicly traded corporations attracted the savings of a wide range of individuals, not just institutions or the very wealthy; these companies dominated the national economy. Indeed, securities investment had become so central to economic and political life that New Deal financial reforms enacted in the wake of the Great Crash of 1929 recognized the desirability of mass investment. New legislation conceded that securities markets possessed the ability to self-regulate, requiring only minimal state oversight. These assumptions would continue to shape ideas about the permissible scope and purpose of economic regulation into the twenty-first century.[6]

After 1900, then, Americans' relationship with—and beliefs about—financial securities and markets were transformed. Corporate need for capital did not call forth popular demand for financial securities spontaneously. The origins of this revolution can be traced to those individuals and organizations that promoted mass investment in the first three decades of the twentieth century: economic reformers and writers, policy makers and government agencies, groups of citizens, and select corporations and financial institutions. Those that promoted investment in financial securities did not view mass investment as a particularly efficient or profitable means of raising capital. Political concerns about public hostility toward corporate capitalism and the future of citizenship proved just as important for animating a host of projects to universalize securities ownership in the United States.[7]

After 1900, a range of intellectual, political, corporate, and financial leaders embarked on a quest to reorient the American political and economic system around universal investment in financial securities. In promoting the idea and the practice of mass investment, they aimed to address many of the most pressing concerns of their day. At the dawn of the twentieth century, industry and corporations eclipsed agriculture and individual proprietorship, raising questions about corporate power and accountability. Mounting economic inequality raised the specter of radicalism, while surging immigration, ethnic diversity, Jim Crow segregation, and women's demands for suffrage sparked fundamental debates about citizenship. Global war stoked anxiety over national unity. According to those who embraced the ideal of *investor democracy,* financial securities offered a tonic for these ailments that modernity inflicted upon the body politic. Mass investment could shore up the propertied foundations of citizenship, preserve economic mobility and autonomy, enhance national prosperity, and make corporations accord with the will of the people.

Progressive-era writers and reformers first recast the financial securities markets as an analog of political democracy and an instrument of economic justice in the years prior to World War I. Their vision of an investors' democracy first inspired the wartime state, then certain corporations, and finally some financial institutions to devise new strategies for the mass distribution of bonds, then stocks. In the War Loan drives of World War I, then in countless campaigns to mass-market corporate shares in the 1920s, distributors of bonds and stocks deployed the rhetoric and imagery of investor democracy, exhorting Everyman to seize hold of his political-economic "stake" in the form of a financial security. Diverse marketing initiatives reframed stocks and bonds as market-based solutions to the social instabilities wrought by industrial capitalism. Securities distributors overcame both their own ingrained business practices and public mis-givings in the first three decades of the twentieth century. The normative figure of the "small investor" encouraged the behavior it purported to describe.[8]

While all investor democrats—including theorists and policy makers along with leaders of corporations and financial firms—envisioned an economy and politics built around securities investment, disagreements arose beneath their capacious rhetorical umbrella. Champions of the investor democracy ideal disputed which securities were appropriate for Everyman. They fiercely debated what role the state should play in directing or regu-lating financial capital, in promoting universal investment, and in protect-ing the interests of citizen-investors. Investor democrats also disagreed on issues of corporate governance, that is, the allocation of authority and re-sources among parties to the corporation. At stake were essential questions about the distribution of economic power and the meaning of citizenship under modern capitalism.

By the end of the 1920s, one particular set of answers—an ideology of *shareholder democracy*—reigned supreme. Promulgated by leading corpora-tions, financial firms, and the NYSE, shareholder democracy ideology found fertile soil in a postwar political climate that grew increasingly inhospitable to government intervention in the economy. It elevated stockowners in mat-ters of corporate governance and economic policy. It pitted mass investment *against* regulation, the welfare state, and labor unions. Shareholder demo-crats urged Americans to renounce the state as an agent for managing eco-nomic risk or allocating economic resources. Universal acquisition of corpo-rate stock via *unregulated* securities markets could accomplish key social goals—individual security and opportunity, macroeconomic prosperity and stability—in a far more efficient and democratic manner, they pledged. Jazz Age stock marketers upheld the maximization of shareholder value as a proper—even primary—goal of state and corporate policy. Even so, they rejected corporate governance and securities market reform—indeed, any notion that the state owed citizen-shareholders any measure of protection. And although 1920s shareholder democrats promised class harmony, they aimed to preserve prevailing hierarchies of economic wealth and power.

The positioning of mass investment against the regulatory and welfare state proved neither inevitable nor enduring. A range of early twentieth-century economic reform programs also looked favorably upon the notion that universal investment could bring corporations in line with democratic political traditions. Even some labor and consumer activists endorsed the project to universalize investment, while progressives raised the banner of investor democracy to demand federal oversight of financial markets and corporate governance on behalf of outsider investors. Ultimately, this very logic bore fruit in New Deal securities regulation.

Versatility broadened the appeal of investor democracy. Ubiquitous claims about the potential for mass investment to revivify democracy and to democratize capitalism—issued from across the political spectrum—provided the context in which a remarkable number of Americans acquired bonds and stocks for the first time. The notion of investor democracy resonated with a generation that struggled to reconcile preindustrial political idealizations of individual property-ownership with modern economic and social realities, yet remained as skeptical of enlarged government as they were of large corporations. Securities distributors and their ideological allies tapped deep-seated fears and fascinations as they retrofitted the time-honored ideal of proprietary democracy with stocks and bonds. After all, investor democrats conceded that industrial corporate capitalism would undermine democracy if citizens lost all connection to property ownership. Financial securities' lingering association with affluence and privilege only enhanced their allure.[9]

Popular receptivity toward investment, then, depended as much upon evolving political thought as it did upon innovations in marketing. Enduring social concerns and political values, shifting cultural norms, the interrelation between government and private-sector institutions, and conflict over economic policy—not merely corporate demand for capital or the aggregate effect of rational individuals striving to maximize their wealth—all of these factors contributed to the first sustained incidence of mass investment in the United States.[10] Of course, fraud and hype pervaded Jazz Age stock marketing, while novice investors of the period certainly displayed a great deal of gullibility and greed. But the broad ideological theme of investor democracy provides a richer context for understanding why stocks and bonds began to make sense to a significant number of Americans for the first time.[11]

This development marked a critical juncture not only in the history of the financial securities markets, but in popular economic thought and political culture as well. In their marketing and public relations campaigns, early twentieth-century securities distributors interjected into the most critical political debates of their day. They endeavored to capture and revise an inherited political vocabulary—at once potent and protean—in light of changing economic and social circumstances. The abstract and intangible nature of financial securities made them effective conduits for an ideology that redefined political liberty and economic equity in terms of securities ownership.[12] Despite the Great Crash of 1929 and the financial turmoil of the early twenty-first century, the notion that a culture of widespread investment confirms the democratic nature of American capitalism endures.

So does the belief that financial markets and institutions constitute the overarching framework of a free enterprise system.[13]

THE phenomenon of mass investment and the notion that financial securities markets afford a realm for the exercise of individual freedom and hold the potential to democratize corporate capitalism did not materialize in reaction to the New Deal, during the Cold War, or with the 1990s dot-com craze. Rather, those seeking regulatory reform of corporations and securities markets first dreamed of an investors' democracy in the early years of the twentieth century. The corporations and financial institutions that promoted stock ownership in the 1920s did so as they engaged in a larger struggle to achieve legitimacy and to maintain autonomy against an expanding state. During the Great Bull Market of the late 1920s, distributors of corporate stock established and promulgated core economic precepts of modern conservatism. The ideology of shareholder democracy embedded in Jazz Age stock marketing did not, at first, *reflect* the existence of a sizable class of corporate shareholders. Rather, it aimed to foster mass investment in the hopes of discrediting modern liberalism, even before the New Deal. Ironically, the ability of these institutions to enlarge the shareholding class in the 1920s depended upon the federal government's successes in mass-marketing its debt and in reshaping popular attitudes toward securities investment during World War I.[14]

The early twentieth-century discussion of the "small investor" did not simply describe an existing population holding predetermined interests. Rather, it involved rhetorical claims meant to cultivate potential political allies. Corporations and financial institutions aimed to nurture political affinities and to shape political culture *through*—not just alongside—their pursuit of new sources of capital and profit. Economic elites did not surrender the reins of real economic power when they offered the middle and working classes access to instruments of corporate wealth. Nonetheless, the quest for an investors' democracy vindicated both publicly traded corporations and the financial securities markets. In consequence, individuals altered their savings preferences, banks and brokerages transformed their practices, and corporate and political leaders identified new policy goals.[15]

Defining characteristics of modern American capitalism took root as securities investment embedded deeply in economic and political culture. From the 1920s, the United States has distinguished itself in comparison to other nations with its above-average ratio of stock market capitalization to gross domestic product (GDP), the extent of stockownership, and the dispersed nature of shareholding in the typical corporation.[16] Since the 1980s, the practice of investment and the figure of "the investor" have occupied positions of highest honor in economic policy and corporate governance. Self-regulating financial markets have been viewed as the engine of growth and innovation, the best mechanism for distributing economic risk, and the source of genuine opportunity and security for individuals. These axioms—with origins in the first three decades of the twentieth century—underlay the free-wheeling securitization that torpedoed the economy in 2008.[17]

Early twentieth-century securities distributors and their ideological allies succeeded in legitimating financial securities investment. But perceptions of investors' interests have been constructed and reconstructed ever since.[18] Advocates of investor democracy have not always privileged investors ahead of other corporate constituencies. The mass investment ideal both inspired demands for government intervention in the economy *and* nourished challenges to the liberal state. In other words, the "investor" has not been aligned with any fixed political-economic agenda. Should Americans continue to prize mass investment, the implications for corporate and economic policy must not be presupposed. Wall Street is a powerful means, but Main Street should decide its ends.

CHAPTER ONE

The Problem with Financial Securities

T HE UNITED STATES stood at a crossroads at the turn of the twentieth century. The traditional ideal of proprietary democracy—a political-economic system in which virtuous, independent citizen-producers exercised free command over their property and the labor of the dependents in their household—seemed increasingly unattainable as a predominantly rural society gave way to an industrial one. The massive industrial corporation stood poised to restructure the economy and to shake the foundations of democracy. National political debate focused on the "trust problem," the tremendous power over economic and political life wielded by colossal corporations.[1]

At the close of the nineteenth century, first railroads and then manufacturers sought sanctuary from cutthroat competition and labor intransigence through various means of consolidation. Transnational rail systems and oligopolistic industrial firms—such as Standard Oil, International Paper, DuPont, and Armour and Co.—rapidly secured dominion over their respective industries, but they failed to stabilize either the economy or labor relations. Severe financial panics in 1873 and 1893 punctuated a prolonged economic depression, as prices, profits, per capita output, and productivity growth fell steadily from 1870 to 1896. Unemployment also rose, but battle for control of the workplace only intensified. Fin-de-siècle labor disturbances evoked the possibility of cataclysmic class warfare: the 1886 general strike for an eight-hour day that culminated in the Haymarket explosion in Chicago, the 1892 shootout at steel baron Andrew Carnegie's Homestead works that pitted unionized workers against Pinkerton detectives and the Pennsylvania militia, the 1894 strike at the Pullman Palace Car Company that halted traffic west of Chicago until federal troops forcibly intervened.[2]

Nationally integrated markets, mass production, and new technologies improved many citizens' lives. Yet the corporations driving these developments lacked political and moral legitimacy. Their economic supremacy and tremendous political influence greatly troubled citizens, as did the vast fortunes amassed by their often ruthless founders. The corporatization of industry propelled the shift from an agricultural-based economy to one dominated by manufacturing. It intensified economic volatility and amplified inequality, displacing the household as the basic unit of the economy and attracting Southern and Eastern European workers that natives perceived as unskilled, radical, and inassimilable. Between 1870 and 1910, the proportion of self-employed in the labor force declined from 67 percent to 37 percent. In consequence, many judged the nation's supposedly egalitarian heritage to be imperiled.[3]

A burning desire to safeguard individual and local economic autonomy against corporate consolidation and the vicissitudes of financial markets suffused the reform movements of the late nineteenth century. Currency reformers, Populists and other anti-monopolists, Progressives, antitrust advocates, and muckraking journalists all sought to expose and counteract the political and economic power of mammoth corporations.

Few matched the fiery passion of Tom Watson, the People's Party candidate for vice president in 1896. Watson refused to sit idly as corporate leviathans overtook proprietary democracy. The Populist movement for which Watson spoke insisted that the federal government institute policies to restructure the economy, so that virtuous independent producers and industrial workers could compete against the "trusts," Watson's epithet for all large corporations. The People's Party platform demanded a ban on subsidies to corporations, the establishment of postal savings and local lending facilities, federal licensing of all interstate corporations, punitive taxes on land speculation, the abolition of the gold standard, a progressive income tax, prohibition of futures contracts, the recognition of labor unions and agricultural cooperatives, immigration restriction, and the nationalization of the rail, telephone, and telegraph systems. Free-market competition did not account for the trusts' ascendance, according to Watson and his supporters. Rather, they believed, monopolistic corporations owed their supremacy to unfair advantages attained through crooked politics and fraudulent financial markets—unjust privileges that the Populists' economic reform agenda aimed to eliminate.[4]

The New York Stock Exchange (NYSE) played a central role in the wicked corporate conspiracy against proprietary democracy, Tom Watson charged. His 1896 interview with the *New York World* illustrated the Stock Exchange as the lair of a vicious serpent. Springing forth from his den of iniquity, this monstrous constrictor squeezed the lives and livelihoods of the three groups that constituted the productive class in the Populists' theory of political economy: farmers, laborers, and independent businessmen. Watson excoriated the syndicates of promoters, NYSE brokerages, and allied investment banks that spawned insidious trusts. Allegedly, these syndicates lured independent proprietors into a horizontal consolidation that engulfed an entire industry by assigning them stock in the integration at prices that greatly exceeded the "intrinsic value" of the companies being combined. Once formed, according to Watson, Wall Street's monopoly-seeking corporate progeny flexed their economic muscle to crush competitors, to raise prices, and to pollute politics.

The idle investor no more counted among the Populists' productive citizenry than did the brokers, bankers, and corporations that Watson so reviled. Only labor created real economic value, the Populists held. "Money withdrawn from circulation and put into partnership with speculators," in contrast, robbed the productive economy of resources. "Not one dollar did the bondholder of Wall Street ever add to the nation's store of wealth," Wilson spat. Instead, this nonproducer stood ever poised to pounce on any opportunity to "relieve" the producer of his wealth in order to "build up a caste, an aristocracy of wealth founded upon special privilege," destroying forever "the spirit and purpose" of the "democratic republic." With stocks and bonds in their bag of tricks, brokers, traders, and owners of financial securities pursued dastardly depredations against virtuous, productive citizens. Ill-gotten gains and paper securities served to bribe "the press, the bench, the Legislature, the ballot," permitting Wall Street to dictate "legislation to the detriment of land, labor, and production"—particularly the gold standard, which protected investors' interest payments from inflation at the expense of debt-burdened producers, Populists believed.

But without the brokers and speculators that traded corporate securities, no "consolidations" could be engineered, or so the Populist standard-bearer imagined. No bribes could be offered. Although abolition of the NYSE was not specified in the People's Party's official platform, the idea could not have been far from Tom Watson's mind.[5]

In many ways, Watson's tirade harkened back to eighteenth- and nineteenth-century economic beliefs and political ideals that embraced independent proprietorship and production. He looked forward, however, by locating the financial securities markets at the root of the trust problem. The People's Party lost the 1896 presidential and vice presidential elections, but nonetheless, a great many Americans agreed that the colossal turn-of-the-century manufacturing mergers were more dangerous than even the largest corporations of the nineteenth century. Through use of the stock market, it seemed, the organizers of these latest mergers could aggregate competitors into a single behemoth virtually overnight.[6]

The great turn-of-the-century merger movement reshaped how Americans understood the role of the financial securities markets, although the vast majority of businesses continued to obtain capital outside of those markets and ownership of bonds and stocks remained quite limited. Still, both critics and supporters of economic consolidation came to view the stock market as essential to the formation of vast, nation-spanning industrial corporations. Even many who embraced this concentration of industry still sought means to contain or reverse its negative social and political consequences. They speculated that widespread ownership of corporate securities might purify corporate culture and reconcile modern capitalism with cherished commitments to proprietary democracy. They called for some form of state oversight over corporate securities issuance, trading, and financial disclosure that would protect, even encourage, the outsider investor of modest means.

The notion that securities ownership might resolve the trust problem and redeem proprietary democracy *predated* the emergence of a sizable investor class in the United States. In the second decade of the twentieth century, both the rhetorical figure of the "small investor" and the practices of the New York Stock Exchange came to the fore of a national debate on economic reform.

From the nation's founding until well into the twentieth century, Americans venerated proprietary democracy, a political-economic ideal that associated citizenship with ownership and control of productive property such as a farm or business. Those who made their living by buying and selling bonds and stocks commonly were perceived as traitors to proprietary democracy. Those who acquired stocks and bonds warranted little consideration in a political-economic system that valorized independent proprietorship and production. Few Americans owned financial securities. The households, proprietorships, and small partnerships that organized the bulk of enterprise made no use of securities markets to obtain funds.

Americans' long-standing commitment to proprietary democracy originated in the classical republican and liberal thought that had inspired the Revolution, along with the comparatively high incidence of land-ownership among free white men in the colonial period. According to the axioms of classical republicanism, property conferred the economic and political independence that a republic required in its citizenry. Self-governance first required self-employment. Possessed of property, a man avoided subjugation to a master's command. Ownership and control of productive resources and dependents' labor secured a man's autonomy and cemented his commitment to private property. Endowed with a vested interest in the fate of the republic, the propertied citizen attained the capacity for autonomous deliberation and public-mindedness in the political realm. Those without property (women, children, servants, slaves), by contrast, lacked the elemental ingredient for self-sovereignty and virtue. This justified their relegation to positions of economic and political dependence. The Lockean, classical liberal notion that men entered the body politic to protect their individual rights—particularly property rights—and to represent their dependents further strengthened associations between proprietorship and citizenship. Independent proprietorship, then, constituted a prerequisite for full inclusion in the body politic according to the canons of classical republicanism and classical liberalism.[7]

Producer-centered theories of political economy complemented the political ideal of proprietary democracy. Well into the twentieth century, most Americans viewed producers and production as the most essential elements in a thriving, equitable economy. Popular economic thinking embraced the labor theory of value, which held that the value of a good or service equaled the amount of labor expended in production. Few Americans, if any, acknowledged any relationship between the forces of production and the oscillations of financial securities markets. Americans generally recognized that banks stored savers' wealth and lent it to those who might produce more wealth. Drawing upon a long tradition of British antispeculative sentiment, early Americans tended to view the speculation that took place on securities exchanges—which were organized in several port cities at the end of the eighteenth century to organize the trading of government bonds—as an improvident diversion of capital.[8]

Similarly, few Americans admitted any affinity between virtuous citizen-producers and those who traded or owned stocks or bonds. The most significant social division recognized by eighteenth- and nineteenth-century Americans pitted producer against nonproducer. Owners of and dealers in financial securities comprised the most dangerous subsegments of the nonproducing class, according to a political-economic worldview that prized production and the property-owning citizen. "Moneyed men" seemingly enjoyed wealth they had not produced, for they had not labored. Bonds, stocks, and the malefactors that traded fictitious paper imperiled civic virtue. The enticing mirage of effortless riches through speculation seemed to undercut all the traits that imbued a productive citizenry with republican virtue: skill, industry, and thrift. Because stocks and bonds conveyed un-earned wealth to dissolute progeny, they admitted an unproductive aris-tocracy into the body politic, eroding the supposed egalitarianism of pro-prietary democracy, according to most.

Financial securities and exchanges found precious few defenders in the early Republic. Even when bondholders were not characterized as nefari-ous speculators, they were not understood as "the people," or any kind of significant, representative sub-segment of the citizenry. For example, when Alexander Hamilton argued that the federal government's assumption of the states' Revolutionary debt would create a constituency of investors strongly committed to the success of the American experiment, he envi-sioned wealthy domestic and foreign investors. Hamilton no more imag-ined that Everyman would own a federal bond than he intended universal suffrage.[9]

So when Tom Watson charged that the denizens of Wall Street corrupted legislators, officials, and judges into advancing policies that impeded the livelihoods of independent producers, he joined a long line of agrarian crit-ics. In Shays' Rebellion, the Whiskey Rebellion, and various other, smaller uprisings of the late eighteenth century, rebel farmers demanded policies to lighten the burden of their taxes, which paid the interest on government bonds owned by the wealthy, influential few. The Jacksonian coalition of skilled artisans, master craftsmen, small manufacturers, and freehold farmers shared the suspicion that fictitious capital advanced corrupt, monopolistic designs against proprietary democracy, embodied especially in the Bank of the United States. Certainly Jackson's supporters appreciated the power of the institutions of modern capitalism to promote economic develop-ment. Through general incorporation and free banking laws, they aimed to ensure that Everyman, not only the wealthy and well-connected, could organize a corporation or bank in their own vicinity. However, support for such reforms diminished neither the Jacksonians' allegiance to proprietary democracy nor their conviction that securities markets stood in opposition to a political-economic culture properly grounded in independent ownership of productive resources.[10]

As states abolished property qualifications for suffrage for men and as waged-labor, corporations, and banks all proliferated across the antebel-lum landscape, the associations between the possession of property, self-governance, and political inclusion shifted. But they were not abandoned. Jacksonian artisans and mechanics demanded universal manhood suffrage by recasting their ability to contract their labor freely as a form of self-ownership. The category of producer-proprietor broadened, yet it remained counterpoised against speculators and idle moneyed men. Throughout the nineteenth century, the vast majority of Americans continued to imagine the ideal polity as populated by autonomous producers, preferably owners of land. "So long as free land exists, the opportunity for a competency exists, and economic power secures political power," wrote Frederick Jackson Turner in 1893, reiterating the connection between landed autonomy and political independence in his famous frontier thesis.[11]

Consistent with the considerable value assigned to proprietorship and production in nineteenth-century political culture and economic thought, both labor and agrarian groups demanded reforms to encourage and to safeguard independent producers, especially yeoman farmers. The presumption that property accompanied citizenship inspired antebellum Free-Soil politics, the Homestead Act of 1862, and Radical Republicans' proposals to provide freed slaves with their own farms. After the Civil War, the identification of full political maturity with independent proprietorship inspired the National Labor Union, the Knights of Labor, a range of currency reformers, and, of course, the People's Party, led by William Jennings Bryan and Tom Watson. These groups perceived their birthright to be imperiled by capital congealing in ever-increasing aggregations: the railroads, the Eastern financial establishment, and massive industrial corporations. They looked to the state to ensure that workers and small-scale producers preserved their autonomy, enjoyed access to adequate credit on equitable terms, and received their fair share of the benefits of economic growth.[12]

Social commentators who opposed such economic reforms also theorized within the popularly accepted framework. William Graham Sumner, arch-defender of laissez-faire and the founder of the discipline of sociology in the United States, concurred that a good political economy safeguarded producers. He ignored securities, financial markets, and investors as he defended capital as stored labor. The "Forgotten Man," that "simple honest laborer, ready to earn his living by productive work," must retain the full fruits of his labor, Sumner insisted. Never should labor's yield be diverted to sustain "the vicious, the idle, and the shiftless." Capital, which Sumner characterized as "labor accumulated, multiplied unto itself," must be left to the industrious man so he could continue to "take care of himself and his family" and perform "his share in the work of society." Sumner's model of society continued to divide those who labored from those who did not. But Sumner's chief malfeasants were idlers living off philanthropy or coddled by government, rather than investors sustained by interest payments. Capitalists he defended as proprietors who themselves worked; their capital derived its legitimacy from its origin in independent labor. Sumner did not include abstract forms—such as stocks and bonds—in his model of what capital was, how it benefited society, or why it must be defended.[13]

The foremost beneficiaries of corporate consolidation followed Sumner's lead, seeking to distinguish themselves from contemptible speculators and eschewing entanglements with Wall Street. Steel magnate Andrew Carnegie, for one, damned "speculators" as innately and "irreparably ruined men, bankrupt in money and bankrupt in character." John D. Rockefeller Sr. prided himself that Standard Oil remained "independent of the Street," financing growth out of its earnings and declining to list its securities on an organized exchange. Americans of all walks of life and political persuasions, then, generally perceived securities owners, brokers, and traders— as well as the paper instruments they dealt in and the securities exchanges they dealt on—as antithetical to independent proprietorship, the engine of production and the wellspring of political virtue.[14]

To be sure, as the nineteenth century wore on, the realities of corporate consolidation, industrialization, waged labor, and southern sharecropping all pushed individual ownership of the means of production beyond the reach of increasing numbers of Americans. The problem of propertylessness grew more vexing, but no less significant, as the ranks of the dispossessed swelled. To be sure, some grew cynical about unskilled, unpropertied workers' prospects for political virtue. Conservative elites of the Gilded Age accepted the formation of a permanent American proletariat and proposed the disenfranchisement of the dispossessed, understood as prone to radicalism. In the South after Reconstruction, poll taxes that disqualified the poor and unpropertied from voting fortified a brutal system of racial apartheid known as "Jim Crow."[15]

In contrast, some nineteenth-century reformers, legislators, and civic leaders began to imagine that new forms of property ownership—including savings accounts and home ownership—might renew democratic citizenship. But in the nineteenth century, no one supposed that ownership of financial securities could bestow political virtue on the dispossessed.[16]

Indeed, such a proposal would have seemed incongruous, for the vast majority of Americans lacked anything resembling a direct relationship with the financial securities markets and continued to look upon them with suspicion. Mass bond drives conducted by investment banker Jay Cooke funded the Union cause during the Civil War, but Cooke's efforts failed to permanently enlarge the American investor class. Around midcentury, certain European and a handful of American writers—including Ralph Waldo Emerson—began to characterize financial securities markets as a means of amassing and directing capital and to assert the scientific nature of financial knowledge and the legitimacy of speculation. Judicial decisions in the 1880s and 1890s bestowed legal personhood and rights on corporations, altered the legal concept of property to include intangible assets like financial securities and their exchange value, and allowed that speculation served a legitimate economic function when conducted by "competent men." But neither these writings nor these rulings made much impact on popular opinion about, or popular participation in, financial securities markets in the United States. Similarly, the telegraph, telephone, and ticker allowed investors across the country to send orders directly to exchange trading floors, but their rapid proliferation after the Civil War failed to increase securities ownership significantly. Rather, these new technologies provided straitlaced Victorians with opportunities to taste economic impropriety in "bucket shops." Here, instead of buying securities for investment, they placed wagers on the movements of securities and commodity prices in violation of many states' anti-gambling laws.[17]

Certainly the market machinations of Daniel Drew, Jim Fisk, Jay Gould, Cornelius Vanderbilt, and the like stirred interest and provided Wall Street critics with plenty of fodder. These Gilded Age robber barons battled one another for controlling stakes in railroad systems. Insider dealings (manipulating stock prices, trading securities on advance information, committing a railroad to contracts with firms that insiders owned) swelled their fat pockets even further, while bribes to politicians and journalists secured favorable rate legislation, land grants, and profitable subsidies for the robber barons' roads. Readers devoured accounts of these great operators' intrigues. Tourists flocked to urban financial districts and stock exchanges, hoping to catch a glimpse of brokers executing the schemes of legendary financial operators like Drew, Fisk, Gould, and Vanderbilt. The financial securities markets certainly fanned mass fascination in the last decades of the nineteenth century, but not mass participation.[18]

For the most part, working- and middle-class Americans steered clear of stocks and bonds before World War I. Probably no more than 500,000 Americans (0.5% of the population or 2.5% of households, using 1910 census data) owned any type of security—corporate or government, bond or stock—even as late as 1917. The value of all stocks listed on the NYSE in 1900 ($2.86 billion) equaled only 2 percent of the value of all assets in the United States ($150 billion). Conventional wisdom held that unless investors knew corporate managers personally, they would be wise not to place their confidence in such enterprises. Consistent with their commitment to proprietary democracy, Americans preferred to invest in tangible assets they controlled: their own homes, farms, or shops. Outside of proprietary enterprises, Americans purchased real estate or insurance, invested in real estate mortgages or building-and-loan shares, and deposited funds in mutual savings banks (which held one-quarter of all financial assets in 1880) or, after 1907, in the U.S. Postal Savings system. At century's turn, government and railroad bonds probably were the most widely held types of security; an estimated 320,000 Americans purchased a federal bond issued to fund the Spanish-American War. Railroad bonds and stocks predominated on the nation's exchanges.[19]

The financial firms involved in the origination and distribution of bonds and stocks largely ignored the American middle and working classes. Beginning in the 1870s, leading investment banks like J. P. Morgan and Co. reorganized bankrupt American railroads, then underwrote and distributed the securities of these new consolidated systems mainly to institutional and European investors. Domestically, institutions like insurance companies, mortgage companies, and savings banks provided most of the demand for railroad and later industrial securities, in which they invested policyholders' and depositors' funds. Toward the end of the nineteenth century, select banks like Lee, Higginson, Kidder Peabody, National City Bank, First National Bank, N. W. Halsey and Co., and N. W. Harris, and specialized investment companies like Investors' Syndicate in Minneapolis, acquired sales forces and advertising space to attract the savings of the professional and white-collar classes residing in their respective cities and surrounding regions, but such firms counted only several thousand customers before World War I.[20]

The clientele of a nineteenth-century securities broker reflected Americans' infrequent use of brokerages and organized securities exchanges. U.S. exchanges' standard minimum transaction value of $10,000 placed stock trading well out of the reach of middle-class Americans, even if they only paid 10 percent margin and borrowed the rest from their broker. The standard $100-per-share size also catered to wealthy and institutional clients. For the most part, members of the nation's securities exchanges traded for their own accounts or brokered the orders of the very affluent, foreign investors, and financial institutions. Banks and insurers also lent funds to exchange members, providing capital for those members' speculations. Because banks invested with and lent to securities brokers, the credit market and, ultimately, the real economy felt the repercussions of stock market bubbles and panics.[21]

Despite these ramifications on the economic well-being of the larger public, those who owned seats on the nation's various exchanges considered themselves members of decidedly *private* associations. Boards of governors, elected by the membership, determined and enforced rules regarding members' conduct and corporations' qualifications for listing their securities for trading. Acting as cartels, exchanges fixed the prices (or commissions) that members charged to execute trades and further limited competition by restricting membership.[22]

Like the vast majority of savers, American business enterprises only rarely made use of the organized financial securities markets before the twentieth century. In the antebellum period, state governments played a crucial role in funneling capital toward large-scale projects like banks, canals, and railroads. Still, households, proprietorships, and small partnerships organized the bulk of economic activity throughout the nineteenth century. Entrepreneurial individuals or groups tended to raise initial capital and to fund growth through loans, family wealth, or retained earnings. Even among manufacturers, only 29 percent of firms owned by more than one person took corporate form in 1900. Even corporations generally remained closely held; any distribution of securities tended to take place within the local, personal, and familial networks of founders and managers. Beginning in the 1870s, transnational railroads turned to syndicates led by investment banks, but these syndicates distributed railroad securities to small groups of clients that could afford sizable subscriptions, mainly wealthy individuals, institutions, and foreign investors. Even for corporations that listed securities for trading on an exchange, founding families and managers quite often retained the majority of shares in order to retain control. Shares of corporate common stock served as a means to transfer control of the corporation between large stockholders. In 1900, only the Pennsylvania Railroad, the Atchison, Topeka & Santa Fe, the New York Central, the Union Pacific, and American Sugar Refining Company counted more than 10,000 shareholders, and it cannot be assumed that each resided in the United States. In comparison, corporations quite commonly tallied over 10,000 shareholders in Britain and France, where share ownership was far more prevalent.[23]

Yet the issuance of financial securities did play an important role in the formation of the industrial mergers that assumed center stage in the nation's economy at the end of the nineteenth century, as critics like Tom Watson recognized. First, the engineers of the turn-of-the-century mergers identified independent firms in an industry that suffered from overcompetition. In exchange for their plants, the proprietors of these firms received stock in a new corporation that absorbed the constituent firms. Merger engineers next sold the shares of the new corporation—now large enough to vie for control over its industry—for much more than the combined purchase price of the original firms, thereby securing a sizable profit. Still, when merger organizers issued stock in their combination, they typically bypassed banks, brokers, and exchanges in favor of independent promoters, who dispensed few shares to the general public. Only toward the end of the merger movement, especially after the formation of U.S. Steel in

1901, did national syndicates of investment banks and brokerages become involved in the distribution of these kinds of stock issues, which some exchanges (notably the Boston Stock Exchange) admitted for trading. Even then, these syndicates continued to look mainly to large institutions and wealthy individuals, often abroad. The general public acquired only 6 percent of the $6.2 billion in preferred and common stock issued by industrial corporations between 1898 and 1902.[24]

Even so, indirect evidence suggests that the efforts of merger organizers and promoters set in motion a trend toward expanded stockownership—or at least stock trading. Trading volume on the NYSE exploded—from 77 million shares in 1897 to 265.6 million in 1901. No New York Stock Exchange member operated a branch office for the convenience of retail clients in 1890. But by 1905, 162 members counted at least one branch office; the total number of NYSE-affiliated branch offices totaled 507. The number of shareholders of record began to climb at some individual corporations after 1900, as well. Ultimately, however, neither transaction volume, the number of brokerage offices, nor counts of shareholders at particular corporations can determine the total number of shareholders in 1900.[25]

Whether or not the number of securities owners multiplied during the upsurge in industrial mergers, it clearly pushed the rhetorical figure of the "lamb" or "small investor" to the fore in discussions of the trust problem. According to many observers, Tom Watson among them, the nation-spanning, monopoly-seeking industrial corporation depended vitally upon the ignorance and greed of outsider investors of modest means. Promoters could only entice independent proprietors into mergers by offering them shares in a corporation that insiders knew to be priced far above the cash value of the constituent enterprises. Because outsiders knew nothing about the assets and history of the merger, they could be lured into buying shares from insiders who wished to cash out at inflated prices. The blandishments of merger promoters and stockbrokers who later traded the shares of the new merger attracted "people of moderate means and moderate intelligence," explained foremost trust observer Edward S. Meade of the University of Pennsylvania's Wharton School. "The seductive spectacle of leisure class consumption" overwhelmed the "small judgments" of "thousands" of "not so shrewd" people "all over the country."[26]

Neither critics like Watson nor academics like Meade mustered much sympathy for the follies of the credulous, or judged their ranks sizable. Editorial cartoonists likewise lampooned naïve lambs who offered themselves to be shorn by promoters and brokers. Securities markets continued to be portrayed as standing outside of the "real" economic realm of production. For, as Meade described it, trust promoters did not "construct" anything.

They merely combined what was "already constructed." Ultimately, only "a change of ownership and organization" resulted. Financial instruments and securities markets enriched merger promoters and stock speculators, but they did not advance productive enterprise.[27]

The modern stock market could not have arisen without the shares of the great combinations, but the massive industrial corporation did not require the stock market for its capital. Even so, because so many of the new industrial mergers listed their shares for trading on the nation's stock exchanges, what took place on those trading floors no longer seemed a matter of solely private concern. At century's turn, even those who endorsed corporate consolidation joined with Tom Watson in contemplating the proper relationship between the financial securities markets, the "real" economy, and the state.

Tom watson and William Jennings Bryan lost the 1896 election. The Populists' fervent commitment to proprietary democracy and their candidates' rousing oratory could not overcome the campaign chest amassed on behalf of Republican William McKinley. Campaign manager Marcus Hanna outspent Bryan (who also ran on the Democratic ticket) in the costliest presidential bid to date. Himself a wealthy industrialist, Hanna disbursed $3.5 million in contributions from businessmen terrified by the People's Party's platform on novel advertising and publicity techniques. The election of 1896 settled the "money question" in favor of the gold standard. But as the merger wave gained momentum, the "trust problem" loomed larger than ever before.

No particular foe of the trusts himself, McKinley nonetheless took action to address public unease over the pace, scale, and social consequences of industrial consolidation. In 1898, the president made nine appointments to the Industrial Commission, established by the U.S. Senate to study existing industrial conditions with an eye toward recommending legislation to ameliorate the "trust problem." Senator James H. Kyle of the People's Party, who moved into the Republican Party in 1900, chaired the tri-partisan committee. Economists Jeremiah Jenks and William Z. Ripley, the leading advocate for corporate governance reform in the 1920s, served as academic advisers.

Most likely, neither President McKinley nor the Republican-controlled Congress intended the Industrial Commission as anything more than window dressing, and indeed, it spent little time considering whether orthodox Republican policies like the gold standard and import tariffs contributed to the "trust problem." But in the end, the commission levied considerable criticism at the financial engineering behind the industrial mergers. Focusing national attention on the treatment of the outsider investor of modest means, the commission's reports identified that investor as a central—rather than peripheral—player in the American political economy. The U.S. Senate Industrial Commission's investigations would serve as the starting point for economic policy discussions in Progressive and corporate liberal circles from the publication of its preliminary report in 1900 until World War I.

The Industrial Commission embraced the benefits of large-scale industrial corporations: economies of scale, increased production, and promotion of technological and managerial innovation. But, the Commission concluded, the mergers that created these corporate giants all too often involved overcapitalization, or the overpricing of corporate stock when issued and when subsequently listed for trading on the nation's exchanges. Only through overcapitalization could industrial combinations grow large and powerful enough to monopolize entire industries. In turn, the need to pay dividends on this "watered" (overpriced) stock led such corporations to seek oversized profits by instituting layoffs, engaging in anticompetitive practices, raising prices, and lowering quality standards.[28]

The Industrial Commission seized upon overcapitalization as the chief "evil of modern promotion" that required redress. Merger promoters were able to "water" stock in the combinations they organized because outsider investors knew little, if anything, about the real value of the actual assets of companies being merged. The testimony of promoters confirmed that outsider investors, bereft of information, acted on sheer faith. William H. Moore, architect of American Tin Plate Co., National Steel Co., American Steel Hoop Co., Diamond Match Co., and National Biscuit Co., revealed his *modus operandi* to the Commission. First, he borrowed money to acquire firms. Then he sold stock in the combined entity to outsiders for amounts that greatly exceeded what he had paid to acquire the constituent enterprises. Examiners did not question Moore's right to secure a profit from his efforts. The problem lay in Moore's inability to justify the valuation of these mergers.

> Q: What, then, is the basis of the value of the surplus . . . over the cost of the properties and the goodwill involved?
> A: I cannot tell you that. I merely know that I had the plants and organized the companies on that basis, and practical men believe in them and subscribe to them.

Following the initial offering of shares, the Commission found, insiders continued to take advantage of their privileged access to corporate information by organizing pools that manipulated stock prices "to the great detriment of other shareholders."[29]

State-mandated reforms in corporate publicity and governance, devised with the outsider investor in mind, might destroy industrial combinations' "power for evil" but preserve "their means for good," the Senate inquiry surmised. The outsider must be equipped with adequate information upon which wise investment decisions could be based. If informed investors declined to invest in corporations at inflated prices, this would compel the merger's underwriters and promoters to lower the price of the offered stock, thwarting any watery designs. If overcapitalized corporations never formed, they could never wield monopolistic market power over competitors, customers, and labor, Commissioners believed. Given the centrality of the outsider investor in the formation of monopolies, he could not be left to the mercy of merger promoters, investment bankers, and brokers who allegedly issued false or insufficient information about investment offerings, then overpriced shares and manipulated trading on the nation's exchanges.[30]

Corporate financial transparency would benefit not only the outsider investor of modest means, but the public at-large as well, the Industrial Commission envisioned. Accurate disclosure of corporate financial data would counteract monopoly by drawing attention to "excessive profits," encouraging competitors to enter the field while alerting consumers about "too high prices." Employees could bargain more effectively when they knew the true "financial condition of the business in which they were employed." Last, transparency in corporate affairs would combat financial oligarchy, the commission advised. When they organized combinations, promoters and underwriters wielded tremendous power and skimmed enormous profits and fees. But if "water" was exposed and drained, these mergers would lose their egregious profitability and so, too, their appeal.[31]

Rather than continuing to defer to the nation's exchanges to determine what kind of financial information publicly traded corporations disclosed to their shareholders, the Senate's Industrial Commission proposed that the government determine and enforce disclosure requirements. Interstate corporations should be required to submit annual audited reports for inspection, preferably by a bureau at the Treasury Department. In addition, regulatory reform of corporate governance practices would empower shareholders to police the actions of corporate directors. Certainly the Industrial Commission recognized that as stockholding in the trusts diffused, "the exercise of power" would tend to consolidate in the hands of "comparatively few men," whether directors or owners of large blocks of stock. Nevertheless, it imagined that if corporate bylaws and the quality of the financial data disclosed by corporations were improved, then stockholders could see to it that corporate affairs were conducted in accord with their interests and, ultimately, "under their lawful control."[32]

While the Industrial Commission emphasized the necessity of enhanced corporate disclosure, it conceded that "the state" could not "act as guardians to foolish individuals" who could or would not analyze corporate reports. Carelessness on the part of perhaps tens of thousands of individuals who had purchased shares in the great mergers was not "a matter that concerns materially the general public." But overcapitalization—which fed on such inattention—clearly compromised "the public interest." Once formed, monopolistic firms enjoyed free rein to abuse consumers, competitors, and workers, along with their investors. Although proposals intended to protect the interests of outsider shareholders would safeguard the public, the Commission did not view the shareholding class as that public at-large. Indeed, the authors of the Industrial Commission's final report scoffed at exaggerated claims about the number of shareholders in the United States made by defenders of the status quo. Stock promoter John Dos Passos, for example, referenced William Graham Sumner as he warned that regulation would strike against "the middle men, the men of small means, the conservative men, the thousands and thousands of stockholders who have invested their money in these corporations, the young and the old, the widow and infant." Dismissing Dos Passos' objections, the Commission noted that no reliable data about the size of the shareholding class were available.[33]

Even though it considered the shareholding class distinct from the public at-large, the Senate's commission nonetheless maintained that the state could best promote an equitable political economy—in which the benefits of industrial consolidation would be widely enjoyed but monopoly would be avoided—by ensuring investors' access to reliable corporate information and by legislating changes in conventions of corporate governance.

As the U.S. Senate Industrial Commission took testimony and published reports between 1900 and 1902, the foremost members of the American economics profession threw their support behind its inquiries. In line with the Industrial Commission, Jeremiah Jenks, Richard Ely, and John Bates Clark embraced economic concentration but rejected laissez-faire. If designed properly, these three believed, regulatory policies and agencies could help to preclude the unfair practices that led to monopoly. Informed by the work of the U.S. Senate Industrial Commission, Clark, Ely, and Jenks concluded that an effective solution to the "trust problem" would hinge, in part, upon securities market reform.[34]

Ely, Clark, and Jenks took one further step. These leading lights of the economics profession imagined that if the financial securities markets were rehabilitated, they could preserve the essence of proprietary democracy in an industrial corporate economy. Other noteworthy social scientists (most influentially, economist Simon Patten) and certain segments of the labor movement took a hard look at the realities of industrial corporate capitalism and boldly severed the link between property and citizenship, recasting economic citizenship as the consumer's claim on a fair share of the fruits of prosperity. But proprietary democracy retained potency for Clark, Ely, and Jenks. True, these three dismissed as outmoded the Populist dream of perpetuating a republic of small producers, along with the labor theory of value. But they revised, rather than rejected, the equation of property ownership with citizenship.[35]

Jeremiah Jenks, John Bates Clark, and Richard Ely conjured a vision of investor democracy, in which Everyman could attain a measure of economic liberty and political virtue as a modern type of proprietor: the owner of financial securities. Ely, for one, reiterated the incompatibility of republican government with an economic system "in which few men are employers and the great body are merely employes or servants." Analogizing between the independent proprietor of old and the modern-day stockholder, Ely recommended that economic policy aim to "multiply the numbers engaged in independent pursuits" *or* sharing "in the profits" of corporate production as stockowners. The "accumulation of capital" from the multitudes might also sustain competition if their funds were funneled to new entrants, Ely opined. John Bates Clark, for his part, presumed that a "proprietary interest in the tools of labor and a share in what the tools produce" would fortify a workingman's "manly development" and "personal independence." When the "great corporate capitals" were "divided, in its ownership, into a myriad of holdings scattered widely among the people" and "the bonds of great corporations, and even the stocks" became "common and safe forms of investment of workmen's savings," then "the old line of demarcation between the capitalist class and the laboring class" would blur, perhaps disappear. "The socialist is not the only man who can have beatific visions," Clark reckoned. The spread of corporate securities ownership would preserve individual property ownership and economic competition, reconcile the laboring and capitalist classes, and disperse corporate wealth more equitably, speculated Ely, Clark and Jenks, even if the nature of property ownership shifted from direct control of physical assets to securitized, fungible financial claims.[36]

Only "very intelligent action on the part of government" would breathe life into this chimera of investor democracy, Clark allowed. Everyman required better financial disclosure from corporations; corporate charters must specify and protect shareholders' rights. And so, while Jenks, Ely, and

Clark eagerly anticipated the emergence of an investors' democracy, they viewed securities market regulation as a critical and necessary precondition for that felicitous outcome.[37]

Jenks, Ely, and Clark first elaborated the ideal of investor democracy, but no man was more important for promoting that vision than U.S. District Judge Peter S. Grosscup. During the 1894 Pullman strike, Grosscup had issued the injunction against Eugene Debs, leader of the American Railway Union, the nation's first industrial union. Grosscup presided over the subsequent criminal trial, in which Clarence Darrow represented Debs, who had converted to socialism in prison. Grosscup's injuction against colluding meatpackers in 1903 established his reputation as a strict enforcer of the Sherman Antitrust Act. As a kind of industrial-age Solomon adjudicating between radicals and plutocrats, no man seemed better suited to opine on the "trust problem" or to recommend remedies for the disenchantment of the dispossessed. In the first decade of the twentieth century, Grosscup did so repeatedly, both in publications and in testimony before conferences on the "trust problem" convened by government bodies and by private associations like the National Civic Federation.[38]

For Grosscup, the "separation" of "labor from proprietorship" presented "the most unrepublican and menacing fact" confronting the nation. Workmen yearned for a "proprietary part in the enterprise in which they toiled," he believed. Under existing corporate finance and governance practices, however, Americans' "innate, persistent, unconquerable" instinct for property could find no outlet. "No decent, honest citizen dare make an investment anywhere in this new property domain that has come to the republic," Grosscup lamented.[39]

"Government supervision and control" of corporate securities issuance would remodel corporations into "safe subjects for public investment," Grosscup contended. Equating the securities markets with the landed frontier of yore, the judge urged legislators to "deal . . . with this new domain of property" with the same spirit of "statesmanship" that had moved their predecessors to parcel out the West to hearty pioneers. Grosscup himself favored a federal incorporation law, a remedy endorsed earlier by William Jennings Bryan, the Democratic Party, and the U.S. Senate Industrial Commission. If the federal government denied or revoked the incorporation charters or licenses of monopolistic, overcapitalized corporations, advocates believed, these companies would lose their ability to conduct interstate business. Prevention of "false capitalization" by publicly traded corporations, moreover, would enable Everyman to invest safely in the nation's industrial growth.[40]

The advantages—and the stakes—could not be greater, according to Grosscup. Broad-based ownership of corporate stock would distribute "the permanent fruits of progress and prosperity" equitably and reposition the corporation upon "republican . . . foundations." Faith in individual opportunity and initiative would revive. Grosscup further anticipated that the "peopleization of the corporate domain" would awaken "a *widespread habit of scrutiny.*" Shareholders would compel the corporation to improve its conduct toward workers, consumers, and competitors.[41] But if "the country's richest property field" remained inhospitable to "popular occupation," Grosscup warned, then "the whole institution of private property" would founder. "Socialism" would triumph.[42]

Before the First World War, those determined to secure antitrust reform would turn time and again to the Industrial Commission's findings and to the writings of Jenks, Clark, Ely, and Grosscup. Progressives of all stripes and corporate liberals embraced the notion that some form of state intervention into the privately administered financial securities markets could preserve competitive markets in the "real" economy and shore up democracy's propertied foundations. Reform of financial securities markets and corporate governance assumed a central place in so many permutations of progressive economic reform because this approach seemed at once effective and indirect, permitting corporations wide latitude in the ordinary conduct of their business, provided that they met certain requirements regarding the terms under which they issued securities.[43] The principle of securing Everyman equal access to truthful, adequate corporate information—corporate transparency—seemed most consistent with the nation's core individualism. The reins of reform, advocates imagined, could redirect the securities markets toward financing innovative, productive enterprises, rather than lining the pockets of promoters and speculators as they largely had done.

For over a decade following the publication of the final report of the U.S. Senate Industrial Commission, congressmen introduced dozens of bills that bore its imprint. Reform of the financial securities markets—particularly stricter standards for incorporation charters and financial disclosure in order to prevent overcapitalization, along with the revision of corporate bylaws relating to shareholders' rights—now stood at the forefront of the progressive economic reform agenda. During the Roosevelt, Taft, and Wilson administrations, the market in corporate securities became not only a matter of public concern, but by Progressive logic a concern of the state.[44]

President Theodore Roosevelt's intended approach—federal incorporation law—offers a case in point. Like Judge Peter S. Grosscup and William Jennings Bryan, President Roosevelt believed that the cure for overcapitalization lay in requiring all corporations engaged in interstate commerce to obtain a federal incorporation charter. Each year, Roosevelt envisioned, chartered corporations would be required to document their financial status, to publish a list of stockholders and the amount of shares held by each, and to submit their books for examination by a federal agency. All the disclosed information would be published for investors' use. No corporation would be able to issue additional stocks or bonds without agency authorization, which would confirm that the corporation's capitalization did not exceed the cash value of its tangible assets. Roosevelt also endorsed the Hepburn Act of 1906, which authorized the Interstate Commerce Commission to supervise and regulate the issuance of railroad securities and to inspect the roads' financial records in order to set "just and reasonable" maximum rates. This represented an unprecedented federal involvement in railroad finance and securities valuation.[45]

President Roosevelt managed to establish a Bureau of Corporations to gather information about the "trusts," but neither he nor Taft secured legislation authorizing the federal government to oversee incorporation, corporate disclosure, or securities issuance in the industrial sector. Still, these presidents' endorsements of such bills sharpened the focus on the treatment of outsider investors and signaled their lack of confidence in privately administered securities markets. Failure to pass a federal incorporation law was not due to a lack of support among prominent corporate executives. The leaders of many of the greatest industrial corporations, including U.S. Steel and Standard Oil, considered uniform federal standards for incorporation and corporate disclosure superior to conflicting state laws and judges' varying applications of the Sherman Antitrust Act. By backing federal incorporation, these "corporate-liberal" industrialists sought to streamline the regulatory environment and to validate their sense of themselves as publicly minded corporate leaders who cooperated with the agencies of government to manage the economy in the public interest.[46]

Roosevelt's closest ally among this group, George W. Perkins, took an additional step. As chairman of New York Life Insurance Co., partner in J. P. Morgan and Co., and director of several industrial giants, Perkins was determined to portray the companies he was involved with as "good trusts." Inspired by John Bates Clark's vision of worker shareownership, Perkins launched employee stockownership plans (ESOPs) as part of larger public relations and welfare capitalism initiatives at U.S. Steel (1903), McCormick Reaper (1903), and International Harvester (1908). Several other large employers with publicly traded stock—DuPont, Commonwealth Edison, National Biscuit, and Proctor & Gamble—soon followed suit, hoping to improve both public and employee relations.[47]

These plans garnered mixed reviews. U.S. Commissioner of Labor Carroll D. Wright endorsed employee stockownership, as did Frank A. Vanderlip, an assistant secretary of the Treasury who later became president of National City Bank and one of the chief architects of the Federal Reserve. Vanderlip even encouraged financial institutions to follow industrial employers' lead and attempt to disseminate financial securities "through the masses." A mere "share or two of stocks" bestowed a "stake in the country" upon a man, he advised. Lifted "into the class of capitalists," Vanderlip conjectured, the small stockholder became "conservative." Banks and brokerages did not rally to his call. Many judged direct investment in corporate securities too risky for the average worker, and proposals to mitigate that risk by reforming corporate disclosure practices too "far-reaching" and radical. "The workman's investment should never be at risk" in the stock market, Andrew Carnegie declared. He criticized U.S. Steel's ESOP, although the Amalgamated Association of Iron, Steel and Tin Workers endorsed it. Stock market mania meant the neglect of "machinery, and machinery, like art, is a jealous mistress," Carnegie warned. For its part, the Industrial Commission dismissed "the philanthropic hope" that "workingmen will attain a share in industrial government" as stockholders. Only "the organization of labor" would provide workers with a voice in "the conditions under which they work" and "introduce an element of democracy" into industrial labor relations in the eyes of the Senate's Commission.[48]

As corporate mergers and employee ownership plans slowly but very modestly expanded the ranks of the American investor class, muckraking exposés lent credence to the Industrial Commission's findings of corporate and financial chicanery. *Frenzied Finance* (1905), maverick stock promoter Thomas Lawson's sensational account of the Amalgamated Copper trust, and Louis Brandeis's 1907 investigation of the New York, New Haven, and Hartford railroad merger divulged further details. These accounts revealed that monopolistic corporate and rail consolidations congealed thanks to the sponsorship of colluding Wall Street banks and brokerages, particularly those led by J. P. Morgan and Co. Morgan's "money trust" allegedly refused to raise financial capital for the rivals of the corporations they held in thrall, thereby erecting barriers to entry against newcomers. *Frenzied Finance* also detailed how the money trust orchestrated depredations against outsider investors. First, aggressive promoters and brokers enticed outsiders to buy watered stock. "Pools" of allied bankers, NYSE brokers, and corporate insiders then used wash sales, false rumors, and phony tips to manipulate stock prices ever higher, which lured more and more lambs to grasp for a piece of the action. These pools next engaged in short-selling to drive prices back down, frightening outsiders to sell out at rock-bottom prices. Lawson also bared the close ties between the investment banks that distributed securities and the insurance companies and savings banks that purchased them. The money trust, Lawson charged, had secured a monopoly over "other people's money."[49]

AND THEN, the Panic of 1907 struck. In October, an unsuccessful attempt to corner the market in the stock of the United Copper Company ended in the failure of participating brokerages. Frightened depositors clamored to recover their savings from banks associated with the scheme. The resulting collapse of the Knickerbocker Trust, the third-largest trust company in New York City, wreaked havoc on the financial system. Faith in financial institutions evaporated; even depositors at sound banks and trusts lined up to withdraw their money. Depositors' demands forced regional banks to call in their reserves from the New York City banks. These, in turn, demanded the repayment of loans made to brokers, corporations, and others who had pledged corporate securities as collateral. The stock market plummeted, and credit markets froze, driving all kinds of borrowers into bankruptcy. With no central bank to step in, it fell to J. P. Morgan to stem the crisis. Morgan organized his associates to lend money to and buy assets from flagging banks, trusts, brokerages, even the City of New York.[50]

In the public eye, J. P. Morgan's efforts confirmed his imperious suzerainty over "other people's money," not his chivalry. The Panic of 1907's collateral damage on the real economy and the behind-closed-doors drama of Morgan's rescue threw even more momentum behind demands for an overhaul of the nation's financial system. The Federal Reserve was one ultimate result. But more immediately, legislation aiming to curtail securities speculation in order to promote macroeconomic stability now took its place alongside the reform of incorporation procedures, corporate disclosure requirements, and corporate governance in the progressive economic agenda.[51]

State legislators took up the anti-speculation cause in earnest. In New York, Governor Charles Evans Hughes convened a commission to investigate the Panic of 1907. The Hughes Commission urged the Exchange to enact measures to curb speculation by vulnerable outsider investors. The Stock Exchange was asked to tighten control over its quotations, to raise its margin requirements (the amount of money customers could borrow from their brokers to trade securities), and to prohibit its members from trading the "unlisted" securities of corporations that disclosed no financial information whatsoever. Apart from closing its unlisted department, the NYSE largely ignored these suggestions. Outside of New York, legislators in Midwest and Great Plains populist strongholds crafted "blue sky" laws requiring brokers to obtain state licenses and establishing state commissions empowered to approve new issues of bonds and stocks.[52]

As reformers took aim at speculation, some observers claimed that multitudes of middle-class bargain hunters had plunged into the languishing stock market in the wake of the Panic of 1907. By this point, estimates of the number of U.S. shareholders had become inextricably bound up in the debate over corporate and financial regulation. Some aimed to quash reform with inflated claims. The *New York Times,* for example, asserted that by acquiring corporate stock, 2 million Americans had signaled their satisfaction with existing, unregulated corporate disclosure practices. But the *Times* failed to adjust for individuals who owned stock in more than one corporation, institutional investors, or foreign investors.[53]

After the Panic of 1907, more Americans may have entered the market, or existing investors simply may have traded more often. As a group, outsider investors acquired one-third of the new stock issued between 1905 and 1914, but the number of outsider investors involved cannot be determined. In 1907, the daily volume of odd-lot trading (trading in less than standard 100-share lots) on the Stock Exchange sometimes reached 200,000 shares per day. If odd-lot investors traded in ten-share blocks, then 20,000 Americans might have been trading stocks through NYSE brokers on the heaviest trading days. The Exchange did not establish a regular procedure for accommodating odd-lot trades until 1914, however, indicating that retail investors remained relatively unimportant to that institution. Still, *perceptions* of rising demand for information about securities investment prompted publishers to insert new investment columns into mass-circulation magazines like *Harper's Weekly, World's Work,* and *Saturday Evening Post* and to launch magazines devoted to investment.[54]

Irrespective of whether the Panic of 1907 attracted an influx of new investors, calls for the reform of the nation's financial system reached a fever pitch. The leading contenders for the presidency in 1912 threw down their gauntlets against financial oligarchy and fraud. Running on the ticket of the new Progressive Party, Theodore Roosevelt accepted economic consolidation as inevitable and proposed a "New Nationalism" economic platform that aimed to counterbalance corporations with social welfare legislation and powerful regulatory agencies, including ones charged with the oversight of corporate disclosure and securities issuance. Democrat Woodrow Wilson's "New Freedom" agenda, in contrast, sought to restore competition in the economy on behalf of independent proprietors. The public might taste the fruits of corporate wealth as employees and consumers, Wilson allowed, but democracy could never "afford to have its prosperity originated by a small controlling class" of corporate and financial elites. Wilson, who studied under Richard Ely at Johns Hopkins, vowed to force a "release of capital" and thereby throw open "the doors of opportunity" to all independent entrepreneurs.[55]

Although Roosevelt and Wilson prescribed different remedies for the "trust problem," both candidates singled out the financial securities markets as a particular object of reform. Much as Roosevelt had done when president, candidate Wilson dismissed as "entirely illegitimate" the notion that corporations with publicly traded securities should enjoy the same privacy in the conduct of their business as simple proprietorships and partnerships. As its stocks and bonds circulated "from hand to hand," the publicly traded corporation entangled its interests with "multitudes of men" and "whole communities." Such a corporation became "in a very proper sense everybody's business," Wilson affirmed. Its affairs must, therefore, be opened "to the inspection of everybody" who might wish to purchase its securities. The "foul means" of overcapitalization employed to seize "control of the market," the "secret arrangements" made with colluding banks to deny financing to competitors, these abuses should "be stopped by law," Wilson promised.[56]

In the end, American voters chose the candidate whose political-economic philosophy adhered more closely to the tenets of proprietary democracy. At inauguration, Woodrow Wilson affirmed that his administration would target the "concentration in the control of credit" that sustained the trusts and stifled the aspirations of independent entrepreneurs.[57]

Even before Woodrow Wilson took office, House Democrats launched an investigation by the Banking and Currency Committee chaired by Arsene Pujo (D-La.). Samuel Untermyer, a wealthy New York trial lawyer who had participated in the 1906 investigation of the insurance industry in New York and the 1911 Standard Oil antitrust case, directed the inquiry as special counsel. The final report of the Pujo Committee, issued in February 1913, affirmed the existence of a J. P. Morgan–led money trust, consisting of a small fraternity of financiers who ruled the economy through a system of "interlocking directorates." Purportedly, these banker-directors stymied competition by denying capital to innovators that might compete with their pet corporations. NYSE members allegedly acted as "money trust" lackeys, admitting watered stocks to trading and orchestrating "pools" to manipulate stock prices to the detriment of outsider investors.[58]

> A very important phase . . . is the manipulation of prices up or down, as desired without regard to the real value of the securities, and the creation of false appearances of activity in particular stocks. Besides inciting, as intended, popular speculation . . . this practice prevents the Exchange from faithfully reflecting the current value of securities—one of its true functions—and gives those controlling the great supplies of capital a further power over the enterprises of the country.[59]

The Pujo Committee concluded that the Stock Exchange diverted savings from productive enterprise into stock gambling, yielding only "moral and economic waste and corruption." The NYSE offered manipulators a mechanism for swindling the "great body of the public."[60]

In many ways, the Pujo Committee's verdict concurred with that delivered by the Senate's Industrial Commission a decade earlier: overcapitalization, manipulation, and monopoly would cease if outsider investors were equipped with adequate financial information about the corporations in which they had invested, or wished to invest. But the Pujo report advised a new strategy, directed against a new target. "Great and much-needed reforms in the organization and methods of our corporations may be legitimately worked out through the power wielded by the stock exchanges over the listing of securities," the Committee concluded, if the exchanges could be obliged to require "complete publicity as to all the affairs" from listed corporations. Believing that the money trust could be defanged if the state compelled its chief instrument to comport itself in the public interest, the Pujo report homed in on that most suspicious and secretive of financial institutions, the New York Stock Exchange.[61]

The Pujo report proposed that all stock exchanges be obliged to incorporate in the state in which they were located and that the use of the mail, telegraph, and telephone be denied to any stock exchange that did not comply with certain rules regarding procedures for listing securities, the information that listed companies must disclose, and members' conduct. The U.S. Postmaster General would censor exchange members' marketing mailings and inspect their books to ensure that the impecunious were not enticed into "unwholesome speculation" in watered stocks. These suggestions aimed to enable investors to identify the assets and earning history of an enterprise, so that overcapitalization could not occur, and to dampen speculation. "Legal supervision" of the nation's exchanges, the Pujo Committee promised, would bolster the "confidence" of the "general public" and yield "a greater volume of business of an investment and otherwise legitimate character."[62]

In the end, the Wilson administration chose different tactics to bust the money trust. The Federal Reserve Act of 1913 created a decentralized national banking system, providing government supervision but leaving operations in bankers' hands. The Clayton Antitrust Act of 1914 clarified which activities would be prosecuted as anticompetitive (including interlocking directorates). Enforcement fell to the Federal Trade Commission, established in 1914.[63]

Still, congressmen and state legislators took up the Pujo report in 1913 and 1914. The Owen bill of 1913 sought to deny use of the mails, telegraph, and telephone to all members of any exchange that did not adopt certain reporting requirements for listed corporations and rules of conduct for members. Various state bills demanded that exchanges reorganize as corporations; others proposed to tax short-selling (bears' favored trading strategy) out of existence. By 1914, twenty-four states had passed blue-sky laws obliging brokers to obtain licenses and creating commissions to approve new issues of stocks and bonds.[64]

Those in support of financial reform turned to the press. Louis Brandeis, Woodrow Wilson's chief economic adviser during the 1912 presidential campaign—considered an "untamed radical" by "the great financial interests"—drew upon Pujo Committee findings to build a case for Wilson's economic agenda in *Other People's Money* (1914). Meanwhile, Samuel Untermyer campaigned for both state and federal incorporation of the NYSE. Both Brandeis and Untermyer asserted that the securities markets served a public interest. Money trust rule over the mammoth corporations *indirectly* harmed "the people" with cutthroat competition that drove out small proprietors and raised prices. "The people" suffered *indirectly as investors*, for when captive insurance companies and banks invested in over-capitalized corporations, they put the funds of policy owners and depositors at risk. Last, Untermyer and Brandeis posited *direct* harm to "the public" *as investors*. Lack of competition in the financial industry allowed NYSE members to overprice new security issues, overcharge for trades, and manipulate stock prices to the detriment of outsider investors.[65]

In the wake of the investigations of the U.S. Senate Industrial Commission, economists Jeremiah Jenks, John Bates Clark, and Richard Ely, along with U.S. District Judge Peter S. Grosscup, eagerly anticipated that reforms in corporate disclosure and governance would solve the "trust problem" and encourage the masses to invest in corporate securities. Several years later, following the publication of the Pujo report, Samuel Untermyer and Louis Brandeis asserted that a large body of aggrieved outsider investors *already* existed, in order to draw attention to the imperative need for immediate reform. Both camps rhetorically recast the investor as a legitimate—even central—player in the political economy, one whose interest were aligned with—rather than opposed to—those of the public at-large. Both camps targeted the financial securities markets for state-mandated reform.

Assertions about the desirability of mass investment and the regulatory needs of the small investor grew out of a larger debate on the "trust problem." Progressive proposals to regulate the financial securities markets marked an enormous departure in thinking about financial securities, exchanges, and investors. Herein lay the precursor of a new political-economic ideal—the ideal of investor democracy—in which mass investment in financial securities would democratize modern capitalism and restore propertied status to the citizenry.

In 1913, the governors of the New York Stock Exchange finally awakened to the looming prospect of federal regulation that would restructure their institution fundamentally. In response to progressive proposals for regulation of the nation's securities exchanges, the governors of the Stock Exchange turned reformers' rhetorical strategy on its head.

CHAPTER TWO

The "Free and Open Market" Responds

L IKE MOST MEMBERS of the New York Stock Exchange, R. T. H. Halsey was inured to the hostility of the public. Popular antipathy toward financial securities, brokers, and exchanges he dismissed as mere ignorance. But unlike his less politically astute colleagues, Halsey—a Republican National Convention delegate—attended closely to how politicians made use of anti–Wall Street sentiment. In the first decade of the new century, Halsey grew ever more alarmed as, in his view, both Democrats and Republicans—not just the Populist fringe—increasingly pandered to public ignorance with such measures as the U.S. Senate Industrial Commission, bills proposing federal incorporation of interstate corporations, and state blue-sky laws. Halsey warned his fellow Stock Exchange governors that legislation directly impinging upon their institution would come, illustrating the threat with a scrapbook filled with editorials and cartoons criticizing the NYSE. But Halsey's counsel fell on deaf ears.

It took the Pujo investigation and the 1912 presidential campaign to capture the attention of Exchange members. Just before the Pujo Committee convened in May 1912, the members of the New York Stock Exchange broke with tradition. With their election of an "insurgent" nominating ticket, they signaled their dissatisfaction both with the "self-perpetuating character of the Governing Committee" and its unwillingness to defend their institution. R. T. H. Halsey held high hopes for the new blood joining him on the Governing Committee, especially William C. Van Antwerp, a former journalist, and the new president of the Exchange, James C. Mabon. Perhaps this "younger element," more "in sympathy with the demands for better methods of doing business on the Exchange," could diffuse demands for government supervision by refuting the allegations of muckraking journalists, crusading politicians, and especially self-styled "people's" lawyers like Louis Brandeis and Samuel Untermyer.[1]

The Pujo hearings dashed Halsey's hopes. Those sent to testify allowed Samuel Untermyer to finger the New York Stock Exchange as the minion of the "money trust." Untermyer emphasized the importance of securities exchanges—the way in which floor trading determined the prices of securities, how banks more readily lent to listed corporations, and how the stock market facilitated corporate mergers, for example—but in a manner that cried out for government oversight. With their clumsy evasions and inept attempts to underplay manipulation in the prices of listed securities, the NYSE delegation came across as arbitrary in their administration of the Exchange and indifferent to the interests of minority shareholders and the public at-large, just as the slippery-tongued inquisitor charged.[2]

That a man like Samuel Untermyer dare question the public-mindedness and patriotism of an institution to which R. T. H. Halsey belonged must have outraged this scion of a wealthy, pedigreed New England family. A long line of bankers and merchants connected Halsey to his Puritan forebears. His grandfather served as aide-de-camp to General George Washington and belonged to the Society of the Cincinnati. His father, like Halsey himself, cherished the Presbyterian faith and the Republican Party. Proud of this heritage, Halsey devoted his time and his fortune to preserving the finest artifacts of the nation's past for public display. In 1906, when no museum in the country displayed any American decorative arts, Halsey donated a sizable amount of funding to the Metropolitan Museum of Art to develop an "Americana side." He penned the catalog for the very first exhibition of Early American silver at the Museum of Fine Arts in Boston. In 1909, Halsey lent his own collection to the Met's Hudson-Fulton Exhibition. It established the reputation of New York City furniture maker Duncan Phyfe and later served as the basis for the early republic period rooms in the Met's American Wing, which Halsey would curate. In 1910, the mayor appointed Halsey Municipal Art Commissioner, charged with redecorating the Governors' Room in City Hall.[3]

The furniture, textiles, prints, silver, ceramics, and architecture produced by preindustrial craftsman embodied for R. T. H. Halsey the essential American traits of simplicity, industriousness, and individualism. Halsey viewed the New York Stock Exchange as just another expression of the unique national proclivity for individual initiative and voluntary association. His governorship seemed to him quite similar to the service that he rendered willingly and without recompense to the Metropolitan Museum and the City of New York.[4]

Provenance and authenticity—in men as in objects—consumed R. T. H. Halsey. He deemed Samuel Untermyer just the kind of "pious fraud" that he abhorred. Untermyer presented himself as a champion of "the people," in particular, the long-suffering "investing public." Yet this son of a prosperous Confederate planter had enriched himself by lending his assistance to some of the largest, most infamous industrial combinations, including Bethlehem Steel and Amalgamated Copper, the very merger lambasted by Thomas W. Lawson in *Frenzied Finance*. Subsequent work representing security holders in corporate reorganizations polished Untermyer's reputation and swelled both his pockets and his head, in Halsey's estimation. The audacious parvenu ensconced himself at his Greystone estate in Yonkers, surrounded by works of European Old Masters, rare orchids, and prized show dogs. With an exterior that suggested "a French chateau," Greystone boasted a vulgar pastiche of Gothic, French Renaissance, Louis XV, Louis XVI, and Pompeiian-styled decor. Gold dripped from the walls of the salon and ebony-paneled "den." Elaborate "stained glass tiles" and "ornamental work" adorned the "turkish bath" and indoor pool. Untermyer's rhetoric paid homage to the general good, but Halsey suspected that partisanship in fact inspired his proposals. After all, Untermyer had served as a delegate to the Democratic National Convention since 1904.[5]

Now, thanks to Samuel Untermyer, the New York Stock Exchange found itself caught in the crosshairs of progressive reform. In 1913, legislators deliberated over bills either drafted or endorsed by Untermyer that would regulate the members and the practices of securities exchanges. In Congress, the Owen bill denied the use of the mail, telegraph, and telephone to securities exchanges that failed to adopt certain rules regarding listing procedures, the information that listed corporations must disclose, and members' trading practices and relations with their customers. In Albany, Governor William Sulzer proposed to force the Exchange to incorporate, which would abolish its distinctive character as a voluntary association of independent firms and subject its membership, governors, and listed companies to rules specified by legislators in the incorporation charter. Meanwhile, more and more states passed blue-sky laws requiring securities brokers to obtain licenses and creating commissions to approve new issues of stocks and bonds.[6]

The future of the New York Stock Exchange now seemed unclear. Whatever their particulars, all the bills inspired by the Pujo Committee jeopardized the Exchange's status as a private, self-governing association, as well as the distinction of a NYSE membership or listing. Any broker and any security traded on any exchange would be subject to the same regulatory and judicial oversight. Any such leveling of the brokerage industry might undermine the NYSE's ability to maintain the fixed commission that members charged customers to execute trades, its governors feared.[7]

For R. T. H. Halsey and his colleagues, more than the traditions of the New York Stock Exchange and the prerogatives of its member-elected governors were at stake. Halsey blamed the 1913–1914 recession on recent economic legislation. The Pujo inquiry, the Federal Reserve and Clayton Antitrust Acts, the Federal Trade Commission, the Newlands Act (to mediate railway labor controversies), and the refusal of the Interstate Commerce Commission to raise railroad rates all demoralized the business community, Halsey believed. Businessmen would only "pluck up their ears and affairs change for the better" if conservative Republicans lured back those that had followed Teddy Roosevelt into the Progressive Party in 1912. For Halsey, the best course of action was clear. The Exchange must adopt the idioms of its Populist and Progressive foes to answer the expansion of the regulatory and administrative state.[8]

R. T. H. Halsey and his fellow NYSE governors determined to turn the charges that Populists and Progressives levied against the Exchange to its advantage. In response to the Pujo report, the Stock Exchange conceded that an "investing public" existed, but it refused to yield to government oversight. Exchange spokesmen redeployed the rhetorical figure of the small investor as a justification for continued self-governance: Everyman must remain free to trade securities in the "free and open market" without paternalistic and inefficient regulatory hand-holding. Given members' expertise, the existing structure of administration by committees of member-governors safeguarded investors best. State oversight, NYSE spokesmen contended, would compromise Everyman's ability to have access to its "free and open market" and interfere with members' optimal distribution of economic resources and risk. Exchange representatives further insisted that the American political economy be organized for the benefit of the "investing public," and that economic policy be judged according to its impact on securities owners. The Exchange's embrace of the small investor proved mostly rhetorical. Believing that lambs' losses only incited meddlers like Samuel Untermyer to clamor for regulatory legislation, the governors of the Stock Exchange simultaneously issued new directives that dissuaded members from pursuing retail brokerage.

The Exchange's campaign to defend itself against regulatory encroachment aimed to incite a conservative insurgence among the nation's businessmen, financiers, and investors. As they construed any form of state intervention in the economy as an elitist attack on individual freedom, the NYSE set itself apart from the "corporate-liberal" executives and bankers who dominated the history of business politics and economic policy in the Progressive Era. During this period, a great many financial and corporate leaders came to doubt the ability of modern industrial capitalism to self-regulate. They began to consider how they might cooperate with the state to stabilize and rationalize the economy. The regulatory and administrative state expanded to address the instabilities of modern capitalism, but it often delegated authority and administration to private groups, as with the Federal Reserve. The Stock Exchange, however, refused any such rapprochement. Its governors considered Samuel Untermyer's notion that incorporation and the oversight of the Postmaster General would transform their institution into an "instrument for carrying out the great reforms in corporate management" simply preposterous and completely undesirable, even if the Exchange was allowed to enforce the provisions of an incorporation charter or the directives of the Postmaster General. Rejecting corporate liberalism, Exchange representatives propagated a fresh, finance-centered version of laissez-faire. It proclaimed that all state interference in the economy crushed individual initiative and private property, allegedly epitomized by the privately administered NYSE.[9]

As the Exchange took steps to repel the regulatory state, it discovered allies among the bankers and publicists of the Pennsylvania Railroad. It also encountered a rival organization—the National Association of Owners of Railroad Securities—that drew very different conclusions about how the state could advance the interests of an imagined "investing public."

IN FEBRUARY 1913, the governors of the New York Stock Exchange launched a public relations department. Chaired by R. T. H. Halsey and staffed by NYSE members, this Committee on Library (COL) aimed to reshape public perceptions of the Exchange and its practices in order to secure legitimacy for their institution and thereby preserve its autonomy. The COL immediately opened an on-site library for use by members and their customers, legislators, and journalists. Publications penned by COL members William C. Van Antwerp and H. S. Martin sought to refute Pujo investigation findings, Samuel Untermyer's speaking tours, and Louis Brandeis's *Other People's Money* series. All promised to galvanize public opinion behind bills that the Exchange governors considered adverse to their institution. "Suggest something along these lines but use your own language," Halsey instructed NYSE members as he circulated COL publications through members' branches and customer lists. Legislators, journalists, academics, libraries, financial institutions, and other stock and commodities exchanges also received COL materials. Halsey urged Exchange members to apply pressure on their elected officials; his connections within the Republican Party proved invaluable. "A very effective argument to use with those active in Republican politics," he advised one colleague in Ohio, "is that it is increasingly difficult for those of us who year after year contribute to Republican campaign funds to remain Republicans" when those elected to office failed to oppose securities exchange regulation strenuously.[10]

In its publications, the NYSE portrayed itself as a "free and open market" for financial securities that performed two essential economic functions. First, members' continuous trading produced securities prices and distributed economic risk to those most able to bear it. Second, the Stock Exchange facilitated corporations' accumulations of capital. By delineating these two functions, the NYSE aimed to refute recurring allegations that members watered stocks, manipulated prices, and orchestrated financial panics. Further, it intended to suggest the futility and danger of state-based regulation.

In the course of competitive trading, Exchange authors posited, "the combined judgment of thousands of experts" was integrated into one "scientific," or objective, price for any listed security. This process constituted a "natural regulator of securities prices." Like economic tea leaves, share prices signaled the most promising investment opportunities. The Exchange's self-administered market offered the best possible mechanism for processing and signaling information so that economic order could emerge spontaneously. The valuation of the worth of a corporation also allegedly depended upon the price-making work of the Exchange. The value of any listed corporation should be determined by multiplying share price by the number of outstanding shares—*never* through the kind of valuation inquiries conducted by the Interstate Commerce Commission and similar regulatory bodies. And as NYSE traders continuously purchased and sold securities, they allegedly took up and redistributed economic risk. Their collective efforts yielded a "free and open"—or, in today's parlance, liquid—market, where any investor theoretically might turn cash into securities (or vice versa) at any time.[11]

In truth, the Exchange assigned responsibility for making a market in each listing to *one* member: a specialist stationed at a post on the floor. At all times, the specialist was required to bid (offer a price at which he was willing to buy) and to ask (offer a price at which he was willing to sell). He acted both as a broker (matching orders between other members) and a dealer (trading for his own account). Because all orders traveled through the specialist, he enjoyed privileged information. He could accept the best bids and ask for his own trades, or even advance manipulations in the prices of his assigned stock. Indeed, specialists played key roles in the insider manipulations of the era. Concerned with refuting accusations of manipulation and insider privilege, NYSE spokesmen typically played down the specialist in their accounts. Often they characterized trading floor activity as continuous competition that ultimately yielded consensus in the form of the executed price. Indeed, the Stock Exchange recast itself as the purest expression of economic competition, despite the fixed commission rate that members charged.[12]

As traders crafted "scientific" prices in many different stocks, the stock market itself was produced, NYSE publicists contended. Aggregate stock market levels served as a "barometer" of future economic conditions, for traders' decisions took into account (or "discounted") anticipated future prospects. Even if would-be manipulators enjoyed a "brief hour" by issuing false rumors, fake trades, and phony reports, the market always responded "to actual conditions and discount[ed] the future of those conditions." Exchange writers asserted that securities prices reflect all known information and prognostications in order to defend self-governance when faced with state-based regulation. For just as artificial manipulation of barometer readings could not alter impending weather, they argued, no regulatory attempt to modulate the volatility of securities markets could ever prevent any economic change those markets had forecast. Even if regulation could be devised to modulate the market, it would replace the "combined judgment of thousands of experts" with the oversight of an inexpert few. And just as a barometer could not be held accountable for impending changes in the weather, the NYSE could scarcely be blamed if a decline in securities prices preceded an economic downturn, it maintained.[13]

Critics of Stock Exchange trading practices most vigorously objected to short-selling, in which traders (bears) borrowed securities from long-term investors and then sold them. Bears did so believing that the price of the borrowed securities would fall. If it did, bears could repurchase the securities they owed at a lower price, return them to the lender, and pocket the price difference. Critics alleged that bears profited from others' losses, expressed unpatriotic pessimism, and drove down the price of stocks. Exchange authors rejoined that, in fact, these "short" sellers prevented bubbles and furnished buying support during stock market panics. Further, they equated both short-selling and speculation (short-term trading, often with borrowed funds) with the typical manner in which merchants commonly used credit to finance commerce. Unless voters intended "to abolish property altogether, do away with the instruments of credit, and suppress all forms of trading designed to supply future requirements," they had better "reconcile" themselves to the NYSE, for it ostensibly embodied all the natural, immutable tendencies of *homo economicus*.[14]

Despite these references to the laws of economics and the veracities of human nature, Exchange claims were hardly based on extensive empirical investigation. Academic economists of the day viewed securities trading as largely unrelated to their discipline's major concerns: production, distribution, and consumption in the real economy. The NYSE culled selectively from the writings of academics and journalists. Its authors appropriated the term "free and open market" from economist Henry C. Emery. The conceptualization of the stock market as a macroeconomic "barometer" originated with journalist Charles A. Conant, the chief theorist of banking reform. Neither writer shared the Exchange's strict antiregulatory stance.[15]

Exchange members laid claim to a second economic contribution as brokers, delivering customers' funds to worthy corporations. Stock Exchange authors posited that "industrial progress" dictated that firms incorporate and list their securities on the NYSE, even as they steadfastly refused the Pujo proposal that the Exchange itself should incorporate. In truth, much of early twentieth-century industry did not assume corporate form. Even many of the largest corporations raised capital to fund growth through private buyouts, independent promotions, or retained earnings.[16] John D. Rockefeller Sr. preferred to remain "independent of the Street," financing Standard Oil's operations out of its earnings. Department store magnate John Wanamaker never sold securities to the public, either. "I shall be better for learning to depend on myself, humanly," he wrote in his diary in 1907, "rather than on the financial system of our country that now operates by the might and money power of a few." Likewise, Henry Ford built his automotive empire without accessing securities markets.[17]

Nonetheless, the Exchange emphasized the process by which corporations raised capital in order to assert a productive—rather than parasitic—identity for itself. Its publications played down the secondary trading (in which money goes from one investor to another as one sells a security and another buys it) that the NYSE could more properly claim to its credit. When NYSE authors did mention speculation, it was defined as holding "securities ready in the market" for multitudes of long-term investors of modest means. Given this intimate coupling of speculation and investment, no legislative attempt to abolish or diminish the former would ever stabilize or promote the latter, Stock Exchange representatives contended. Instead, state-based regulation would choke the flow of the masses' savings to corporations, the NYSE swore.[18]

Stock Exchange writers asserted that when insurance companies, banks, or individuals utilized NYSE brokers, "the public" determined "the direction which new capital shall be applied to new undertakings." Exchange members simply executed the investing public's plans for national economic development. Society as a whole benefited when men tested by experience and recognized by colleagues and customers valued and circulated financial capital. These stewards piloted corporate capitalism *for* the people, even if this economy was not constituted of all the people acting as direct investors. With these arguments, the NYSE reframed itself as a kind of an investors' republic. This move foreshadowed the Exchange's celebration of itself as the embodiment of a shareholders' democracy in the 1920s.[19]

At the pen of Exchange authors, then, the "small investor" and the "investing public"—rhetorical figures first conjured to support demands for legislative reform—justified rejection of those same proposals. In the 1910s, NYSE publicists conceded the existence of *an* investing public—composed of financial institutions that invested depositors' funds and *some* individuals investing directly—but avowed that Exchange self-governance best served that public and expressed its will. After all, Everyman (or at least the institutions that held his funds) had *chosen* to trade on the unregulated NYSE.

Even so, Exchange spokesmen trod carefully. They aimed to establish that the NYSE served but never abused the public, was not a monopoly, and therefore required no state oversight. On one hand, the Stock Exchange stressed its members' caution in dealing with inexperienced clients. On the other hand, the NYSE trumpeted how Everyman enjoyed the very same access as the "the richest investor in the land." In the end, it scarcely mattered whether sizable numbers of Americans actually invested. The point was to reconfigure individual economic freedom as the *possibility* of trading stocks and bonds—win or lose—through privately administered markets. True economic freedom involved assuming the risk of failure. If the state excused the individual from consequences, "society" would become "more solicitous of the man who fails than the man who succeeded . . . is this not dangerous ground?" R. T. H. Halsey asked the editor of the *Saturday Evening Post*. If the ignorant "proletariat below the stairs" indulged in unwise speculations, this provided no justification for politicians to meddle with critical and delicate economic processes, the Exchange insisted.[20]

Having enshrined the Exchange as the cornerstone of modern capitalism, NYSE publicists tapped traditional aversions to strong central government to dismiss abuse allegations and reform bills. They scoffed at Samuel Untermyer for his alleged belief

> . . . that government can set everything right, and that through all wise and beneficent lawmaking the ills of society can be cured. It is an ambitious programme, affording a view of a distant Utopia and of the delectable mountains of humbug. No government can be better than the governed; no government is all wise and few are beneficent . . . [government] is not a philanthropic agency, it cannot . . . protect the individual against himself.[21]

"Demagogues and self-seekers" like Untermyer misrepresented the Stock Exchange, its spokesmen charged. Proposed legislation could scarcely improve—and most likely would impair—member-experts' fulfillment of their critical economic functions. The machinery of financial securities markets proved too delicate for politicians' bumbling hands, insisted Exchange writers. They flung mud back at the farm-bloc congressmen most committed to securities market reform. Blame for distressed economic conditions lay in the inherently wasteful tendencies of the state, the NYSE claimed. Retail investors' losses in the stock market paled in comparison to the costs of "all these junkets, all these investigations, and all these political excursions" and frivolities such as civil servant and veterans pensions, agricultural programs, transportation infrastructure and post offices. Private capital, the Stock Exchange averred, financed essential expenditures far more efficiently. This alleged contrast between the expert, mechanical, and free nature of privately administered markets and the inefficiency, corruption, and oppression of the state lay at the heart of the NYSE's new institutional identity as the "free and open market."[22]

As its second task, the Committee on Library worked doggedly to induce others to accept and to propagate its portrayal of the New York Stock Exchange as the "free and open market" for financial securities. With the assistance of NYSE members across the United States, the COL monitored newspapers, advised reporters, editors, and publishers on articles, rewarded allies with exclusive material, and forwarded favorable clippings as models. Columnist Albert Atwood at *Harper's Weekly* (which had first published Brandeis's *Other People's Money*) and the *Saturday Evening Post* soon became the COL's most favored recipients for story suggestions and "assignments." The COL challenged depictions of the NYSE as a "gambling hell" or a stockyard where voracious bulls and bears fleeced lamblike small investors. Chairman R. T. H Halsey even threatened a libel suit against the producers of a 1914 film adaptation of Frank Norris 1903 novel, *The Pit*. Scenes in which trading pits yielded psychological dissolution—rather than scientific prices—were eliminated. Never again would a yuletide lamb slaughter take place on the trading floor of the New York Stock Exchange. Instead, *The New York Stock Exchange* (1919) presented empty, tidy trading floors and groups of neatly attired clerks calmly operating pneumatic tubes, tickers, and telephones.[23]

But of all the misperceptions about the Stock Exchange, the public's alleged inability to distinguish between NYSE brokerages and nonmember bucket shops troubled Exchange leaders most. According to the legal definition, a bucket shop accepted wagers on the movement of stock prices as recorded on the ticker tape, with no physical transfer of stock. Exchange spokesmen, however, deemed any nonmember firm that offered generous credit a bucket shop. The ruse of a small "margin" (or down payment) enticed the incompetent, the NYSE charged. When stock prices fell, buckeeters called for more margin. If customers did not put up more money, their accounts were liquidated. The Exchange accused bucket-shop customers of gambling on price movements; the "margin" actually constituted a wager.[24]

In 1913, Governor William Sulzer introduced legislation that strengthened New York laws against bucket shops. As NYSE governors knew quite well—and as bucketeers reminded the press—certain Exchange practices easily could be interpreted as wagering on the movement of stock prices. Some NYSE commission houses allowed clients to open accounts on minimal margin. Short sales between Exchange members settled without physical transfer of stock. NYSE odd-lot houses (which executed trades in less than the typical 100-share lot) based prices on the last sale of a stock, and not on the current bid or ask offered in the regular, full-lot market. Unfriendly judges might classify any of these practices as illegal, governors feared.

To avoid running afoul of the new law, the COL took measures to differentiate members' brokerages from bucket shops. Exchange publications contended that members, as craftsmen of prices and bearers or risk, had earned an exclusive right to the fruits of their labor: the securities quotations recorded on the ticker tape. Because a NYSE member's "willingness to assume economic risk actually creates values," William Van Antwerp claimed, "he has the right to profit, since he has really earned it." By contrast, when bucket shops accessed NYSE quotations, they secured "an unfair return for labor performed by others." Emboldened by this argument, the Stock Exchange demanded a new contract with Western Union that permitted NYSE officials to veto any request for tickers delivering NYSE quotations. Hoping to induce the courts to order the Exchange to share its quotations, bucket shops styled themselves "poor man's stock exchanges" and decried an Exchange "monopoly" in market data. So the Stock Exchange turned to the muckraking expose—that favored technique of its Progressive foes—to publicize the losses of bucket shop customers. The COL delivered a report on "two extensive chains of bucket shops" to "federal authorities" and Albert Atwood at *Harper's*. Police raids closed the identified establishments.[25]

By deflecting attention, the Exchange secured a truce with the regulatory state. The members of the NYSE Committee on Library certainly believed that their efforts had altered both public opinion and the political environment. Samuel Untermyer agreed that the COL had stymied his agenda. By emitting "false distress signals at every attempted economic reform," Untermyer charged, the COL misled the public and stirred up among legislators "a degree of uncertainty and alarm" that was "grossly disproportioned" to the actual economic significance of the Exchange. Concerned with the outcome of the midterm elections, President Wilson grew wary of deepening the recession and failed to endorse bills to regulate the exchanges. The Owen bill died, and neither the Federal Reserve Act, nor the Clayton Antitrust Act, nor the Federal Trade Commission impinged upon NYSE self-governance. In the state of New York, prospects for reform dwindled with Governor Sulzer's impeachment in 1914.[26]

Both Committee on Library and its adversaries believed its efforts had improved relations with voters, journalists, and legislators. In many ways, this task proved easier than convincing the membership to jettison cherished aspects of their occupational identities. For when NYSE spokesmen refigured the Exchange as a "free and open market" where Everyman might trade, they cast aside members' long-standing sense of themselves as fellows in a private club, a place where beastlike brokers locked horns, bared claws, and ravaged an ovine public. Given the Exchange's status as a private association, many members disagreed that it should change its culture or even defend itself. When NYSE governors strengthened internal systems of restraint so as to avoid external regulation, many members resisted. Some clung tenaciously to their old ways. Others demanded a different reformulation of the Exchange's institutional identity.[27]

Members voiced differing critiques of the governors' strategy. Investment banks and wholesale brokerages that owned NYSE seats feared that the governors' newfound sensitivity toward public opinion would prompt closer scrutiny of new issues of securities. Many NYSE traders and specialists relished bulls-vs.-bears imagery and counted pools and corners among the tricks of their trade, even if some of these practices stood in violation of the formal rules of the Exchange. Accordingly, they resented the governors' resolve—to appear, at least, to forestall manipulation by establishing another new committee, the Committee on Business Conduct (CBC) in 1913. NYSE commission and odd-lot houses likewise damned the CBC, which received retail customers' complaints and investigated NYSE firms that failed to require "adequate margin" from customers, committed "improper use" of a customers' securities, or issued advertising "not of a strictly business character." Censorship particularly vexed NYSE commission houses that wished to pursue retail investors. Odd-lot houses offered the mechanism through which commission houses executed trades in less than the 100-share standard (retail investors generally could not afford a full 100-share lot) and therefore sided with the commission houses. To these groups, it made no sense that the Stock Exchange should proclaim itself a "free and open market" if the CBC impeded retail brokerage.[28]

Ultimately, an "Old Guard" coalition of individual traders, most specialists, investment banks, and wholesale brokerages held the balance of power at the prewar Exchange. Because retail investors played little role in the business models of this dominant coalition, the CBC curtailed advertising by the NYSE commission houses. It forbade the use of "catch phrases," illustrations, narrative, ornate fonts or borders, and "rumours of a sensational character," for such devices drew "a class of business" deemed "not desirable." Retail brokerage required firms to borrow heavily in order to lend heavily to their customers. Should such a firm fail, it might bring shame upon the Exchange. If small investors' losses inspired demagogues to jump on the NYSE-reform bandwagon, then members should avoid the retail segment, the Old Guard believed. No matter if this policy ran against the grain of the Exchange's new institutional identity as a "free and open market" that welcomed the trades of Everyman.[29]

Commission houses, odd-lot houses, and their advertising agencies balked. "Maligned and misrepresented," the Stock Exchange required "not less advertising, but more" to broaden "the market beyond the group surrounded by ticker tapes," these members insisted. Every modern technique of consumer enticement should be employed to promote securities ownership, advertising agents urged. For when the "the ownership of our great corporations" became "democratized," the nation would achieve equitable distribution of wealth and attain true economic democracy.

> We talk about our labor unions, we talk about the growth of Socialism. [Yet] Capital . . . insists on 1000 dollar bonds, it insists on narrow professional minds, it insists on . . . making the field of finance some sacred precinct into which people must have a passport to enter.

An employee of John Muir and Co.—a large NYSE commission house that often ran afoul of the CBC for its steep interest charges, rude collection letters, and use of catch phrases—concurred about the "important political consequences" of securities ownership.

> The man who owns a few shares of stock . . . is a great big island of common sense . . . He thinks intelligently on business subjects, and he votes intelligently, and he influences other people.

To democratize corporations and to restore proprietary democracy in the form of universal securities ownership—this was the proper institutional mission for the NYSE, according to its commission and odd-lot house members.[30]

While Exchange members and governors wrangled over the place of the small investor, the NYSE Committee on Library turned its attention to regulation pertaining to listed corporations, particularly railroads, which composed a large proportion of NYSE listings. Stock Exchange representatives joined forces with publicists and bankers from the Pennsylvania Railroad to demand that federal transportation and tax policy prioritize the interests of the investing public. As R. T. H. Halsey had hoped, Exchange public relations contributed to a larger backlash against the regulatory state. Even so, the NYSE and its allies soon encountered formidable competition for the role of the voice of the investing public. In 1917, the National Association of Owners of Railroad Securities (NAORS) also demanded recognition as the due representative of a legitimate—indeed, vital—investing public. With its corporate liberal orientation toward economic policy, NAORS would achieve far more success in shaping transportation policy.[31]

In 1914, the outbreak of war in Europe flooded the American financial markets. Europeans unloaded American securities in return for cash and gold, while belligerent nations jockeyed to market their war bonds to American investors. As prices of outstanding rail securities declined precipitously, American railroads found it impossible to raise new capital abroad and very difficult to do so domestically. The introduction of the federal income tax in 1916 made matters worse, as investors replaced railroad securities with tax-exempt state and municipal bonds.[32]

But the NYSE and the Pennsylvania Railroad circle blamed misguided federal transportation policy and hostile regulators exclusively. If investors entertained any other explanations for the poor performance of their railroad securities, these self-styled mouthpieces of financial capital endeavored to correct them. They argued that when the Interstate Commerce Commission set railroad rates (as authorized under the 1906 Hepburn Act), it deferred to shippers and undervalued invested capital, thereby yielding insufficient returns for investors. This assessment was based on the Advance Rate Case of 1910, when Louis Brandeis (representing shippers) waylaid a rate increase by asserting that the railroads could save $1 million per day by implementing scientific management techniques.[33]

In 1914–1915, Pennsylvania Railroad publicist Ivy Lee and Otto Kahn of investment bank Kuhn, Loeb joined the NYSE's William C. Van Antwerp for a cross-country tour. In speeches, in publications and communications with the press, and as they lobbied congressmen and regulators, these spokesmen portrayed investors as worthy of consideration, even priority, in matters of economic policy. These three traversed the country to explain to newspaper editors, chambers of commerce, and railroad industry groups exactly how the ICC was "strangling the railroads" through over-regulation and failure to raise rates.[34]

To establish the presence, legitimacy, and grievances of an investing public, NYSE spokesmen designed to publicize financial losses suffered by public—that is, nonprofit—institutions. Before a 1914 ICC hearing, in which Louis Brandeis again appeared as special counsel for the "public interest," R. T. H. Halsey twisted the arm of president Reverend Charles A. Richmond of Union College:

> I imagine that your institution's investments are largely in railroad securities, and that the funds for your running expense . . . come largely from [the donations] of those interested in the railroad situation.

In case Richmond missed the hint, Halsey informed him that those "attempting to handle the railroad credit situation" had chosen him to testify before the ICC. Publicists from the NYSE, Pennsylvania Railroad, and Kuhn, Loeb also disingenuously characterized railroad investors as middling individuals who bought "railroad stock to pay . . . rent," rather than institutions or the affluent. Lee urged railroad executives to publicize "the number of shareholders railroads have; how they are increasing and the number of women among them." Under Lee's guidance, the Pennsylvania Railroad established an employee shareownership plan to increase its number of shareholders to accord with his arguments.[35]

Having dismissed the notion that the railroads were "owned in Wall Street" solely, Stock Exchange and Pennsylvania Railroad representatives advanced a case for the economic importance—even centrality—of their imagined investing public. ICC decisions directly robbed a large body of direct investors of their dividends. In doing so, the Commission also injured those lacking any direct investment in the rails. Insufficient rates yielded paltry returns, Lee explained. This, in turn, prompted capital to flee the sector. Unless this trend reversed immediately, Lee and his colleagues argued, rail facilities and service would deteriorate to the detriment of commerce, agriculture, and industry, indeed, the very "growth of the country." Railroad employees would be thrown out of work.[36]

Because the entire nation's economic well-being demanded the recognition of investors' supreme importance, Lee, Kahn, and Van Antwerp insisted that the ICC raise rates immediately. Judging the Commission to be hopelessly incompetent, Van Antwerp demanded that the roads be removed from its jurisdiction and placed under a new agency staffed by "businessmen, railway men, and public-spirited citizens," modeled after the Federal Reserve. Instead, in 1916, news arrived of Louis Brandeis's appointment to the Supreme Court and the passage of the Adamson Act, which instituted an eight-hour day for interstate railroad workers, with additional overtime pay. The Adamson Act enlarged the roads' labor bills without any offsetting increase in rates.[37]

But worst of all, from the point of view of the NYSE and the Pennsylvania Railroad circle, their actions raised the ire of financial institutions holding sizable amounts of American railroad securities that were rapidly losing their value. In 1917, the NAORS organized in Baltimore under the leadership of S. Davies Warfield, president of the Continental Trust Company. Fire and life insurance companies, savings banks, trust companies, and mutual savings banks constituted the membership of the Association. None other than Samuel Untermyer served as legal counsel.[38]

Members of the Owners Association rejected the NYSE-Pennsylvania Railroad claims and designated themselves as the delegates of all railroad investors—individuals and institutions, large and small, stockowners and bondholders. An insurance company was nothing but a "device" whereby "33 million people . . . erected a great sociological plant which in turn has become a great investor," explained one NAORS member. Another insisted that "the poor man, the man that has his money deposited in a savings bank, is the man who is, after all, interested in these railroad companies." The Interstate Commerce Commission consulted "time and again" with railroad executives and managerial and labor organizations. NAORS demanded it now hear the "real owners of the railroad properties, the owners of the securities."[39]

By forming NAORS, institutional investors issued a strong vote of no-confidence in the NYSE and its colleagues affiliated with Pennsylvania Railroad, as well as associations representing transportation executives and managers, including the American Railroad Association and the Association of Railway Executives. With their intransigence on the Adamson Act, resistance to full-crew laws, and antagonism toward the ICC, all these groups had created "a hostile state of mind" toward the roads among voters, regulators, and legislators, according to the Association of Owners.[40]

Yet Warfield and his colleagues agreed with their rivals on certain fundamental matters of political economy. NAORS spokesmen also demanded that regulators prioritize investors' interests. The Owners Association also articulated an investor-centered theory of railroad economics. If the railroads failed to make their interest payments, or if railroad securities continued to lose value, investors would lose their "maintenance" and financial institutions might fail to meet their obligations to their depositors and policyholders, NAORS held. The Association of the Owners also endorsed the notion that the economic welfare of the public at-large was aligned with, rather than opposed to, investors' interests.

But with its far more accepting attitude toward the regulatory and administrative state, the Owners Association parted ways with the NYSE and the Pennsylvania Railroad circle. Allowing that the railroads constituted "public service carriers" in which "the first consideration should be the public interest," NAORS embraced the ICC and sought to expand its mandate. The ICC *should* value capital and determine rates. Rates should guarantee a minimum return for investors, so that the railroad sector could retain and attract the capital required to provide shippers and workers with the best possible treatment.[41]

Given NAORS's more cooperative demeanor, the ICC agreed to admit its representatives to testify on behalf of investors, beginning in June 1917. Soon after, the United States entered World War I and the federal government assumed control of the nation's rail network. The Owners Association participated in negotiations over the U.S. Railroad Administration's (USRA) leasing contract. Ultimately, that contract stipulated guaranteed standard returns, a policy NAORS championed over the objections of the American Railroad Association and the Association of Railway Executives. In March 1918, the Federal Control Act guaranteed that owners of railroad securities would receive a return equal to each road's average earnings over the highly profitable years 1915 through 1917. In May 1918, USRA Director-General William G. McAdoo ordered a rate increase to cover wage hikes for workers and guaranteed standard returns for investors. As the United States entered the Great War, NAORS had mobilized an institutional investor constituency, refused to defer to railway management, financiers, or the New York Stock Exchange, and scored a victory on rate setting.[42]

Despite the disagreements that divided the National Association of Owners of Railroad Securities from the NYSE and the Pennsylvania Railroad circle, these groups' equally firm commitments to the primacy of investors' interests signaled the arrival of a new way of thinking about political economy. To be sure, popular economic thinking, political action, and economic policy all continued to feel the influence of producer-centered theories that held that labor created all economic value and accepted state intervention in the economy to protect the interests of producers. Consumer-oriented theories that viewed consumer demand as the source of economic value and growth and specified widely distributed material prosperity as the proper goal of economic policy also gained ground in the Progressive Era. But on the cusp of the Great War, NAORS, the NYSE, and the bankers and executives of the Pennsylvania Railroad advanced a third, investor-centered manner of conceptualizing political economy. Their rhetoric placed the small investor in the driver's seat of the economy, although in fact, no more than 500,000 Americans directly owned stocks or bonds before World War I.[43]

THE GREAT WAR presented both challenges and opportunities for the New York Stock Exchange. In 1914, a global financial meltdown forced the Exchange to suspend operations. After trading resumed and the United States entered the war in 1917, the NYSE seized the opportunity to achieve recognition in the War Loan drives to fund the war. But the subscription totals ($500,000) secured by even one of the largest NYSE commission house (J. S. Bache and Co.) paled in comparison to the millions raised by banks, corporations, labor unions, women's groups, and ethnic associations. Yet sales mattered less than stature. By lending its trading floor for major Liberty Loan rallies, the NYSE positioned itself as the crux of financial mobilization.[44]

Stock Exchange leaders spied an opportunity to advance their political agenda in the War Loan campaigns. Committee on Library Chairman R. T. H. Halsey penned irate letters to the Interstate Commerce Commission regarding "the hysterical state of mind which exists among the large investing public owing to the long delay in action of the proposed freight rate increase." Halsey warned that a "country-wide demoralization among investors" would undermine efforts to "interest investors in the new Liberty Loans." Despite Halsey's dire predictions, citizen-investors clamored to buy war bonds, inspired by astounding spectacles, mass assemblies, sensational advertising, and local community policing.[45]

The success of the wartime state in distributing its small-denomination bonds to roughly 30 million Americans enhanced the allure of the small investor in the eyes of NYSE commission houses. Unprecedented federal incursions into markets drew the governors' attention, however. During the war, Congress considered exchange incorporation, regulation, and closure in the interest of economic stabilization. These bills met defeat, but the commodity prices were fixed and commodity exchanges closed under Food Administrator Herbert Hoover. Worse, the Federal Reserve's Capital Issues Committee (CIC) monitored new securities issues to ensure that capital was directed toward War Loans and enterprises deemed essential for the war. All these precedents greatly alarmed the governors of the Stock Exchange. The Great War would deepen their commitment to public relations as a means of challenging federal forays into the economy. But it would not cause the governors to reconsider their reservations about retail brokerage.[46]

THE RHETORICAL FIGURE of the small investor first appeared in early twentieth-century discussions of the "trust problem." Antitrust theorists and reformers integrated government regulation of the financial securities markets—including reform of corporate financial disclosure, corporate governance, and the securities exchanges—into their reform agenda. Both supporters and opponents of securities market regulation pressed exaggerated claims about the size of the American investing class. Prewar political controversies over the desirability of such regulation elevated the small investor as a legitimate player in the American political economy, despite the small size of that body in fact. By the eve of the Great War, a new, investor-centered manner of conceptualizing political economy had emerged.

In the War Loan campaigns of World War I, the federal government would further develop and widely propagate an investor-centered theory of political economy. The ideal of an investors' democracy would become reality as millions of American citizen-investors acquired war bonds and dramatized the nation as a financial market in War Loan pageantry and publicity. The War Loan drives encouraged new, positive ways of thinking about the relationship between the practice of investment and the process of democracy. Americans were encouraged to incorporate financial securities ownership into their understandings of national citizenship and national community and to anticipate that widespread ownership of federal debt might transform their society and their state.

As Americans mobilized to fight and to fund World War I, the debate over the interests of "the investor" would grow more vociferous and encompass even more voices. After Armistice, the New York Stock Exchange and its allies would continue to compete with the National Association of Owners of Railroad Securities for recognition as the due representative of the nation's investor class, which grew dramatically and gained considerable legitimacy on account of the War Loan drives. Just as before the war, these groups would by no means agree upon policy matters, even as both groups elevated the figure of the small investor in their rhetoric. The institutional investors represented by NAORS would continue to assert that an active, properly oriented regulatory and administrative state could best promote investors' welfare. The Exchange and its Pennsylvania Railroad allies would continue to judge unregulated markets as best equipped to advance investors' interests.

CHAPTER THREE

"Be a Stockholder in Victory!"

N O ONE HAD ever seen anything like Victory Way. During the last week of April 1919, Park Avenue closed to streetcars, automobiles, and carriages between Forty-fifth and Fiftieth streets. Columns embellished with colorful swags lined the thoroughfare. Behind these, enormous murals depicted scenes of both military *and* industrial glory. After all, workers' labors had contributed as much to victory as soldiers' feats. Overhead, "air displays" simulated aerial engagements. On the ground, a "Panorama of Victory" revealed "the whole picture of the war." Servicemen stationed on floats staged key battles, demonstrated the use of gas masks, and reenacted how they had charged "over the top" of the trenches to engage the loathsome Hun. Other floats informed veterans and their families about the challenges of postwar economic "reconstruction and methods of getting employment" in peacetime. Spectators promenaded through a veritable petting zoo of vanquished German war machines "all taken by Americans." A pyramid of 85,000 German helmets—intended for a triumphal entry into Paris but captured in Coblenz—marked the terminus of Victory Way. The helmets would be distributed to reward Victory bond salesmen, in return for $1,000 bond purchases and for use in ongoing publicity to promote the Victory Loan. This would be the last of five such drives to mass-market federal war debt. Together, the proceeds of the four Liberty Loans, the Victory Loan, and an additional War Savings program paid for roughly 60 percent of the costs of the Great War.[1]

Twice Treasury Secretary William G. McAdoo addressed the crowds assembled on Victory Way, urging citizen-investors to settle "the final accounting and reckoning with the money side of this great war" by purchasing the bonds of the Victory Loan. His wife, Eleanor, daughter of President Woodrow Wilson and chairman of the National Woman's Liberty Loan Committee, spoke before assemblies of women in which female Liberty Loan canvassers received special recognition. "Ethnic Honor Day" concluded the week. "Speakers from many lands" urged the "loyal to lend freely for victory," for the government required still more funds to bring the boys home. Attired in traditional costume, groups representing twenty-nine nationalities marched down Victory Way, in alphabetical order to avoid any appearance of hierarchy. At parade's end, the chairman of the War Loan Organization's Foreign Language Bureau delivered a speech on how "Victory Loan subscriptions make the world safe from Bolshevism," the great peril that democracy faced still.[2]

How incredible to see thousands of citizen-investors inspecting the return on their investments on Victory Way. How inspiring to imagine millions more dispersed across the nation, and to consider how so many of these had, at first, opposed American participation in the Great War. But most remarkable was to witness how the wartime state and fellow citizen-investors paid homage to groups otherwise marginalized in political and civic life. The wartime state sought their funds, and their support, too. The War Loans redrew the boundaries of civic inclusion, admitting workers, women, and recent immigrants as equals in a new national imaginary.[3]

Despite the nation's triumph over German autocracy, many of the original concerns that motivated the administration's decision to mass-market the debt accrued to pay for the war remained unresolved. The recent general strike in Seattle involving 65,000 workers, for example, convinced a great many Americans of the necessity of continued vigilance against the rising cost of living that incited labor strife, as well as the radicalism of foreign-born subversives. As it had during the war, the Wilson administration looked to universal ownership of federal bonds, stamps, and certificates to meet these threats against the nation by conveying to every American a portion of property and a stake in lawful government.

When the subscription books for the Victory Loan closed, Treasury Department officials rejoiced in the successful distribution of federal war debt across the population. In the four Liberty Loan and the final Victory Loan campaigns that took place between June 1917 and May 1919, an estimated 20 million subscribers (82 percent of U.S. households or roughly 20 percent of the population) pledged to buy a federal war bond. These drives raised $21.4 billion. The second program of the Treasury Department's War Loan Organization, War Savings, collected roughly $1 billion during the war through the sale of savings stamps and certificates to as many as 34 million men, women, and children (nearly a third of the population). Neither financial reformers, nor their opponents, nor those firms that marketed financial securities had ever dreamed of such a sizable retail market. Before the Great War, no more than 500,000 Americans had owned any type of publicly traded financial security—stock or bond, government or corporate.[4]

Mass distribution of war bonds had not been necessary from a practical standpoint. The cost of distant military excursions might have been met through taxation, by printing money, or by relying on wealthy individuals and institutions to purchase federal debt. But these other methods would not have addressed critical political goals of the wartime state. Policy makers looked upon mass investment in federal war debt as a means of encouraging a widespread sense of identification with the war effort and the nation itself. Through mass distribution of Liberty bonds and War Savings stamps and certificates, the Wilson administration aimed to mobilize and to bind all the inhabitants of the United States, even those lacking full political rights.[5]

In doing so, the wartime state loudly interjected into a contentious conversation about the nature of citizenship and nation at a moment when those concepts possessed tremendous fluidity. In the decades preceding World War I, few issues engaged Americans as deeply as those related to American identity, citizenship, and nationhood. The great political controversies of the Progressive Era—women's suffrage, Jim Crow racial segregation, eugenics, immigration, the draft—all raised fundamental questions about the markers and meanings of civic inclusion. Americans debated which groups might achieve citizenship and which should be considered irretrievably unfit. Even immigrants asked what preparation was required for incorporation into the polity, and whether American identity and national allegiance meant jettisoning ethnic heritage and solidarity. Americans grappled with the very definition of citizenship. Which political, civic, and socioeconomic rights and obligations bound individuals to the state and to fellow citizens? Was every citizen entitled to an identical bundle of protections and privileges?[6]

The War Loan campaigns advanced new models of citizenship and nation in answer to those perennial questions. The wartime state instructed Americans that investment constituted a fundamental component of their civic obligation to contribute to the war effort. Investment both made and manifested citizenship, as the citizen-investor assumed full membership in the polity with his or her acquisition of federal war debt. War Loan rhetoric, imagery, and spectacle thereby revised the traditional ideal of proprietary democracy—which grounded citizenship in the ownership and control of property—to accommodate financial securities. Shared investment practices, in turn, constructed a sense of national community among a dispersed, heterogeneous populace, War Loan architects believed. The War Loans modeled the nation as a financial market that integrated every inhabitant as a citizen-investor. In return for their funds and fealty, the federal government assumed responsibility for protecting citizen-investors from fraud and loss.[7]

Many objected to American involvement in the Great War; others rejected the mass-marketing of small-denomination federal debt as improper war finance policy. Domestic criticism compelled the Treasury Department to defend the merit of investment as a set of attitudes and practices that would yield a better future for individuals and for the nation as a whole. Federal securities were promoted as tools of individual economic freedom and national economic stability. The investor-centered theory of political economy embedded in War Loan rhetoric and imagery figured citizen-investors as holding the reins of the nation's economy. The War Loan campaigns encouraged Americans to anticipate that widespread ownership of federal debt would not only win the war, but also transform their economic system and their state.

WHEN Congress declared war on Germany and its allies in 1917, President Woodrow Wilson vowed to make the world "safe for democracy." Yet the American electorate did not stand solidly behind its president. After all, Wilson's victorious 1916 reelection campaign had featured the slogan, "He Kept Us Out of War." Neither could Wilson claim that the millions denied the right to vote—women, African Americans, children, and the newly immigrated—had endorsed the war. Outright resistance ran deep. Pacifists in the Progressive, women's, and socialist movements decried that humble American youth were dying to protect plutocrats' financial interests. Millions of Irish and German Americans steadfastly opposed alliance with the British. To cultivate public support, Wilson established the Committee on Public Information to conduct a sweeping domestic propaganda campaign. As a second measure to engineer and to make evident popular consent, the administration determined to distribute the debt of the wartime state as widely as possible. Countless speeches, posters, and sundry other forms of publicity and pageantry bombarded Americans with constant reminders that "the backbone of the whole matter will be the small investor."[8]

The administration's decisions to rely mostly upon borrowing and to mass-market federal war debt were not foregone. Specific political considerations drove this finance strategy. Apart from cultivating public support for the war, War Loan leaders aimed to integrate noncitizens into the polity and to fold disparate social groups into the nation by fostering a culture of mass investment. Universal ownership of federal securities would stabilize society by forestalling radicalism and curbing inflation, the engineers of the War Loan programs advised. They drew inspiration from the glorification of property ownership that reached back to the American Revolution, as well as the new way of thinking about securities investment as a social stabilizer that reform-minded economists and political commentators first articulated at the opening of the twentieth century. The War Loan drives identified the practice of investment with the process of democracy, urged Americans to recognize investment as a distinguishing feature of the nation's culture, and equated the figure of the investor with that of the citizen.

The architects of the War Loans sought universal investment because they imagined that robust subscription totals both encouraged and expressed broad-based consent and national unity. By distributing its securities "among the people and not among the members of the 'money trust' solely," the wartime state answered domestic criticism that "Wall Street" had "manufactured" the war and lent support to "the President's declaration that this is a people's war," according to one speakers' handbook. Although America's enemies abroad falsely characterized her as "a heterogeneous people incapable of united action," she "revealed herself to be a solidified, homogenous, altruistic, and unselfish nation" when citizen-investors pledged billions. Pervasive bondholding in the United States responded to enemies and allies alike, demoralizing the German people and heartening the Allies. War Loan publicity presented subscription totals as a pronouncement of the vox populi, crafting an analogy between investment and vote. Americans voted in favor of the war "more effectually as if they put a piece of paper in the ballot box" when they subscribed to Liberty Loans. In this formulation, the financial market disclosed consent *more* effectively than democratic political mechanisms. As an added benefit, if citizen-investors lent all that their government required, then the wartime state would not need to commandeer resources and productive capacity. Widespread acquisition of federal debt would bolster administration claims about the consensual and democratic nature of economic mobilization in the United States, in contrast to the autocratic methods employed in Germany.[9]

Mass distribution of federal war debt appealed to the administration because acquisition seemed an ideal method for signifying the loyalty of those denied suffrage: children, women, African Americans, Native Americans, and the newly immigrated. The War Loan drives' financial market model of polity and nation incorporated these previously marginalized groups. By establishing "a point of contact between the government and the individual," War Loan publicity aimed to open a direct line of communication and sense of connection between all citizen-investors and their debt-issuing state. Citizen-investors' shared financial relation with the state, in turn, brought them into closer identification with each other, cementing "the sentiment and population of the country," in the words of Treasury Secretary William G. McAdoo. The leaders of the War Loan Organization envisioned that as individuals acquired and promoted war bonds, stamps, and certificates, they would gain a sense of participation in a national public culture distinguished by the shared practice of investment. This would differentiate the American people from others and overcome the particularities of Americans' various ancestries. Neither shared ethnicity, nor history, nor language knit the national community together. Rather, possession of securities bound citizen-investors as a nation.[10]

The outbreak of the Russian Revolution in November 1917 heightened the administration's anxiety about the loyalty of propertyless immigrants. "The peace of the world is now threatened by this new group of dissatisfied individuals whose creed is MAKE THE OTHER FELLOW DIVIDE WHAT HE HAS SAVED," warned one War Savings tract. Mass investment would nurture "a citizenry of individual responsibility founded on individual ownership," War Loan officials anticipated. Bondholding would inoculate the masses against the virulent utterances of both German agents and Communist agitators by establishing direct, individual financial relationships with the federal government, along with personal "stakes" in the success of the war and the American economic system. "Anything that tends to destroy or disrupt the Government," explained one War Savings bulletin, "destroys or disrupts the individual, and he realizes this more quickly when his investment is in danger of being lost." One Liberty bond speaker proclaimed that a "nation where every man is a capitalist is a sound nation, economically, socially, politically." Indeed, Federal Reserve Governor Robert F. Herrick identified widespread distribution of federal securities— rather than meeting the costs of the war—as "the most important financial project" facing the home front, for universal investment would stir among all inhabitants a "patriotic and political interest in the affairs of the country" and distribute the "steadying influence of owning property" across society. By extending the opportunity to acquire property in a new form, the wartime state aimed to nudge those prone to radicalism into a classic liberal social contract, in which individuals submitted to the rule of law in order to preserve their property. With its small-denomination securities, the wartime state aimed to demolish "the barriers between bondholders and the rest of the people," bridging the chasm of class that might otherwise engulf the United States as it had Russia.[11]

The War Loans embraced all manner of men, women, and children as citizen-investors. But it remapped the imagined social geography of the nation without reexamining existing economic or political inequalities. The War Loans' financial market model of the nation set aside the disparities in the privileges and duties that the state conferred on different categories of Americans. Ownership of federal securities presented a form of obligation and a basis for inclusion more fundamental than, and prior to, traditional modes of political engagement like voting, or military or jury service. Indeed, a "Share in America" trope—employed widely in War Loan rhetoric and imagery—cast federal debt as a more direct stake in the polity than even the vote itself.

> Democracy is meaning more and more . . . formerly it meant only the vote and the right to have a part in the making of laws. Today it means all this and more. It means proprietorship—which comes with the actual owning of the nation's securities . . . A financial interest in the Government, large or small as it may be, helps to make better citizens.[12]

Share in America stretched the ideal of proprietary democracy beyond tangible assets to encompass financial securities—specifically federal war debt—as a suitable qualification for civic inclusion. The War Loans' new ideal of investor democracy grounded citizenship in investment and expanded the categories of persons eligible.

Just as it equated investment with vote and investor with citizen, "Share in America" refigured the state as a corporation and conflated debt and equity. Speakers likened the Liberty bond to a share in "the greatest, the most glorious, the most honorable and most successful corporation in the world." NYSE brokerage John Muir and Co. likewise equated the state with a corporation "which has adopted the policy of sinking earnings into a new enterprise," that of erecting "a structure of democracy in Europe and for the world." On National War Savings Day (June 28, 1918), the War Loan Organization called for "the number of 'stockholders' in the Government" to be "still further increased through the sale of War Savings stamps." Employed in innumerable speeches, images, spectacles, and tracts, Share in America constituted nearly as central a theme in the War Loans as the Great War itself.[13]

War Loan propaganda emphasized citizen-investors' obligation to acquire a Share in America by equating investment with the sacrifices of life and limb made by the young men who discharged the ultimate duty of citizenship on the battlefields of Europe. In films distributed by the War Loan Organization—including "Scrap of Paper," starring popular comic Fatty Arbuckle—cash and bonds morphed magically into soldiers. Treasury Secretary McAdoo enjoined his audiences to "enlist" their "dollars for the period of the war." Even the largest bond purchases amounted to a "small contribution compared to the sacrifice" of the "dying soldier," he contended. Elsewhere, McAdoo contrasted the situation of "volunteers of money," with their "principal impregnably protected," quite favorably to the conscripted soldiers facing death and worse at the hand of the Hun. "Property in America" must not be "less patriotic than the men who are shedding their blood," he declared. War Savings societies encouraged citizen-investors to "join a company of savers" that backed "a company of fighters," while President Wilson demanded that all citizen-investors enlist "in the great volunteer army of production and savings" on National War Savings Day. War Loan rhetoric and imagery idealized the soldier as the unifying figure around which diverse civilians could be rallied to meet their obligations to the wartime state.[14]

The vision of investor democracy propagated in the War Loan campaigns associated a new form of property—financial securities—with the qualifications and responsibilities of citizenship. It also redefined the nature of the sovereignty that property bestowed upon its possessor. The traditional ideal of proprietary democracy had conceived of property as the source of its owner's sustenance, autonomy, and authority over his dependents. In the investor democracy figured in the War Loan drives, by contrast, investment conferred economic freedom in the form of self-restraint, economic stability, social mobility, and individual security.

Foremost, investment conveyed economic freedom by necessitating economic self-mastery, or thrift, the engineers of the War Loans believed. Between 1916 and 1918, the cost of living rose by nearly a third, setting off a series of popular protests. The Treasury Department concluded that the middle and working classes stoked rampaging inflation with their reckless expenditures of high wartime wages. While the Food and Fuel Administration struggled to enforce explicit price controls, the Treasury resolved to absorb consumers' profligate dollars with the War Loans. Even the smallest denomination of Liberty bonds ($50) remained beyond the means of a great many Americans, however. And so, in December 1917, the Treasury Department launched the War Savings program, directed by Frank A. Vanderlip, the Chairman of National City Bank, a former financial journalist and Assistant Secretary of the Treasury, and a key player in the development of the Federal Reserve. The War Savings program sold twenty-five-cent thrift stamps, which could be accumulated into interest-bearing certificates, priced at $4.12 and redeemable in five years for $5.00. Twenty of these could be converted into $100 savings certificates.[15]

From the outset, Vanderlip and his staff and advisors conceived of War Savings as something more than "a war measure." The War Savings program intended to train Americans to invest habitually, in order to augment the nation's "reservoir of capital" permanently and to ensure the "financial future" of every citizen-investor. Even as War Savings pursued its near-term goals of collecting funds, combating inflation, and encouraging the conservation of materials and manpower for the war effort, it endeavored to "press upon the nation for all time the habit of thrift." If Americans continued to "demand the things of luxury, of comfort, of convenience," Vanderlip explained, their purchases would compete against those of the wartime state, undermining the war effort and fueling inflation. The financial obligations of citizenship included a "personal responsibility" to "govern" expenditure in order to cede "the Government free right of way" as it mobilized the economy for war, he maintained. Citizen-investors held "a duty to society, a duty to the Nation—indeed, a duty to the world" not only to purchase small-denomination war debt, but to forgo "unnecessary expenditure" in order to invest to the utmost. Together, thrift and investment would yield economic and social stability, along with military victory, War Savings propaganda promised. Inflation would diminish as demand for consumer goods abated. Citizen-investors would ignite "a backfire against the inevitable wave" of postwar "industrial and political confusion and unrest," for their invested reserves would maintain their purchasing power and compensate for diminished government employment and expenditures after the war.[16]

By practicing thrift and investment, citizen-investors attained economic freedom in the form of social mobility and economic security, according to War Loan propaganda. "Intelligent and consistent saving," one War Savings bulletin advised, offered "the most vital practical step towards personal success" and served as "the foundation" for each citizen-investor's "future independence." To inspire thrift and investment, the War Savings program circulated "stories of business opportunities, where a man investing $1,000 in a small enterprise he built up acquired a fortune—an opportunity that he never could have grasped unless he had first saved the $1,000." It asked newspapers to interject "thrift propaganda" into "stories and editorials." Citizen-investors exercised self-sovereignty by insuring themselves against "all hard knocks," especially dependency in old age, this propaganda suggested, reversing older notions of economic independence that involved command of dependents' labor or self-employment. The War Loan Organization stoked fears of destitution in old age by circulating statistics regarding the debasement of the nation's elderly. Investment in small-denomination

federal securities guarded against just such calamities, War Loan promoters promised. In one Liberty Loan film, "Ready Money Ringfield"
(played by silent Western star Dustin Farnum) and his wife rescued themselves from homelessness and penury in old age with the Liberty bond
that Ringfield discovers in the inside pocket of an old coat. The couple
had acquired the bond thirty years prior, when they foresightedly declined an extravagant wedding. The War Loans vowed to slay both German autocracy and "Want in Old Age," figured as hideous twin vultures.
As Everyman assumed the secure, independent economic position of
citizen-investor, a modern form of proprietary democracy—an investors'
democracy—emerged.[17]

Looking back upon the War Loan experience, Treasury Secretary William G. McAdoo recalled proudly that he had directed "the whole energy
of the Treasury" toward "the heart of the nation, to make the men and
women who bought bonds, or got others to buy them, feel that they were
doing service to their country." By soliciting subscriptions from "the people . . . everybody . . . the average man and woman," the War Loan Organization sought to "acquaint the country" with "the purposes" of the Great
War and to mount a "financial front" of citizen-investors exhibiting the
"same inspiration and morale as the military front of the army." For Mc-
Adoo, mass investment engendered a "quality of coherence" that fused "the
nation together," despite the heterogeneity of the population and the prevalence of opposition to the Great War at its outset. This opposition pushed
the Treasury to mass-market federal war debt and to formulate appeals
that avoided mention of the war but rather positioned securities markets as agencies of democracy and investment as a liberating practice. All
across the United States, War Loan rhetoric and iconography recast both
citizenship and nationhood as it promoted universal ownership of federal
war debt. In the War Loans' vision of the United States transformed into an
investors' democracy, universal investment improved society by restoring
property to the citizenry and restoring their economic freedom. During
World War I, Americans were instructed that the privilege and obligation of
investment extended beyond the immediate crisis. So, too, did the federal
government's responsibility toward citizen-investors.[18]

IF BOND purchases evinced the unity and resolve of the financial nation,
did sales imply a crisis of faith in the war and the administration? After
the federal government issued each series of Liberty bonds, their price
promptly fell below par as they traded on the nation's securities exchanges;
$100 Liberty bonds reached a wartime low of $92.25 in 1918. Modern
observers might find it unremarkable that many investors sold their bonds

and the market price fell as a result, considering that both individuals and institutions were pressured into subscribing for more than they could easily afford. But at the time, the decline in the market value of Liberty bonds presented an enormous problem for the Wilson administration. Critics alleged that the fall in prices proved that Liberty bonds had been overpriced or should have carried a higher rate of interest.[19] While Secretary McAdoo denied that "fluctuations in the market price of government bonds on the Stock Exchange" determined "the patriotism of the American people," Treasury officials fretted that citizen-investors would feel "that the bonds in some way had been misrepresented" and charge their debt-issuing state with betrayal. Losses might also undermine faith in private property and financial markets, turning the "financially ignorant" against "not only Government bonds but against all kinds of securities." In response, the Treasury Department took up new commitments toward citizen-investors. In the War Loan vision of the United States transformed into an investors' democracy, investment constituted not just an obligation, but also a right of citizenship that the federal government was bound to safeguard.[20]

As the war progressed and Liberty bond prices fell, War Loan propaganda cast blame upon nefarious swindlers, those who accepted war bonds as payment for other securities or merchandise. From the first Liberty bond drive, swindlers pursued a variety of schemes. Targeting farmers on account of their bulging pocketbooks and their financial naïveté, swindlers descended after the harvest to peddle get-rich-quick schemes. New "enterprises" accepting Liberty bonds in exchange for stock attracted investors by fraudulently listing trusted figures such as Treasury Secretary William McAdoo and War Savings Chairman Frank Vanderlip as directors. Other schemes were less deceptive, but the Treasury judged them equally undesirable. Retailers that used Liberty bonds as a mode of extending credit to their customers were also charged with swindling. A customer might use bonds to pay for a fur coat while still owing hundreds of dollars on that bond. "When the bonds are exchanged for merchandise," McAdoo explained, "it discourages thrift and increases expenditures, thus depriving the Government of labor and material needed for war purposes." Worse, merchants immediately sold bonds that they accepted for merchandise, depressing "the market price of the issue." All these intrigues amounted to financial sabotage in the eyes of Treasury officials. By enticing citizen-investors to part with their Liberty bonds, swindlers sapped the nation's financial vitality and weakened the ties of securities ownership that bound citizen-investors to each other and to their federal state.[21]

To excise the swindling excrescence from the body politic, the Treasury Department parried with War Loan propaganda. As it sounded the alarm against swindlers, the War Loan Organization explicitly denied that the Treasury had mispriced the bonds or misled citizen-investors. Speakers refuted any "suggestion" that "the present price decline" indicated "that the Government" had "failed to live up to the agreement it made with the investors of the nation." If anything, backsliding citizen-investors were to blame. The disloyal, fair-weather citizen-investor failed to "live up to his agreement" when he dumped his bonds in favor of "extravagance and reckless spending" or "speculative stocks of alluring but highly uncertain promise" or "get-rich schemes of the wildest nature." In an attempt to staunch sales and stabilize prices, War Loan publicists enjoined citizen-investors to hold their bonds. "Any man who sells Liberty bonds below par stabs at the very lifeblood of the nation," McAdoo declared. "You must not sell your bonds," demanded a notification card signed by Secretary McAdoo and mailed to citizen-investors. "Every unnecessary sale" depressed the market price, damaging both "government credit" and "the genuine interest of the people of the United States." The War Loan Organization emitted propaganda that stigmatized bond sales as insufficient patriotism, greedy gullibility, and abandonment of personal economic discipline.[22]

The Treasury Department also attempted to stimulate price-sustaining demand for previous series of Liberty bonds. War Loan speakers and publications implored citizen-investors to recall their financial commitments to the nation and the war and purchase *more*, given the "additional investment opportunity" presented by bargain prices in the aftermarket. Liberty bonds were intrinsically "worth considerably more than the market price," temporarily depressed only because a "great many foolish people" had "thrown their bonds upon the market," editorials advised. This diagnosis amounted to a critique of the price-setting action of "free" securities markets.[23]

Such criticism of privately administered securities exchanges for failing to protect the interests of citizen-investors soon prompted demands for stronger state interventions into the nation's securities markets. In the fall of 1917, financial reformer Samuel Untermyer blamed short sellers, not swindlers, for the subpar price of Liberty bonds. He called for the abolition of short sales or the closure of the New York Stock Exchange, observing, "the country experienced no great discomfort" when the NYSE closed briefly in 1915 to check a European sell-off in American securities. In December 1917, Representative William R. Wood (R-Indiana) introduced a bill criminalizing any dealings in Liberty bonds below par, which he characterized as "German selling."[24]

Wood's bill did not pass, despite Secretary McAdoo's endorsement. In its place, two novel federal interventions into the financial securities markets aimed to fulfill the debt-issuing state's newfound obligation to limit citizen-investors' losses. At McAdoo's suggestion, Congress authorized the Treasury to create a special state-administered fund to purchase Liberty bonds in the aftermarket in order to support their prices; 5 percent of the proceeds of the Third Liberty Loan were set aside for this purpose. Ultimately, the Treasury's bond purchase fund acquired $1.7 billion in Liberty bonds, while the Federal Reserve increased its holdings of federal debt sixfold (from $57.1 million to $352.3 million) between 1916 and 1920. In addition, the Federal Reserve established a new body to "regulate the issue of securities in competition with the Government's loans" early in 1918. This Capital Issues Committee (CIC), composed of Federal Reserve members and an advisory group of bankers, influenced the allocation of capital by limiting the amount and types of securities that corporations, states, and municipalities were permitted to issue during the war. Although Secretary McAdoo preferred to grant the CIC the power to levy criminal penalties, it ultimately relied upon voluntary compliance from those seeking to raise capital. Entities petitioning to issue stocks or bonds were asked to provide a prospectus that established the profitability of the enterprise and the character of its management. The CIC approved only those issues it deemed essential to the war and rejected those it deemed risky or fraudulent schemes that might prey upon citizen-investors. Between May and December 1918, the CIC dismissed $917 million out of $3.8 billion of proposed capital expenditures.[25]

The War Loan drives forged a new chain of obligation linking citizen-investors to their debt-issuing state. Citizen-investors lent their funds. In return, the federal government assumed responsibility for issuing appropriate securities and protecting citizen-investors in their quest to invest. This new relationship permanently altered the federal government's role in the nation's securities markets. The Treasury Department continued to sell small-denomination federal securities until 1924. In 1922, the Federal Reserve assumed control of the bond purchase fund established during World War I. Beginning in 1923, the Fed's Open Market Investment Committee began to orchestrate the trading of federal bonds by Federal Reserve banks with the aim of influencing interest rates. Seeking to promote economic stability and growth, the Federal Reserve affected the price of money (the interest rate) through coordinated purchases and sales of federal bonds. The Federal Reserve, originally designed to act as lender of last resort, now became a tool of federal monetary policy. The success of the CIC convinced many of the need for ongoing federal regulation of securities issuance and corporate reporting practices. Both Secretary McAdoo and the members of the CIC urged Congress to empower a permanent government agency to perpetuate the Committee's work in peacetime. "The wide distribution of Liberty bonds . . . placed upon the Government" a definite "obligation" to "protect its public from financial exploitations by reckless or unscrupulous promoters," the CIC advised Congress. The War Loan experience not only encouraged Americans to rethink the meaning of nationhood and citizenship, but to expect that the federal government would extend its role in the economy and act as the guardian of citizen-investors.[26]

FROM THE OUTSET, the Wilson administration's decisions to assume a large burden of indebtedness and to parcel that debt across the populace raised controversy. Throughout the war, congressional and academic progressives repeatedly demanded that income and business taxes be increased in order to tap wealthy and corporate pockets bulging with war profits. Critics in languishing industries alleged that by exporting dollars abroad, the War Loans sapped the vitality of the domestic economy. The War Savings program in particular faced resistance from purveyors of consumer goods and services. They were shocked to learn that the Treasury planned to "spoil as much Christmas trade as possible" by launching War Savings in December 1917. They rightly perceived federal stamps and certificates as competition for Americans' disposable income. Savings banks also balked at War Savings at first, fearing that federal stamps and certificates would erode demand for existing savings products and services.[27]

To press their demands for a change in war finance policy, consumer marketers urged "business as usual." They issued propaganda encouraging Americans to spend buoyant wartime paychecks in order to grow the economy and thereby increase tax receipts and create "a background of good business to sell securities" to fund the war. These arguments reveal the increasing salience of consumer-centered theories of political economy. This set of assumptions—which originated at the turn of century with the work of economist Simon Patten and the "living wage" demands of organized labor—elevated the consumer as the pivotal actor in the economy and identified Everyman's enjoyment of material prosperity as the rightful goal of properly designed economic policy. Influenced by these ideas, retailers hung "Business As Usual—Beware of Thrift and Unwise Economy—Money Breeds Money" signs in shop windows across the nation in the fall of 1917 and spring of 1918. Newspapers joined the retailers' campaign, for publishers feared they would offend advertisers and scare away ad revenue if they acceded to the War Loan Organization's requests to counsel modest consumption and robust investment.[28]

The War Loan Organization sought to mollify "business as usual" opponents, for the success of the War Loans required their cooperation. It suggested models for integrating War Loans into in-store merchandising, as in an elegant "furniture display" in which mannequins dressed as a fashionable husband and wife sat down to together to "figure out how the family" could save money to purchase a Liberty bond. Such incongruous proposals, however, merely provoked retailers to bemoan the loss of precious display space. To reassure financial institutions, Treasury staff compiled data to prove that War Savings sales were not drawing money from hinterland savings accounts. Officials promised that the proceeds of the War Loan drives would be kept on deposit in the banks of the originating community, not whisked away to Washington, D.C., or New York City. War Loan leaders also assured financial institutions that the War Loans would sow seeds of thrift that would blossom in peacetime. War Loan publicity placed the private financial industry in a favorable light, delineating a natural evolution of savings, beginning with small, price-stabilized, secure government securities, advancing through savings deposits, home ownership, and insurance. When citizen-investors attained a high level of sophistication and diversification, they might even entertain more complicated, riskier corporate bonds and stocks. Eventually, publishers warmed to the War Loans as retailers, banks, and brokerages purchased space for War Loan advertisements.[29]

But advocates of "business as usual" were not swayed by the War Loan Organization's suggestions, or by its assertions that small-denomination war bonds would knit the nation and enhance citizenship. The choice of borrowing over taxation would need to be defended directly, on purely economic grounds. So, too, would investment. The War Loans transmitted an investor-centered alternative to the consumer-centered theory of political economy circulated by the champions of "business as usual." The figure of the investor and the practice of investment were assigned central positions in the War Loans' model of a properly functioning economic system, one grounded in mass investment.

"'Business as Usual' a Delusion!" the War Loan Organization declared. The money borrowed then "put back into circulation" by the wartime state more effectively stimulated the economy into employing more labor and producing more goods than would consumer demand, while heavy taxes would rob firms of resources before they could be invested in expanded capacity and additional workers. Federal borrowing also invigorated foreign trade, as the wartime state lent citizen-investors' funds to its Allies. The money lent returned immediately into "the channels" of American business, War Loan propaganda instructed, despite the Allies' pesky proclivity to contract war supplies and materiel however they saw fit. Last, War Loan leaders contended that large levies of taxes would place the financial burden of the war "entirely on this generation" unfairly. Large-scale borrowing, in contrast, "placed part of the burden" on future generations of citizens, whose taxes would help to pay off the principal and the interest.[30]

As it took on its "business as usual" challengers, the War Loan Organization endeavored to prove that from a purely economic point of view, a political-economic system grounded in mass investment was superior to one driven by mass consumption. In doing so, the wartime state devised and disseminated a new investor-centered theory of political economy. War Loan propagandists identified investment as the individual's most essential economic role. They identified investment as the most powerful of economic functions and presented universal investment as essential for a properly functioning political-economic system.

In order to heighten the appeal of investment, the War Loans rhetorically raised it above all other economic acts. Investment in financial securities— rather than in tangible assets or savings accounts—seemingly evidenced superior moral character, self-control, masculinity, even whiteness. Indeed, the practice of investment revitalized American manhood by nourishing self-discipline and serving as handmaiden to individual ambition. In contrast, mass consumption eroded republican gender norms to the detriment of national character and vigor. One War Savings society organ observed that "owing to long continued prosperity," America had approached "the condition of luxurious degeneration, which spelled the downfall of the Roman Empire." Men grew "flabby both physically and morally." Boys failed to respect elders or the law, while girls "indulged in luxurious tastes in dress." But by acquiring War Savings stamps and certificates and Liberty bonds, citizen-investors might "emulate the simple virtues" and self-denial of their republican forebears, "who with axe and rifle conquered the American wilderness" and, in the process, "mastered themselves." Wartime financial mobilization would reinvigorate "the inherent vitality of the race" and halt luxury's rot.[31]

The power of the investment extended beyond the vitality and discipline it nurtured within individuals. According to War Loan propaganda, investors directed the course of the national economy by determining the flow of capital. Invested dollars "set labor to work" making "producers' goods," according to Thomas Nixon Carver, the David A. Wells professor of political economy at Harvard University, whose wartime writings served as the primary basis for War Loan thrift propaganda. More investment meant more of these capital goods, which multiplied the nation's productive capacity, the economy's aggregate demand for labor, and the total output of goods and services available to consumers. Consumption, by contrast, represented a far less enduring—and therefore less fruitful—economic activity, Carver and his fellow War Loan propagandists asserted. Expenditure "for the means of facilitating production is a good thing, but exchange for its own sake is not," Carver argued. "When it interferes with production it is a bad thing." Investment discouraged "the wasting of manpower in the selling and production of non-essentials" and "released manpower from the non-essential industries making it available for the essential industries." Dollars expended in consumption did nothing to ensure production and employment in the future. Invested dollars—by virtue of not being consumed—prevented the squandering of labor and materials in the production of frivolous, ephemeral things. The significance of the small investor, therefore, derived not only from his contribution of savings to productive enterprise, but also from his refusal to indulge in consumption that might cause misallocation of labor and capital.[32]

In wartime, there could be no question that the federal government constituted the "essential industry" toward which citizen-investors properly directed their savings. Citizen-investors thereby equipped the wartime state with the resources to command the nation's productive capacity and workforce. The practice of investment also advanced economic mobilization by discouraging expenditures on consumer goods and services. When "we loan to the Government," explained Frank A. Vanderlip, "we do two things: we give the government credit" and "we release material" and manpower so that the wartime state might acquire them. Stories, cartoons, and posters circulated by the War Loan Organization aimed to illustrate "the fundamental principle underlying the Liberty Loan—the government's imperative need for labor and materials for which the proceeds of the bonds will be used—and the consequent duty of all citizens by self-denial to release" the labor and materials that they ordinarily might consume to satisfy "their own desires for comforts and luxuries." In Liberty Loan films, the biggest stars of the silent screen dramatized the War Loans' refutations of "business as usual." Mary Pickford's character in *100% American*, a working-girl named Mayme, gains admission to "a grand ball given to the 100% Americans," soldiers and savers, by forgoing "clothes, ice cream sodas, and other luxuries" in favor of Liberty bonds and War Savings stamps. In *The Spirit That Wins*, a society maiden played by Elsie Ferguson (known to her fans as "the aristocrat of the silent screen") resolves "to make even greater sacrifices to help the soldiers," releasing "her maid for service in the Red Cross and her chauffer for the army." And in *The Bond*, Charlie Chaplin watches in delight as Uncle Sam passes the little tramp's money to "Industry, who quickly outfits the soldier with a gun." All these movies illuminated how, by investing in war debt, citizens stopped themselves from hiring men "to do non-essential things" and allowed the wartime state "to set men to work winning the war." Secretary McAdoo made no secret that the War Loan Organization counted among its "chief activities" the "reduction" of the "normal needs of our population" in order to create space in the economy for the government's nearly insatiable demand for men and material.[33]

Investors and investment proved equally essential in the peacetime economy, War Loan propaganda asserted. "Money saved" provided enterprises with "the capital" to create "jobs" and fortified individuals against "unexpected emergencies." Citizen-investors should not feel "confined to the government" for "opportunities for the productive use" of savings, Thomas Nixon Carver advised. He recommended they invest "in the tools of production," although Carver and his colleagues failed to specify how this might be done or to theorize about the relationship between abstract financial securities and the tangible means of production.[34]

Before the Great War, both supporters and opponents of financial reform had asserted the existence of an investing public and proclaimed the legitimacy of financial securities and markets. During World War I, the wartime state sought to transform prewar fantasies of widespread investment into reality. The Wilson administration determined to induce all Americans to become investors, to think of themselves foremost as investors in the conduct of their financial affairs, and to consider matters of political economy from the viewpoint of an investor. By associating investment with patriotism and civic engagement, the wartime state established that financial securities and markets might advance the public good, not just individual economic interest. The War Loan drives identified individual restraint and accumulation—and their manifestation in financial securities—as the proper means of exercising economic self-sovereignty, allocating economic resources, and containing inflation.

Although the War Loan drives identified federal war debt as the most suitable type of financial security for Everyman, especially in the time of war, its celebration of the practice of investment embraced financial securities categorically. Because the War Loans expounded the benefits of investment in general, postwar corporate stock distributors easily laid claim to the ideal of investor democracy. After Armistice, War Loan analogies that equated the state with a corporation and that likened the exercise of democracy to the process of investment lost their moorings in the wartime experience. As postwar securities distributors appropriated these War Loan marketing conventions, they endeavored to erase any regulatory implications and to refute wartime critiques of privately administered financial markets. Even so, the corporate capture of retail investors and the conservative capture of investors' mentality were hardly foreordained.

In World War I, the federal government played an important and innovative role in cultivating a mass market for financial securities. Federal policies have promoted corporate capitalism in the United States in a wide variety of ways throughout history: land grants to the railroads, the provision of free rural postage and interstate highways, granting limited liability and legal personhood, bestowing tax breaks and military contracts. But something even more fundamental took place during the Great War. Neither demand for capital from private corporations nor the organic machinations of a free market drew millions into the financial securities markets for the first time. In the War Loan campaigns, the wartime state prodded Americans to invest in financial securities, to claim the protection of the state as investors, and to understand themselves as collectively directing the national economy through their investment choices. Publicity, imagery, and spectacle pushed the figure of the investor and the practice of investment to the forefront of public thinking. The federal government nurtured both the practice of investing and an investors' mentality as part of its conduct of war.

It did so aiming to reinforce and redefine citizenship and nationhood for a dispersed, heterogeneous, often contentious and sometimes hostile population. In the place of tangible property, the wartime state offered the waged and salaried masses its small-denomination securities as an emblem and agent of citizenship. War Loan publicity suggested that these securities would fortify the nation by absorbing the dispossessed, the disenfranchised, and the disaffected into the social contract. In the crucible of war, the traditional ideal of proprietary democracy—in which ownership of productive property and command of dependents' labor secured the political virtue and independence required in a citizen—was reshaped into an ideal of investor democracy. The War Loan Organization presented investment in financial securities as a fundamental basis for civic inclusion and a defining characteristic of the nation's culture.

The cultivation of investment as a national custom and the support of citizen-investors in their quest to invest became objectives of federal policy during World War I. Citizen-investors now warranted new protections from the state. Accordingly, the federal government intervened in the financial securities markets of behalf of citizen-investors, rejecting the laissez-faire status quo preferred by the New York Stock Exchange. Resolving that war-born habits of thrift and investment should become permanent features of American life, the federal government continued to promote those practices and to provide citizen-investors with its small-denomination securities until 1924.

In imagining the nation through the financial market and equating investment with citizenship, those charged with devising a war finance strategy tapped progressive faith in a unitary people's will. Their investment-centered conceptualizations of citizenship and nation sought to transcend class divisions but ignored ethnic cultural persistence and the circumscribed nature of women's and African Americans' rights.[35]

Citizen-investors would not mobilize as the single, indivisible public of progressives' dreams, however. Victory Way marked the culmination of nearly two years of sensational spectacles, rousing oratory, and arresting propaganda that private bodies—including ethnic societies, African American groups, women's clubs, churches, businesses, trade organizations, and labor unions—devised to induce their members to acquire war bonds, stamps, and certificates. As they mustered the financial nation, citizen-investors revealed the cultural pluralism of America's peoples. They competed to specify the consequences of their financial enfranchisement. And even as War Loan publicity and pageantry cast the financial market as an instrument and an analog of freedom and democracy, citizen-investors actualized the financial nation through compulsion as much as celebration.

CHAPTER FOUR

Mobilizing the Financial Nation

A S NANNIE BURROUGHS took the stage to address a "mammoth mass meeting" of African Americans during the third Liberty Loan drive, she stepped into a fray over whether the "War for Democracy" abroad would reconfigure racial relations at home. Recent migrants from the rural South filled the seats of Philadelphia's Olympic Theater. Between 1915 and 1921, the Great Migration funneled close to three-quarters of a million such African Americans into the nation's cities, where they sought jobs made newly available by wartime labor shortages. This mass exodus from the indignities and violence of Jim Crow, and the enlistment of nearly 400,000 black men in the U.S. military, challenged white supremacy and racial apartheid both in the southern countryside and in the neighborhoods, ports, and factories of cities across the United States. Activists seized upon the Great War as an opportunity to press burning questions about African American citizenship and rights. Newly mobile, uniformed, and emboldened, African Americans met with an upsurge in lynchings and riots at the hands of whites and heightened surveillance on the part of the wartime state. Antagonism and brutality toward black Americans would plague the home front, then explode in a series of urban race riots after Armistice.[1]

But when Nannie Burroughs announced to the crowd that the National Woman's Liberty Loan Committee (NWLLC) "had found out 'who could get the colored American's coin,'" selecting her as chairman of its new Colored Women's Committee, "quite three thousand people stood and cheered." With Burroughs's appointment, the federal government finally affirmed African Americans' contribution to the war effort and their place in the nation. It meant a great deal that "the race was receiving consideration in handling the Liberty Loan work," Burroughs reported to the NWLLC in Washington, D.C. When she solicited African American churches, schools, clubs, lodges, businesses, and community leaders for their cooperation, she heard time and again, "'I'll gladly subscribe now that they have appointed one of ours.'"[2]

For her entire adult life, Nannie Burroughs had dedicated herself to the "uplift" of African Americans, helping to establish the National Association of Colored Women in 1896 and founding the National Training School for Women and Girls in Washington, D.C., in 1909. There, pupils were drilled in the "three B's"—the Bible, the Bath, and the Broom—as they prepared for vocational employment. Now, deputized by the War Loan Organization's National Woman's Liberty Loan Committee, Burroughs traveled to cities across the country, organizing African American clubwomen to teach thrift and investment to those escaping the cotton fields. By subscribing for Liberty bonds and War Savings stamps and certificates, African Americans would improve themselves financially and earn the respect and gratitude of the nation, Burroughs and her agents believed. Their faith in the socially transformative potential of the War Loans was naïve, perhaps, but hardly surprising. After all, the endless flow of publicity materials and suggestions that poured out of the War Loan Organization's offices in Washington, D.C., equated investment with the obligations and rights of citizenship.

The Treasury Department's War Loan Organization determined the goals, terms, quotas, and key themes for the Liberty and Victory Loan drives and the War Savings program. But Treasury officials rather quickly recognized the difficulty involved in distributing federal war debt across all segments of the population and all regions of the country. "The problem would have been hopeless," Treasury Secretary William G. McAdoo later wrote, "if we had not had the willing cooperation of thousands of people. It was the business of the Treasury to organize this outpouring of energy and willingness; to organize and instruct an army of volunteer salesmen." Women's clubs "turned themselves into selling agencies. Factories and workshops stopped their plants and assembled their workmen so they might listen to Liberty Loan speeches and subscribe for bonds," McAdoo remembered in his memoirs. "Newspapers and billboard" companies "contributed space" for War Loan messages; Americans could not avoid advertisements posted in very conceivable public space. "In every city and sizeable town in the country," Liberty Loan and War Savings committees imbued with "patriotic fervor" contacted "every home in the United States and every adult person," McAdoo recollected with pride. One wartime survey by the U.S. Bureau of Labor Statistics revealed that 68 percent of urban-dwelling, wage-earning families owned a Liberty bond, and nearly 50 percent participated in War Savings.[3]

During World War I, investment became both a mass practice and a ritual of national belonging. On the ground, Americans conducted the War Loan campaigns through the broad array of private associations that organized public life. Groups representing those whose fealty the state especially sought to secure—women's, labor, African American, and ethnic associations—proved particularly important in the financial mobilization of the home front. As these groups mobilized their members to raise money for the war, they advanced a wide range of answers regarding which political, social, and economic rights the citizen-investor could claim. The architects of the War Loans could not control how citizen-investors defined the terms of their financial enfranchisement, nor the manner in which they policed the boundaries of their financial nation. Policy makers figured the small investor's subscription as a freely cast vote in favor of a war for democracy. But to secure subscriptions, grassroots rituals of financial nationalism mixed celebration and exhortation with heavy doses of emotional manipulation, social ostracism, and even physical coercion.[4]

ALTHOUGH the Treasury launched a new agency, the War Loan Organization, and transformed existing government agencies into points-of-sale, it depended upon private institutions and associations to mobilize citizen-investors. The War Loan Organization identified labor organizations and large employers, foreign-language press and ethnic societies, African American institutions and associations, and women's clubs as its most promising allies. These organizations seemed best positioned to staunch the riotous spending of the working classes and to secure the loyalty of nonvoting groups. However, as these organizations conscripted their members to promote and acquire war bonds, stamps, and certificates, they competed to fix the meaning and consequences of financial enfranchisement in a manner consistent with their particular political agendas.

The expansion of the Treasury Department involved the establishment of the War Loan Organization, which included two programs, Liberty Loans and War Savings. Leading investment and commercial bankers served on the National Liberty Loan Committee. It assigned sales quotas to both Federal Reserve districts and states. It appointed district and state Liberty Loan committees in consultation with the governors of the Federal Reserve banks. State committees divided their territories into county or school districts, appointing a local committee for each. Working with private organizations, local committees received publicity from Washington, devised their own propaganda and pageantry, and solicited donated advertising.

War Savings distributed its publicity and securities somewhat differently. National War Savings Director Frank A. Vanderlip knew from his experiences as a financial journalist, as an assistant Secretary of the Treasury (where he organized a popular $200 million loan to fund the Spanish-American War), and as the chairman of National City Bank that leading bankers and brokers—heavily represented on Liberty Loan committees—knew little about marketing to the masses. Accordingly, Vanderlip looked to mass retailers, union leaders, life insurance executives, and large employers to provide counsel and distribution channels for War Savings. Retail and insurance executives pledged salespersons, agents, and direct mail facilities. Chain store clerks pushed War Savings securities over counters with a "'personal touch' to folks they see everyday." Restaurants added thrift stamps to their menus; stores offered them as change. Industrial corporations sold War Savings in their plants, while American Federation of Labor–affiliated unions reached out to "local men." In addition, voluntary associations, unions, employers, and schools established roughly 150,000 War Savings societies during the war. Supplied from Washington, these societies helped members to budget for investment and taught the "principles of sound economics," including judicious shopping, conservation, recycling, and basic facts about financial institutions and markets.[5]

The umbrella War Loan Organization in Washington, D.C., provided a publicity clearinghouse for both programs. It issued millions of speaker handbooks, press releases, records, pledge cards, posters, motion pictures, slides, placards, and buttons in dozens of languages. Staff suggested cartoons, contests, editorials, window displays, and angles for press coverage. In return, local committees and societies shared their locally devised materials with the national office in Washington, D.C. Citizen-investors read about their fellows' doings in the press and in War Loan Organization bulletins. They appropriated ideas and proudly reported their successes to Washington. This circulation of ideas and materials encouraged identification with the imagined national community. War Loan activities and ephemera constituted the stuff of national consciousness, the practices and materials with which Americans collectively experienced themselves as national subjects.[6]

The War Loan Organization also garnered speakers for both programs. During the first two Liberty Loan campaigns, "bond dealers and bankers from the large cities" dominated the roster. Unfortunately, these experts spoke "over the heads of the people" and raised suspicions—

particularly among Midwest farmers—that the "whole project" might be a Wall Street plot. Accordingly, speakers with broader appeal were added after the Second Loan, including Treasury Department personnel, servicemen, diverse political figures such as William Jennings Bryan, Samuel Gompers, William Howard Taft, and Samuel Untermyer, as well as celebrities such as Mary Pickford, Charlie Chaplin, and Douglas Fairbanks, along with revivalist minister Rev. Billy Sunday. Local Liberty Loan and War Savings societies called upon local "molders of sentiment," such as clergy and educators, to inspire purchases.[7]

To distribute both publicity and securities, the War Loan Organization made use of those sites where Americans already came into contact with their federal government. Points-of-sale were established at the post office and at military sites, through the mail, and, most especially, in the public schoolroom.

The nation's public education system occupied a central place in the War Loan Organization's plan to stem radicalism by promoting investment. Educators were seen as manning "the trenches" of intellectual warfare against "vicious and selfish" bolshevist and German "falsehoods." Through English-speaking children, the wartime state sought to reach foreign-born parents, vulnerable to pernicious bolshevik agitation, German sedition, and riotous consumption. John H. Pulicher, War Savings director for Wisconsin, recalled a speaking contest organized among immigrants' children. "Little tots ranging from 8 to 14, they told their foreign born parents truths about our country, such that had we uttered them, we would have been pointed out the door, and the parents cheered them." War Loan pedagogy aimed to Americanize and de-bolshevize the nation's immigrants.[8]

Across the nation, schoolteachers collected children's pennies, earned through chores or coaxed from relatives, then sold them War Savings stamps. The War Loan Organization circulated innumerable ideas for lessons, contests, craft activities, and texts. These encouraged children to perform chores or to collect scrap to earn their share of the war debt. Children performed plays and took lessons and savings banks home. These illustrated how investment improved a household's standard of living and social prospects. Prodded by homework assignments or by organizations like the Boy Scouts and the Girl Scouts, American youth solicited family and neighbors for Liberty bond and War Savings subscriptions.[9]

However useful the public school system or other existing state agencies, neither Liberty Loan or War Savings committees could achieve broad-based distribution without the assistance of private institutions and associations. Stores, churches, colleges, universities, chautauquas, patriotic organizations, fraternal societies, farmers' granges and alliances, women's clubs, political parties, science societies, labor unions, ethnic societies, professional groups, corporations, banks, retail and commercial associations, scouting and other youth groups, and the press: all these groups worked with War Loan committees to devise and distribute publicity, to organize events, and to solicit sales.

Given concerns about inflation and the allegiance of nonvoting groups, the War Loan Organization specifically cultivated relationships with foreign-language press and ethnic societies, African American institutions and associations, labor organizations and large employers, and women's clubs. It crafted specific images and arguments to appeal to these subsegments. In turn, these groups seized hold of War Loan metaphors equating investment with citizenship, financial market with national polity. They competed to specify the consequences of their financial enfranchisement, particularly whether universal investment would upend or uphold existing economic and social hierarchies. They issued demands as they acquired their Share in America.

Fear of subversive foreign elements prompted the War Loan Organization to turn to ethnic societies and the foreign-language press to mobilize dollars and to mold sentiment among the recently immigrated. Although War Loan engineers' national imaginary comprised atomistic *individual* citizen-investors, in reality, financial mobilization absorbed groups as groups and allowed that ethnic pride was not at variance with national allegiance. Although the War Loan campaigns aimed to encourage an overriding sense of national loyalty, they did not exclude identifications with homeland and heritage. Indeed, the War Loan drives harnessed ethnic difference even as they attempted to construct a single nation.

Throughout the war, Liberty bond subscriptions were totaled and reported according to ethnic group. The Treasury viewed the results as a gauge of immigrants' allegiance. Speakers demanded that immigrants demonstrate the depths of their loyalty through the size of their subscription. Addressing a polyglot group of workers in Jersey City, New Jersey, machine gunner Arthur Empey rejoiced when a "citizen in his working clothes laid down $50."

> And he's a Greek; come on, come on, you Americans! Who's going to follow Greece? If you are an American, declare yourself one. If you call yourself one and don't intend to subscribe to this Liberty Loan . . . you are a traitor!

Leading men of each nationality issued War Loan endorsements in native languages. Many linked fund-raising efforts to the plight of the homeland or cited the economic opportunity found on American soil. "Liberty money" earned in "liberty land" necessitated "American savings in American bonds."

Immigrants owed the United States; Liberty bonds and War Savings securities would settle the debt.[10]

America's ethnic groups seized upon the suggestion that investment conveyed consent and conferred citizenship. They demanded full recognition and inclusion in the body politic. I. J. Paderewski, "the world's foremost living pianist," advised Polish Americans that they would "prove" they deserved "respect and honor" as "first class citizens" if they achieved first place on the subscription lists. The *New York Times* related how Tie Sing, a fifty-year-old "Chinese born in Virginia City, Nevada" had "invested all his savings in the Second Liberty Loan." Sing hoped that publicity of his deed might yield information verifying his "American birth." Under his current alien classification, Sing could not "bring to this county from China his wife and daughter."[11]

Although "100% American" campaigns sought to suppress foreign cultural and political traditions during World War I, ethnic groups retained the right to celebrate their heritage as they mobilized their members to acquire war debt. Even Germans, whose tradition of foreign language instruction came under fire during World War I, received and devised publicity in their mother tongue. In any given Loan drive, cities commonly assigned different days to distinct ethnic groups for public exhibitions of foreign language speeches, "choruses and solos," parades in traditional garb, and various other "demonstrations" of cultural heritage. In Buffalo, New York, for example, thousands of Polish Americans dedicated a "replica of the U.S. Treasury Building" before enjoying Polish music and speeches. The "foreign born population" of St. Louis paraded before a Statue of Liberty replica. Each group "placed a memorial wreath at the feet of Liberty" as bond salesmen "circulated through the crowd." The War Loan drives offered immigrants an opportunity to pledge fealty to the nation-state without jettisoning ethnic heritage. The cultural pluralism modeled in War Loan assemblages—quite similar to that theorized by progressives like Horace Kallen, Randolph Bourne, and John Dewey—allowed that ethnic identity and difference could be consistent with American-ness.[12]

So, too, could African American pride and demands for racial justice. At the national level, the War Loan Organization delegated responsibility for the financial mobilization of the African American community to the Colored Women's Committee of the National Woman's Liberty Loan Committee, which worked in conjunction with National Association of Colored Women. Local Liberty Loan and War Savings committees, however, sometimes admitted prominent black men. As American cities swelled with those carried along by the Great Migration, African American institutions and organizations—banks, businesses, women's clubs, fraternal orders, newspapers, labor unions like the Brotherhood of Sleeping Car Porters, Civil War veterans groups, colleges and vocational schools—formed War Savings societies and urged black Americans to subscribe. Whenever possible, these groups sought to make visible the capabilities of black men as a "matter of race honor," something the War Loan Organization declined to do when it designated the Colored Women's Committee as its official envoy. The *Savannah Tribune*, a weekly newspaper serving the black community, called upon all black Savannahians to bear witness to the "merit and power" of the "Negro leadership of the pulpit, business, and industry" by subscribing for the War Loans under that leadership. War Loan publicity and events devised by Americans of African descent celebrated the manhood of the 400,000 black men who challenged Jim Crow by enlisting in the Great War to affirm their fitness for full political rights.[13]

The War Loan pageantry and rhetoric produced by African Americans made visible and gave voice to demands for civic inclusion, political rights, and the destruction of Jim Crow. Twenty thousand marched through the streets of Savannah, Georgia, in a War Savings parade on May 8, 1918. "Over one hundred different organizations" represented "the Savannah Negro in all his better and loftier aspects," demonstrating "his loyalty to the nation, his unity and solidarity of race, his strength, his capacity for organization and system, his self reverence and self respect." This momentous parade prompted the editor of the *Savannah Tribune* to "dream dreams" about the "tremendous advantages which are to be derived from the great War Savings and Bond Campaigns." If "wealth is power," then "the vast wealth and improved economic and industrial status which will come to the Negro race" as a result of the War Loan drives would reshape "the future alignment of men and the hierarchy of groups in America." Surely, this editor continued, racial "troubles and friction and oppression" would diminish as Americans of African descent attained "greater wealth, increased economic power, and wider industrial opportunity." African Americans' "greater independence" would command "greater tolerance and respect." In a more pointed and poetic appeal, this same editor called upon "every Negro man and Woman of the State of Georgia."

> Come with your unmeasured determination to pour out your money that in the close of this world struggle and international carnage and war, the flickering rays of the Star of Hope may scintillate into a fully and complete brilliancy of rights and privileges, long longed and prayed for by our fathers and mothers who sleep beneath the soil of a country, made rich by the labor and toils of a race which has never produced a Benedict Arnold, an assassin of a president or a thrower of bombs to destroy life and property.

A more specific demand for racial justice was issued by Professor L. R. Thompson during a Liberty Loan speech at the State College of Georgia. African Americans had exhibited "no incendiarism" during the war; they had "done their bit in the Liberty Loan." Thompson perceived a "great power for the achievement of manhood rights vested in the 'almighty dollar'" that the African American had relinquished to the wartime state. Now he offered this "this simple plea" to the nation: "Oh flag! My flag! . . . vouchsafe to me and to those who are to come after me, every right and every privilege that are guaranteed to me in the Constitution and laws of the land." These included "equality before the law," wages and public expenditures commensurate with those received by whites, "equal accommodation on the highways of travel," the "right to work along any line," and, of course, the "right to register and vote."[14]

As Americans of African descent took to the streets during the War Loans in ways unthinkable under Jim Crow, the African American press closely monitored the response of the white community. A "large concourse of people many of whom were whites" viewed a mile-long War Savings parade in Statesboro, North Carolina, listening "intently" and "heartily applauding" leaders of the black community. White political leaders who probably never had set foot in an African American neighborhood now addressed rallies packed entirely with black bodies. After Liberty Loan speeches by the "eloquent race general Col. Roscoe Conkling Simmons" and Mayor Harry Mendenhall, Kansas governor Arthur Capper assured the congregants of the African Methodist Episcopal Church in Kansas City that "the loyalty that American Negro has shown far surpasses the white man and all the expectations of the world." During a War Savings rally in Dale, South Carolina, state Representative J. Coney promised "that when the war is over there will be many things accorded to the Negro which he is denied today." In many cases, the War Loan campaigns facilitated collaborations between white and black male civic leaders, which rarely took place under Jim Crow. The interracial War Savings Committee of Atlanta, Georgia, even convened its meetings at Big Bethel Church. During the War Loan campaigns, African Americans had reason to believe that finally, their contributions to the nation were being made visible and their demands were being heard.[15]

Still, black Americans mostly (but not always) paraded separately from whites. Southern landlords and urban employers solicited their African American tenants and workers however they saw fit. This meant that "the race" failed to receive full credit for tens if not hundreds of thousands of dollars, the African American press complained. According to the NAACP, it also meant that exclusively white committees visited "brow-beating tactics" upon blacks with impunity. Indeed, the *Shreveport Times* encouraged whites to "Adopt Force to Get Negro to Buy War Savings Stamps." Although black men sometimes were invited to serve on Liberty Loan and War Savings committees, it seems only black women were permitted to solicit on the streets, as their presence seemed a lesser affront to Jim Crow.[16]

As these women canvassed the streets of cities across the country, they crossed paths with black-faced minstrels selling War Savings stamps from sidewalk booths. War Loan publicity included malicious racial imagery that coded investment as a marker of civilized whiteness and racial progress, possibly to appeal to European immigrants seeking confirmation of their own whiteness. Propaganda produced in the South employed racial allusions to suggest parallels between the situation in Europe and the social disruption of the Civil War and Reconstruction.[17]

Native Americans fared even worse. The Department of the Interior refused to credit subscriptions to particular tribes, deeming such a strategy disharmonious with its "plan for developing the Indian's citizenship." Rather, the Commissioner of Indian Affairs hoped that war debt acquisitions would "dissolve tribal bonds, remove inter-racial barriers, rescue the Indian from his retarding isolation, and absorb him into the general population with full rights and immunities" as a fully assimilated, property-holding individual citizen-investor.[18]

To capture the wages of workers, the War Loan Organization turned to labor unions, the labor press, and employers. Amidst fierce debates over the nature of "industrial democracy" and as union membership doubled, employers and organized labor jockeyed to shape the meaning of the War Loans. Both sides feared that whoever captured the workingman's wage would gain the upper hand in a larger contest over authority in the workplace—a battle that grew more pitched after the wartime state endorsed workers' right to organize. Representatives of organized labor and industry quarreled over whether employers or unions should take responsibility for conducting War Loan drives within plants. American Federation of Labor leaders worried that employer-organized initiatives bound "the employee too tight" and "gave the employer a sort of hold on him." Employers, on the other hand, grumbled that the War Loans either stirred "antagonistic feelings among employees" (who resented payroll deductions) or encouraged labor organizing (if workers were allowed to canvass each other for subscriptions).[19]

The War Loan Organization endeavored to produce publicity palatable to both sides, alternatively presenting federal debt as an instrument of labor empowerment *and* pacification. On one hand, federal securities might act as "a bridge to a new job, a ladder to climb by, a tool to grasp opportunity." Still, War Loan leaders assured employers that "men who are in the habit of saving" would not rattle "around from job to job" or disrespect "the tools and materials put into their hands." Even as the War Loan Organization associated thrift and investment in federal debt with economic freedom, it struggled *not* to intimate that universal bond holding would undermine employee loyalty or managerial prerogative.[20]

Labor unions played a critical role in mobilizing the funds of the working class. The War Loan Organization established labor bureaus—populated largely by AFL leaders—to conscript the workingman's dollar. AFL organizers and staff acted as sales agents and established War Savings societies in union halls and places of employment. With their coffers swollen with the dues of millions of new members, local unions acquired Liberty and Victory bonds to augment their strike and relief funds. Lacking any other storage space, the Seattle machinists' union piled their Liberty bonds into wastebaskets at the union office. AFL President Samuel Gompers and other labor leaders endorsed the War Loans and appeared in advertisements. Many employed a "Back of it All" trope, which depicted the magnificent apparatus of war production and cast workers as the linchpin in economic mobilization.

> Back of all of the armies of this nation going to France is ocean shipping—back of ocean shipping, labor—back of labor, transportation—back of transportation, the nation's natural resources. But back of all of these . . . is the financial strength of the United States of America, whose actual active and numerical terms are Liberty Bonds.

War Loan literature and imagery promised workers a greater voice in America's political economy and improvements in working conditions. They consistently invoked the AFL's wartime goal of industrial democracy, which aimed to defeat employer "autocracy" in domestic labor relations through the spread of trade unionism under the protection of the wartime state. Workers themselves claimed new rights and protections as they purchased bonds.

> Just like a horse and wagon, work all day . . . For why this war? For why we buy Liberty Bonds? For the mills? No, for freedom and America—for everybody. No more horse and wagon. For eight-hour day.

Workers' own articulations figured the acquisition of federal war debt as a route to industrial democracy at home, as much as political democracy abroad.[21]

But even as it supported unions in their quest for industrial democracy, the War Loan Organization demanded quid pro quo. The Treasury expected hearty subscriptions from railroad workers and their unions, on account of the privileges they enjoyed under federal operation of the railroads. These included wage increases, recognition of the Railroad Brotherhoods as collective bargaining agents with rights to organize, and labor mediation by the federal government. Furthermore, the Treasury insisted that Brotherhood-led initiatives stress the importance of uninterrupted, efficient labor.[22]

Despite the War Loans' embrace of organized labor, large industrial employers proved just as essential to capturing the wages of the laboring multitudes. Employers of all sizes were asked to acquire large blocks of bonds and to extend credit to employees so they might acquire bonds on partial payment plans. Employers encouraged employee subscriptions with payroll deductions, bonuses, competitions, and War Savings societies.[23]

Eager to capitalize on requests for assistance, business leaders demanded war orders when their locality exceeded its Liberty Loan quota and issued a host of grievances related to labor relations. Apart from expressing irritation over the ways in which the War Loans emboldened organized labor, local elites' complaints revealed the ways in which economic mobilization disrupted social relations. They looked to federal stamps, certificates, and bonds to shore up class, racial, and gender status quos.[24]

Business leaders in Columbia, South Carolina, reported that war orders buoyed cotton prices, the mills ran day and night, and three training camps were under construction. The resulting demand for labor had deranged "the normal scale of wages," while all the "off-season" work relieved farmers "from the necessity of borrowing in order to finance the planting of their crops." Worst of all, "negroes" refused to labor unless paid "in actual cash" at "high prices." Black women luxuriated, refusing to "work at any price." Black families, determined to obtain "easy money" from soldiers' wages and insurance policies, allegedly forced their young men to enlist, while "the young women" lured "soldiers who they have known very slightly" into marriage. The local Liberty Loan committee spied "disastrous" consequences for "the usual relations between employer and employee," debtor and creditor, husband and wife, and white and black. It demanded that War Loan publicists and propaganda urge "people" to "sacrifice to the limit," invest excess wages in federal securities, and resume appropriate social roles.[25]

Similar complaints flooded in from employer and financier-dominated Liberty Loan committees across the nation. Allegedly, the "the wives and the daughters" of farmers and "better-paid working people" in Richmond, Virginia, spent "more money than ever" on "dresses" and other items never before "bought except by the rich." In the industrial Northeast, agents reported, workers expected wage increases sufficient to cover the demands for investment, a situation that threatened to exacerbate wage inflation. At one early War Savings conference, Lawrence Priddy of the National Life Insurance Underwriters Association asserted that "domestic maids of this country" held "the money and lots of it." He demanded that the War Savings program design to "get it away from them." When Priddy related how his own overly "independent" help had "skinned" him "to death," another voice joked tellingly, "scared you to death, you mean, don't you?" Like Priddy, many business leaders hoped stamps, certificates, and bonds would absorb workers' profligate dollars and sustain existing power relations, which wartime economic mobilization had destabilized with high wages, labor shortages, and federal support for unionization. But elite complaints illustrate that working people were determined to use wartime economic conditions and War Loan rhetoric to challenge those very power relations—to advance organized labor's wartime goal of industrial democracy, to shield wives, mothers, and daughters from the necessity of work, or to purchase elite goods never before attainable.[26]

Through ethnic associations, labor organizations, and employers, the War Loan Organization endeavored to capture the wages and to mold the sentiment of workers, especially those born abroad. But to parcel war debt among scattered rural inhabitants and anonymous urban multitudes, the War Loans also required a cadre of grassroots agents. "I knew [women] could be quickly wielded into a powerful force," Treasury Secretary William G. McAdoo later recalled, if they were marshaled "through their clubs." With men drawn away to the frontlines and the factories, the War Loan Organization looked to the well-organized national culture of women's voluntarism.[27]

DURING World War I, more American women volunteered as War Loan agents than in any other form of home-front service. In the Fourth and Fifth Liberty Loan drives, nearly 1 million women agents were credited with roughly 25 percent of sales. Given how deeply entrenched the culture of voluntary association was among women all across the United States, women's clubs presented an ideal partnership opportunity for the War Loan Organization. To stir these organizations on behalf of the financial nation, the Treasury Department established the National Woman's Liberty Loan Committee. This separate and autonomous structure organized sales of war bonds, stamps, and certificates by and to women. Through NWLLC, the wartime state tapped the political culture and institutions of the "maternal commonwealth," which embraced voluntary civic service and reform as an extension of domesticity. At the same time, NWLLC encouraged women to act in socially and politically unconventional ways in order to

coax war stamp, certificate, and bond sales. Since women's suffrage constituted one of the greatest citizenship questions of the Progressive Era, it
comes as no surprise that the National Woman's Liberty Loan Committee became a battleground upon which women on both sides of the issue
fought to specify whether women's wartime service and investments would
alter their place in the postwar polity.[28]

Mrs. William C. McAdoo chaired the National Woman's Liberty Loan
Committee. Its executives included bankers' wives as well as leaders of
national women's organizations, such as Carrie Chapman Catt, president
of the National American Woman Suffrage Association (NAWSA). NWLLC
leaders reported directly to War Loan Organization Director Lewis B.
Franklin. Despite objections and resistance from male War Loan committees, NWLLC developed its own publicity and organized local, state, and
Federal Reserve District women's committees, which reported directly to
Washington, D.C. Women's committees drew from existing women's
associations, ranging from those defined by ethnicity or religion, to those
devoted to specific political causes (Woman's Christian Temperance Union),
to those defined by profession or economic function (Women's Trade
Union League). Still others were auxiliaries to men's associations (Ladies
Auxiliary Order of Railway Conductors of America) or primarily social in
nature (women's clubs and their confederations).[29]

The War Loan Organization judged American women uniquely suited
to the task of converting every inhabitant into a citizen-investor. "The
greatest glory of the women's work lies . . . in the large number of subscriptions" that female agents secured, Mrs. McAdoo surmised. After all,
"from the standpoint of the wakening of a national spirit," dollar totals
mattered far less than the number of *persons* that subscribed. Through the
national network of women's clubs, the wartime state could reach women
all across the United States. Through women, the wartime state might tap
the pocketbook of every home, capturing dollars before they were spent.[30]

Despite NWLLC's autonomy, conventional assumptions about women's
distinct and fundamentally maternal and wifely nature underlay its formation and its activities. War Savings understood women to hold "the purse
strings" of the family budget and targeted the woman-of-the-house in innumerable budgeting and wise-shopping lessons, pamphlets, demonstrations, and plays. Women's clubs marketed war debt by invoking thrift's relation to home ownership, home economy, and genteel domesticity. Consistent
with traditional beliefs about suitable forms of female political engagement, NWLLC propaganda urged women to pressure their husbands, fathers, and sons to subscribe to the utmost. Women best advanced the nation's well-being when they influenced men from their perch of moral

superiority within the private sphere, NWLLC averred. With testimonies of loss, bereft mothers and wives might compel commensurable financial sacrifice from others. Liberty Loan parades assembled tens of thousands "of wives and mothers of soldiers," with "each woman carrying her service flag" emblazoned, "We have given our men. They are more precious than dollars," or, "We give our sons—they give their lives—what do you give?" NWLLC harnessed belief in the distinct nature of men's and women's privileges and obligations as citizens to stress American women's *individual* duty to solicit and to subscribe. Although they were exempt from military conscription, women would reap the benefit of victory "no less than men."[31]

NWLLC activities also adhered to gendered conventions regarding public space. While men's committees solicited industrial and commercial establishments and sold bonds at banks and station booths, women's committees organized and canvassed churches, private homes, schools, women's clubs, as well as employment sites and trade unions dominated by women (as in the clerical, retail, and needle trades). Women sold bonds and stamps from sales booths erected at sites of consumption, such as retail establishments, hotels, and theaters. On occasion, however, women's lack of formal authority in "male" sites succeeded where the techniques of men's committees—such as working through employers—generated resentment or resistance. When miners in Colorado struck during the Victory Loan, for example, "women continued their work" promoting the War Loans and ultimately "broke the ice" for resuming negotiations over labor conditions.[32]

Conventional assumptions about women's fundamental domesticity led War Loan officials to view women's War Loan work as strictly volunteer. Herein lay the appeal of women agents. At once, women's unpaid labor "saved money for the government" while freeing men for factories, farms, and battlefields. Women workers felt compelled to forgo reimbursement for travel or publicity materials whenever possible.[33]

Still, the voluntary and unpaid nature of women's War Loan work served to justify their unprecedented enlistment as agents of the wartime state. NWLLC encouraged women to demand respect as envoys of the federal government.

> Be conscious always that you are a representative of the United States Treasury and that the work you are performing is of vital importance to the prosecution of the war. You have the right to confidently expect . . . the people of our county to purchase stamps to the full amount of the quota allotted to them.

Emboldened by their quasi-official status, women canvassed house-to-house, conducted mass parades, spoke in open-air meetings, and even participated in episodes of physical coercion. Female clerks in Canton, Ohio, for example, helped wrap one of their own in an American flag. Dragged through the streets to the local bank, this "dollar slacker" finally purchased her bond.[34]

Despite their inability to cast votes for President Wilson, NWLLC agents nonetheless defended his policies. Women workers were trained to "discuss with the farmers and other residents" the reasons for the United States' participation in the Great War: "to safeguard our Liberty, our homes, our person." NWLLC even deployed female agents to counter an anti–League of Nations propaganda campaign, conducted by nationalists led by Senator Henry Cabot Lodge (R-Mass.) and industrialists Henry Clay Frick and Andrew Mellon. Women canvassers fanned out to convey the necessity of the "President's peace program," associating "the success of the Loan" with "the strengthening of the hand of the United States at the peace-table." They explained why "American democracy," the safety of Americans serving abroad, and the rehabilitation of Europe all depended upon Wilson's beleaguered vision. Ultimately, Wilson's peace program failed. The Victory Loan, however, exceeded its target.[35]

The National Woman's Liberty Loan Committee encouraged women to view War Loan work as "a new proving ground" where "women of the Nation" might demonstrate "their patriotism, their ability, their consciousness of the obligations of citizenship, and their steadfastness of soul." Neither the Treasury nor the NWLLC endorsed women's suffrage explicitly. Nevertheless, publicity hinted that impressive subscription totals would present a convincing case for enfranchisement. One standard newspaper ad run by women's committees noted that previously, men had "hesitated" to enfranchise women on "the grounds that women are unable to defend the country in WAR." But modern war demonstrated that "money to warm, feed, clothe and transport troops" proved as indispensable "as soldiers." If conscripted dollars and financial sacrifice were commensurate with conscripted bodies and physical sacrifice, then female citizen-investors could expect to acquire the full privileges of citizenship, NWLLC publicity intimated. With peace secured, "the grateful nation" would grant women's "highest aspirations in the way of social and political standing."[36]

Awake to such possibilities, suffragists turned out in droves. Indeed, the Wilson administration had intended to marginalize more radical elements in the women's suffrage and peace movements by establishing NWLLC and appointing Carrie Chapman Catt to its executive committee. As president of the National American Woman Suffrage Association [NAWSA], Catt led that organization to support the war in the hopes of attaining the vote for women. In contrast, the militant National Woman's Party [NWP] picketed the White House and maintained its strident antiwar stance throughout the war, its members drawing violent reprisals from crowds, ad hoc protective leagues, and police alike. During the First Loan, Mrs. Henry O. Havemeyer, wife of the sugar baron and member of the National Advisory Committee of the NWP, urged suffragists to boycott the War Loans. "I haven't the nerve to ask money for a battle for democracy when we who demand true democracy are thrown into jails for doing so," Havemeyer avowed. In response, members of the National Society Opposed to Woman Suffrage flooded the Treasury with telegrams endorsing the loans and branding *all* suffragists as disloyal. NAWSA denounced Havemeyer, while Carrie Chapman Catt protested that Havemeyer's comments did not represent the suffrage community at large.[37]

Throughout the war, pro-suffrage and anti-suffrage groups vied to raise funds and to shape the meaning of financial mobilization. In the end, the better-organized forces for suffrage won. In the Fourth Liberty Loan campaign, the Women's Equal Suffrage Association amassed $5 million in subscriptions in comparison to $50,000 collected by the Association Opposed to Woman Suffrage. Suffragists symbolically linked the War Loans to their cause; NWLLC provided a new network to promote women's suffrage. During national conventions, NWLLC delegates lunched at the "Suffrage House" following receptions at the White House and the McAdoo home. Far more accustomed to public action than their opponents, suffragists led women's Liberty Loan parades and open-air meetings, spoke at bond rallies, and donated materials. Suffragist techniques that once had appeared so scandalous and unwomanly were validated and conscripted in the service of the wartime state. And by suspending the ideological boundaries between private and public, wartime financial mobilization allowed women's suffrage groups to claim legitimacy and authority as never before. Even so, the NWLLC shaped the suffrage movement, further estranging the more radical, immediatist, and pacifist National Woman's Party.[38]

Although NWLLC played with notions of gender—sometimes reflecting and other times subverting traditional assumptions and norms—it adhered strictly to the same assumptions about class, ethnic, and racial hierarchies that permeated the suffrage movement and the larger culture of women's voluntarism. Well-to-do and professional white women were deputized to "enlighten" wage-earning and recently immigrated women, those considered the "weaker links" in the chain of wartime civic unity. Similarly, educated middle- and upper-class black women fanned out to canvass the African American community through the NWLLC's Colored Women's Committee in conjunction with the National Association of Colored Women (NACW). In the Fourth Liberty Loan drive, the NACW raised a total of $5 million, earning a fifth-place rank among women's organizations.[39]

Wartime financial mobilization relied upon certain gender conventions even as it challenged others. The War Loan drives politicized traditional female social roles, such as shopping and budgeting, even as new political relationships were created between the federal state and women canvassers, agents, publicists, and investors. Women's centrality in the War Loan campaigns had a crucial symbolic effect. By pushing those who lacked suffrage to the fore, the War Loans engendered its own claims regarding the inclusivity of financial nationalism and investor-citizenship.

THE WAR LOAN Organization drew heavily upon existing private institutions and associations to raise money speedily from as many as possible. But Americans would not be roused by exhortation alone. Liberty Loan committees and War Savings societies employed a range of social and emotional inducements—emulation, excitement, shame, guilt, and fear—through a range of cultural technologies—visual, material, dramatic, and rhetorical—in order to emphasize the obligation to invest and to manifest the financial nation.

War Loan boosters favored visual media, which they believed to be effective with the illiterate and foreign-language speaking. Posters, ads, cartoons, films, billboards, slides, window displays, handbills, and pamphlets all conveyed the imperative to invest and invited vicarious participation in the war. The War Savings program invited Americans to "lick the Kaiser" as they licked their thrift stamps. War Loan publicity associated the citizen-investor's funds with soldiers' exploits and the machinery of modern industrial warfare. War Loan marketing enabled the citizen-investor to visualize how the state spent the funds lent. To illustrate the importance of even the smallest subscriptions, War Loan publicity specified what certain denominations bought in terms of food, clothing, tanks, planes, ships, armaments, surgical instruments, machinery, artillery, and so on. Another trope allowed citizen-investors to imagine themselves halting the kaiser's innumerable depredations against the weak and the innocent. Countless images and stunts invited citizen-investors to enact violence, humiliation, and vengeance upon the kaiser and his son, Prince William. In one typical exercise, Liberty Bond subscribers drove one nail into the kaiser's coffin for each purchase. A moving billboard in Memphis even depicted Uncle Sam anally penetrating the kaiser with a bayonet.[40]

Three-dimensional spectacles added a tactile dimension. In-store dioramas recreated the typography and progress of key battles. New York City's Loan committee staged reenactments complete with soldiers, trenches, mortars firing blanks, "liquid fire display," and a "Breath of Death" demonstration of "the most modern poison gas and gas defense equipment." Highly popular "war relic" tours materialized the contributions of citizen-investors. "War material, soldiers' and soldiers' equipment, ordnance, and ammunition" collected from American, Allied, and enemy forces toured the country, "enabling the people, particular in the more remote districts, to inspect some of the things" the Loans bought. Similarly, a captured UC5 German mine-laying submarine was rechristened "U-Buy-A-Bond" and served as a Liberty Loan sales booth in Central Park. Those presenting a Liberty Loan button or other proof of purchase enjoyed free admission.[41]

War Loan Organization publicists preferred to render the battlefront as antiseptically as possible, but citizen-investors hungered for gorier accounts of the supreme brutality of modern industrial warfare. They clamored for American and Allied soldiers' testimonies to the inhumanity of the kaiser's forces. They flocked to motion pictures in which Norma Talmadge and Lillian Gish played innocent maidens menaced by "lust-maddened Huns" and American troops arrived just in time to rescue the fair one "from the fate that has befallen so many women 'over there.'" But no one moved audiences to tears quite like Marie Van Gastel. Tens of thousands gathered at Liberty bond rallies to hear this Belgian Red Cross nurse "of striking beauty, youth and charm" recount the atrocities suffered by brave Belgium at the hand of the "mad hun" and her sleepless nights tending to thousands of shredded bodies.[42]

Soldiers and scenes of war were oftentimes absent, however. War Loan imagery and pageantry instead displayed the financial nation itself, aiming to elicit allegiance of groups by making them visible. In parades and assemblies, citizen-investors manifested the financial nation as a plurality of diverse groups acting in concert to achieve a common cause. The financial nation embraced distinctly women, ethnic groups, and African Americans, along with different religious faiths and economic functions. Ten different "patriotic-religious meetings" representing "all religious sects and beliefs" were held in Cincinnati during the Fourth Liberty Loan. Each employed "the same program . . . devised and timed" so that the 150,000 participants "would be doing exactly the same thing at the same time." In Omaha, various trade union and trade associations joined to erect Liberty Tower. The groups alternated installing one block for each $10,000 raised. Upon completion, the Hohenzollern family was hung in effigy. In many ways, the War Loans anticipated Mary Follett's and John Dewey's theorizations of a pluralistic state comprising competing associations and interests—none enjoying an absolute claim to a citizen's allegiance—which the state sought to balance.[43]

The War Loan campaigns' stagings of the financial nation dramatized investment as an exercise of political rights. In Lynn, Massachusetts, for example, the local Liberty Loan committee opened the polls for a "Liberty election." For the first time ever, inhabitants practiced "universal voting—equal suffrage." Men, women, and children entered the voting booths to answer "'yes' or 'no' on the greatest question before the world—'shall democracy live?'" By subscribing to bonds at the polling place, citizen-investors voted in favor of the "thousands of men" who protected the "interests," lives, "liberty and happiness" of the nation.[44]

In contrast to the patriotic revelry and democratic excitement of Liberty Loan events, War Savings cast the mobilization of the financial nation as a dire civic obligation. National War Savings Days dourly summoned all adults to "meetings at school houses and polling places at 2 o'clock to secure subscriptions." Local employers and civic leaders led the roundup, while the Treasury mailed direct summons to every American household. These somber exercises approximated Registration Day on June 5, 1917, when almost 10 million men publicly enrolled in the draft. In comparison, the first National War Savings Day on June 28, 1918, mobilized roughly 34 *million* men, women and children.[45]

Quite often, War Loan features showcased neither the war, nor the financial nation, nor even the precepts of thrifty forbearance and wise investment. Rather, a spontaneous street theater of financial nationalism simply aimed to capture attention and arouse enthusiasm in order to inspire sales. Nothing worked so well as displays that contravened gendered conventions of respectability and vulnerability. Attired as sailors or soldiers, young women sold bonds and stamps from "war relics" converted into sales booths. During the Fourth Loan drive, Frances Helen Kelly donned "a military uniform" and "rode the good horse 'Thrift' across the state" of New Jersey, collecting $3 million in subscriptions. Female stunt pilots flew scout and bombing planes at state fairs, while Miss Ruth Law's "spectacular flying tour" dropped "paper bombs calling attention to the Liberty Loan" across the Midwest and Southwest. Women even exposed themselves. Six scantily clad burlesque entertainers performed feats of "fancy diving" on "State Street" in Albany, while "society belle volunteers" climbed fire ladders above crowds in Austin, Texas. William Howard Taft's niece also revealed her underskirts, ascending one rung of fire ladder outside the Woolworth building in New York City for every $500 bond. Over in Harlem, "kisses sold above par when a score or more of the prettiest" African American girls auctioned their affections to Italian passersby. These types of shocking acts "sold bonds where every other effort" failed.[46]

But celebration, solicitation, and conscription only went so far. War Loan committees and societies also employed a range of more coercive techniques—including guilt, shame, competition, fear, even violence—in order to enforce the obligations of financial citizenship and to quash dissent regarding the war or the methods of its financing.

No group disappointed the War Loan Organization more than American farmers. Publicists struggled to secure appealing speakers (including implacable Wall Street foes Samuel Untermyer and William Jennings Bryan) to stage accessible spectacles and to organize War Savings societies in rural areas. Propaganda devised for rural audiences sought to stimulate feelings of guilt over how European food shortages benefited American agriculture. Only through War Loan subscriptions could American farmers sanctify their newfound wealth.[47]

Where celebration and sensation failed, local committees and societies sought to stoke desire for social recognition. Even so, they backed their efforts with provocations of guilt, shame, and sometimes with force. School programs exposed parents' investment decisions to offspring, classmates, and teachers so that children might goad parents into further sacrifice. War Savings societies aimed to shame the "extravagant" individual, one War Savings leader explained, "as extravagance will mark him or her as unpatriotic and will be so designated by the fellow-members."[48] In an effort to "create desire" for social recognition, the War Loan Organization induced local papers to print the name of every Liberty bond subscriber. Each citizen-investor received a button, while Victory Loan canvassers were awarded medals "struck from captured German cannon." Buttons and badges stirred the longing to look like everyone else along with fear of suffering (sometimes violent) reprisals. "'We don't sell Liberty Bonds, we sell buttons,'" reported New York agents. In one Buffalo, New York, plant, "every employee" but one wore such a button. When asked, "'where is that man?'" the manager confessed, "'he's in the hospital!'"[49]

In urban areas, spectacles of shame forced "dollar slackers"—an epithet commonly leveled at those who refused to subscribe—to run a gauntlet of dishonor. In Houston, Texas, where the African American population swelled and black troops revolted in 1917, pedestrians could not cross downtown intersections unless they presented proof of purchase to white volunteers positioned at barricades. In smaller and rural communities, shame could be applied even more effectively. In Northern Iowa, one prominent farmer who refused his quota received arson threats and found his "cattle driven out of the local stockyard and scattered throughout the country." Townspeople erected a "yellow monument" in the "center of town" inscribed with the names of family members. Episodes of public shaming were so common that Philadelphia introduced "Conscience Day," so citizens might avoid solicitation on the city streets by pledging voluntarily.[50]

While some dramatizations of financial nationalism performed unity, others harnessed—even encouraged—competition and rivalry. States, towns, factories, corporate divisions, chapters of clubs and unions, ethnic groups, War Savings societies, classrooms, and even family members were pitted against each other. Locales and groups competed to win honor flags for meeting or exceeding quotas. To compel railroad labor subscriptions, the Treasury published figures regarding workers' daily wages and urged railroad companies to subscribe liberally and to challenge employees and the Railroad Brotherhoods to match. Ethnic leaders, in particular, stirred competitive pride to induce subscriptions. "We Croatians by blood and race, American citizens by free choice and oath, must not be left behind the others," declared Don Nike Grskovia, Supreme President of the Croatian League. In New York City, Hungarians and Italians vying for the honor of leading a Liberty Loan parade nearly erupted in street violence. In Atlanta, the black press boldly reported that in "out of a population of 75,000 the Negroes of Atlanta had 15,000" in their War Savings parade, whereas "the white citizens, with a population of 150,000, had in line less than 10,000." And in homes across the United States, window placards recorded each bond purchased by each resident. This produced rivalry between family members, while a lack of sufficient placards "created such unfavorable neighborhood comment" that "indifferent persons" quickly became hot prospects.[51]

Although War Loan architects dreamed of a polity in which citizen-investors entered willingly and joyously, local agents and committees did not hesitate to frighten the populace into union. To open the Fourth Loan drive, the New Orleans Liberty Loan committee fanned out across the city before dawn, lighting smoke bombs. A special morning edition of the *Times-Picayune* alerted alarmed residents to the ruse. Demonstrations of the omnipresence of the federal government likewise aimed to incite fear and awe to coax sales. In Dallas, Texas, Southwestern Telegraph Company donated operator time to deliver a stern "subscription reminder . . . at the request of the U.S. Government" to every subscriber. Those seeking to redeem War Savings stamps at the post office after Armistice received this notice:

> I regret to learn from the records at the Post Office that you have served notice of your intention to surrender the War Savings Stamps purchased by you . . . The war is won, but it will NOT BE OVER until ever American fighting man is safely returned . . . YOUR government needs the money . . . you imperil its plans for the reconstruction of the affairs of the country on a Peace Basis. YOU WILL KEEP THEM when you consider what there is at stake!

Intimidation, guilt, and fear were employed to steel citizen-investors' resolve.⁵²

War Loan agents and committees worked closely with the groups that Americans established to perform war service and to maintain vigilance against disloyalty and sabotage during the war. These vigilance societies—variously called home guards, protective leagues, security leagues, and councils of defense—harassed pacifists, those suspected of German or bolshevist sympathies, slackers who failed to register for the draft, striking workers, and prostitutes lingering around military camps. Members of vigilance societies served as War Loan agents. War Loan committees called upon such groups to impress the obligation to invest upon the recalcitrant. During the Second Loan, the Nebraska Council of Defense performed "intensive and vigorous work" in "securing subscriptions from lax or half-hearted individuals" as they "rigorously" investigated and punished "cases of treasonable or seditious conduct." South Dakota's council organized "intensive campaigns by automobile patriots" to canvass "counties where considerable pro-German sentiment existed." The War Loans were a key component of the culture of obligation, surveillance, and vigilantism upon which home-front mobilization depended.⁵³

Although they lacked formal authority, War Loan canvassers nonetheless issued vague threats of official reprisals by the distant federal state. Forbidden to "extract a promise of more than the person is fairly able financially," they brought "the matter to a head by asking the person if he or she is for the Government or against it." Agents—mostly women—collected names and reasons when refused, as directed by the Treasury Department. "Say . . . that his refusal and the reasons therefore will be reported to the State Director and by him sent on to the Department at Washington." Such information was not systematically reported to or acted upon by the federal government. Still, the Treasury notified War Loan agents, "the Government wants to know who is supporting this war and who is refusing to support it," concluding ominously, "we do not know what action will be taken." Local committees recorded the names of those who refused to pledge on a dreaded "yellow card." In Oregon, these were "turned over to military and intelligence officers" to pursue, while in Iowa, yellow cards were posted "in conspicuous places" to invite action by vigilance groups or mobs.⁵⁴

Threats and intimidation were most effective when local War Loan committees devised methods to assess individuals' purchasing ability. Assessment committees included civic leaders such as bankers, clergy, lawyers, police chiefs, large employers, and ethnic leaders. Drawing upon both informal local knowledge and official data about individual assets and debts, these committees set target quotas for individuals and households.

Any who disagreed with his or her quota was required to prove publicly an inability to pay.[55]

Equipped with such assessments, local committees performed rituals of accounting and shaming, enacting threats and feats of violence to force subscriptions. A "joint committee of men and women" in Tishomingo County, Michigan, rounded up "dollar slackers." Delivered by the committee to a public meeting, these slackers' "patriotism" soon "blossomed." Similarly, in Iowa, "a committee of two or more persons" called upon individuals "to ascertain the reason" for their failure to subscribe. If this visit failed, "a larger committee" returned, resorting to "persuasion, argument, cajolery, and finally threats as to what the government and his neighbors would do" if a subscription was not forthcoming.[56]

Mimicking the procedures of the state and claiming its authority, kangaroo courts punished breaches of financial nationalism. In Iowa, an extralegal jury—comprising 10 men who had purchased "generous amounts of bonds" and whose sons were "in the military service"—sat in judgment of those on the "yellow list," who "claimed to have subscribed but did not." The summoned were ordered to bring "a statement of all property and debts." When they reached the courthouse steps, those who refused bonds encountered "a picture of a real patriot; a widow whose only son is in the army and who now washes" to afford her allotment of bonds. The prosecution next asked to photograph slackers, their homes, automobiles, and stores, in order that "the contrast" might be illustrated "at the next local patriotic meeting." Out of 400 persons thus summoned, no one failed to subscribe following such a trial.[57]

"Dollar slackers" encountered coercion in the workplace as well. Employees risked the loss of jobs and military exemptions when they failed to display their loyalty with generous subscriptions. They might also expect a coat of yellow paint from "some gang from another department of the works." Slacker employers and businessmen suffered bricks thrown through storefront or parlor windows, the loss of patronage, or the cancellation of both government and private contracts.[58]

When individuals refused to join the financial nation, swift reprisals ensued. Brutal repressions of labor, pacifism, socialism, ethnic difference, and assertions of African American independence took place throughout World War I. Crowds also meted out violent retribution to "dollar slackers," similarly perceived as disloyal, subversive, and bolshevist. These associations were strengthened by the tendency of critics of the war to refuse investment. During the first Loan, Adolph Cabet, a Socialist candidate for alderman in the Bronx, expressed his opposition to the capitalists' war by denouncing the Liberty Loan:

Liberty Bonds is a false name. They are not Liberty Bonds. They are slavery bonds; they are black slavery bonds. Men working for $17 a week are forced to take them or they will lose their jobs. They pin a button on you. I tear the button from me. I tell you to tear the button from you. They are damned hypocrites. Don't take their bonds. They are a fraud. They will never pay the principal or the interest.

Cabet faced arrest, but other "dollar slackers" were not so lucky. During the Third Liberty Loan, a mob in Camden, New Jersey, nearly lynched a Russian, a German, and an Austrian who had refused subscription. Thirst for vengeance against belligerent nations—or those that had abandoned the cause—clearly incensed the throng. So, too, did War Loan propaganda, which offered for emulation the "methods of treatment" and "retribution" due to dollar slackers. In one film, "Liberty Bond Jimmy," played by Harold Lockwood, casts "the disloyal American" who refused both bond and button "into the street," inspiring his own father to make "an unusually large subscription." Roused by warnings issued from the Treasury Department, stalwart citizen-investors also took action against those who attempted to induce others to part with their Liberty bonds. Just as they ferreted those who refused to subscribe, local patriotic groups—whose ranks swelled with returning servicemen after the war—identified and captured swindlers for similar extralegal prosecution.[59]

To be sure, strongly coercive measures of financial mobilization met criticism. Senator Warren G. Harding called the Liberty Loan drives "hysterical and unseemly." Harding's public criticism greatly angered Secretary McAdoo, but in private, War Loan leaders worried that coercive approaches might alienate workers politically and undermine efforts to promote *permanent* habits of thrift and investment. *Atlantic Monthly* denounced such tactics as "prussianized . . . borrowing with a club." Indeed, its editors blamed strong-arm tactics—"mob rule by the rich, with the able assistance of hoodlums"—for the postwar appeal of socialism in Wisconsin and elsewhere.

It is not difficult to image the effect upon the farmer's ideas of a federal administration to which he attributes such methods. Would you vote for the party in power? I trow not. You would vote *Socialist* until the cows came home.

Yet critics and skeptics concurred that universal investment in federal war debt—if freely chosen—would enrich citizenship, enhance civic culture, and repel bolshevism.[60]

The use of coercion at once advanced and subverted War Loan's equation of citizenship with investment, adding more members to the financial nation, but against their will. Given the centrality of coercion, the creation of a mass market for financial securities—a necessary precondition for the explosion in corporate stock ownership in the 1920s—can hardly be understood as the result of rational deliberation by profit-seeking individuals. But whether citizen-investors found themselves enticed or compelled, the War Loans introduced tens of millions of Americans to financial securities investment for the first time.

GIVEN THE ABSENCE of a strong federal government and deep-seated fears of expansive federal power in the United States, the wartime state ceded a great deal of control over financial mobilization to a fractured citizenry, which could only be organized through preexisting, often conflicting, civic associations. Accordingly, the capacious rhetoric of the War Loans accommodated multiple visions of how universal ownership of federal debt might upend or uphold existing social conventions and hierarchies of power. Ultimately, the War Loan campaigns succeeded in attracting so many millions precisely because the investor democracy ideal remained so open to interpretation.[61]

Debate over the political implications of the creation of a mass investment society grew only more pitched after the Allies declared victory. At the Armistice, investors seemed to comprise a broad-based constituency whose economic well-being ensured national economic vigor. The War Loans raised expectations for permanent federal agencies and regulations to support and to protect citizen-investors, even in their private-sector investments. Neither nationalized enterprise nor the welfare state appeared fundamentally inconsistent with a mass investment society at first. In the tumultuous period of postwar economic readjustment, recommendations for how the state might advance investor democracy in peacetime—ranging from providing its own securities to educating investors, regulating the securities markets, and employing citizen-investors' funds in state enterprise—abounded. They would be challenged.[62]

NYSE member Charles E. Knoblauch as depicted in *Stock Exchange in Caricature*, a limited edition commissioned for the membership (New York: A. Stone, 1904), 79.

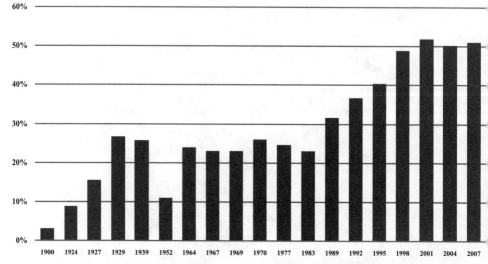

Percentage of U.S. Households Owning Equity, 1900–2007

Note: *Equity ownership includes both direct ownership of corporate stock as well as indirect ownership through investment vehicles such as mutual funds; 1900 includes both bond and stock ownership.*
Source: *John V. Duca, "Why Have Households Increasingly Relied on Mutual Funds to Own Equity?" The Review of Income and Wealth 51 (September 2005): 375–96; U. S. Census, 2010 Statistical Abstract, Table 1174, "Stock Ownership by Age of Family Head and Family Income, 2001–2007" at http://www.census.gov/compendia/statab/cats/banking_finance_insurance.html; Edwin Burk Cox, Trends in the Distribution of Stock Ownership (Philadelphia: University of PA Press, 1963), 28–33; Lewis H. Kimmel, Shareownership in the United States (Washington, D.C.: Brookings Institute, 1952), 89; Twentieth Century Fund, The Securities Markets (New York: Twentieth Century Fund, 1935), 50, 56–57, 735; New York Stock Exchange, A Detailed Look at the Individual Investor (New York: New York Stock Exchange, 1971).*

Graph by Alejandro Falchettore, Russell Sage Foundation.

Percentage of U.S. households owning equity, 1900–2007.

Bulls, bears, and lambs chase each other in a fruitless exercise. W. A. Rogers, "Great Activity in Wall Street," *New York Herald,* March 19, 1908, 7.

Lambs are lured and shorn. "Wall Street," *Judge*, May 1901.

The denizens of Wall Street beg from productive workers. W. A. Rogers, "The Makers of Wall Street," *New York Herald,* October 16, 1916, 15.

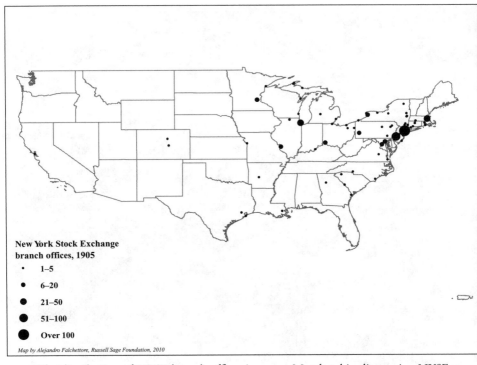

Map by Alejandro Falchettore, Russell Sage Foundation, 2010

The distribution of NYSE branch offices in 1905. Membership directories, NYSE Archives.

Victory Way in New York City, terminating in a pyramid of captured German helmets. *New York Herald,* April 22, 1918, Guy Emerson scrapbook, vol. 7, Library of Congress, Washington, D.C.

EFFECTIVE VACCINATION

War Savings stamps depicted as offering protection against bolshevism. Folder "Cartoons Used in Newspapers in Twelfth Federal Reserve District for Victory Loan," box 27, General Files Relating to Liberty Loan and War Savings Bonds, 1917–1925 (Entry NC-120, 622), Records of the Bureau of Public Debt (Record Group 53), National Archives, College Park, Md.

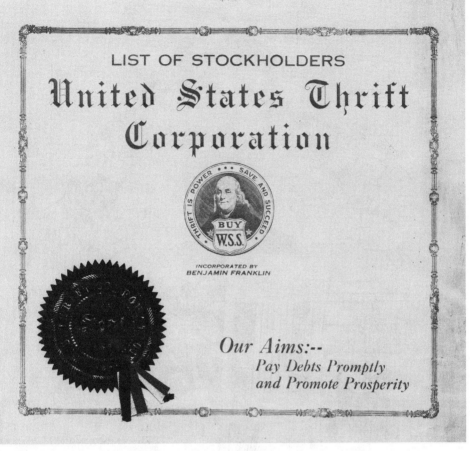

A "stock certificate" in the United States, issued in return for a War Savings pledge. Folder "Thrift—General Twelfth District," box 17, General Files Relating to Liberty Loan and War Savings Bonds, 1917–1925 (Entry NC-120, 622), Records of the Bureau of Public Debt (Record Group 53), National Archives, College Park, Md.

Boardroom USA, a cartoon published to promote the Victory Loan. Folder "Cartoons Used in Newspapers in Twelfth Federal Reserve District for Victory Loan," box 27, General Files Relating to Liberty Loan and War Savings Bonds, 1917–1925 (Entry NC-120, 622), Records of the Bureau of Public Debt (Record Group 53), National Archives, College Park, Md.

"Buy a Liberty Bond and Kill 2 Birds with One Stone," *Evening Mail* (New York), April 15, 1918, Guy Emerson scrapbook, vol. 2, Library of Congress, Washington, D.C.

"Echoes of the Loan's Call from Chinatown," *New York Tribune,* April 28, 1918, Guy Emerson scrapbook, vol. 2, Library of Congress, Washington, D.C.

The Savage Lives Within His Income

··Are You Doing Better Than That?

"The progress of to-day is made possible by the savings of yesterday."

This economic maxim is plainly portrayed by the cartoon above.

The savage, with no more worry than accumulation of food for to-day, since to-morrow's food is always hanging on the trees, has made no progress through centuries of existence.

He eats the same food his great-great-grandfather did, fights with the same crude spears, wears the same crude ornaments in lieu of clothing.

The first slow steps in civilization introduced men to things which could not be had for the taking; things which required labor to make, and which therefore had a price.

The more thrifty of our early ancestors soon acquired more goods and valuables than their careless neighbors; and in time tribes and peoples became marked apart from others less industrious in the gathering of wealth.

They built ships, dug mines, hired the less-developed people of other nations to work for them or enslaved them with the armies which their wealth enabled them to equip.

The railroads, telephones, and steamships of the present day could not have been built if in previous centuries enormous savings had not been laid up.

The law of civilization is the law of saving, and the individual's prosperity and progress as well as that of a nation is dependent upon his living, NOT WITHIN HIS INCOME, as does the savage, but far enough within so that he can lay up savings which work for him.

WASHINGTON : GOVERNMENT PRINTING OFFICE : 1919

Investment portrayed as civilized whiteness. *Thrift* (Portland, Ore.), 1919, folder "Bulletins," box 36, General Files Relating to Liberty Loan and War Savings Bonds, 1917–1925 (Entry NC-120, 622), Records of the Bureau of Public Debt (Record Group 53), National Archives, College Park, Md.

The War Loans' "Back of It All" trope, celebrated workers' contribution to wartime economic mobilization. Box 131, General Files Relating to Liberty Loan and War Savings Bonds, 1917–1925 (Entry NC-120, 622), Records of the Bureau of Public Debt (Record Group 53), National Archives, College Park, Md.

The grandson of two Confederate generals assists at a Liberty Loan sales booth in Richmond, Va., flanked by two wounded Civil War veterans. Box 126, General Files Relating to Liberty Loan and War Savings Bonds, 1917–1925 (Entry NC-120, 622), Records of the Bureau of Public Debt (Record Group 53), National Archives, College Park, Md.

OUR UNCLE SAM EVENTUALLY BAYONETTED FRIEND KAISER

4,000,000   4,250,000   4,500,000

Sketch of a moving billboard used to chart Liberty Loan subscription totals in Memphis, Tenn. Second Federal Reserve District Liberty Loan Committee, "Feature Publicity (Stunts) Others Have Used Successfully," folder 9, box 1, Walter W. and Lillian F. Norton papers, Manuscripts and Archives, Yale University Library, New Haven, Conn.

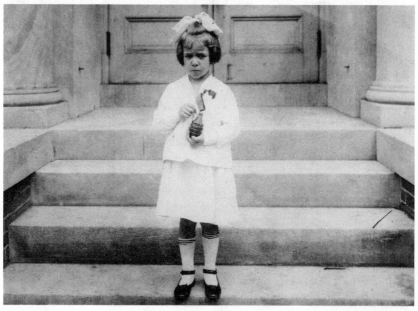

A first-grade pupil displays her savings bank, made from an unused hand grenade shell. Box 126, General Files Relating to Liberty Loan and War Savings Bonds, 1917–1925 (Entry NC-120, 622), Records of the Bureau of Public Debt (Record Group 53), National Archives, College Park, Md.

Let Uncle Sam help build your future

The Treasury Department promoted its War Savings program as a route to economic and social mobility. Folder "Miscellaneous War Savings Advertising," box 42, General Files Relating to Liberty Loan and War Savings Bonds, 1917–1925 (Entry NC-120, 622), Records of the Bureau of Public Debt (Record Group 53), National Archives, College Park, Md.

These groups of stockholders illustrate the rapid growth in ownership of the Bell System.

A Community of Owners Nation-wide

"Who owns the company?" "What is behind it?" These questions are asked in appraising the soundness of a business and in determining its aims.

The American Telephone and Telegraph Company is owned by more than 270,000 people living in every state in the Union. Could the stockholders of the Bell System be gathered to one place, they would equal the population of a city about the size of Providence or Denver.

They constitute a representative cross-section of American citizenship. Among them, of course, are bankers and men of large affairs;

for the idea of ownership in the Bell System appeals to sound business judgment and a trained sense of values.

In this community of owners are the average man and woman, the storekeeper, the clerk, the salesman, the professional man, the farmer and the housewife—users of the telephone who with their savings have purchased a share in its ownership. The average individual holding is but twenty-six shares.

No institution is more popularly owned than the Bell System, none has its shares distributed more widely. In the truest sense it is owned by those it serves.

" BELL SYSTEM "

AMERICAN TELEPHONE AND TELEGRAPH COMPANY
AND ASSOCIATED COMPANIES

One Policy, One System, Universal Service, and all directed toward Better Service

AT&T depicted its shareholders as co-extensive with the nation. Folder 3, box 21, N. W. Ayer Advertising Agency Records, Archives Center, National Museum of American History, Smithsonian Institution, Washington, D.C.

12   E H   1920

Our Triple Responsibility

The three great purposes of the Bell telephone organization, the three united interests which the management must ever keep in the fore-front, are: service to the public, justice to the employees, security to stockholders.

Service to the public must be as continuous, dependable, and perfect in speech transmission, under all conditions and during all emergencies, as it is humanly possible for science and skill to produce.

Justice to employees requires their careful training for the work expected of them, agreeable and healthful working conditions, adequate pay, an opportunity for advancement, cordial relations between managing and other employees, and every facility for properly performing their duties.

Security to stockholders demands earnings to provide dividends with a margin for safety and the stability of market value which goes with a large number of shareholders with a small average ownership.

AMERICAN TELEPHONE AND TELEGRAPH COMPANY
AND-ASSOCIATED COMPANIES

One Policy   *One System*   *Universal Service*

And all directed toward Better Service

An AT&T shareowner portrayed as worthy of managerial consideration as much as the customer or the worker. Folder 2, box 21, N. W. Ayer Advertising Agency Records, Archives Center, National Museum of American History, Smithsonian Institution, Washington, D.C.

Our Stockholders

There are over 135,000 stockholders who own the American Telephone and Telegraph Company. This great body of people, larger than the entire population of such cities as Albany, Dayton or Tacoma, share the earnings produced by the Bell System.

More than 45,000 of these partners are workers in the telephone organization. They are linemen, switch board operators, clerks, mechanics, electricians.

The vast property of the Bell System represents the savings of these thousands of people, in many cases *all* their savings.

In the truest sense of the word this big public service corporation belongs to the people. The people own it and the people receive the profits. More than 93% of its stock is owned by persons holding, each, less than one-ninth of one per cent.

The Bell System is a real industrial democracy. On its economic operation depends the future independence of many citizens of small means, as well as the profitable employment of thousands of other men and women.

AMERICAN TELEPHONE AND TELEGRAPH COMPANY
AND ASSOCIATED COMPANIES

One Policy   *One System*   *Universal Service*

The AT&T stockholder figured as a dependent woman with child. Folder 2, box 21, N. W. Ayer Advertising Agency Records, Archives Center, National Museum of American History, Smithsonian Institution, Washington, D.C.

A pamphlet advertising Mitten Bank Securities Corporation stock. Folder "Mitten Bank Securities Corp.," box 38, Albert Greenfield papers (Mss 1959), Pennsylvania Historical Society, Philadelphia, Pa.

A stock certificate issued by American Trustee Share Corporation. Folder "American G to American Z," box 1, Edgar Higgins Investment Trust Collection (Mss 783), Baker Library Historical Collections, Harvard Business School, Boston, Mass.

A billboard advertising the retail brokerage services of National City Company, in which successful investment funds the family's enriching adventure abroad. Investment Research Committee of the Financial Advertisers Association, *Advertising Investment Securities* (New York: Prentice-Hall, 1928).

"What is back of these bonds?"

When you buy bonds from The National City Company you get something more than dependable income and adequate security of principal. You get a broad choice of issues, and personal contact with bond men well qualified to help you select suitable offerings; you get quick service through a chain of investment offices in over fifty leading American cities, offices interconnected by thousands of miles of private wires; you get ready access to up-to-date information on your various bond holdings; and, finally, you get the broad benefits which come from dealing with an organization having a background of over a century of financial experience and maintaining close contact with investment conditions throughout the world.

Our monthly list of recommended issues will keep you informed on attractive current offerings. It will be sent upon request.

The National City Company
National City Bank Building, New York

Offices or representatives in the principal cities of the United States, Canada, Europe, China, Japan, India, Australia, South America, Central America and the West Indies.

—for suitable bonds

Some bond investors demand the utmost in security—others look more to income. Some need ready marketability—others place tax-exemption first among their requirements. The National City Company always offers a wide choice of bonds of the various types, some meeting the needs of one investor, some the needs of another. Competent bond men at any National City office will gladly help you make a suitable selection. Ask for current list of recommended issues.

The National City Company
National City Bank Building, New York

OFFICES IN 50 AMERICAN CITIES INTERCONNECTED BY 11,000 MILES OF PRIVATE WIRES. INTERNATIONAL BRANCHES AND CONNECTIONS.

The investor and his advisor master the industrial landscape. Carl Hundhausen, *Kundenwerbung Amerikanischer Banken* (Berlin: L. Weiss, 1929).

"The Nation's Market Place" (1928), NYSE Archives, New York.

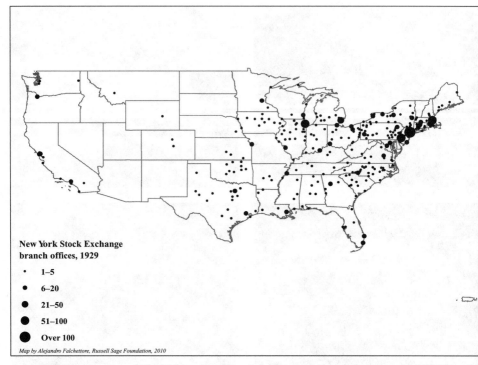

Map by Alejandro Falchettore, Russell Sage Foundation, 2010

The distribution of NYSE branch offices in 1929. Membership directories, NYSE Archives, New York.

CHAPTER FIVE

The Postwar Struggle for the Financial Nation

DURING THE winter of 1918–1919, millions of Americans braved the great influenza pandemic—which killed six times more than did the war—to celebrate the Armistice. Mammoth military parades staged in major U.S. cities hailed successive waves of returning soldiers. Smaller towns arranged more modest but no less dramatic commemorations. In San Joaquin County, California, children clutched precious hand-grenade savings banks as they celebrated alongside their parents and neighbors on the streets of rural towns. The 15 million banks distributed by the Treasury's War Loan Organization—"weapons of war" transformed into "weapons of peace" unleashed "against waste"—embodied "American determination to perpetuate the lessons of self-sacrifice learned in the war." Overhead, planes released aerograms from President Woodrow Wilson onto the crowds and farms below:

SUBJECT: THE HIGH COST OF LIVING
RETURN ADDRESS: OUT-OF-THE-AIR

"A country worth fighting for is a country worth saving for," Wilson's communiqué read. Through "rigid economy," manifested through continued regular purchase of War Savings stamps and Liberty bonds, citizen-investors would vanquish the "burdensome cost of living" now "weighing down" the otherwise victorious nation.[1]

Hopefulness marked Americans' Armistice jubilees, yet the challenges of economic readjustment and simmering sociopolitical conflicts troubled the

Wilson administration. A postwar economic downturn might easily detonate racial and industrial strife. The menace of bolshevism remained. Treasury officials continued to believe that the federal government could safeguard against these perils by conferring upon every American an interest in lawful government and private property in the form of small-denomination federal securities. To do so, the Treasury Department maintained its War Savings program—renamed U.S. Government Savings—until 1924. As part of this ongoing commitment to investor democracy, the Treasury also endorsed federal regulation of the financial securities markets in order to protect citizen-investors from risky and fraudulent promotions. Indeed, in the uncertain years immediately after the Great War, the notion that mass investment held the potential to improve American capitalism and belief in the import of investors' interests moved to the fore in a range of contests over postwar economic readjustment. Americans would engage in crucial debates about how the wartime birth of a nation of investors might alter the course of American capitalism.[2]

Soon after Armistice, jubilation and optimism degenerated into discord and violence. Four million servicemen returned home, only to face shortages in housing, growing unemployment, and surging inflation. Just four days after the Allies' declaration of victory, Samuel Gompers, the president of the American Federation of Labor, warned that labor unions would not accept layoffs, reductions in wages, or increases in hours. American workers fulfilled Gompers's promise. Four million men and women—nearly one-fifth of the labor force—joined approximately 3,500 strikes in 1919. In February, the demands of Seattle shipbuilders for shorter hours and more pay sparked a general strike of 65,000. Fulminating against the strikers as foreign revolutionaries determined to sabotage American institutions, Seattle mayor Ole Hanson vowed to crush the walkout with soldiers stationed at nearby Camp Lewis. Hanson's intransigence pushed Gompers to press Seattle's Central Labor Council to call off their uprising, catapulting Hanson to national fame. Then in April, phone lines in New England fell silent when 20,000 telephone operators put down their headsets to protest their wages and working conditions. Just a few weeks later, postal workers intercepted thirty "May Day" bombs addressed to a range of eminent financiers, industrialists, and politicians, including the mayor of Seattle.

The citizen-investors who mobilized to promote the Victory Loan during April and May of 1919 were, in the words of columnist Walter Lippmann, "the most frightened victors the world ever saw." A nation that so recently had basked in the glow of victory might dissolve in social enmity, perhaps even bolshevist revolution, many feared. The ranks of socialists, communists, anarchists, and militant unionists had begun to recover from the extensive harassment, vigilante violence, arrests for treason and sedition, and deportation that radical groups had experienced during the war. Their meetings and offices were attacked by their indignant opponents, including scores of ex-servicemen. Seattle mayor Hanson, meanwhile, emerged as the most popular speaker of the Victory Loan campaign. Addressing the multitudes gathered on Victory Way in New York City, Hanson urged the federal government to ferret out and deport the "seditious aliens" who were "advocating and planning and attempting to overthrow this government." Soon after, Hanson declared his candidacy for president, championing immigration restriction to bar allegedly inassimilable radicals from eastern and southern Europe whom Hanson blamed for militant unionism and terrorism. Hanson failed in his bid, but the Immigration Act of 1924 largely accomplished his goal.[3]

The Victory Loan drives revived wartime rituals of financial nationalism, but most failed to achieve social cohesion as intended. In Cleveland, Ohio, the vicious collision of a Victory Loan parade with a socialist May Day march forced authorities to commandeer tanks and trucks deployed for display to restore order. During the summer and fall of 1919, brutal conflicts pitted blacks against whites and unions against their employers. Race riots engulfed twenty-six U.S. cities, killing hundreds of African Americans and injuring thousands more. Across the country, a resurgent Ku Klux Klan proliferated, while in Arkansas, a bloody massacre crushed attempts to organize a sharecroppers union. Meanwhile, the U.S. government launched a counteroffensive against the radicals it believed to be poisoning both labor and racial relations. After bombs exploded in seven American cities on June 2, 1919—one sheared the front off of the house of Attorney General A. Mitchell Palmer—the Justice Department launched raids against those suspected of advocating or plotting the overthrow of the U.S. government. Thousands were detained, hundreds deported.[4]

The Red Scare pushed the labor movement into a defensive posture by the end of 1919. But even as Samuel Gompers moved to purge left-leaning elements from the American Federation of Labor, he could not prevent AFL members from endorsing the "Plumb Plan" to nationalize the railroads or silence the United Mine Workers' calls for a federal takeover of the mines. Nor could he control the Boston police, who struck in September for the recognition of their AFL-affiliated union. After several nights of chaos, Boston mayor Calvin Coolidge rose to national prominence when he refused to negotiate, called in federal troops, and fired the strikers. Nationwide walkouts by 365,000 steelworkers and roughly 400,000 coal miners later that fall represented the short-lived apex of postwar industrial unionism. Although union membership had increased to 5.1 million in 1920 from

2.7 million in 1914—with 1 million joining in 1919 alone—labor's bargaining position deteriorated rapidly in the devastating economic recession triggered by the Federal Reserve's sharp hike in interest rates after the Victory Loan concluded. Industrial production fell 23 percent, the wholesale price index fell 37 percent, and unemployment rose to nearly 12 percent by mid-1921. The loosened labor market emboldened employers to reintroduce nonunion laborers into workplaces that had been "closed," or completely unionized. Assisted by the National Association of Manufacturers, employers in 240 cities established "American Plan" leagues to promote the "open shop" by 1920.[5]

Just a little more than a year after Armistice, then, the United States seemed to be perched on the precipice of social enmity and economic collapse. Questions about the future of American capitalism loomed as large as ever. Many urged the federal government to adapt wartime techniques of economic management to address peacetime problems. Validated in the War Loan drives, investors now seemed to amount to a broad-based constituency whose economic well-being could ensure social peace and economic vibrancy. Accordingly, the War Loan experience raised expectations for federal agencies and laws that would serve and protect citizen-investors. The War Loan funding model of mass investment in state debt percolated into postwar proposals to transform American capitalism even more fundamentally. Progressive reformers and rail unionists proposed that soldier bonuses and a federal buyout of the railroad system (the Plumb Plan) be funded through massive public bond sales, just as the war had been. Investor activists in the railroad industry—namely, the National Association of Owners of Railroad Securities—endorsed the nationalization of some transportation infrastructure as they pressed for policies that would stabilize returns on their investments.[6]

In the aftermath of the Great War, it was by no means clear what a postwar investors' democracy would look like. However, most envisioned that the federal state would expand in some capacity to support citizen-investors. In 1919, few anticipated that the private administration of the financial securities markets would endure, much less that a broad-based shift to corporate stock ownership would occur.

THE BATTLEFIELDS of Europe stood silent, but domestic wars against bolshevism and inflation raged still. Against these threats to political and socioeconomic stability, the Treasury Department determined to deploy the "great army of thirty millions of temporary investors" roused by the War Loan campaigns. The "expensive period" of postwar "demobilization and reconstruction" necessitated an abiding commitment to the "continuing practice of thrift" on the part of citizen-investors. Universal investment would fortify the nation against "world-wide unrest and anxiety"; it offered "tangible means of combating high prices and extravagance and the ills that follow in their train." Only when "the people" resolved to "produce more, save more, and spend less" would the economy revert to a "normal, healthy" condition, advised Carter Glass, who replaced William G. McAdoo as secretary of the Treasury in December 1918. As labor relations soured and the economic horizon darkened after Armistice, the Treasury renewed its efforts to mass-market federal stamps, certificates, and bonds and to influence popular economic thought and practice in favor of securities investment. Secretary Glass and his colleagues envisioned that War Savings might be adapted into a peacetime tool for safeguarding political citizenship and managing postwar economic and social readjustment, just as War Loan propaganda had always promised. The Treasury maintained War Savings—renamed "U.S. Government Savings" in 1922—until 1924.[7]

As during World War I, the propaganda emitted by the Treasury Department cast investment in federal securities as one of "the obligations of citizenship," an essential attribute of American culture and character. U.S. Government Savings publicity continued to equate small-denomination federal debt with a "share" in the nation-state, modeled as a corporation. In the postwar climate of economic and political uncertainty, officials continued to anticipate that by creating "stockholders in our great Nation," federal bonds, stamps, and certificates would secure the "loyalty and solid patriotism" of every inhabitant. The purchase of federal securities promoted "Americanization in a very practical way," Government Savings marketing literature contended, for he who acquired a "personal stake in his government" proved "less susceptible to insidious suggestion" and became "a more interested, more constructive, more active citizen." As Guy Emerson, the director of publicity for New York, explained, the spread of "capital" in "small units throughout the majority of our country" offered "a very practical step towards the Americanization" of immigrants, as well as "the best practical guarantee" against "social unrest . . . radicalism and Bolshevism." Universal bond holding reduced "to the minimum that type which makes the Government unstable, that type which is never ahead of the game, which is restless, that type which is poor." The broad-based practice of investment ensured that "in this country, those who have something" remained "in the majority" against "those fellows that go out burning haystacks, barns and factories," Federal Reserve governor James K. Lynch concurred. With its small-denomination debt, the federal government sought to counteract the financial carelessness that supposedly engendered poverty and alienation, which in turn bred industrial strife and political radicalism.[8]

Just as War Loan propaganda had done during the war, publicity devised for the postwar U.S. Government Savings program characterized the liberty that investment conferred upon citizen-investors as social mobility, economic security, and self-mastery. "Who wants to be a partner with government?" one tract inquired. "Who wants an old age pension guaranteed? Who wants to be his own boss?" By offering an "investment for the multitude," Government Savings claimed to endow "all sorts and conditions of men with the wisdom and power to succeed" and the ability to "control . . . their affairs." Through investment, individuals exercised "command of opportunity, command of one's own resolution, command of the present and the future." Instead of being "tied down to a weekly payroll," citizen-investors stood equipped to take "advantage of opportunity as it presents itself," Government Savings proclaimed. By accumulating financial reserves in federal bonds, the enterprising employee enhanced his bargaining power with his employer. "If you can control the dollar in your pocket, you can pick your own job," advised one pamphlet published in Chicago, "and get the upper hand." The citizen-investor derived autonomy and satisfaction from the financial securities he owned, rather than from the labor he performed or commanded, according to Government Savings.[9]

In the estimation of Treasury officials, the ongoing march of inflation—accelerated by the removal of wartime price controls and the Federal Reserve's decision to keep interest rates low to encourage Victory bond sales—most threatened citizen-investors' security, undermined prospects for national prosperity, and fueled disharmonious industrial relations. Accordingly, the Treasury continued to urge citizen-investors to exercise economic self-discipline, or thrift, throughout the tumultuous postwar period. U.S. Government Savings sought to "enforce [the] realization" that investment in federal bonds, stamps, and certificates presented the "most direct and potent means of solving this pressing economic problem" of the high cost of living. The program called upon "each man, woman and child" to assist in "reducing prices" by lessening their demand for goods and services and redoubling their investment efforts.[10]

Government Savings advised citizen-investors that "the only way to get along" under inflation "is to do without some things that are not necessary." But distinguishing between necessity and luxury proved problematic. Thomas Nixon Carver, the Harvard professor of political economy whose writings on thrift heavily influenced both War Loan and U.S. Government Savings propaganda, counseled citizen-investors to limit themselves to "right consumption," which he defined as consumption of goods and services of "real or lasting" economic or moral "value." Carver's category of "right consumption" included traditional capital assets like farmers' trucks and tractors, to be sure. But "right consumption" also encompassed education, books, music, and other trappings of middle-class respectability. In this formulation, individuals and nuclear families—characterized as discrete entrepreneurial units—increased their stock of social and cultural—as well as economic—capital when they invested in federal securities.[11]

In other words, U.S. Government Savings defined indulgence rather indulgently. Sales agents even invited Americans to envision future consumption as a motivation for current investment. One found that a "save-to-spend" argument appealed strongly to "the cotton mill people" in his district. By picturing "to them their need of a suit coat next year," he successfully organized mill workers "into the society of savings for [that] certain purpose." In the end, what a consumer purchased seemingly mattered less than whether funds first spent some time invested in securities. After a proper period of forgoing, citizen-investors might finally reward themselves with "something worthwhile," such as an automobile, home, or vacation, or "anything else that will bring joy into the lives of yourself and family." The only certain diagnosis of extravagance involved the violation of class- or gender-based conventions of proprietary, as with the "cheap finery and jewelry" purchased by "workmen," or the "'beauty doctors' and dealers in cosmetics" patronized by "prosperous women workers" damned in one press release. Still, only a "prussianized mind" would countenance the publication of a "definitive list of luxuries" to avoid, Thomas Nixon Carver advised. "People, in general, can decide more intelligently than Washington officialdom what they want to buy with their reduced incomes," he concluded. In a democracy, mass investment offered the only appropriate remedy for the ravages of inflation, according to Government Savings.[12]

In promoting mass investment as a means of combating inflation, U.S. Government Savings leaders and boosters perpetuated the investor-centered theory of political economy first disseminated in the War Loan campaigns. As in War Loan imagery and rhetoric, Government Savings understood the aggregate actions of the investing public as determining national economic conditions. As investors, citizens wielded the ability to improve American capitalism. Broad-based investment acted as "a great stabilizer," the program contended, for disciplined consumption both dampened inflation and permitted the accumulation of financial reserves that an individual could draw upon to maintain a "usual mode of living" during an economic downturn. Taken together, these reserves maintained aggregate "purchasing power" and kept "business moving," lessening the depth and length of recessions. In the investors' democracy envisioned by the U.S. Government Savings program, "the most stable and permanent prosperity" resulted from Everyman's habitual exercise of thrift and investment. The affluence engendered by universal investment would be enjoyed broadly and equitably, Government Savings suggested, for investment would improve the position of labor vis-à-vis capital. According to Thomas Nixon Carver, investment offered "the means by which tools, that is, capital, increase faster than men," compelling employers to raise wages and improve working conditions to attract workers as they became relatively more scarce. Still, in the immediate postwar period, Carver did not counsel workers to acquire the means of production or employers' stock. Rather, he continued to recommend government securities.[13]

In the context of postwar union militancy and antibolshevist frenzy, U.S. Government Savings strongly stressed the theme of individual responsibility. William Mather Lewis, director of Cooperating Organizations for Government Savings, viewed "the question of the high cost of living and various other great economic questions" as "largely individual questions" that would be resolved only in "so far as the individual is concerned [and] must depend on the way in which those individuals use their money." The emphasis on thrift and investment by individuals as the proper means of taming economic volatility aimed not only to refute militant unionism and "red" radicalism, but also the consumer-centered and more statist prescriptions put forward by the Labor Bureau and Herbert Hoover's Commerce Department.[14]

In the economic turmoil of the immediate postwar period, left-leaning, pro-union economic writers established the Labor Bureau, which identified mass purchasing power as the key to sustained national prosperity. These "purchasing power progressives" blamed recessions on the inability of wages to keep up with prices and posited an essential right to an American standard of living. Their consumer-centered theory of political economy envisioned that a strong industrial union movement and state-based national industrial planning could maximize employment, and thus mass purchasing power. In the estimation of Treasury officials, the Labor Bureau's recommendations for economic recovery—influential within the U.S. Department of Labor and among many rank-and-file union members—would "create an era of extravagant expenditure" and interfere with the "return to normal conditions, of wise economy, of saving and investing, instead of wasting and gambling." Similarly, the Treasury looked askance at remedies for recovery originating from the Commerce Department in the early 1920s. Commerce Secretary Herbert Hoover and his staff maintained that economic recovery and rationalization could be achieved through public-private sector cooperation; countercyclical public works projects intended to stabilize employment and purchasing power could be funded through federal, state, and municipal borrowing, rather than taxation. Influenced by Hoover's Conference on Unemployment, the governors of thirty states announced bond-financed roads projects to boost employment by the end of 1921. The total sale of municipal bonds in the United States in 1921 amounted to $1.4 billion, double that of any previous year. By 1927, the total amount of debt owed by U.S. state and local governments equaled more than three times 1913 levels. Treasury officials worried that such tax-exempt bond issues—and even more so, the mammoth ones proposed to fund bonuses to soldiers and the nationalization of the railroads—would impede recovery by competing with private businesses' securities offerings, thereby driving up the cost of borrowing money (that is, interest rates) and, ultimately, resulting in inflation. Even so, the Treasury opposed the National Association of Manufacturers, the Chamber of Commerce, and other business and financial archconservatives regarding the necessity of layoffs and wage *cuts* for containing inflation and reviving industry.[15]

Apart from the noticeably heightened emphasis on individualism, the mission and message of Government Savings remained much the same as that of the wartime War Savings program. In the several years after Armistice, the expectation that the federal government would permanently provision citizen-investors with small-denomination securities was widely shared. "The power to accumulate a reasonable reserve against" unfortunate contingencies constituted "a natural right" that the federal state should support with appropriate investment products and services, declared *New Republic* editor Alvin Johnson in 1920. Educators, among others, urged the Treasury to maintain its commitments to the promotion of thrift and the sale of federal securities, which would reach "full fruition" as the nation's children matured.[16]

Treasury Secretary Carter Glass and his supporters concurred with these assessments. Novice retail investors remained skeptical about purchasing securities from banks and brokerages, they observed. Citizen-investors preferred "an absolutely safe security" and the feeling that "they are doing something patriotic," U.S. Government Savings Director Lewis B. Franklin surmised. Government Savings sales agents similarly judged the private financial sector ill-equipped to "bring about an active interest in saving and thrift, which, under the leadership of the Government, has been brought about in two years." If the Treasury should forsake new citizen-investors, they might shift their savings into risky or doubtful securities.[17]

A permanent national investment program raised prospects of bureaucratic expansion and competition with the private financial sector. During the War Loan drives, women agents had proven their merit, and Secretary Glass encouraged leaders of the National Women's Liberty Loan Committee (NWLLC) to expect that their organization would become a permanent division at the Treasury Department. This new Women's Bureau might address the unique savings needs of the nation's working women, mothers, and widows, as a kind of counterpart to the Labor Department's Women's Bureau. Fiscal conservatives within the Treasury Department, however, favored cooperation with private associations and institutions to control costs. But without the urgency of war, U.S. Government Savings struggled to maintain its connections with the wide range of private groups that had mustered the financial nation during World War I. Ultimately, this allowed banks and corporations to shape the U.S. Government Savings program to suit their own purposes in the 1920s.[18]

Glass's decision to perpetuate a national investment program met with skepticism from within the Treasury and the Federal Reserve system, most notably from fiscal conservatives like Russell C. Leffingwell (assistant Treasury secretary), Benjamin Strong and Warren G. Harding (Federal Reserve governors), Orrin C. Lester (associate director of the Savings Division), and later, from Glass's successors, David F. Houston and Andrew Mellon. As the nation turned away from progressivism, antistatist conservatism revived, and the power of organized labor ebbed in the 1920s, these fiscal conservatives gained prominence, especially under Republican administrations. Rapid retirement of the federal debt and tax reductions held a central place in fiscal conservatives' plan to stimulate the economy. They judged existing private institutions to be adequate agencies for thrift education and investment activity.[19]

Citing the administrative expense, fiscal conservatives recommended that banks be tapped to distribute small-denomination federal securities. U.S. Government Savings would liaise with roughly only 35,000 institutions, rather than individual investors. Assistant Treasury Secretary Russell Leffingwell advised that Government Savings also instruct the public on how to purchase federal bonds in the secondary market through banks and brokerages. By thus stimulating demand, the Treasury might support the price of prior issues and avoid competition with the private sector's new issues.[20]

By mid-1919, prodded by the fiscal conservatives, Treasury leaders resolved to attempt to persuade banks, large corporations, schools, and women's organizations to assume more responsibility for U.S. Government Savings in the hopes of maintaining the voluntary organizational structure of the War Loan Organization. This compromise sought to control costs by maximizing the number of unpaid (female) volunteers and streamlining distribution. But given continued resistance from consumer retailers and renewed skepticism from the competing financial industry, the voluntary publicity and distribution apparatus quickly atrophied. When recession hit in 1920, redemptions of War Savings and Government Savings stamps and certificates increased dramatically, while purchases of Government Savings securities ground to a halt. Although citizen-investors were drawing upon the program as intended, those who advocated expanding the program found it difficult to justify their position in the face of a sales slump.[21]

Moreover, the compromises that sustained the program generated internal dissension. U.S. Government Savings Director Franklin and Treasury Secretary Glass continued to endorse a permanent Women's Bureau, with a paid force of female agents reporting to Washington. But fiscal conservatives and some local male agents balked. "We want to appoint them and want to control them," demanded one staffer, "we do not want anyone in Washington or a national body here in Philadelphia of women giving orders." Glass and Franklin relented in the face of similar objections across districts. Ultimately, the Treasury advised women to continue to teach thrift on a volunteer basis in their local schools, homes, and churches—as private citizens, not as government officials or agents.[22]

After the National Women's Liberty Loan Committee disbanded in 1919, many NWLLC leaders and staffers shifted their attention to U.S. Government Savings. Still, they lamented that without an official, direct "national connection" to the federal government, women would never manage "real achievement." NWLLC executive Mary Synon urged "the maintenance of a national board" of women because of "a certain kink in feminine psychology which values a definite national connection, the more because of an inability to visualize the Federal Reserve center as an inspiration point." She surmised that Federal Reserve directors would prove "quite hopeless in getting the women of the country interested." Synon proved correct regarding their inability to mobilize the maternal commonwealth for the benefit of U.S. Government Savings.[23]

This left the nation's schools as one of the few promising bases for the program. Although savings and investment curricula did become part of the national education landscape in the 1920s, U.S. Government Savings encountered difficulties regarding how to dictate content, specify government securities, conduct accounting, and ensure participation among sundry state and local boards of education. Furthermore, private bankers and brokerages inserted themselves and their products into thrift curricula, so that school savings programs no longer focused exclusively on government securities in the 1920s.[24]

And as banks and brokerages became more interested in the retail market that the War Loans had nurtured, they grew increasingly wary and weary of Treasury requests. At a 1919 conference with the Savings Section of the American Bankers Association (ABA), William Mather Lewis begged delegates to offer small-denomination federal securities and to evangelize for thrift. Bankers should not consider U.S. Government Savings competition, Lewis counseled, for banks and brokerages might stimulate demand for saving accounts and even corporate securities as they promoted thrift. Banks that participated in U.S. Government Savings also encouraged "Americanization," helping to prevent a recurrence "of the situation in Russia" in America, Associate Director Orrin C. Lester averred. "John Jones Levinsky or any of those people who may have a hundred . . . dollars more or less invested with the Great Father at Washington, I can't conceive of them doing anything very desperate or rash to overturn things," such as "shying a brick through the plate glass window" of a bank branch.[25]

Treasury Department leaders implored banks to appropriate the rhetoric of the War Loans and Government Savings. "Put a little joy into thrift," advised U.S. Government Savings Director Franklin. He urged bankers to make investment "a happy word, an encouraging word, a bright word, the word of opportunity." Franklin suggested the recycling of save-to-spend themes, linking the process of savings with a "'right" consumption goal. "Put a little human interest in it," Franklin advised, "Don't say 'build up a savings bank account' but save for that new home, save to send the boy through college, save for something worthwhile."

But the American Bankers Association's response to U.S. Government Savings was lukewarm, and it grew colder. The ABA pledged "advice" and a measure of sales cooperation, but it refused to take "any responsibility for the success or failure" of the program. Fearing political "misunderstandings," the ABA also refused any commission on the sale of small-denomination federal securities. These decisions ultimately limited the degree to which ABA members participated. In the later part of the 1920s, however, the financial sector would take up the Treasury's advice and appropriate War Loan and Government Savings marketing tropes that associated the state with the corporation, citizenship with investment, and the polity with the financial securities markets—but to promote corporate securities.[26]

And so, large industrial corporations—rather than women's associations, the public school system, or financial institutions—became the closest allies of U.S. Government Savings. As early as June 1919, personnel across Federal Reserve districts reported they had already organized hundreds of thousands of workers into thousands of savings societies—modeled upon War Savings societies—by securing support from "heads of corporations." Alliances with employers only grew stronger after Andrew Mellon assumed the post of Treasury secretary in 1921. As employers launched "American Plan" counteroffensives against organized labor, the retrenched U.S. Government Savings program cast its lot with management.[27]

True, Samuel Gompers and the American Federation of Labor, the chiefs of the Railroad Brotherhoods, and officers of various state labor federations and central labor unions continued to endorse U.S. Government Savings. Treasury officials continued to contend that leaders of organized labor would find it "vital" that the rank and file should "practice thrift" because savings reserves provided the "ability to meet industrial crisis, either individual or of the union, without fear of financial intimidation." *New Republic* editor Alvin Johnson confirmed that in 1919, union locals borrowed money against Liberty bonds "held by the collective membership" in order to sustain strikes; in Seattle, Mrs. C. Y. reported to the *Union Record* that her husband's savings emboldened him to refuse work as a scab.[28]

But in 1919, insurgent locals and rank and file just as often turned away from state-sponsored options in favor of their own experiments in "labor capitalism," as Dana Frank calls it. The "way labor bought liberty bonds demonstrated that we can raise funds for any undertaking," declared Seattle longshoreman Percy May. Entrepreneur George Listman similarly declared that labor's assistance "in financing the world war" proved that "labor has the financial power to launch its own industries." In Seattle, workers could acquire shares in dozens of companies—including Listman's stock brokerage, a salvage company, a newspaper, a laundry, a bank, a theater—which claimed to be owned and operated by organized workers, for the benefit of the union cause, rather than depositing their funds in banks that loaned to "open shop" employers. Similarly, the Black Star Line sold $500,000 in $5 shares to thousands of African Americans who rallied behind Marcus Garvey's call to establish an independent Caribbean produce trade in the service of black self-sufficiency, separatism, even repatriation to Africa. Few experiments in labor or black capitalism survived the recession of 1920–1921, however. The Black Star Line succumbed to mismanagement and harassment by J. Edgar Hoover's Bureau of Investigation in 1922. Garvey was convicted of mail fraud in connection with literature promoting Black Star Line stock—essentially, swindling—in 1923.[29]

And as organized labor lost both political power and membership after 1919, large employers seemed to offer U.S. Government Savings a more economical and effective conduit to workers. "Heads of large corporations" astounded staffers with their effusive support and cooperation; these employers relayed that War Savings had created "a better labor situation for them." The enthusiastic interest of employers confirmed for Mellon that management presented the most efficient route for reaching the largest number of workers. Organized labor lost its place at the U.S. Government Savings table.[30]

After 1919, the program associated thrift with managerial license and labor pacification, consistent with the resurgence of the "open" or anti-union shop. Where War Savings literature once spoke to and through unions in support of industrial democracy, U.S. Government Savings promised owners and managers a "contented," rather than empowered, workforce. "The Man Who Saves" possessed "too much respect for time to squander it" and "too much respect for his job to quit it for a roving notion." He exercised a "steadying" influence over "his fellows," Government Savings maintained. Pamphlets like "Steady Workers" presented the Government Savings program as an alternative to raises, which only encouraged workers to shop for jobs. Publicists and agents suggested that workplace savings societies be integrated into open-shop initiatives, with foremen speaking "directly to the men," cutting out union representatives.[31]

As the industrial economy revived after 1921, U.S. Government sales increased dramatically. In fact, sales exceeded wartime levels in 1922 and 1923. Ironically, this turnaround sealed the fate of the program. Bankers in agricultural sections alleged that it drained local capital away to Washington, inhibiting local lending and recovery. They demanded suspensions of sales in ten states. Government Savings leaders strongly disagreed with this assessment, but acquiesced. In February 1924, another eleven states were added to the suspension list, with a "passive program" adopted in remaining states. Faced with mounting bank opposition, the Treasury announced the termination of the securities component of U.S. Government Savings on July 15, 1924.[32]

Both patrons and laid-off publicists and agents lamented its demise. E. C. Kibbee of the Federal Reserve of Minneapolis found "the suspension . . . most regrettable. Some people were just beginning to understand what savings means through the purchase of these small securities." After "tenderly laying to rest the Treasury Savings Organization of the 8th Federal Reserve District" in St. Louis, Hugh B. Werver took a new position at Union Electric Light and Power "in the Securities Department selling their 6 percent Cahokia preferred stock" on commission. He hoped that someday he might "have another trial at the missionary work that has been done with the War Savings stamps and Savings certificates." In the meantime, Werver told Mellon, he would substitute the Cahokia shares "where I can." Before tendering his resignation as director of the U.S. Savings system, Captain Lew Wallace complained bitterly of the western bankers who killed the program through their representatives in Congress. He alerted Mellon to "innumerable inquiries" and complaints from citizen-investors. "Individuals who could only save a little at a time" needed their government to provide "an absolutely safe security . . . not subjected to market fluctuation." The

United States had "barely made a beginning" in creating "millions of better citizens by having them hold a financial interest in the welfare of their Government." Prescient patron Signe A. Berve of Germantown, Minnesota, served Mellon a piece of his mind:

> I may add that the whole withdrawal is simply disgusting. You are trying to force the people to keep their money in unsafe banks and if you think the Government is following a wise policy you are mistaken. People are going to resent you before long.

And indeed, Mellon's decision left millions of investors primed toward investment in financial securities but bereft of state-sponsored options.[33]

THROUGHOUT its lifetime, the U.S. Government Savings program maintained that investment amounted to a right and a duty of citizenship in peacetime as much as during war. The "teaching [of] thrift throughout the country to our citizens" remained "a proper obligation" of the state, one sales agent asserted, "because it makes better citizens." Equipped by the federal state with the appropriate financial tools, the "good citizen" was obliged to remain "self-sustaining" throughout his life. If shackled by "financial worry," uncertainty, or dependence, a citizen could not perform his duties "to his country and his community." These included the resolution to "take advantage of business opportunity," the achievement of old-age security, and the protection of dependents from penury. In return, the state assumed reciprocal obligations in an investors' democracy, Government Savings allowed. Appropriate economic policies were those that cultivated thrift as a national habit and enabled the citizen-investor to amass sufficient reserves.[34]

At the close of World War I, most commentators concurred that the federal government's ongoing responsibility to support citizen-investors in their quest to invest should include a regulatory component. Even prior to World War I, many Progressives and corporate liberals took up investor protection—especially federally mandated and monitored disclosure of corporate financial data and the regulation of securities exchanges—as a means of preventing monopoly, wresting control of the economy away from the "money trust," and perhaps even encouraging Everyman to acquire a "stake" in corporate capitalism. The War Loan drives validated financial securities and markets and vastly increased the incidences of investment. State-based safeguards for citizen-investors now seemed desirable in their own right. Accordingly, the Treasury Department called for the establishment of a federal commission modeled upon the wartime Capital Issues Committee (CIC) to approve sworn financial disclosure documents prior to any public offering of securities. Many prominent journalists and financial figures, including Paul Warburg of investment bank Kuhn, Loeb and J. P. Morgan partner George W. Perkins, concurred that Congress owed citizen-investors a measure of regulatory protection. In January 1919, when the CIC disbanded, its members joined in demands for federal corporate disclosure law.[35]

Mounting concerns over political alienation and radicalism—as well as falling Liberty bond prices—threw even more momentum behind demands for federal oversight of the financial securities markets. As during the war, commentators and policy makers continued to believe that citizen-investors' faith in private enterprise and their fealty to their debt-issuing state were imperiled by swindlers, those individuals who accepted Liberty bonds in exchange for stocks in risky or fraudulent enterprises. As during the war, lawmakers, officials, and journalists maintained that federal regulation of securities issuance and corporate reporting would equip investors with the information they needed to resist swindles. "The government, which has had the united support of the people in financing the war, must now protect those people from the loss of their Liberty bonds," insisted Louis Guenther in *World's Work*. Until the passage of federal regulation, the U.S. Government Savings program resolved to "protect the secondary market" for all federal bonds, stamps, and certificates with a propaganda campaign to "defeat the efforts of traffickers who attempt to obtain the securities for less than the market value or in exchange for worthless stocks or shares in fraudulent promotions."[36]

If Americans today are at all aware of the post–World War I swindling menace, they probably think of Italian immigrant Charles Ponzi, who raked in millions with a fraud involving international postal-reply coupons in 1920. In his classic "pyramid" scheme, replicated in its basic form by Bernard Madoff many decades later, Ponzi paid "returns" to existing investors out of funds collected from newer investors, rather than from returns on investments that he claimed to be making. Yet Ponzi is simply the best-remembered of scores of swindlers who preyed upon naïve citizen-investors both during and after World War I, inducing them to swap their Liberty bonds and War Savings stamps and certificates for stock in uncertain, worthless, or even nonexistent enterprises.[37]

The governors of the New York Stock Exchange recognized that the activities of Ponzi and his ilk sparked calls for the regulation of corporate disclosure, especially the bill proposed by Representative Edward Taylor (D-Colo.) requiring corporations to file a registration statement with the secretary of the Treasury prior to any new issue of securities. Exchange governors feared that demands for federal incorporation of the NYSE would follow. Both legislative prospects threatened to replace Exchange self-governance with state oversight. Moreover, in the weak stock market of late 1918 and early 1919, any losses suffered by any investors who had liquidated their war bonds risked characterization as a swindle, even if such a trade was executed through a NYSE member. Therefore, after Armistice, Exchange publicists focused on shaping an issue that might impinge upon NYSE self-governance into a platform for burnishing the image of the Stock Exchange and its members. Exchange leaders judged these efforts critical for repelling regulatory incursions into the privately administered securities markets.[38]

Instead of overtly opposing the passage of a federal corporate disclosure law, Exchange officials determined to issue publicity that might cause legislation to appear unnecessary. In February 1919, the NYSE organized the Business Men's Anti-Stock Swindling League (BMASSL), which characterized itself as "a necessary adjunct to eventual legislation." Seeking to take advantage of the linkages it had forged with other organizations during the War Loan campaigns, the Exchange solicited support from "Chambers of Commerce, financial associations, and industrial establishments" across the nation. The executive roster of BMASSL even included William Green, vice president of the American Federation of Labor, and W. G. Lee, president of the Railway Brotherhood Association, most likely at the suggestion of former Treasury Secretary William G. McAdoo, who also joined. Leaders of the Associated Advertising Clubs of the World, who had engaged in a "systematic" war on "fraudulent stock promotions" since 1912 as part of their truth-in-advertising initiative, were included as well.[39]

BMASSL leadership called on the members of their respective national associations to join with the Treasury Department to publicize the threat of stock swindling just as widely and loudly as they had promoted the War Loans, urging the "same elements of decency in this country" that joined to "defeat the Hun" to "unite to suppress the private promoter and his tool, the smooth-tongued salesman." BMASSL notices advised citizen-investors to trade securities only through established banks and brokerages, never through "strange and doubtful channels." Communications identified stock swindlers as treasonous, even seditious. Of course, "draining the people's savings" undermined "the foundation upon which all prosperity rests." But far worse, swindlers' depredations caused "millions of innocent victims who were taught to practice patriotic self-denial" to lose "confidence" and to turn against American "institutions" and "Government." Much like the bolshevist agitator, the financial fraud undercut citizen-investors' faith in private property. Indeed, NYSE commission house A. H. Bickmore and Co. equated stock swindling with the Soviet repudiation of Romanoff debt, while Exchange publicist Jason Westerfield proclaimed widespread postwar social and political "Unrest Due to Fakers" and "Stock Frauds . . . [a] Spur to Bolshevism." As BMASSL echoed War Loan associations between investment and political quiescence, it offered businessmen and financiers criminal causes for postwar social instability. It ignored structural explanations, such as labor relations.[40]

Although BMASSL publicity echoed War Loan associations linking the democratic process with the practice of investment, it never allowed that the tremendous growth of the investor-citizenry necessitated any new regulations. Instead, BMASSL insisted that voluntary, cooperative effort by enlightened private actors protected novice investors best, without saddling the securities markets with the intrinsic inefficiencies of regulatory red tape. And despite the nominal inclusion of labor leaders and government officials, BMASSL publicity cast a single, unified national business/financial community as the stalwart defender of the financial nation in a moral equivalent of war against stock swindlers.[41]

Inspired by BMASSL publicity and testimony, newspapers across the United States published maudlin tales of losses suffered by the helpless and the dependent in the spring of 1919. Still, BMASSL failed to receive much in the way of financial contributions from participating organizations. Some suggested that "for the movement to be successful it must spring from Washington and be national in scope under a Government Department." Former Treasury Secretary William McAdoo proposed that more "representatives of Farmers and Labor" be added. These recommendations stood at odds with what the NYSE intended. BMASSL pursued neither course. Participation atrophied until only the New York Stock Exchange remained committed to the venture.[42]

Yet the Exchange viewed BMASSL as highly successful. Throughout 1919, press coverage trumpeted Stock Exchange leadership in the protection of citizen-investors. R. T. H. Halsey, chairman of the NYSE Committee on Library, certainly relished chastising adversary Henry Ford for his unfavorable comments about the NYSE in his *Dearborn Independent*:

> Surely to continue to represent the underworld of finance as Wall Street is unfair to both Wall Street and the public which it serves . . . why not cooperate in the movement against fraudulent swindlers . . . Your magazine is betraying your readers into believing that the excrescence is in the body. It is not. It is the body's worst enemy.

Press coverage and BMASSL publicity prompted an increase in prosecutions of non-NYSE brokers under existing New York criminal law.[43]

As the stock market recovered at the end of 1919, the perception of swindling receded, in part because stocks fell less often after purchase with a war bond. The Taylor bill and federal and New York state bills proposing securities commissions died at the end of 1919. In New York State, an advisory committee that included NYSE President William Remick (1919–1921) and other Wall Street leaders rejected corporate disclosure legislation. "The way to stop stock frauds is to provide a flexible, virile, fraud hunting state machinery driven not by statute but by human intelligence and human activity"—in other words, to pursue incidences of criminal fraud under existing laws. Unlike "Western States," the nation's financial center could not afford to adopt "experimental legislation," the report sniffed. While the War Loan drives yielded a nation of investors, the Business Men's Anti-Stock Swindling League helped to deflate the expectation— encouraged in the War Loan campaigns themselves—that securities market regulation need follow. New York Stock Exchange self-governance survived.[44]

IN THE YEARS immediately following the Great War, the federal government upheld its war-born responsibility for aiding citizen-investors by provisioning its small-denomination securities and by propagandizing for thrift and against swindlers. Treasury Department officials sought—ultimately without success—to meet the widely held expectation that the federal government should subject the financial securities markets to regulatory oversight. The War Loan experience also inspired proposals for the federal government to reshape American capitalism in even more dramatic ways. The success of the War Loan campaigns persuaded many Progressives that mass bond drives offered a better alternative than taxation for financing government projects to enhance public welfare, such as soldier bonuses, farm mortgages, even a federal buyout of the nation's transportation infrastructure. The National Association of Owners of Railroad Securities agreed with organized labor that investors—who now, on account of the War Loan drives, seemed to embody "the public interest," rather than a special interest—also would benefit from government ownership of some aspect of the nation's rail infrastructure. Some of the most significant debates over postwar economic readjustment, then, revolved around the possible transformative potential of mass investment and the proper understanding of citizen-investors' interests. Having entered the political lexicon during the War Loan campaigns, the rhetorical figure of "the investor" was referenced by a range of groups in the immediate postwar period as they made—and refuted—new claims upon the state.

As the military demobilized after Armistice, legislatures at the state and national level debated the merits of granting veterans some form of additional compensation as a reward for service and to ease their reintegration.

Both state and federal soldier bonus bills proposed bond issues as their source of funding. By 1922, thirty-eight states had made some provision for a soldier bonus. Federal bills overcame repeated presidential vetoes in 1924. The bonus marked an unprecedented federal foray into social policy, anticipating later twentieth-century entitlement programs. Ultimately, it would cost the equivalent of the 1924 federal budget. By 1927, total government expenditures on services for veterans stood at more than three times 1913 levels.[45]

War Loan drives also inspired proposals for the federal government to fund social reform by issuing new securities. In 1920, Congress amended the Federal Farm Loan Act to authorize the federal government to sell bonds paying 4.5 percent interest in the affordable denominations of $20, $40, and $100. Proceeds from the bonds were to be invested in farm mortgages. At once, the federal government provided farmers with a new source of credit while offering retail investors an affordable and safe investment vehicle. In addition to helping agriculturalists escape bankers' clutches, the Federal Farm Loan program might liberate African American tenant farmers from the sharecropping system, editor of the progressive standard *New Republic* Alvin Johnson believed. Encouraged by the Federal Farm Loan amendment, Senator W. M. Calder (R-N.Y.) proposed that the federal government similarly finance the mortgages of building and loan associations to promote home ownership. Both the Federal Farm Loan program and Calder's plan looked to the federal government to encourage property ownership by issuing appropriate securities. By introducing small investors to small borrowers in the financial markets, Calder and others envisioned, the state might universalize individual property-ownership—in both traditional, tangible and updated, securitized forms. The privately administered financial markets, in contrast, seemed incapable of nourishing this vision of investors' democracy alone.[46]

Meanwhile, other postwar Progressives—also ruminating on the War Loan experience—argued that if thrift and investment now constituted civic obligations for citizen-investors, then the state must support the thrifty when private financial markets failed them. For John A. Lapp, managing editor of *Modern Medicine,* professor at Marquette University, leader of the Federal Council of Churches and the National Catholic Welfare Council, and a key figure in the revived Progressive Party of 1924, "the advocates of individual savings as a means of providing against the hazards of life" erroneously assumed that "these hazards confront everyone to a like degree," ignoring "the unequal distribution of the burden which the contingencies of unemployment, sickness, old age and death throw upon certain people." While "individual thrift" could never provide a fail-safe protection against every misfortune—whether illness, infirmary, "fire, business failure [or] stock swindlers"—state-administered contributory social insurance programs could forecast and insure against such "calamities" across society. Lapp found it distasteful that private financial intermediaries should be allowed to profit from citizen-investors' efforts to meet their civic duty to invest for future needs and contingencies. The thrifty should not be compelled to "pay tribute" to private insurers, he believed. Rather, the state should "safeguard" citizen-investors "by means of public, mutual, social insurance," in recognition of their fulfillment of their obligation to invest, Lapp argued.[47]

The belief that investors warranted heightened consideration in economic policy and the notion that mass investment in federal securities could transform American capitalism also influenced postwar debates over the fate of the nation's railroads, the economy's largest sector with the largest number of investors. Impressed with the federal government's ability to improve railway operations and labor relations during World War I, the Railroad Brotherhoods representing nearly 1.5 million workers came forward in 1919 with their Plumb Plan—named after author Glenn E. Plumb, legal counsel to the Brotherhoods—to nationalize the railroads permanently through a federal buyout, to be funded with a mass-marketed bond issue. The prospect of railway nationalization immediately raised questions about possible consequences for the nation's investors. The interests of investors—previously understood as marginal—became a critical matter for economic policy in the aftermath of World War I.[48]

The National Association of Owners of Railroad Securities (NAORS)—which represented a constituency of insurance companies and savings banks that invested in railroad securities—conceded that wartime financial mobilization *had* created a new relationship between the citizen-investors and the federal government, one that dictated structural transformation of the railroad industry. Like those who supported the Plumb Plan, members of NAORS were impressed by the benefits of systemwide integration that had been achieved under federal control. Accordingly, the Owners Association demanded new federal policies, both to stabilize returns on railroad investments and to establish some degree of state ownership of transportation infrastructure (although it rejected a complete federal buyout, as in the Plumb Plan). Both the Plumb and NAORS plans met opposition from groups seeking immediate and total reprivatization, including the Association of Railway Executives (ARE), the American Railroad Association (ARA), and financial institutions that sold and traded railroad securities, especially the New York Stock Exchange, the Guaranty Trust Company, and investment bank Kuhn, Loeb.[49]

In the 15 million pieces of literature that NAORS distributed through member institutions to depositors, borrowers, policyholders, and individual retail investors, NAORS made the case that the investing class constituted *the* public interest, a claim made plausible by the War Loan celebration of the investor and elevation of investment. The Owners Association demanded that the federal government intrude into rail financing, operation, and ownership in order to protect the interests of that investing public. It directed regulators and lawmakers to prioritize investors' interests above those of shippers-consumers or workers-producers. The Owners Association *broadened* the wartime concept of the financial nation—the notion that the investing population amounted to the analogue of the polity—to encompass those who invested in corporate securities, not just federal bonds.[50]

NAORS argued that the railroad sector required a comprehensive overhaul in regard to operation, finance, and regulation. Its proposed solution—dubbed the "Warfield Plan" after NAORS president S. Davies Warfield—specified excess-earnings regulation. Under excess-earnings regulation, the Interstate Commerce Commission (ICC) would set rates at a level targeted to guarantee railroad investors a fixed minimum return upon invested capital, which would be valued by ICC investigation. Excess-earnings regulation aimed to stabilize returns and to insure the payment of interest to bondholders and a moderate dividend for stockholders. NAORS anticipated that predictability of returns would attract the capital necessary to address the costs associated with reconversion to peacetime operations. In return, the Warfield Plan gladly surrendered any further potential upside (or "excess profits").[51]

Investors should be recognized as the paramount public interest under which all others should be subsumed, NAORS contended, because investor-centered railroad policy would ensure a healthy flow of capital to the sector, for the benefit of all. If additional capital could not be attracted, the roads would fall further into disrepair. Shippers would find themselves without transportation service, and workers would lose their jobs. And if investors did not receive adequate interest payments or dividends, the savings and insurance institutions that invested in the rails would be unable to extend credit or to meet the claims of their depositors and policyholders.[52]

To advance its excess-earnings regulation proposal over the Brotherhoods' Plumb Plan, the Owners Association mimicked organized labor's language of the living wage. Paying a "living rate" upon fairly valued capital to ensure a "living return" would attract capital and allow the roads to "maintain their properties and give proper service." Should a road earn a return above the fixed minimum, the Warfield Plan specified that the excess should be divided equally between that road's owners, that road's workers, and a collective fund. The ICC would disburse this collective fund to make improvements and to acquire facilities to benefit the rail system as a whole. And so, even as NAORS rejected the Plumb Plan for the federal government to acquire the railroads entirely, it envisioned some degree of state ownership of transportation infrastructure.[53]

The Warfield Plan embodied the desires of NAORS's constituency, the "buy-side" savings and insurance interests that purchased and held railroad securities for long-term investment. They sought steady, fixed returns from which depositors and policyholders might be paid. Owners Association arguments rested on its claim that its membership—and not railroad executive and managerial associations—truly spoke for the investing public. Thus, NAORS insisted that "no class of institution" dwelled "so close to the people as the mutual savings bank and the mutual insurance companies" that its membership comprised. Not less than a third of the American population patronized such institutions. Indeed, these patrons "largely constituted what is termed the public; they own the investments their mutual institutions hold," albeit indirectly. Whether these institutions held rail bonds or stocks, their depositors and policyholders came "pretty near to being the real owners of the railroads."[54]

NAORS's claim to represent the owners of the rails depended upon rhetorically blurring the differences between stocks and bonds and redefining the relationship between owners and creditors. "If the title of owner means anything it is reflected in the bondholders," for bondholders had contributed roughly three-fifths of all railroad capital, asserted John J. Pulleyn, vice president of the American Bankers Association and a key player in NAORS. And although bondholders held no right to elect corporate boards and executives, "when those managements" mismanaged the roads, bondholders could not be expected "to stand by and see chaos overtake" them. Indeed, the Owners Association judged bondholders *more* qualified to claim the mantle of ownership than the typical stockholder, who sought "speculative gain," not permanent investment. The impermanence of stock speculators' holdings degraded any pretext of ownership, especially in contrast to the fortitude of bondholders, NAORS contended.[55]

Although NAORS, railroad management, and railroad financiers all recognized a common enemy in the Plumb Plan to "russianize the railroads," the Owners Association found few allies. Associations of railroad executives and the "sell-side" financial institutions that underwrote, distributed, and traded railroad securities demanded an immediate return to the prewar status quo of private control, private finance, and privately managed labor relations. While sell-side institutions also called for policies that privileged investors, they rejected any hint of government administration or ownership in the railroad industry. As in the prewar period, the most vocal of NAORS's financial industry opponents included the New York Stock Exchange, the Guaranty Trust Company of New York, and the investment bank Kuhn, Loeb, financial advisor to the powerful Pennsylvania Railroad.[56]

Because it placed a ceiling on returns, these banks and brokerages that underwrote, distributed, and traded railroad securities could not swallow Warfield's proposal for excess-earnings regulation. Fixed returns, valuation of capital by federal commission, and federal regulation of railway securities issuance might make them superfluous. Just as the New York Stock Exchange had asserted before the war, sell-side institutions and managerial associations in the railroad industry insisted that the state could simply not be trusted to perform the required valuations of railroad properties. The *market* established the current value of capital invested in railroads, as trading continually repriced outstanding railroad securities. Moreover, sell-side critics predicted that the federal government would expend any excess-earnings fund to buy up lines and equipment. Inevitably, this back door would admit complete government ownership. For the financial interests and managerial organizations that lined up against it, the Warfield Plan represented a dangerous compromise, a "step in the direction of outright Government ownership," nearly as socialistic as the Plumb Plan itself.[57]

Executive and managerial associations and financial interests opposed to the Warfield Plan mimicked NAORS's investor-centered strategy and lexicon, citing the same statistics exaggerating the size and diversity of the investing public. But they asserted managerial protection of that class. Otto Kahn, a partner in Kuhn, Loeb, also called for "living rates" in order to attract new capital to the roads. However, Kahn decried Warfield's excess-earnings regulation proposal for its "timid opportunism" and characterized it as a "government guarantee of earnings" akin to "bureaucratic management" and fundamentally irreconcilable with "private management," private ownership, and "individual effort." Kahn begged railroad investors not to be "bribed" by the Warfield Plan.[58]

In response to Kahn and his sell-side and managerial allies, S. Davies Warfield scoffed that the "great body of investors" and "the trustees of institutions occupying fiduciary relations to the great mass of people" greatly preferred a "sound basis for credit" to the "opportunity for excessive return." True, a valuation commission might initially undervalue investors' holdings when gauging the worth of a road's capital in order to calculate rates. However, NAORS found such valuation "by public authority" preferable to the uncertain, fluctuating, and allegedly manipulated values produced by secondary trading of railroad securities. For decades, the Association of Owners charged, speculative orgies, managerial incompetence, and the resulting hostility of regulators had prevented security prices from reflecting the true value of the roads. In consequence, insurance companies found themselves unable to formulate decent projections about the future value of their investment holdings, from which future claims must be paid. NAORS preferred "honest" regulation—of rates, working conditions, wages, and railroad financing—to the chicanery and chaos of private *mis*management.[59]

Ultimately, the National Association of the Owners of Railroad Securities scored a major victory in the Esch-Cummins Transportation Act of 1920, which included excess-earnings regulation. In accordance with the Warfield Plan, Esch-Cummins directed the ICC to set minimum rates in order to guarantee a 5.5 percent return on investment, plus an addition 0.5 percent to fund improvements. If a road managed to achieve a higher return, half of that return was "recaptured" by the ICC for a common fund to supply weaker roads with loans. Whereas earlier ICC policy sought to protect farmers and shippers from predatory rates by monopolistic carriers by setting *maximum* rates (as authorized in the 1906 Hepburn Act), the Transportation Act of 1920 authorized the ICC to establish *minimum* rates, in recognition of investors' right to a "living return." It also authorized the Interstate Commerce Commission to regulate railroad securities issuance and to conduct a valuation of all railroad property in order to determine the amount of capital invested in the railroads, upon which to calculate returns, just as the Owners Association had recommended.[60]

NAORS declined to rest on its laurels after the passage of Esch-Cummins in 1920. It proposed amendments and articulated positions on rate and wage inquiries, valuation investigations, and proposed rail consolidations. It turned its attention to the federal transportation fund created by 1920 Transportation Act. The Owners Association demanded the creation of a National Railway Service Corporation (NSRC) to distribute the "recapture" fund established by the Transportation Act. The state-owned, nonprofit NSRC would purchase "cars, engines, or equipment," then lease this "floating equipment" to individual roads to "meet seasonal or abnormal requirements." Individual roads would continue to procure their own equipment "to meet their normal requirements." NSRC would coordinate jointly used terminal facilities and service. The NSRC solution sought to extend wartime experiments in federal ownership and operation without impinging upon private "incentive and initiative" on individual roads, according to Warfield and his allies.[61]

Not surprisingly, managerial and executive associations balked once again. The American Railway Association, for example, judged NRSC "contrary to the fundamental principles of private and competitive operation of the American railroads." Sell-side financial interests, meanwhile, objected to federal intrusion into railroad financing. Warfield recognized that Wall Street would never countenance even a partially state-funded corporation "since it might interfere with their financial relations" as underwriters and distributors of the securities of particular lines. NAORS, however, demanded that rail financiers recognize the need to stabilize transportation credit and operations on a broader, national scale.[62]

Ultimately, NAORS failed to amend the Transportation Act to establish a National Railway Service Corporation. After crushing the railroad shopmen's strike of 1922, railway management stabilized relations with workers and regulators. NAORS gradually receded from the political scene. Still, it left behind an impressive legacy. It broadened the notion of an investing public to include those holding *private*-sector securities, although it by no means allowed that privately administered markets best safeguarded those citizen-investors' financial well-being. It secured lasting institutional change in the railroad industry. The Transportation Act's excess-earning stipulation undercut management's ability to influence returns on their particular roads. It also undermined the role of the private financial markets in establishing the value of capital invested in the rail sector. And throughout the 1920s, regulated corporations in the transportation and utilities sectors would draw inspiration from NAORS's victory on excess earnings, demanding that regulatory commissions set rates to ensure shareholders a "fair wage." Indeed, light and power corporations would take a further step by launching plans to increase their numbers of shareholders in order to buttress their demands.

The National Association of Owners of Railroad Securities held its own in crucial ideological debates about what sort of political economy should emerge out of the war. Moreover, it challenged the conventions of corporate governance by driving a rhetorical wedge between corporate managers and securities owners. Warfield and his colleagues questioned executive prerogative and claims to represent investors, albeit in an effort to substitute another relation of dependency for "the small investors of the country." Through NAORS, a significant segment of capital rejected laissez-faire precepts advanced by railroad executives and sell-side financial institutions: the necessity of the maximization of return-to-investors and the efficiency of laissez-faire financial markets. In the estimation of the Owners Association, the "free" securities markets held little legitimacy, produced unreliable values, and yielded few benefits either to investors or to society-at-large. Unlike railroad executives and sell-side financiers, NAORS welcomed state intervention in railroad operation and finance. In this instance, the "capital" represented by NAORS judged the risk and potential upside of privately administered markets far less attractive than the stability ensured by state involvement. The NAORS narrative recovers a key contest between liberal and conservative variants of an evolving investor-centered theory of political economy in the immediate postwar period. The more liberal NAORS won an important battle with the Transportation Act of 1920. But its opponents had not lost the ideological war. Their fortunes would soon revive.[63]

WHEN THE GREAT WAR ended, it remained uncertain whether War Loans' success in increasing the number of American investors and in disseminating a new investor-centered theory of political economy would support the expansion or the contraction of the federal government. The National Association of Owners of Railroad Securities succeeded in increasing federal interventions in railroad finance by building upon the wartime validation of the investor. NAORS established that investors held a plausible claim to constitute the public interest and therefore warranted policy consideration, even protection, even in private-sector investments. On the other hand, fiscal conservatives within the Treasury Department and the New York Stock Exchange managed to repel efforts to extend the administrative and regulatory state on behalf of the nation's novice citizen-investors.

Obviously the death of U.S. Government Savings did not dictate that the American masses would plunge into the corporate stock market in the 1920s, although the closure of this alternative path certainly helped. Citizen-investors holding excess cash from Liberty bond, War Savings, or Government Savings redemptions and interest payments were met by corporations and private financial institutions holding War Loan subscriptions lists. Both were equipped with War Loan-inspired marketing, advertising, and financing techniques. But wider participation in the stock market also required significant shifts in perception—from debt to equity and from the state to private corporations. These modifications in investor perception evolved gradually; they depended upon the capture of War Loans' ideology of investor democracy, its investor-centered theory of political economy, and its marketing tropes and techniques.

In the first half of the 1920s, a range of economic thinkers seized upon corporate stock as a superior vehicle for propertizing the masses, advancing investor-citizenship, and democratizing the political economy. This proposition—labeled "the New Proprietorship" by contemporaries—was most associated with the leading theorist of the War Loan and U.S.

Government Savings programs, Harvard professor Thomas Nixon Carver. In the 1920s, first corporations and then private financial institutions appropriated rhetoric, imagery, and techniques pioneered by the War Loan campaigns—then reshaped by apostles of the New Proprietorship—to promote corporate stock ownership. As they did so, they promulgated a new ideology of shareholder democracy.

CHAPTER SIX

Swords into Shares

T HOMAS NIXON CARVER remembered "the years immediately follow- ing World War I" as the "most active" and happiest of his life. Between 1919 and 1921, Carver "brought out three textbooks" in high school and college-level economics, published a series of short articles in *Youth's Companion,* and contributed editorials and articles to the Boston *Herald,* the New York *Herald-Tribune,* the Hearst newspaper syndicate, and *Reader's Digest.* He ranked among the most popular professors at Harvard, making such an "impression on the student mind" that some "began to call themselves Carverians, and to be called Carverians." In all this work, Carver emphasized the centrality of thrift and investment for the betterment of society, just as he had done when promoting the War Loan campaigns and the postwar U.S. Government Savings program. But beginning in 1919, as the nation descended into Red Scare hysteria, labor strife, racial violence, and xenophobia, Carver began to entertain the notion that shares of corporate stock might convey a political-economic stake in American capitalism more effectively than federal bonds, stamps, or certificates. In the 1920s, corporate stockowners moved to the fore of Carver's investor-centered theory of political economy, which his adherents dubbed the "New Proprietorship."[1]

Carver's postwar professional success was complemented by personal joys, including the nuptials of beloved children and the births of eagerly anticipated grandchildren. Second son Emmet K. Carver wed Ruth Ripley, the daughter of William Z. Ripley, Carver's esteemed colleague in the Harvard economics department. A mutual interest in the writings of social Darwinist Herbert Spencer and racial sociology first brought Ripley to Carver's attention. Carver met his son's future father-in-law in 1900, when Ripley delivered a summer course at the University of West Virginia on the "Races of Europe," based upon Ripley's highly influential book. After serving as an advisor to the U.S. Industrial Commission, Ripley's focus shifted to railroad operations and finance. Upon Carver's recommendation, Harvard's economics department admitted Ripley as a full professor in 1902–1903. Together with C. J. Bullock, F. W. Taussig, Edwin F. Gay, and O. M. Sprague, Thomas N. Carver and William Z. Ripley constituted the "backbone" of the "strongest department of economics in the country" until the 1930s.[2]

Given the length and depth of their relationship, Carver and Ripley were shocked to find that some judged them to be antagonists in the mid-1920s. True, Carver considered himself a champion of the "old healthy American individualism," whereas Ripley consistently advocated the expansion of the regulatory state, especially legislative reform of corporate financial disclosure and governance to protect shareholders. Still, Carver endorsed the passage of such laws to encourage and to protect those "productive individuals" who acquired shares in American corporations. And Ripley's widely read exposés of the means by which corporate executives "disenfranchised" their shareholders—which even captured the attention of President Calvin Coolidge—by no means indicated the he opposed the diffusion of shareownership that Carver celebrated as a "silent revolution" in American business. Indeed, Ripley took great offense that Henry M. Brundage, vice president of State Gas and Electric Association and vice president of Consolidated Gas of New York, accused Ripley of berating Carver's work "'with a violence of invective and an indiscriminateness . . . that would make a socialist orator blush for shame.'" Ripley sought only to alert Americans to "the prime fact confronting" the nation: "the progressive diffusion of ownership on the one hand and the ever-increasing concentration of managerial power on the other."[3]

Indeed, more united Carver and Ripley than divided them. Both men believed that the diffusion of corporate stock ownership would improve social, political, and economic life in the United States. Carver's theory of New Proprietorship reassigned to corporate shares all the potential for economic reform that he had claimed for small-denomination federal debt when he promoted the War Savings and U.S. Government Savings programs during and immediately after World War I. In the 1920s, Carver and his adherents envisioned that mass distribution of corporate stock would redeem American democracy by enabling salaried or waged citizens to regain a classical republican sense of political stake-holding, along with the economic autonomy that only property ownership could convey. Widespread acquisition of corporate stock would redistribute the nation's wealth peacefully, and in accordance with natural market mechanisms, Carver and his apostles imagined. This "silent revolution" would institute a mode of collective ownership of the means of production that respected individual private-property rights, in accordance with American political traditions. Carver and his disciples also envisioned that broad-based stock ownership would enhance American corporations' sense of accountability toward the public. Ripley, for his part, simply demanded that the law ensure that corporations did so, by improving their corporate governance and financial disclosure practices for the benefit of outsider investors of modest means. William Z. Ripley served as loyal critic to Carver's New Proprietorship.

Taken together, the work of Carver and of Ripley provided the stock market with a legitimizing ideology. Without it, the advent of broad-based, direct investment in corporate stock in the 1920s could not have occurred. Certainly, the War Loan drives had established the basic political, cultural, and moral legitimacy of financial securities and markets. They had validated the marketing, advertising, and financing techniques required to capture and service the retail market. And certainly, broad-based participation in the stock market also required the closure of certain alternative postwar paths, particularly U.S. Government Savings. And yet, none of these factors—even taken together—determined that American investors would seek shares of domestic corporations instead. The expansion of corporate stock marketing and ownership in the 1920s cannot be understood apart from the elaboration and criticism of the theory of New Proprietorship.

Shifting retail investors' attention from debt to equity and from the state to corporations depended upon the capture of the War Loan notion of investment as citizenship, as well as its investor-centered theory of political economy. In the first half of the 1920s, the War Loan model of investor democracy—which celebrated ownership of state debt as an exercise of political citizenship—was transformed into a theory of New Proprietorship, which reconceptualized economic citizenship as direct investment, particularly in corporate stock. The work of Carver and Ripley narrowed public discussion about the nature and the goals of the corporation. Before World War I, when Americans engaged in debates over the role of the corporation—the "trust problem," in the parlance of the day—they considered corporations' proper relationship to consumers, employees, competitors, and local communities more often than they deliberated over managements' responsibilities to shareholders. In Carver's and Ripley's influential postwar writings, by contrast, corporate accountability meant attentiveness to the concerns of outsider shareholders. For those, like Ripley, who considered corporate reform necessary, this meant enhancing those shareholders' influence within the corporation.

The New Proprietorship guided a remarkable transformation in financial culture, serving as the rationale for retail marketing by countless stock distributors during the 1920s. Emboldened by the claims of Carver and his disciples and confident that Ripley's loyal criticism only confirmed the fundamental desirability of widespread stockholding, corporations and financial institutions seized hold of the iconography and rhetoric of the War Loan drives to promote investment in corporate enterprise in the 1920s. In doing so, corporate stock distributors once again revised the ideal of investor democracy to elaborate a new ideology of shareholder democracy. Despite William Z. Ripley's cogent, constructive criticisms, a more conservative vision of shareholder democracy—which rejected *any* state oversight of the financial securities markets—achieved supremacy in the late 1920s.

THOMAS NIXON CARVER, the David A. Wells Professor of Political Economy at Harvard University, was a key theorist of thrift and investment for the War Loan drives of World War I. In the postwar period, Carver further refined his investor-centered prescriptions for political economy in a wide range of articles, textbooks, and forums and books published for popular audiences, including *Elementary Economics* (1920) and *The Present Economic Revolution in the United States* (1925). In the early 1920s, Carver emerged as the progenitor of the theory of "New Proprietorship," which trumpeted the democratizing potential of universal ownership of corporate stocks, rather than federal debt. Carver's revised investor-centered theory of political economy envisioned that widespread distribution of corporate shares held even *more* potential to realize such economic reforms as the elimination of class strife, the redemption of proprietary democracy, and the subjugation of the business cycle.

For Carver, economic reform meant securing a "wider diffusion of prosperity" and ensuring that all classes enjoyed equal access to the inherent "advantage" of American capitalism, but without recourse to statist appropriation or violent revolution. The key to this kind of "constructive" reform lay in making labor scarce in relation to capital. "In proportion as capital is scarce relatively to the labor supply, in that proportion will capitalists be well off and laborers badly off." What the laborers needed most was "more capital," which they could provide for themselves by saving and investing in employment-generating enterprises. Thrifty laborers might even make capital "so abundant" as to significantly "reduce the share of the capitalist class" such that capitalists would be compelled to seek waged or salaried employment themselves. The universal exercise of thrifty habits would enlarge the nation's stock of capital and thus increase the demand for labor and expand Americans' economic opportunities. Furthermore, by urging Americans to "buy things that will give [them] more buying power next year and every year"—i.e., interest-bearing or income-generating investments—the state and private institutions would stimulate future consumption, thereby improving standards of living and guaranteeing steady employment, macroeconomic growth, and widely enjoyed prosperity.[4]

Both before and during World War I, Carver had written about the need to encourage "saving and the accumulation of capital" in order to make "capital so abundant" that it would "cease to be the limiting factor in production." But before 1920, Carver always characterized capital as the physical means of production, and investment as the literal "buying of tools," while praising thrift as abstention from extravagant consumption that misapplied or misdirected both capital and labor. After 1920, however, Nixon surmised that the best tonic for the ailments that corporate aggregations of wealth had inflicted upon political democracy lay in the dispersion of corporate shares (Carver also supported broad-based ownership of insurance policies, savings accounts, homes, and small businesses). As "a democratic institution," corporate stocks provided "individuals with only small sums of capital" the opportunity to participate in the profits of corporatized mass production. Otherwise, the profits of "large scale production" would continue to accrue to "only a few very wealthy men." But if the masses came to share the financial privileges of the wealthy, labor and capital would no longer find themselves at odds. In particular, if corporate stocks trickled down the economic ladder, "so many laborers" would become "capitalists, and so many capitalists laborers, as to make it difficult to tell" where to demarcate between groups. When this "blending and overlapping of so-called classes" occurred, Carver concluded, "class consciousness," class antagonism, and class revolution would become impossible in the United States. As the New Proprietorship unfolded, "the world quietly turn[ed] over" while "professional reformers bark[ed] at the moon."[5] In contrast to violent revolution, Carver's "higher strategy" took into account natural, immutable, and "permanent economic forces," but was not bound by "*a priori* theory," he contended. Enthusiasts judged the New Proprietorship's promise of peaceful, natural practicality its most appealing aspect.[6]

Much as it had in the War Loan model of political economy, ownership of financial securities reoriented the individual economic self in Carver's vision of New Proprietorship. Individual ownership of dividend-paying stocks would liberate workers from total dependence on wages, modestly redistribute wealth without the paternalistic intervention of the state, and increase the demand for labor so as to enlarge economic opportunities and improve working conditions without the paternalistic intermediation of labor unions. Once liberated from dependency on wages or salary, Carver's new economic man engaged questions of political economy from the viewpoint of the investor, rather than consumer or worker.

> When his wages are high, when he has a few hundred dollars saved and bearing interest, when he knows that there are several other jobs waiting for him, and he knows that when he quits his boss will have a hard time getting another man [he will] feel free and be free in fact . . . If the laborers should spend their surplus incomes for income-bearing securities, they begin to assume another economic status.

Under the New Proprietorship, individuals would look to the returns of their investment portfolio to gauge their own economic well-being and that of their nation. But corporate stocks would now dominate the contents of that portfolio. Carver's model citizen-shareholder, however, did not engage in active stock trading, or speculation. He held his economic-political stake in perpetuity.[7]

Ultimately, the implementation of the New Proprietorship through the dissemination of corporate stocks would nurture and empower an entirely new economic class: citizen-shareholders. Carver recognized that because shareowners only voted in proportion to the number of shares they held, any broad-based movement toward corporate stock ownership could not be considered democratic in a literal sense. And he allowed that the individual votes of small investors might count for little in the shareholder meetings of great corporations. But in the aggregate, Carver claimed, their investment choices would put Everyman in control of the national economy. "They who spend their money for securities" tended "to control or influence business" by determining which corporations and industries received capital. Investors' exercise of this "financial power" put "laborers in a strong position" to influence the operation of the means of production, even if they held only nonvoting stocks. Given the financial power of their aggregate potential savings, laborers might, "any time [they] decide to do so," buy out any number of "industrial corporations, railroads and public service companies, and actually control a considerable number of them," if they chose. That no group of workers had done so already suggested (at least to Carver) that the rank and file understood that "their own interest" required "the best management that can be secured," not worker-management.[8]

To improve the ratio of labor to capital, Carver recommended that the state conduct "an aggressive and permanent thrift campaign" to shape social mores, continue to alert citizen-investors to "fraudulent promotions," fund the educational programs to train workers for the most promising fields, and restrict the flow of "cheap labor from Mexico." Carver countenanced securities market and corporate governance regulation to protect small investors, because "bad investment" misdirected "productive energy," causing "fundamental irreparable loss to society." But otherwise, the government should not interfere in the economy, Carver stressed. "Private investors" alone should direct the flow of capital through their individual investment decisions. For investment, in Carver's assessment, represented "competitive bidding for the productive energy of society," which "in the long run" placed the economy "in the hands" of the most "efficient directors." Carver also opposed social welfare legislation and the guarantee of the rights of workers to organize independent labor unions. As *individuals*, laborers must "insist on breaking up the old personal relationship" with employers and learn to treat their own labor "as a commodity, selling it in the highest market." Carver advised labor organizations to contribute to the New Proprietorship through voluntary initiatives such as labor banks, which would preserve workers' capital and help them to accumulate funds from which they might subsequently purchase corporate securities.[9]

The New Proprietorship rejected both the welfare state and collective bargaining as paternalistic and unnatural. Carver and his adherents understood legislative proposals to address economic inequality—such as adjusting wages to the cost of living or legislating minimum wages or maximum working hours—as undermining economic self-sovereignty and, ultimately, political democracy. "Purchasing power progressives" within the labor movement and Commerce Department suffered Carver's harshest criticisms, however. Those who advocated high wages and robust consumption as a means of augmenting and equalizing the benefits of industrial capitalism only discouraged thrift in favor of "hand-to-mouth extravagance," ensuring that capital remained scarce relative to labor. Carver classified purchasing power progressives among "those enemies of American labor who oppose the restriction of immigration or the control of the birth rate among the poor." In the final analysis, Carver's New Proprietorship looked relatively antistatist and antilabor, in comparison to the War Loan model of an active security-selling federal government that supported the cause of organized labor.[10]

THE MUSINGS of Thomas Nixon Carver met with wide-ranging enthusiasm, by no means limited to his academic milieu. New Proprietorship enthusiasts hailed from the advertising industry, the financial sector, corporations, government, the media, academia, and even from organized labor. Inspired by Carver's writings, they seized upon corporate stockownership as the natural palliative for the nation's social and economic ills. Mass investment in corporate stock stood at the center of the just and thriving political and economic system envisioned by Thomas Nixon Carver's adherents. They viewed the implementation of the New Proprietorship as a means of revising and restoring proprietary democracy, fortifying economic citizenship, and liberating individual economic selves. They portrayed universal stock ownership as consistent with America's essential national character, rooted in its propertied past. They envisioned that the realization of the New Proprietorship would put Everyman in the pilot's seat of the national economy, convey to workers an active interest in their work, and engender a New Era of economic stability and growth. However, Carver's apostles derived several new claims for universal stockholding that were not located in his original gospel. Champions of the New Proprietorship promised that mass investment in corporate stocks would diffuse not only the threat of socialism, but also "socialistic" demands to regulate corporations. They cast stock trading as a constant mass referendum on the performance of corporate management and the state of American capitalism-at-large. These elaborations would greatly inspire corporate stock distributors in the 1920s.[11]

The fate of proprietary democracy—which linked political citizenship with property possession—concerned Carver's devotees most. Subscribers to the New Proprietorship invented a past in which universal independent proprietorship fell before corporate concentration and waged employment. During America's formative "pioneer days, individual ownership and opportunity" had been impressed forever upon the collective, essential American psyche, according to William L. Ransom, former Justice of the City Court of New York. In these fictitious bygone days, farms and firms remained small and local, "owned and controlled by the men who did the work in them." Obviously, this mythical past ignored the fact that early American proprietorship rested upon command of dependents' labor—whether enslaved, indentured, waged, or familial. Nonetheless, adherents to the New Proprietorship pretended that every early American worker shared "in the ownership of the enterprise" and therefore possessed a "proprietary sense." New Proprietorship enthusiasts' elevation of the individual as the basic economic unit in early America bore little relation to historical reality. But erasing historical proprietors' reliance upon domination allowed theorists to ignore questions of authority and control in their visions of the New Proprietorship.[12]

Having rewritten history, New Proprietorship adherents imagined a bright future in which a nation of citizen-shareholders would secure their economic birthright—a share in America's certain economic progress and future prosperity—in the form of corporate stock. "The public seems to have a profound faith in the future growth and prosperity of the United States and wants to share in such prosperity" through "ownership of common stock," declared Professor Charles Amos Dice, the author of the popular *New Levels in the Stock Market* (1929), the standard text of the Roaring Twenties bull market. Under the New Proprietorship, citizen-shareholders gained much more than regular dividend payments or steady appreciation in the market value of their investments. They also shared "in part, at least, in the risk of progress. They are usually for their company and take an interest in it," Dice observed. Corporate share ownership promised to eradicate the passivity that marked economic life in the corporate age.[13]

Devotees judged the New Proprietorship consistent not only with the Americans' political heritage, but also with uniquely American modes of political action and social change. Mass acquisition of corporate stocks suited a dynamic, democratic polity far better than the state-based social insurance devised for Europe's teeming unskilled hordes, or the state socialism for Russian peasantry, or even France's system of small-denomination government securities for petty farmers and the bourgeoisie. Those without property lacked an essential, foundational aspect of democratic citizenship. At the root, social alienation and political disaffection could be traced to propertylessness. But by transforming the masses into "capitalists," the advent of the New Proprietorship would correct the political outlook of unpropertied voters.[14]

Otherwise, the communist threat would grow. For New Proprietorship adherents, strong socialist showings in national and local elections in 1920 and 1924 proved that those lacking property had become "receptive soil for seeds of discontent and destructive" communist-tinged radicalism. As Pierrepont B. Noyes of Oneida put it, the "disinherited voters" had turned "in desperation" to "use the power which democracy" gave them to attempt to "equalize wealth by national ownership and national operation of industry." But when Everyman achieved propertied status by acquiring corporate shares, he quickly recognized the sanctity of private property and became a "better citizen and particularly a better elector." Predictably, the citizen-shareholder would demand "proper safeguards" for his property against the machinations of the "shiftless agitator who wants the whole social order upturned." *Commerce and Finance* even predicted that "a nation of investors" would "necessarily" become "a nation of political conservatives," indeed, "a nation of conservative Bourbons." Citizen-shareholders would "safeguard" both personal *and* corporate property from *any* form of state encroachment, whether communistic, socialistic, or merely regulatory in nature.[15]

For as citizen-shareholders acquired corporate stock, they cast "yea" or "nay" votes on particular corporations or sectors and they issued a general endorsement of the private corporate enterprise system. For Charles Amos Dice, the presence of Everyman in the stock market disproved every "accusation socialists may hurl, whatever criticism labor leaders may raise." Dice swore that citizen-shareholders' intertwined political and economic assent would sustain late-1920s stock market levels. Indeed, as an unmediated register of vox populi, stock market levels signaled Americans' implacable, united determination toward economic growth and progress.

> There is no institution in this country that is so sensitive to all economic changes and social and psychological developments as the Stock Market. Almost at once it registers on the ticker tape every hope and fear, every constructive plan or destructive scheme, every surge of confidence or every wave of alarm . . . The ticker registers the pulse of the nation . . . in terms of dollars and cents. And so before the politicians, the newspaper reporters, and even before businessmen themselves realized what had really happened . . . it was registering . . . a new world of business, a new standard of living, and the fact that the American people are only beginning to appreciate their tremendous power in invention, in industry, and in commerce.[16]

With this social-psychological safety net in place, New Proprietorship extremists like Dice found it acceptable that even more small investors enter the stock market, even as prices rose to dizzying heights after 1927. In turn, this inexorable inflow of small capital purified, legitimated, and stabilized the securities markets. Even as infamous operators such as William Durant, Michael Meehan, Jesse Livermore, and Clarence Saunders titillated the public by orchestrating pools to manipulate the prices of stocks in companies such as Durant Motors, RCA, and Piggly Wiggly, New Proprietor stalwarts like The *Magazine of Wall Street* declared that small investors, "the real owners of Wall Street," stood mightier "than the mightiest clique of capitalists." This "general public" would "break the back of the biggest speculation pool" now that the New Proprietorship had arrived.[17]

MORE REFLECTIVE commentators probed questions left unanswered by Carver and his staunchest supporters. Certain quandaries stymied consensus among those drawn to the dream of New Proprietorship. If the form of ownership upon which democracy rested should change, would that transformation alter the nature of political democracy in the United States? What other sorts of institutions or interventions would be required to nurture politically meaningful proprietorship among the masses? Even if shares were distributed widely among all classes, would—and *should*—managers' autonomy over waged workers subside? Would it undermine managerial prerogatives or lead to control of corporations by shareholders? Over the course of the 1920s, the parameters of the New Proprietorship were debated among the theory's enthusiasts.

The most fervent supporters of the New Proprietorship simply ignored such questions; corporate stockownership approximated traditional notions of proprietary democracy closely enough. In this formulation, shareowner-ship imparted some vague sense of participation in larger economic institu-tions and forces. The economic citizenship, or "stake," acquired resembled the mere right of petition. For example, employee-owners at New York Edison "manifested" their new "interest" in the company through (unen-forceable) "suggestions for improvement," according to Vice President Ar-thur Williams. In this view, the New Proprietorship democratized industry without the interference of labor unions implicit in demands for industrial democracy. More conservative New Proprietorship disciples cared little about Carver's goal of increasing labor's relative value in comparison to capital. The precise nature of the ownership involved in the New Propri-etorship mattered far less than the placating effects if promised, if privately implemented.[18]

But the power of the New Proprietorship in the 1920s may be grasped more by analyzing its critics rather than by focusing on its most sanguine adherents. In truth, very few public figures—whether politicians, journalists, activists, labor leaders, corporate and financial leaders, or academics—discarded the New Proprietorship entirely. Given the wartime validation of the small investor and the scorn heaped upon any suspected of socialist or communist leanings in the 1920s, almost none were prepared to reject the New Proprietorship outright. Even Carver's critics agreed that he might be on to something. Perhaps universal corporate shareownership could reconcile corporate capitalism's tendency toward concentration and depersonalization with American commitments to political democracy and economic individualism. Moderate skeptics wondered whether stocks were really suitable for small investors. More cynical observers like iconoclastic economic theorist William Trufant Foster and labor leader Sidney Hillman contested the notion that pervasive investment in corpo-rate stock would, or should, subsume the unique interests of workers or consumers. But this line of criticism lamented the New Proprietorship's capture by conservative welfare capitalists more than it rejected corporate stock ownership's inherent potential for effecting a positive transformation of the American political economy.

Some mild critics of the New Proprietorship such as Warren S. Stone, grand chief of the Brotherhood of Locomotive Engineers, judged corporate stocks unsuitable for the rank and file. Yet Stone did not reject the New Proprietorship; he simply preferred bonds, homes, and accounts in labor banks to stock market forays. After the Brotherhood of Locomotive Engineers partnered with the National City Bank to distribute Northern Pacific bonds among its workers, Stone observed that while he appreciated the "partnership which stocks confer," he did not "believe that many workmen can afford to assume the risks involved." Bonds could also convey "that sense of responsibility which workmen ought to have," but they were far safer investments. For Stone, corporate bond ownership could create a unity of interest between employees and employers just as well as stocks.[19]

Proponents of new consumer-centered theories of political economy found common ground with the New Proprietorship. Leading "purchasing power progressive" William Trufant Foster of the Pollak Foundation for Economic Research allowed that wider distribution of corporate securities could play a role in sustaining prosperity and ending economic cyclicality. But Foster integrated his mild endorsement of the New Proprietorship into a progressive, pro-consumer framework, which asked for state action to adjust wages to increases in the cost of living, public works to sustain employment, and concern with overcapitalization and overproduction. The "end of all economic activity is consumption," wrote Foster. If consumers possessed enough money, then producers would easily attain "enough money to produce; *but the reverse is not true,*" he avowed. Overproduction constituted a very real and very alarming possibility, unless both policy makers and corporate leaders took action to sustain consumer demand.[20]

Foster granted that broad-based ownership of corporate stock might offer part of the answer. Since "income from securities" flowed "more steadily" than wages, a "more extensive" and "more equitable distribution of securities" might augment "purchasing power" and maintain it during downturns. Distribution of securities among the lower classes was critical, for these investors would be more likely to spend rather than reinvest their investment returns. Thus, a broad distribution of investment income might mitigate shocks to consumption due to wage fluctuations or unemployment. However, Foster warned, consumers would always spend money from wages more quickly, and in greater proportion, than money received from investments. Robust wages, therefore, remained more important than returns to invested capital in Foster's fundamentally consumer-centered model of the economy. Moreover, most corporate profits were not paid out to consumer-investors as dividends or interest anyway, Foster remarked. Rather, corporations retained and reinvested earnings to expand production, compounding the problem of overproduction and ultimately exacerbating economic volatility. Foster, therefore, did not endorse investment merely for the sake of investment.[21]

Intellectuals favorably disposed toward organized labor subjected the New Proprietorship to criticism as well. Donald R. Richberg—one of the nation's leading labor lawyers and who would later help to draft Franklin D. Roosevelt's National Industrial Recovery Act—mocked certain fantasies of the New Proprietorship cult. Employees would never surrender their quest for higher wages, better working conditions, and workplace democracy even if they acquired shares in corporations. "An employee who becomes a fractional employer" attempted an "embarrassing" and functionally impossible "acrobatic feat" of economic self-division. Richberg disagreed that "a New Proprietorship" would "transform the conflicting interests of seller and purchaser, or the employer and employee, into the common interest of genuine cooperators." While an employer and an employee might "cooperate in making profits," the "competitive spirit of the free worker, which makes him efficient" would never be satisfied with anything less than "a maximum wage" and a secure right to organize. Similarly, the *North American* sniffed at the "fatuous" assumption than any "stock-selling plan could in any way weaken the consumer's determination" to resist fare, rate, or price increases.[22]

The most cynical pro-labor discussants suspected that the New Proprietorship might be tainted at its core, a reactionary plot to strengthen the hand of management against unionization efforts, shareholder activism, and regulatory oversight. If corporate managers really wanted to enhance workers' interest in employing enterprises, they should "recognize and deal with the organizations they have formed for that purpose," averred George Soule, director of the Labor Bureau. Lewis Corey of the *New Republic* asserted that American industry would never be democratized "by the multiplication of stockholders deprived by all functional obligations to industry." Such a development would only intensify "the separation of ownership and management, concentrating control in an oligarchy composed of practically self-perpetuating management and their financial overloads." Corey also observed that if some kind of "silent revolution" were taking place, it was not affecting the overall concentration of wealth in America. For these most suspicious observers, the promise of the New Proprietorship had a very long way to go to escape the conservative machinations of its allegedly reactionary implementers.[23]

Nevertheless, it did not seem impossible, even to these pro-labor cynics, that the "full advantages of" the New Proprietorship *might* be achieved if workers who acquired their employers' stock also enjoyed some form of "appropriate participation in management." For Amalgamated Clothing Workers of America (ACWA) leader Sidney Hillman—the nation's leading advocate for industrial unionism—true New Proprietorship demanded "a fair day's wage for a fair day's work," coupled with a share in the "responsibility of management." Only by assuming substantial managerial "responsibilities" could workers attain meaningful proprietorship in the industrial workplace. If coupled with industrial unionism, employee-ownership might indeed rescue proprietary democracy from the dustbin of history. Hillman proposed institutional innovations to secure a New Proprietorship for American workers, particularly labor banks, which aimed to enable unions to retain control over, and to protect, locals' and members' savings. Furthermore, Hillman's ACWA established a labor-run investment trust. Amalgamated Investors Inc. invited union members and locals to invest their money in a professionally managed fund that purchased both bonds and stocks. Hillman advised that labor investment trusts provided a more independent, safer, and more lucrative alternative to corporate-managed employee stockownership plans, in which workers found both their wages and their investments dependent upon the success or failure of their employer.[24]

Just as in the ideological struggles to specify the precise implications of wartime financial nationalism, the key questions posed in critiques of the New Proprietorship involved the policy and social consequences of its implementation. William Ransom warned against surrendering the noble ideal to an "ultra-conservative group of capitalists" who sought to "silence, through a false and narrow economic sense of self-interest in ownership, the individual who would protest against abuses in management of capital or demand its regulation in the public interest." Similarly, Commerce Secretary Herbert Hoover surmised that privately administered markets would never yield a true New Proprietorship. A noxious but natural economic tendency toward "further and further concentration of ownership" would, if not countered by appropriate laws and regulations, cause the "ultimate destruction of democracy." The state might rightly intervene to ensure that the "tendencies of the diffusion of ownership" would exceed these "tendencies of concentration." For Hoover, state policy must direct, promote, and protect the diffusion of all forms of ownership, whether involving a home, land, or corporate stocks.[25]

These loyal critics of the New Proprietorship worried that, at present, corporate stockownership represented a shadow, even a debasement, of proprietorship in the traditional sense (in which owners assumed some degree of control or influence in the enterprise in which they had invested). At present, owners of corporate stocks did not exercise any real initiative. They concerned themselves only with returns, rather than the quality of the corporation's goods or services, or whether corporate activities fulfilled broader social needs. Unlike their propertied forbearers, investors did not individually pursue opportunity and assume risk and control in order to gain a measure of economic independence and self-sufficiency for themselves and their progeny. Instead, as both employees and investors, Americans had become "dependent" on corporate managers and financial institutions for both their wages and their interest income.[26] Both "impersonal ownership and irresponsible management" threatened that sense of independent responsibility for private property upon which the republic depended.[27]

Shareholders' passive, ignorant condition bore no relation to the kind of active command of physical assets that the Founding Fathers had exercised, Carver's loyal critics lamented. The shareholder viewed his holdings as mere instruments of income-generation. He knew "almost nothing of what goes on in his company," and management encouraged his ignorance, maintained Herbert C. Pell, chairman of the Democratic Committee of New York. The body of shareholders became too "scattered" and fractured to effectively counter the machinations of the minority control of financial and managerial overlords. Furthermore, the diffusion of ownership made "any real personal relations" between employees and their real employers, the stockholders, impossible. Directors and executives, meanwhile, looked out only for themselves and freely engaged in "every form of political corruption and journalistic subsidy." Instead of elevating the American polity, Pell lamented, the dissemination of corporate stocks had opened the door to managerial malfeasance, which "paved the way for a greater toleration of the principle of government control." Subjected to little oversight or accountability, corporate misdeeds undermined faith in private property and free markets, inflaming rather than dousing bolshevism.[28]

According the loyal opponents of the New Proprietorship, the mass distribution of corporate stock might as easily undermine as uphold democratic political traditions, unless new laws and regulations introduced state oversight over the "silent revolution." Skeptics certainly denied that the New Proprietorship would unfold organically and correctly if abandoned to corporate or financial leadership. But they did not deny that if proper policies were implemented, the New Proprietorship just might work. Perhaps all that was missing from Carver's idea, suggested George Soule, was some way "to increase the interest and responsibility" of shareholders in the "conduct of our industries," so as to improve management "not only in producing material things but also in producing happy citizens." William Ransom wondered whether the corporation might still offer "instrumentality for restoring popular ownership," if share ownership might somehow include a "sense of participation" and "command" in the nation's industries. But how could this be accomplished?[29]

HARVARD economics professor William Z. Ripley offered the most influential set of answers in his *Main Street and Wall Street* (1926). Like other loyal critics of the New Proprietorship, Ripley averred that under present conditions, the diffusion of corporate stock actually threatened to dissolve, rather than revitalize, the connection between property ownership and political virtue. *Main Street and Wall Street* recommended new federal policies to restore shareholder potency and realize the potential of a true New Proprietorship.[30]

Largely forgotten today, Ripley's book was serialized by *Atlantic Monthly* and presented to U.S. senators by Robert La Follette Jr. upon its publication. Ultimately, it would inspire Ripley's student, Adolph A. Berle, to write *The Modern Corporation and Private Property* (1932) with economist Gardiner Means. Berle and Means's book became the foundational text of New Deal economic reform and the most cited work on corporate governance in the period of its publication. When Ripley first published his indictment of corporate governance in 1926, he already enjoyed an established reputation as a Brandeisian critic of big business and financial oligarchy. He had served on the staff of the U.S. Senate's Industrial Commission of 1899–1900. His *Trusts, Pools, and Corporations* (1905) had condemned the watering and insider manipulation of corporate stocks and demanded federal oversight of corporate reporting. Building upon this earlier work, *Main Street and Wall Street* focused on questions of corporate control and accountability. It contended that a mass investment society required enhanced state oversight of the securities markets, specifically, reforms in corporate governance and reporting.[31]

Main Street and Wall Street picked at the New Proprietorship's central analogy between the ownership of physical property and the holding of corporate stock. For Ripley, proprietorship could not exist in any meaningful sense if outsider investors were denied sustained input in the enterprise in which they owned shares. The diffusion of corporate stock might increase the number of citizens entitled to income from corporate property, but it would not provide them with any degree of influence over managers' conduct, their use of corporate assets, or their treatment of workers. But rather than rejecting the New Proprietorship, Ripley looked to the state to legislate reforms in corporate reporting. Then, Ripley and his adherents believed, the New Proprietorship might serve as a safe, worthy substitute for the Old. Just like Carver, Ripley reasoned within a thoroughly investorist framework and reiterated that widespread distribution of corporate stock could revitalize economic citizenship and modernize proprietary democracy in the corporate age. In other words, he questioned the policy implications of the New Proprietorship, but he did not jettison its central tenets.

Ripley's investigations revealed that by issuing no-par stock, nonvoting stock, and stock lacking the right to participate in future issues, corporate management systematically prevented shareholders—especially outsider investors holding small, minority stakes—from exercising any influence over corporate policies. The fact that American firms incorporated according to state rather than federal incorporation laws produced a race to the bottom in standards of corporate disclosure and governance.[32]

Main Street and Wall Street aimed to expose the "disfranchisement of the public shareholder" by tracing the methods by which the "rape" of shareholders' "voting power" had been actuated. For Ripley, the erection of holding-company pyramids and the execution of mass mergers—so intriguing to the financial press and so appealing to small investors—proved worst of all. Through these stratagems, Ripley wrote in true Brandeisian form, financiers aggrandized themselves and reduced "the great body of shareholders . . . to subjects." Harkening back to the findings of the Industrial Commission on which he served, Ripley detailed how higher-than-market valuations offered for the companies to be merged easily lured shareholders into accepting such deals. In return, they surrender their voting shares in the old company for nonvoting shares in the merged holding company. The financial oligarchy thereby "hoodwink[ed] the shareholders out of the franchise." Meanwhile, press and financial marketing coverage of the merger enticed even more small investors to buy the new, watered, nonvoting shares. The subsequent widened distribution of shares only further nullified the small investor. With control of the holding company now firmly vested in a small group of "organizational capital," only "the doubtful protection of private consciences" protected shareholders' interests. Shareholders stood powerless while corporate insiders suspended dividend payments and retained earnings to indulge in more orgies of overpriced acquisitions and overexpanded production.[33]

Ripley labeled the passivity of corporate shareholders a "disenfranchisement." In doing so, he, too, advanced the fiction that American firms had once been run in the fashion of New England town meetings, as much as the most sanguine New Proprietorship stalwart. Ripley's rhetoric, however, cast a spotlight on the dangerous political consequences of the managerial license and shareholder submissiveness produced by the diffusion of corporate shareholding. The more numerous and diffuse shareholders became, the more easily a small group of financial and managerial oligarchs

could control the corporation, Ripley surmised. These plutocrats hid behind masses of indifferent and disenfranchised shareholders, plundering
companies and abusing consumers. Meanwhile, relations between labor
and capital worsened as "absentee owners" and the employees found themselves unable to communicate. Worst of all, managerial miscreants oriented
the companies under their control toward "quick turnover" and short-term
profits rather than "long-time up-building" of the American economy.[34]

Political citizenship could not withstand this degradation of corporate
citizenship, Ripley warned. Far too often, shareholders displayed little interest in the details of corporate policy and strategy, and exercised their
voting power infrequently. Like S. Davies Warfield and those connected
with the National Association of Owners of Railroad Securities, William Z.
Ripley categorically rejected the "hackneyed argument that at bottom management and public shareholders have an entire unity of interest" that
made the exercise of shareholder rights irrelevant. By abdicating their rights,
stockowners gave "themselves over, body and soul" to corporate managers,
becoming their "mere wards, *non compos mentis.*" Indeed, Ripley judged
the proliferation in the number of women stockholders—celebrated by the
New Proprietorship cult as indicative of the democratization of the American corporation—as illustrative of this degradation. "Ill-fitted by training—
begging the moot point of sex," female shareholders would improve corporate governance even "less so than . . . politics," Ripley sniffed.[35]

Despite the dire picture of misgovernance and disenfranchisement that
he painted in *Main Street and Wall Street,* Ripley considered these developments neither natural nor irreparable. He certainly did not reject the New
Proprietorship's goal of distributing corporate stock among all Americans.
Rather, Ripley emphasized the necessity of preserving—even enhancing—
shareholders' rights within the corporation. He urged investors to rally in
their own defense by "boycotting" all offerings of nonvoting stock, as well
as any offering by a corporation that published inadequate financial reports. He also demanded changes in the law to revitalize shareholder rights,
especially enhanced federal regulatory oversight of corporate reporting and
legislative reform of corporate governance practices.[36]

Ripley's writings kept the prospect of corporate reporting and governance reform alive throughout the 1920s. He proposed regulatory reforms
that aimed to empower outsider investors of modest means, whose interests
he understood as identical with the interests of dissenting minority shareholders. Ripley did not anticipate that improvements in corporations' disclosure of their financial data would lead shareholders to seize control of
the corporation. Rather, the dissemination of such data, translated "into
terms that will be intelligible to all" by "specialists, analysts, bankers and

others," would inform the trading decisions of scattered individual investors, "leading inevitably to the quotation of a just and true price based upon" the real condition of the corporation, rather than the "rigged market prices, based upon inside information," that too often prevailed on the nation's exchanges.

Increasing the influence of shareholders within the corporation would require other kinds of corporate governance reform, and not just enhanced disclosure, Ripley argued. Ripley sought an "orderly way to render minorities at least reasonably articulate" by putting an end to "absolute governance by a majority" within corporations. His platform included the introduction of cumulative voting to elect corporate boards of directors, the extension of the right "to call meetings and to initiate proposal for actions" to groups of minority shareholders, the "creation of a permanent shareholders' representation committees to function alongside" the board of directors, and independent audits of corporate reports. Additionally, permanent arbitration bodies might mediate disputes between minority and majority groups of shareholders.[37]

For Ripley, federal oversight was the key to substantial reform of both corporate governance and reporting. He decried that "nation-wide private industrial corporations" conducted "business all over the United States, cloaked and hooded like the despicable Ku Klux Klan." National corporations should incorporate under federal law, and the Federal Trade Commission should assume administrative responsibility and oversight of enhanced, standardized corporate reporting. Although Ripley praised the New York Stock Exchange for toughening its listing requirements, he judged the disenfranchisement and subsequent abuse of the small investor far too grave to be solved by the voluntary actions of private associations like the NYSE or the Investment Bankers Association. After all, NYSE requirements did not affect nonlisted corporations, and accessing NYSE listing information—however helpful it might be for investors—required a visit to the Exchange's on-site library.[38]

Even so, bankers, brokers, and corporate executives scoffed at Ripley's "grave charges." Insofar as they even entertained any need for change, they advocated voluntary reform—although some branded Ripley a communist instead. Ripley's opponents charged that he confused and "startled the investing public" needlessly. No individual or administrative body could ever possibly devise "a general and sweeping rule" for corporate reporting that could apply to the multitudinous forms of industrial enterprise. When *Industrial Management* asked Thomas Lamont of J. P. Morgan to respond to Ripley's charges and recommendations, Lamont gladly obliged. Modern corporations could not be managed according to "rules and formulas" laid "out on paper" in "by-laws" formulated in "stockholders' committees," Lamont sniffed. The character of management offered most important safeguard for investors, best gauged by experienced financial intermediaries. The NYSE, for its part, asserted that the information required for listing on the nation's exchanges already proved sufficient for investors, who rarely examined such documents, in any case. The "free and open" securities markets corrected managerial wrong-doings in a more natural and democratic manner. Eventually, the Exchange contended, investors learned to avoid the securities of corporations that gained a reputation for malfeasance.[39]

But Ripley was far from alone in believing that implementation of the New Proprietorship would require regulatory expansion. In New York, Public Service Commissioner William A. Prendergast, for example, anticipated that the arrival of the New Proprietorship would "vindicate . . . the regulatory principle," for broad-based corporate stockownership would not flourish without a rigorous regulatory structure to enhance public confidence. Prendergast concurred with Ripley that minority shareholders and retail investors would require "definite representation in the boards of directors" because true "democratization of ownership" would require a "democratization of responsibility." The NYSE's perennial antagonist, Samuel Untermyer, heartily endorsed Ripley's call for federal "control, supervision, and regulation" of corporate incorporation procedures and the reporting of corporate financial data to shareholders. Even Arundel Cotter of the *Wall Street Journal* lent his support to certain aspects of Ripley's platform, particularly cumulative voting and standardization of corporate reporting. Ultimately, the issues of managerial accountability and control vis-à-vis outsider investors would be picked up by Gardiner Means and Adolph A. Berle in their seminal *The Modern Corporation and Private Property*, which would serve as the basis of New Deal securities market reform.[40]

CLEARLY, those who agreed that corporate stocks—rather than federal debt—offered the best mechanism for universalizing property ownership stood at odds about the possible regulatory implications of Thomas Nixon Carver's New Proprietorship. Yet the reform-minded William Z. Ripley and the ebullient Charles Amos Dice may be understood as opposite sides of the same New Proprietorship coin, or rather, the same stock certificate. Even the most enthusiastic acknowledged that ancient models of proprietary democracy—in which independent citizens pursued entrepreneurial activity through the command of tangible assets and others' labor—had become atavistic in a modern corporate economy. Even the most exacting critics of existing corporate governance practices allowed that the dissemination of corporate stock offered the last, best hope for preserving a propertied republic and for improving corporate behavior. Ripley did recognize that stockholders proved "hopelessly indifferent" and "no one expects it to be otherwise." Nonetheless, he emphasized the importance of the *possibility* that "once in a blue moon some resolute individual or stockholder could . . . organize a protective committee or dissenting group—and if nothing else happened, at least there was a thorough ventilation of what sometimes proved to be a musty or unsafe tenement." With the exception of Thorstein Veblen in *Absentee Ownership* (1922), those commenting upon the diffusion of stock ownership in the 1920s acknowledged the desirability of widespread corporate stockownership, at least in theory. Widespread assent to this core precept of the New Proprietorship assured the legitimacy and enhanced the desirability of corporate stocks.[41]

The elaboration and criticism of the New Proprietorship inspired and encouraged the efforts of corporate stock distributors in the 1920s. But it would take sustained ideological work to overshadow Ripley's calls for regulation. In the 1920s, employee stockownership plans (ESOPs), customer ownership plans (COPs), investment trusts, and retail brokerages all claimed to advance Carver's vision. But as these four strategies put the New Proprietorship into practice, they bent its ideals in conservative—that is, antistate, anti-union, and antiregulatory—directions.

CHAPTER SEVEN

The Corporate Quest for Shareholder Democracy

WHEN WARREN G. Harding was sworn in as the twenty-ninth president of the United States in March 1921, David F. Houston left the Treasury Department, where he had overseen the U.S. Government Savings program. But when Houston stepped down as Treasury secretary, he did not relinquish the public spotlight. A new post as chairman of Bell Telephone Securities Company—AT&T's stock-distribution subsidiary— beckoned him. Houston did not, however, mean to abandon his commitment to public service when he entered the private sector.

Houston understood his new mission to be quite similar to the one he had pursued as secretary of the Treasury. Ever the fiscal conservative, Houston continued to speak out in a range of public forums against extravagance in both government and personal expenditure, illustrating his comments with Treasury Department statistics on Americans' "unreasonable and extravagant expenditure" for candy, tobacco, soft drinks, perfume, and cosmetics. At the time the total public budget stood at 4.3 percent of GDP (up from 0.2 percent in 1914), and Houston vocally upheld the position that the Harding administration must quash proposals for soldier bonuses, practice "rigid economy in government expenditures" and maintain "taxation upon a level sufficient to meet" government expenditures, "including interest" charges on the debt accrued during the war. Tax cuts proposed by the new treasury secretary, Andrew Mellon, as a means of stimulating the economy would yield deficits and diminish the progressivity of the tax code, Houston warned. Even after economic recovery began in 1922, Houston continued to counsel individual and government frugality in order to combat inflation and to perpetuate economic prosperity. But now, according to the chairman of Bell Telephone Securities Co., American corporations' plans to make "every worker a capitalist" by promoting stockownership—rather than the federal government's sale of its debt—sustained a thrifty investor-citizenry and ensured the "democratization" of the American economy.[1][2]

Thomas Nixon Carver's notion of New Proprietorship influenced a wide variety of opinion makers in the 1920s, but none were as prominent or influential as David F. Houston, who had served as Woodrow Wilson's secretary of the Treasury (and before that as secretary of Agriculture). Under Houston's guidance, AT&T became the first of a large number of corporations that seized hold of Thomas Nixon Carver's theory in the first half of the 1920s. Before banks or brokerages began to successfully mass-market corporate stocks to retail investors, these corporations dispensed their own shares directly, through employee-ownership and customer-ownership plans. Following the lead of AT&T's Bell Telephone Securities Co., these corporations repurposed the rhetoric and imagery first pioneered by the War Loan campaigns and then reshaped by New Proprietorship theorists. They reworked Carver's theory into an ideology of *shareholder democracy,* which portrayed the corporation as a commonwealth of shareholders and characterized the stock market as a real-time referendum on the performance of management and a mechanism for democratizing corporate wealth. Sponsoring corporations contended that customer-ownership and employee-ownership schemes would harmonize relations between labor and capital and between corporation and consumer.[3]

But as they put the New Proprietorship into practice, Houston and the corporate executives he inspired bent Thomas Nixon Carver's ideas toward more conservative goals. The need to raise capital did not motivate the corporations that established plans to dispense their shares in the early 1920s. In fact, large industrial corporations of the period typically funded their capital outlays with retained earnings and sold additional shares to retire their debt. Corporations sought after mass shareownership after World War I to buttress their assertions that privately administered corporate capitalism best served the public interest. As they implemented plans to increase the ranks of their shareholders, AT&T and the corporations that followed its lead all sought to foster affinity with one party to the corporation—shareholders—that had been far less politically mobilized than either workers or consumers, both of which had exhibited a history of political activism against corporations.[4]

Corporations deployed employee shareownership plans in the hopes of repelling unionization and federal intrusions into labor relations. By distributing shares among their customers, adopters of customer-ownership plans sought to secure cheaper financing, to stave off antitrust suits, to avoid unfavorable regulatory action, and to refute proposals for government ownership of utilities. Houston and his imitators largely ignored the concerns about the governance of corporations and the administration of financial securities markets raised by loyal critics of the New Proprietorship such as William Z. Ripley. Instead, these ideologists of shareholder democracy dismissed the state both as a distributor of securities and as a regulatory protector of citizen-shareholders. Ultimately, corporate schemes to distribute shares directly to retail investors played a key role in separating ownership from control within the modern corporation.

After 1922, robust economic growth coupled with the remarkable expansion in corporate stockownership—8 million American households would own stock in 1929—confirmed for Houston and his followers the rightness of their cause. Throughout the 1920s, Houston expressed pleasure over Americans' increasingly positive attitudes toward large corporations. No doubt the countless corporate public relations campaigns of the era played a considerable role in improving public opinion. Houston, for one, believed that Americans now understood fully "the advantages of large scale production" under corporate organization, which they enjoyed as voracious consumers of an unprecedented material boom. Through radios, record players, and movie theaters, most Americans sampled the delights of mass entertainment in the age of Jazz and "talkies." The standard of living rose. The proportion of houses with electric lighting increased from 35 percent in 1920 to 68 percent in 1930. Expenditures for consumer durables exploded, averaging $7.06 billion per year between 1918 and 1929, compared to $4.29 billion between 1909 and 1918 (in 1929 dollars). Most iconic of this "New Era" of mass consumption was the automobile; nearly three times as many cars could be found on American roads in 1930 as in 1920.

Yet the gains from 1920s economic expansion were not evenly distributed. Neither did the fundamental distribution of economic power change during that decade. The farm sector continued to languish, one-fifth of the country lived in poverty, the rich got richer, and the 200 largest nonfinancial companies amassed almost one-quarter of the nation's wealth in a flurry of merger activity. Moreover, the stunning growth of the consumer durable market depended upon an explosion in borrowing. Outstanding consumer debt as a percentage of household income doubled, from 4.6 percent in 1919 to 9.3 percent in 1929. Total outstanding consumer debt reached $7.6 billion by the end of the decade. But on these points, Houston did not dwell.[5]

In Houston's final analysis, it was not corporate public relations campaigns or the marvels of mass consumption that secured legitimacy for the American corporation. Rather, he identified the change in "the character of ownership" as the "most important" factor in enhancing Americans' attitudes toward big businesses like AT&T. Even so, the advantages of broad-based stock ownership far exceeded these public relations benefits according to David Houston and those corporations that copied AT&T. Investment in corporate stocks offered Everyman "salvation against dependence" and thus fortified "the foundation of democracy itself" by conferring "a stake in society" upon all those willing to exercise thrift and initiative, Houston avowed. Dispersed shareholding reestablished the link between property ownership and citizenship, albeit in a form quite different than the Founding Fathers had known.[6]

As secretary of the Treasury, Houston had promoted small-denomination federal debt as the best investment for average citizens. But in the 1920s, he conceived of corporate stockownership as the *sole* means of resurrecting a propertied republic in a corporate-industrial era. American political traditions had long judged independent proprietorship—involving ownership and control of tangible productive assets—as a prerequisite for full political citizenship. Americans had long fretted about whether civic virtue, political independence, and economic self-determination could survive in competition with corporate consolidations. Between 1919 and 1929, corporations like A&T overcame a lengthy history of widespread antipathy by promoting investment in their stock, which they presented as synonymous with the ancient ideal of proprietary democracy.

THE CREATION of Bell Telephone Securities Co. can only be understood in the context of the uncertain economic and political climate of the immediate postwar period. In 1919, AT&T faced demands to make wartime nationalization of the telephone system permanent along with a rebellious unionized workforce (20,000 telephone operators walked out in Boston in 1919). To meet these crises, AT&T determined to showcase its shareholders in its institutional advertising while increasing their numbers through employee and customer ownership programs, in line with Thomas Nixon Carver's theory of New Proprietorship.[7]

Beginning in 1919, the company's publicists laid claim to War Loan Share in America iconography, likening AT&T to a political nation and depicting its shareholders as citizens of that democratic polity. Institutional advertising proclaimed AT&T "a Democracy—of the people, by the people, for the people," and, hyperbolically, "a democratic instrument of democracy." Bell Telephone Securities Co.'s efforts to distribute AT&T stock among customers and employees amassed a corporate citizenry that included "people of every walk of life in every state," of "every class . . . trade, profession and business." Broad-based shareownership seemingly unified a new, single public interest that subsumed prior, more contentious relationships between AT&T and its workers or customers. AT&T now embodied "a new democracy of public service ownership . . . a partnership of the rank and file who use the telephone service and the rank and file employed that service," its institutional advertising proclaimed.[8]

Through frequent references to the size and diversity of its shareholder base, AT&T established the investor as a legitimate economic position vis-à-vis its workers and customers. Managers were charged with balancing the needs of these three parties to the corporation. By asserting that the "future independence of many citizens of small means" depended upon the "economic operation" of AT&T, that corporation suggested that the interests of those investors might even constitute management's foremost concern. And while AT&T could not claim that its shareholder lists included every American, its corporate imagery suggested that its body of shareholders at least offered "a representative cross-section." Like the post–Nineteenth Amendment voting population, women constituted "half of its owners." On one hand, showcasing female shareholders suggested the modernity and inclusivity of the AT&T shareholder-polity. But on the other hand, the feminization of the AT&T stockholder also underscored both her dependency and the modesty of her means. By figuring the investor as a vulnerable woman, AT&T again intimated that investors warranted as much—and perhaps even *more*—consideration from management than did customers or workers.[9]

Assuming the chairmanship of Bell Telephone Securities Co. in 1921, David F. Houston portrayed AT&T's share-distribution initiatives as merely one example of a broad corporate commitment to fulfill the promise of economic democratization made in the War Loans and by New Proprietorship theorists. He cited Thomas Nixon Carver frequently and explicitly. Houston avowed an identity of interests between the shareholders of *all* American corporations and "the public" at large. Silently and sanely, and without the input of "ignorant individuals [who] have been unable or unwilling to sense it," he contended, the U.S. corporation had become "the vehicle through which laborers and other smaller investors" had "become owners and capitalists," to a far greater extent than ever before, "anywhere, at any time in history." But when Houston trumpeted an explosion in the number of American shareholders, he failed to adjust for individuals owning stock in more than one corporation, foreign investors, or institutional investors. These strategic omissions implied not only that everyone was acquiring corporate stocks, but that everyone should.[10]

For Houston, these little corporate commonwealths proved more democratic than any antecedent, or alternative, forms of economic organization. Although "demagogues" aimed to vilify corporations as "menaces" to the public, those very enterprises enabled men of small means "to acquire a financial stake in society" through stock investment. In doing so, corporations were resolving successfully the perpetual "problem of the relation of labor and capital." Such corporate efforts would vanquish socialism forever, for a far superior form of public ownership emerged as corporations dispersed their shares. By showcasing shareholders in its institutional advertising and by characterizing Bell Telephone Securities Co. as a project of economic democratization and political renewal, AT&T presented itself as providing a service to society that transcended mere profit-making. At the same time, it defended profits as valid payments owed average folks, rather than the ill-gotten gains of plutocrats.[11]

In Houston's formulation, the advent of "true" public ownership of corporate enterprise depended solely upon small investors' individual initiative. Corporate shareholders gained "ownership of one's self," an economic "independence" that assured both "the financial salvation" of "the individual" and "the permanence of democracy." Houston's language of free markets and individual initiative characterized economic freedom, equity, and security as transcendent ends that could only be compromised by state intervention, whether these interventions took the form of government ownership, state-mandated reforms in corporate governance or reporting, or increased regulation. Indeed, Houston predicted that employee and customer owners would defend AT&T against any such political threats.[12]

Bell Telephone Securities Co. campaigns sidestepped the distinction between ownership and control that troubled critics of the New Proprietorship like Harvard economist William Ripley, who spearheaded demands for corporate governance reform to protect minority investors in the 1920s. In framing shareholding as corporate enfranchisement, Houston expressed none of the skepticism about minority investors' ability to exercise influence in corporate affairs that marked Ripley's work. AT&T simply declared itself "controlled not by one, but controlled by all," while Houston dismissed concerns that too few shareholders actually voted. AT&T shareholders' "very keen interest" in "the business and problems" of the company and their willingness to defend it against criticism from customers, employees, and politicians testified to their political commitment to the corporation, Houston maintained. As far as shareholders' actual input was concerned, Houston contended that the widening of a corporation's shareholder base engendered "a striking advance in ideals, standards, and practices of management" on its own, thereby dismissing the possibility that reform of corporate governance practices might be warranted.[13]

Thanks to the efforts of David F. Houston and Bell Telephone Securities Co., AT&T became the most widely owned corporation of the period. Indeed, it retained its reputation as a "widow and orphan" stock throughout the twentieth century. In 1929, AT&T boasted that a half million persons owned its stock, having added roughly 400,000 shareholders since World War I.[14] In 1931, AT&T became the most widely held stock in the world, counting 642,180 shareholders. *Printer's Ink* credited AT&T's shareholder-centered institutional advertising campaigns with "stopping government ownership talk," and, indeed, the United States remained alone among major industrial nations in retaining private ownership of its telecommunications infrastructure. The size of the AT&T shareholder base—and former Treasury Secretary Houston's affiliation with the project—inspired a wave of customer and employee-ownership plans among American corporations and blazed an ideological and iconographic trail for 1920s securities marketing by corporations.[15]

IN THE POSTWAR period, many corporate executives deliberated upon the War Loan experience, the ideals of the New Proprietorship, and the examples of the U.S. Government Savings program and Bell Telephone Securities Co. All these suggested that workers' acquisition of financial securities might whittle away at organized labor's strength, facilitate the Americanization of immigrant workforces, forestall bolshevism, and provide means for individuals to achieve economic autonomy and security. Both the Treasury's War Loan Organization and its postwar U.S. Government Savings program had sworn that a metaphorical "stockholder" in the federal state would never "throw a brick through the window of his company or apply the torch to the warehouse." After the war, corporate executives and managers ruminated over such assertions. If ownership of federal debt would inspire an otherwise incendiary worker to "strengthen" the enterprise in which he was employed, might stockownership in that employing enterprise improve that laborer's attitude and productivity even further? An affirmative answer informed the employee-ownership "movement" among large American corporations after 1919.[16]

Most historians hold that employee stockownership plans proliferated in response to immediate postwar labor militancy. In truth, many industrial managers continued to integrate workplace sales of U.S. Government Savings securities into their Americanization, open shop, and welfare capitalism initiatives throughout the tumultuous 1919–1921 period. The Treasury Department's decisions to scale back U.S. Government Savings in 1921 and then to terminate the program in 1924 threw considerable momentum behind the corporate employee-share ownership "movement," which AT&T's highly publicized ESOP also encouraged significantly. Of the 337 employee-ownership plans with known dates of establishment, more than half were established in 1921 or after. By 1928, nearly 800,000 employee-owners at 315 firms held $1 billion of employers' stock.[17]

The Liberty Loan and War Savings drives offered templates for corporate managers devising ways to administer and publicize their employee share-ownership plans in the 1920s. "Usual procedure" involved "a campaign to arouse the interest of the workers," including "mass meetings, personal talks by executives, articles in the employee magazine, the distribution of literature, payroll inserts, and posters on bulletin boards." Partial payment plans were common, as were investment support groups modeled on War Savings societies.[18]

Corporate managers believed that employee ownership offered a straightforward, affordable answer to the problems of worker motivation, morale, efficiency, and turnover that welfare capitalism had sought to resolve since the 1880s. The acquisition of employer's stock would plant the "profit motive" in workers' hearts, according to ESOP enthusiasts. The practice of making the opportunity to invest conditional upon the length of employment aimed to encourage employee retention among skilled workers perceived as at-risk for trade unionism. Employee ownership assigned individual workers the responsibility of providing for their own and their family's economic security in the case of sickness, periodic unemployment, accident, old age, and death. Each received his share of corporate profits in the form of dividend payments or share-price appreciation, in proportion to his individual resolve to forgo expenditures and invest in his employing corporation.[19]

And so, by the mid-1920s, large corporations had rushed in to assume the burden of shoring up the foundations of American democracy by distributing their stock to employees. Corporations promised to propertize the masses and to rescue laborers' nest eggs from "wildcat investments" with stock plans—formerly commitments the federal government had met with its own small-denomination stamps, bonds, and certificates. When U.S. Steel's CEO, Elbert H. Gary, testified in the Senate in the aftermath of the steel strike in 1919, his portrayal of employee ownership at U.S. Steel could have been lifted straight out of War Loan or Government Savings literature.

> [It] makes the wage earner an actual partner . . . a real capitalist. . . . They have as keen a desire to see the institutions of this country protected as those who have greater riches, and they may be relied upon to lend their influence and votes in favor of the protection of property and person.

In Gary's articulation, however, corporate employment strongly mediated workers' relation to the polity. ESOPs bound workers more firmly to particular employers, instead of the state.[20]

Corporations addressed public and labor relations simultaneously when they assumed the state's role as conveyer of financial securities to those allegedly lacking both property and civic virtue. Enthusiasts maintained that employee shareownership would reform an industrial system that all too often pitted worker against owner, but in a peaceful, privately conducted manner. Management consultant Thomas E. Mitten, who devised ESOPs and COPs for the Philadelphia Rapid Transit (PRT) Co., detailed how employee ownership had transformed "a group of under-paid, disgruntled street railroad men"—who had robbed shareholders of dividends when they stormed "their bloody striking way through the streets" of Philadelphia— into "a body of self-respecting, efficient and courteous employees." Employee ownership refined these thugs' manners by reorienting their economic perspective, without addressing larger structural issues of economic equity. Employees learned to "give before they get," according to Mitten. "No man" would steal or strike when he realized he stole "his own money." Arundel Cotter of the *Wall Street Journal* agreed. After laborers acquired stock, they saw "things from the point of view of the corporation" and grew to "appreciate the problems and difficulties" of capital. To promote "understanding" between and align the interests of labor and capital, ESOPs targeted only the hearts and minds of workers, leaving management to pursue an unchanged course.[21]

Despite talk of forging a new partnership between labor and capital, ESOP rules ensured that worker-ownership never translated into worker-owner management. ESOPs did not "mean a soviet of workers holding the reins," clarified Mitten. Managers retained full control, although Mitten hoped that once employee-owners knew what they were "talking about," they might "act as a purifying and improving tonic to management." In truth, very few firms made any effort to share—much less explain—corporate information such that worker-owners might evaluate the performance of management or the current worth or future prospects of employers' stock. Only managerial employees ever attained a controlling stake through any corporate shareownership plan.[22]

Those firms that instituted ESOPs presented themselves as sponsors of a social policy based on individual acquisition of financial assets in private securities markets. In the 1920s, states added worker's compensation and mothers' pensions, along with old-age insurance programs. Meanwhile, the federal government provided funding to improve maternity and child health under the Sheppard-Towner Act of 1921. Corporations positioned employee ownership against this quiet, localized expansion of the welfare state, maintaining that ESOPs offered a "private enterprise" answer to the challenge of how to achieve social security. Advocates claimed such plans spared the public purse from "periodically recurring pleas" for state-based social insurance. At the same time, an ESOP compared favorably to "the uncertain sea of pension promises" and group insurance as a solution to the "problem of old employees," supporters maintained. Employee ownership aimed to free firms from the extended, expensive commitments of pension benefits or group insurance, while still deepening workers' financial dependency on employers.[23]

ESOPs had additional financial advantages. By selling stock to its employees, a corporation might circumvent financial intermediaries (and their fees) to raise new capital. Widening the distribution of a corporation's stock might modulate the volatility of—and prevent manipulation in—that stock. If workers received something in the way of corporate dividends, the denial of wage increases, or even wage reductions, might be made more palatable, if only in the field of public relations. And if employee ownership did increase worker productivity, or even just public goodwill, then the price of a corporation's stock might increase, a desirable outcome in the minds of manager-owners.[24]

Thus, corporations typically launched worker-ownership plans to deepen wage-earners' dependency and to strengthen managerial prerogative. Managers intended to fence workers' economic citizenship even more strictly within the bounds of the employment relation. Despite promises to educate and acclimate workers to the capitalist system, corporate ESOPs did not encourage workers to become free agents in an open labor or investment market. Rather, ESOPs sought to tip the scales further in employers' favor. When laborers subscribed to employers' stock, they gained something more to lose if they left, or if they were fired. Employee ownership conceived of a worker's acquisition of a financial security as a vote of confidence in a private-property system grounded firmly in individualism, but this assent involved acquiescence to managerial authority and waged employment.

Accordingly, employee ownership drew the ire of organized labor, especially since ESOPs quite often played handmaiden to the open shop and company unions, both of which gained ground over the decade. "This 'me and

Rockefeller' consciousness is Standard Oil's patent substitute for class-consciousness and labor unionism," ESOP critic Robert W. Dunn sniffed. He greeted a "movement" led by such anti-union stalwarts as Du Pont, Standard Oil, U.S. Steel, Bethlehem Steel, Pacific Mills, and A&P with heavy skepticism. Only in a very few cases did employee-ownership coexist with independent labor organization. The Amalgamated Clothing Workers of America—whose vision of industrial unionism embraced modern management techniques, sought joint deliberation with management, and created worker-run ventures like labor banks, insurance, and investment funds to pool and protect workers' financial resources—accepted employee stockownership at some firms. But even in these exceptional cases, foremen acquired most of the stock. Most typically, white-collar and managerial employees dominated ESOPs.[25]

Accordingly, the leadership of the American Federation of Labor (AFL) denounced ESOPs, believing that such plans eroded the fundamental distinction between labor and capital, upon which collective bargaining depended. A rhyme in the *Federated Press* communicated the AFL position:

> You take sum savings from your sock and buy an ounce of bosses' stock. It's printed in sum colored ink and all lit up to make you think, that you're as rich as all creation and goin' strong to own the nation.
>
> I hope you don't gulp down the dope that buyin' stock is workers' hope. It's precious little you can get from your weekly wage, I bet. And there ain't any chance in hell that them what owns will really sell enough so that they will lose their grip on railroad, factory, mill and ship. So long as they can run the show, they just as soon such stock should go to the workers, with a purse what's thin as into bankers' box of tin. In fact, they really want us guys to make a few investment buys, and read our share of stock each night, instead of this here dope I rite. Keep cool in your financial collar; the world ain't offered for a dollar.

Employee ownership would never redistribute power or wealth to workers, either within a particular corporation or across the larger economy, the AFL held. ESOPs might, however, lead workers to forget their essential economic identity and interests *as workers,* so that the AFL's vision of industrial democracy through craft unionism would never materialize, it feared.[26]

But the AFL failed to recognize that worker-owners could take the stock but leave management's definitions of partnership and security behind. Following fluctuations on the financial pages, employee shareholders might locate an alternative source of economic gain or articulate an alternative definition of stockownership. Rather than pursuing economic security as employers defined it, workers could pursue excitement when they acquired their employers' stock. The possibility of capturing speculative profits constituted an entirely different notion of economic freedom, emanating from another source, utterly distinct from the employment relation. If, as the AFL feared, stockownership led worker-owners to think individualistically rather than collectively on economic matters, this did not necessarily entail acquiescence to management.[27]

Ultimately, employers' intentions made little impact on the decisions and motivations of worker-investors, the National Industrial Conference Board reported in 1930. Workers most often acquired shares at the urging of "fellow employees, chance acquaintances, the newspapers, the 'boss' (foreman), the wife or husband, the family generally, [or] the family friend, who set himself up as the one versed in financial matters and might be termed the 'neighborhood economist.'" Forty percent reported that they bought employers' stock because they "believed in stockownership" in a general sense, rather than on account of faith in their employer specifically; 19 percent considered the stock a "good investment"; 19.7 percent invested because "everyone else did"; while 11.9 percent made no answer. Only 9.4 percent invested in order to put themselves "in right with the company." Fifteen percent admitted that they borrowed against the value of their holdings in "complete disregard" of agreements not to do so.[28]

Indeed, ESOP observers noted that worker-owners tended to choose quick profit over "partnership" as defined by management. Some actively traded employers' stock, chasing profits from short-term fluctuations in stock price. Those who acquired shares through an installment plan sometimes sold partially paid-for shares short, anticipating a fall in the market price of their employer's stock. Employee-owners thereby negated the stock market's estimate of their employer's worth. Accordingly, ESOP architects attempted to devise restrictions to limit employees' ability to recast the meaning and purpose of their stock acquisitions. Plan sponsors generally made little effort to educate worker-owners about the risks of stock investment, the prospects of their shares, or the benefits of other kinds of saving vehicles, lest they embolden workers to sell or trade their shares.[29]

But when employees sold, shorted, or speculated in their employers' stock, they rejected welfare capitalism's central tenet: that workers should consider their employing corporation the central economic and social institution of their lives. The stock market offered alternatives; another source of income, however small. An alternative economic self—one that stood apart from the wage relation—emerged when a worker traded stocks or just followed their movements in the market. The stock market offered a different, seemingly direct and neutral, relationship to the corporate economy. Workers who "played" the market with their employers' stock rejected the suggestion that they should soberly save for a rainy day. This was not the financial freedom that ESOP engineers intended. But it associated financial markets, individual freedom, and economic self-realization all the same.

CORPORATIONS inspired by AT&T's conception of shareholder democracy—as well as AT&T's success in sidestepping undesirable legislation by scattering its stock—interpreted large numbers of shareholders as an endorsement, each share registering another citizen-shareholder's vote of confidence in management. According to one of the greatest stock promoters of the Roaring Twenties, Samuel Insull of Consolidated Edison, a wide investor base indicated that "the industrial captain" had been chosen "by his fellow workers and proprietors but so chosen in a way that theorists have never dreamed of." Apart from workers, customers constituted another potentially disaffected group capable of cloaking themselves in the "public interest" mantle. So they, too, became targets of corporate stock distribution programs: customer ownership plans (COPs). By 1929, the National Electric Light Association (NELA) claimed almost a million and a half customer-owners in 230 utility corporations.[30]

Utilities launching COPs in the early 1920s enthusiastically deployed mass-marketing techniques inspired by the War Loan drives: direct mail solicitation, partial payment plans, sales contests, sensational giveaways, thrift education campaigns. Customer ownership campaigns innovated with new media, as well. Utility holding company Cities Service Company sponsored radio concerts, for example. Announcers identified the sponsor but never "directly urged" audiences to purchase Cities Service securities. Rather, announcers reiterated the "importance of thrift" and offered free thrift aids, thereby associating Cities Services with that War Loan keyword. Cities Services deliberated upon "buying motives" rather than "the actual selling features of the stock." "Emotional appeals" advised customers that stock investment increased "the opportunity for greater leisure" and made "home comforts possible" by supplementing "regular income from work." Customer ownership campaigns encouraged stock ownership in general, not only investment in specific corporation.[31]

Following the lead of Bell Telephone Securities Co., most corporations instituted customer-ownership and employee stockownership plans together. Any interaction with a customer provided an opening for the employee-owner to make a stock sale, often on commission. The meter man taking a reading, the telephone operator placing the call, the train conductor attending to travelers, the clerk selling a ticket—any might extend the hand of partnership along with service. If a customer accepted the invitation to invest, they joined "in a democracy of industry," in the words of the Philadelphia Rapid Transit Co. Surely "no corporation could claim better assurance of safety and high return" for its stock than one in which investment aligned the interests of workers, management, and customers. While ESOPs reformed behemoth corporations into equitable industrial democracies without state or union interference, COPs extended the financial, political, and moral benefits to the wider community.[32]

Customer-ownership advocates presumed that the investor identification would supersede any prior—and potentially more fraught—relationship that consumers might have had with the corporation previously. Antagonists could be transformed into allies as they assumed a new status as shareholders. To encourage political sympathy, corporations inserted information "combating attacks on the company whether political, business, or personal in character" into dividend-check envelopes and annual reports. NELA viewed the customer-owner as a "political asset" for his company, claiming that he would cast his vote more "intelligently" in regard to policies affecting utilities. Of course, this line of reasoning assumed that customer-shareholders would understand their interests as defined by managers. Customer-ownership boosters quickly forgot the antimanagerial politics of the National Association of the Owners of Railroad Securities. Or rather, they learned the lesson that elite-directed political mobilization of investors could plausibly claim to represent the "public interest."[33]

The desire to shape views about what constituted the public interest—in particular, to define the meaning of public ownership—lay at the heart of the customer ownership "movement." None other than New Proprietorship originator Thomas Nixon Carver claimed that a widely owned corporation achieved true "direct public ownership—real ownership by the public—each in his own right, as against collective political ownership with its attendant wastefulness and inefficiency." Throughout the 1920s, executives and publicists in the utility and transportation industries parroted Carver as they opposed municipal, state, or federal-owned power and transportation facilities, resisted regulatory incursions, and sought favorable action in regard to rates. Railroad lines, for example, introduced employee and customer-ownership plans in the aftermath of the 1919 Plumb Plan to nationalize American transportation. Albert H. Harris of the New York Central favorably compared the "direct and voluntary" form of "public control and public ownership" achieved by distributing shares to customers to the "indirect and involuntary public ownership and control" that "the advocates of government ownership" espoused. In the power and light industries, the National Electric Light Association promoted customer-ownership as it lobbied in favor of the privatization of the Muscle Shoals hydroelectric dam and nitrate plants. NELA further positioned customer ownership in opposition to the Swing-Johnson bill proposing federal development of a dam on the Colorado River to supply power to the cities of southern California.[34]

Corporations that promoted customer-ownership against national, state, or municipal ownership contended that government-owned and -operated utilities would inevitably "succumb" to "inertia," inefficiency, and ineptitude. Americans' "vast supply of low-priced power" would be impeded, warned NELA. COPs, in contrast, secured "'public ownership' in its true sense." These plans involved only "individuals who desired to become partners," whereas the inherently coercive nature of "political ownership" *forced* taxpayers to become owners. Last, individuals' acquisitions of utility stocks properly rewarded "private initiative" as investors delivered capital to successful corporations. In return, this "private capital" was rewarded for choosing wisely and assuming risk.[35]

A successful customer-ownership plan could also serve as a weapon in battles over rate-setting in situations where government agencies determined utility rates. Obviously, NELA reasoned, protecting the genuine interest of "the public" in the utility industry required utility rates set to ensure a "fair wage," or return, for the capital contributed by that investing public. AT&T put it quite bluntly in a 1922 advertisement: "the rates must furnish a new return sufficient to induce you to become a stockholder, or to retain your stock." NELA alleged that rates charged to customers or wages paid to workers affected only special or class interests but not the general welfare. A broad shareholder base made demands for rates to be set to achieve a "fair" return on invested capital more viable politically. NELA imagined that corporations that publicized their efforts to distribute their securities improved relations with "the non-investing public" as well. That mass of voters came to understand that neither the idle rich nor Wall Street malefactors controlled or profited from the nation's utility and transportation infrastructure.[36]

Thus, the National Electric Light Association and its members cast shareholders' interests as the public interest, much as the National Association of Owners of Railroad Securities had in the immediate postwar period. But utility corporations went further, taking steps to enlarge the numbers of shareholders in the industry. By 1925, NELA widely publicized the 2.5 million American owners of utility securities as evidence that "true people's ownership" in the light and power industries had been achieved through employee and customer-ownership plans. But just like employee share-ownership, customer-ownership never reworked corporate governance. The prospect of shareholder activism troubled managers introducing COPs as infrequently as those launching ESOPs. Neither did corporate directors anticipate that financiers would interfere on behalf of customer-shareholders, for COPs quite often bypassed financial intermediaries entirely, avoiding both their underwriting fees and their input. This held great appeal in the capital-intensive but regulated utility and transportation industries, where rate regulation limited return on capital and dampened investment banks' interest in those sectors in the 1920s.[37]

Indeed, many corporate executives and managers aimed to evade contests for control with bankers and owners of large blocks of shares by instituting COPs and ESOPs. With stock "widely distributed," management became "self-perpetuating and independent of scattered shareholders whether they be employees or outsiders." Apart from offering COPs and ESOPs, corporate managers seeking to reshape corporate governance in the 1920s also priced new issues in smaller denominations, or split each outstanding share into several shares priced more cheaply. *Coast Investor and Industrial Review* praised corporate managers' initiative:

> Splitting shares to fit the purses of the public . . . is manifest evidence that the corporations are adjusting themselves to the era of the small investor. For several years it has been giving the stock market a patronage that brokers and investment bankers long shunned. They believed that the business in which they were engaged had to do only with the rich . . . The entire point of view has been changed since the corporations began, not more than a half-dozen years ago, to eschew short-term loans and seek their capital by the sale of common stocks. In the process not only the small investors but the bankers and the brokers have been educated. It is all part of the great movement.

Such glowing commentary cast corporations as the great democratizers of finance, yet ignored the way in which the diffusion of corporate stock increased the number of Americans entitled to corporate income without providing them with any means to influence corporate policy.[38]

General Motors serves as a case in point. GM added employee share-ownership to its welfare capitalism offerings in 1919. In 1923, it launched a massive public relations campaign to enhance its image and to boost the integration and morale of its internal divisions. Its institutional ads ran beside financial columns and in leading financial journals, promoting GM stock to current and prospective customers. When General Motors' shareholder base took off, CEO Alfred P. Sloan and CFO John J. Raskob established Managers' Security Company (MSC) to inspire top executives and to ensure their devotion. General Motors lent MSC $28 million to purchase GM stock. MSC shares were then distributed to executive management. No matter how numerous GM shareholders became (176,693 in 1928), key executives secured full authority by voting the GM stock held by MSC as a single block.[39]

Ultimately, then, the employee- and customer-ownership "movements" of the 1920s were instrumental in the consolidation of power over the corporation in the hands of management. The separation of ownership from control—lamented most famously by Gardiner Means and Adolph Berle in *The Modern Corporation and Private Property* (1932)—was not an unintended by-product of an increase in the prevalence of corporate stockownership. Rather, many corporate executives intentionally resolved to distribute their shares to as many investors as possible—in blocks as small as possible—in order to augment their power vis-à-vis financial intermediaries and large shareholders.

BOTH EMPLOYEE and customer-ownership conceived of stockholding as a vote of confidence in the corporation issuing the shares. Both "movements," however, sought to cement a bond with that corporation alone. The vast remainder of American corporate economy remained as remote as ever to Everyman. Despite the claims of enthusiasts, neither COPs nor ESOPs nurtured individual entrepreneurialism or independence. The stockholding employee's primary identity remained that of employee, while COPs associated stockownership with consumption and all its traditionally feminine connotations. Corporations' emphasis on the aged widows "whose life savings of a few thousand dollars" were invested in the stock of her local utility, telephone provider, or street railway made it unlikely that customer-ownership would provide an effective grounding for masculine economic realization. Neither customer- nor employee-ownership promoted meaningful interaction among investors or encouraged their contribution to corporate strategy. As one critic of AT&T explained it:

> At times I am greatly puzzled by my woeful lack of intellectual or spiritual contact with agencies upon which I am clearly dependent for the maintenance of my present standard of living . . . as a human being with average capacity to think with other human beings about things in which our concern is common, and to work with them, when there is occasion to do so, or when joint effort is called for; as a man who, besides paying his pew rent, on special occasions, at least, occupies the space paid for . . . as a citizen who, rain or shine, votes at national, state, and municipal elections; who in the past has organized small business enterprises, and helped to make them successful; who is member of clubs and assists in running them; who cheerfully transfers some of his annual income to [charity] . . . I wonder why it is that I cut so indifferent a figure as a joint owner of enterprises from which I derive an annual income . . . The dividend for the last quarter, now lying somewhere among the papers that clutter my desk, has no connection with anything that I do or anything that I am . . . I lack the consciousness of primal responsibility that ordinarily goes with possession.

As the citizen-shareholder meekly collected dividends from the company from which he received his paycheck or to which he paid his bill, was proprietary democracy preserved? Would Everyman seize hold of his Share in America as a worker-owner or consumer-shareholder?[40]

Private-sector financial institutions answered with a resounding no. By mid-decade, they had introduced new retail-investor–oriented products and greatly expanded their provision of brokerage services to investors of modest means. In doing so, financial firms offered employee- and customer-owners bolder experiments in corporate stock investment. Their forays were validated by the flourishing discourse of shareholder democracy, which asserted that corporate stock represented a political-economic stake in America-at-large. Just like the corporations that preceded and inspired them, Jazz Age financial firms resolved to reach out to potential shareholders to promote a particular conservative political agenda.

CHAPTER EIGHT

Finance Joins in the Quest for Shareholder Democracy

A S CANDIDATE FOR president in 1920, Warren G. Harding promised a return to "normalcy" after the disruptions of war and the instability of the post-Armistice moment. But Harding's assurance did not portend that in the 1920s American government would revert to its prewar size and scope. When Harding's successor, Calvin Coolidge, pledged that the "chief business of the American people is business," this did not signal a retreat of the state from the economic realm.

World War I marked a turning point in government spending and capacity in the United States. For the remainder of the century, the federal government would rely primarily upon direct, progressive taxation of personal and corporate income for revenue (rather than regressive import duties and excise taxes as it did in the nineteeth century). By 1929, per capita federal expenditures net of military and interest expenses stood at four times pre–World War I levels. Under the direction of Secretary Herbert Hoover, the Commerce Department tripled its spending during the Harding and Coolidge administrations. The Sheppard-Towner Act of 1921—the first piece of federal social welfare legislation pertaining to nonveterans—authorized the federal government to provide states with matching funds to improve maternal and child health. The social welfare benefits provided by states expanded. Five states added worker's compensation programs after the start of World War I, nine added mothers' pensions, and twelve states passed laws to provide assistance to the elderly poor. Between 1922 and 1927, combined government spending on nonveteran pensions—disabled, government employee, maternal, and old age—increased by 65 percent. President Harding even proposed the establishment of a federal bureau of social welfare and one of education. Still, with memories of the Red Scare still fresh in Americans' minds, charges of "red radicalism" and "paternalism" would limit progressive legislators' attempts to expand government interventions into the economy during the 1920s. Even so, Robert M. La Follette Sr. managed to capture 16 percent of the popular vote in the 1924 election as the candidate of the Progressive Party, which advocated government ownership of the rails, mines, and utilities. And the passage of the federal soldiers' bonus in 1924 established a $2.25 billion, twenty-year commitment to 4.7 million veterans, signaling an important federal foray into social policy.[1]

Just like the corporations that marketed their shares directly to retail investors in the first part of the decade, Jazz Age financial firms reached out to potential investors in the second part of the 1920s with particular political goals in mind. Brokerages, banks, and investment trusts presented mass investment as superior to this quiet—yet historically significant—expansion of the welfare state. Their marketing coded shareownership as masculine initiative and familial stewardship. Banks, brokerages, and investment trusts figured the stock market as the route to social advancement and abundance in old age. These financial firms concurred with corporate stock distributors that stock ownership could shore up the propertied foundations of American democracy. Retail-oriented financial firms also championed the stock market as a mechanism for subjecting corporate capitalism to democratic discipline. Just like the corporations that preceded and inspired them, banks, brokerages, and investment trusts promulgated an ideology of shareholder democracy as they developed new channels for distributing corporate securities to retail investors during the Roaring Twenties.

The unprecedented influx of new investors into the stock market in the later part of the 1920s can best be understood through an analysis of the ideals, symbols, and rhetoric that suffused stock marketing, rather than by charting the dizzying fluctuations of stock prices or hypothesizing about the "correct" valuation of securities relative to the growth rates of particular corporations or the economy at large. Investment in corporate stocks first began to make sense to a significant number of Americans because of certain recurring stories that stock marketers told about the potential for universal investment to make corporate capitalism more equitable and more stable while preserving entrepreneurial individualism. Brokerages, banks' trust departments and securities affiliates, independent investment advisory firms, and investment trusts all framed stock market investment as a stake in corporate wealth and growth, as a means for Everyman to access both consumer abundance and economic security. These narratives constructed stockownership as a social norm; investors drew upon them as they formulated their savings preferences. Retold countless times by a large number and wide range of financial institutions, these stories gained plausibility because they sounded and looked so familiar, employing tropes first developed in the War Loan campaigns and referencing the New Proprietorship.[2]

Jazz Age financial marketing offered not only a new interpretative framework for understanding the stock market and negotiating a changing economic world, but also a model for thinking about particular social and political issues. Through their advertising and marketing, early twentieth-century securities distributors interjected into the most significant political debates of their day. Their stock market narratives aimed to influence both Americans' saving practices *and* their political attitudes. The stories they told about the desirability of universal stockownership resonated with Americans because they connected with widespread concerns about the future of democracy and opportunity in a modern corporate economy. By the end of the decade, perhaps 2 million Americans had acquired shares in an investment trust, while 3.5 million had opened a brokerage account (for the purpose of acquiring financial securities) with a brokerage firm, a bank, a bank's security affiliate, or some other investment firm.[3]

DURING WORLD WAR I, banks and brokerages took notice of the way in which mass-marketing techniques were applied successfully to financial products and services. The War Loan campaigns familiarized the masses with abstract, divisible forms of property. Financial industry executives and advertising agents further recognized that the War Loans had established the basic moral and political legitimacy of achieving monetary gain through the ownership of financial instruments, rather than through labor or independent proprietorship of tangible assets. New York City financial institutions secured patriotic validation by positioning themselves as the locus of the nation's financial mobilization. All the major Liberty Loan and War Savings committees in the second Federal Reserve District had been packed with the representatives of these firms. The most spectacular and heavily reported Liberty Loan rallies—which included performances by motion picture stars Mary Pickford, Charlie Chaplin, and Douglas Fairbanks—had taken place on the sub-Treasury steps at the corner of Wall and Broadway. When the second District contributed one-third of the value of all subscriptions to the first Liberty Loan, its Publicity Committee gushed in *Life* about the significance of "this phenomenon" for refuting any who might denounce "New York as the enemies' country," or "the next time Wall Street is pictured as the worm that lies in wait to bite the head off American industry." New York City's leading banks, trusts, and brokerages contributed heavily toward advertising space for the War Loans; only the nation's top retailers rivaled Wall Street firms. And by spearheading an antiswindling blitz during and in the immediate aftermath of the war, Wall Street polished its image even further.[4]

In the immediate postwar period, then, the financial industry stood well positioned to take advantage of the enhanced image it had gained in both War Loan and antiswindling campaigns. Eager to capitalize on this improved standing with the American public, many firms did, in fact, utilize War Loan subscription and mailing lists to pitch other kinds of securities to citizen-investors in the years immediately following Armistice. When firms like Kidder, Peabody mailed Liberty bond interest payments and redemption notices to their customers, they compared the prices and yields of various securities and offered their advisory services should clients prefer something "yielding a higher income return" than Liberty and Victory bonds, given how inflation eroded the purchasing power of the interest paid on the bonds. Apart from direct mail solicitation, postwar banks and brokerages adopted other War Loan promotional techniques. They inaugurated savings clubs, recommended investments as gifts, and incorporated patriotic iconography into their ads, publications, and on-site displays. Throughout the 1920s, the American Bankers Association and the YMCA teamed to sponsor a nationwide National Thrift Week, held in honor of Benjamin Franklin's birthday. Participating institutions drew inspiration from the War Loan drives. Thrift Week in Geneva, New York, for example, included the distribution of Liberty Bell home savings banks, use of the Boy Scout troops to solicit savings pledges, and hot-air balloon launches to raise awareness.[5]

As the 1920–1921 recession darkened the national economic horizon, financial leaders worried about how to sustain the new relation of mutual acceptance—even admiration—between Wall Street and Main Street, especially as political agendas that they perceived as hostile gained ground. Proposals to nationalize certain economic sectors, to increase regulation, or to expand benefits to soldiers, mothers and children, and the aged would increase government indebtedness and drive up taxes, stifle "large industrial institutions in their legitimate expansion," "strangle" the railroads, and, worst of all, "permit the menace of government ownership, and its assured inefficiencies and political tragedies," warned Frank H. Sisson of the Guaranty Trust. Financial institutions could not afford to remain idle "while the organized might of labor and of other class interests works its way at the public expense," Sisson declared. With mass advertising, some argued, the financial industry might counteract the "economic illiteracy" that allegedly undergirded such proposals, even as it sustained and extended retail demand for financial securities. The retail distribution networks of the financial industry—forged in the crucible of war but not yet fully developed—would become frontlines in a battle over peacetime political economy, imagined financial executives and advertising agents in the immediate postwar period.[6]

Political concerns, then, attracted many financial executives and advertising agents to the New Proprietorship's ideal of universal investment in corporate stock. Through "insistent and persistent publicity" and advertising, Frank H. Sisson recommended, the financial sector could promote universal investment *and* shape "enlightened public policy," lest economic ignorance yield its "inevitable harvest" of "industrial and social disaster." Similarly, Herbert H. Houston, president of the Associated Advertising Clubs of America, advised that if Everyman held "a stake in the country" in the form of corporate securities, bolshevism would never make "the slightest inroads" in the United States. Aggressive advertising would broaden corporate stock ownership. The shareholding-citizenry would issue "the answering challenge" to "Red Russia" just as surely as wartime financial mobilization had once served notice "against imperialistic Germany." The postwar stock-swindling menace provided further validation for forays into retail marketing of corporate securities. Only through mass advertising could Americans learn "what to buy, where to buy, and why to buy" from established, reputable banks and brokerages. For financial advertisers, the triple threat of enlarging government, stock swindling, and bolshevism justified an increase in postwar advertising budgets.[7]

In the immediate postwar period, however, the financial industry still faced significant practical challenges in targeting the retail segment successfully. These would not overcome until the second half of the decade. Brokerages holding seats on the New York Stock Exchange remained constrained by the advertising censorship policies of the NYSE's Committee on Business Conduct until about 1922. Even nonmember firms found that the conventional pricing of securities in denominations of $100 or more tended to make them too expensive for retail investors of modest means. This required firms to extend a great deal of credit to retail customers. Soliciting, administering, and financing the tiny accounts of retail investors proved very expensive.

Still, the War Loan drives had endorsed certain techniques—previously considered disreputable—for financing the accounts of retail investors, specifically, partial payment plans and the use of margin (or borrowed funds) in investment accounts. For example, despite the disapproval of Exchange governors, NYSE commission house John Muir and Co. had played an instrumental role in devising and promoting partial payment plans during the war. The firm donated copious amounts of literature and administered plans on behalf of many large employers. Like many other firms after Armistice, Muir urged potential customers to apply the wartime lessons of financial discipline and borrowing-to-save to other forms of financial securities. "You know now that you can invest. You have learned that the small capitalist" enjoyed the same "opportunity" to invest as "the large capitalist," advised the brokerage's advertisements. "You will invest again—if you are anxious to get on in the world." Muir and Co. recommended that citizen-investors place their Liberty bond in "good company with securities having an open, established market." But borrowing-to-save required that citizen-investors pledge collateral to attain credit. Much to the chagrin of the NYSE Committee on Business Conduct, and not unlike nefarious stock swindlers, John Muir and Co. and similar firms allowed clients to borrow against the current market value of their Liberty bonds in order to purchase other kinds of securities.[8]

In many ways, Stock Exchange governors' skepticism toward retail brokerage proved wise. The costs of administering small retail accounts remained too expensive to pursue profitably in the immediate postwar years. Firms borrowed heavily in order to lend heavily—an expensive proposition after the Federal Reserve raised interest rates to dampen inflation after the Victory Loan closed. High levels of indebtedness led several NYSE brokerages—including John Muir and Co.—to fail during the 1920–1921 depression. One of the largest NYSE commission houses—J. S. Bache—found itself $45 million in debt after aggressively pursing retail investors with offers of easy credit. Bache only narrowly avoided bankruptcy in 1921 after Exchange governors organized a private bailout.[9]

And so, despite the wartime validation of mass advertising and marketing techniques, partial payment plans, and margined brokerage accounts, the financial sector made only limited headway in developing a retail market for corporate securities in the first half of the 1920s. After 1922, the Federal Reserve's commitment to maintain relatively low interest rates for most of the decade made it cheaper for firms to borrow money to lend to retail customers. Most importantly, banks, brokerages, and investment trusts benefited as corporations piqued investors' interest in stocks through corporate employee ownership, customer ownership, and other direct-to-investor distribution plans. Sometimes financial intermediaries even administered employee and customer accounts on behalf of corporations, which yielded a new group of potential customers to whom other financial products and services could be marketed. In any case, corporate efforts to widely distribute stock solidified mass-market demand for corporate securities by greatly expanding the ranks of those who already owned shares. Corporate schemes to promote shareownership also established the basic rhetorical and iconographic conventions of Jazz Age stock marketing, which financial firms put to use in the second half of the 1920s.[10]

After 1924, banks, brokerages, and independent investment firms introduced investment trusts. In exchange for shares in the investment trust, investors contributed their savings to a common portfolio that professional managers invested in a range of securities. Trusts drew inspiration from Edgar L. Smith's *Common Stocks as a Long Term Investment* (1924). Smith—along with Yale economist Irving Fisher and financial journalist Kenneth Van Strum—argued that a portfolio of corporate common stocks best protected the future purchasing power of invested savings from erosion by inflation, that great economic scourge of the war and immediate postwar periods. In 1924, several investment trusts opened in Boston. Their location proved a great selling point. Investors simply "didn't trust the New Yorkers," viewing them as "slick Wall Street fellows who take the shirt off your back," trust innovator Paul Cabot later recalled. But soon, New York banks and brokerages joined the trust "movement." Before 1927, no more than a few dozen trusts were established in any one year, together issuing no more than $40 million in shares. Then, in the watershed year of 1927, 140 were established, issuing at least $300 million in shares. Investment trusts in the United States raised approximately $3 billion in 1929 alone. By decade's end, nearly 2 million American households owned shares in 770 investment trusts. Dillon, Read and Co., F. J. Lisman and Co., Brown Brothers, Stone and Webster, Bonbright and Co., Blyth Witter, National City Bank, Goldman Sachs, and Guaranty Trust emerged as leading investment trust underwriters and distributors.[11]

Investment trusts did not become a sensation simply because they objectively met middle-class Americans' preexisting need for an affordable, professionally managed, diversified investment vehicle. In fact, trusts often pursued risky trading strategies and charged rapacious fees. Nor did investment trusts gain popularity simply because they echoed War Loan Share in America imagery and rhetoric. Rather, securities *salesmen* found trust shares exceedingly appealing, given their "romantic sales story" publicized in "national advertising" campaigns, as well as the bountiful incentives provided by trust sponsors, which included banks, brokerages, and other independent investment houses. NYSE members could circumvent the advertising censorship of the Exchange's Committee on Business Conduct by establishing investment trusts outside of their NYSE-registered firm. Exchange governors did not require members to submit any materials related to investment trusts that members might organize until August 1929.[12]

To appeal to investors, the new trusts strove to overcome lingering reservations rooted in the old populist critiques of Wall Street as a thievish gambling den. Trust managers and promoters labored to associate their product with insurance, to disassociate it from speculation and stock watering, and to claim professional expertise. Investment trust marketing touched upon certain intractable quandaries of corporate capitalism. Purportedly offering Everyman a direct, entrepreneurial stake in the *entire* corporate economy—rather than a relationship with *one* corporation, as in employee or customer stockownership—the investment trust promised to inaugurate an equitable shareholders' democracy in accordance with natural market mechanisms. Harking back to War Loan and New Proprietorship claims about the potential of universal investment for reforming modern capitalism, Jazz Age trust sponsors and managers claimed that their new product would resolve animosities based in class, disparities of wealth, and the endemic cyclicality of modern industrial capitalism.

During the Roaring Twenties, investment trust boosters incanted the mantra "diversification" incessantly. They equated diversification—investing in a range of stocks—with "the principle of insurance applied to investments" in order to associate their new financial product with one already familiar to working and middle-class Americans. Retail investors lacked the requisite knowledge, time, and funds to achieve diversification on their own, trust promoters alleged. Emphasis on diversification sought to refute the allegation that the market prices of trust shares included fictitious, or watered, value. In exchange for contributing their capital to the common fund, investors received shares in the investment trust. However, the combined market value of all the trust shares was higher than the combined market value of all the underlying corporate shares owned by the trust. Supporters of the "trust movement" asserted that this premium reflected the intangible—but very real—value of trust managers' expert ability to achieve diversification.[13]

The principle of diversification across industries conceived of the economy as something that could be modeled and represented—broken down into constituent sectors or parts, those parts classified, representative examples selected within categories, examples reconstituted into a model that functioned in a manner analogous to the invisible, abstract whole. Investment trust advertising suggested that by acquiring a share in a diversified trust, the investor came to comprehend, and in some sense, gain a measure of power over what it modeled: the vast, abstract, powerful national—even international—economy. Many trusts added just a touch of international diversification so that American investors might imagine themselves assisting in the reconstruction of a war-torn world, but without subjecting their pocketbooks to heavy risk. Internationally diversified trusts invited retail investors to profit from the United States' ascendance as a global creditor and to imagine themselves as masters of the global economy.[14]

Trusts in which managers actively traded the collective portfolio—known as "managed trusts"—labored to assuage investors' concerns by crafting distinctions between speculators and professionals. Their marketing aimed to avoid accusations of speculation by recasting managers' trading as the "active supervision of holdings." American Founders Corp. affirmed a professional distinction separating trust managers from wild and wily speculators. With "prudent caution," American Founders managers traded only securities that would "possess greater intrinsic values as the years go on," the firm swore. Given the vigilance of its sagacious professionals, investors could ignore "market fluctuations" and hold shares "for the long pull," the firm concluded. Trust managers' expertise was further confirmed in contrast with the capricious behavior of inexperienced small investors. Prior to World War I, the association of retail investors with fear, panic, and volatility had served as a rationale for barring them from the market and as an explanation for their losses. But in the 1920s, many trusts reiterated these same associations to underscore Everyman's need for their expert services.[15]

Trust managers further sought to establish their expertise and professional status by populating their advisory boards with leading financiers, academic economists, corporate leaders, and recognized financial journalists. Purportedly, these professionals conducted disinterested, judicious, and rigorous analyses of opportunities and trends with the assistance of highly trained research staffs. Trust boosters positioned their firms as little economic research laboratories that allegedly put the best minds of the technical elite to work for Everyman.

"Fixed" trusts, in contrast to "managed" ones, sought to lay to rest all allegations of speculation by forswearing *any* trading and maintaining their initial portfolio choices. American Basic-Business Shares, for example, claimed that by committing its portfolio to 132 major American corporations in 30 industries, the firm enabled its investors to avoid dependency "on the judgment and integrity of management." Paul Cabot judged the fixed trust a ridiculously unwise instrument, as managers could neither dispose of a poor investment nor pursue more profitable opportunities as they arose. Nevertheless, the fixed trusts' populist rhetoric attracted those

unimpressed by managed trusts' claims of expertise. Investors could decide for themselves what form of investment trust best advanced their interests and furthered shareholder democracy.[16]

Whether they be of the fixed or managed variety, all investment trusts
sought to downplay the risks of stock investment by claiming the ability to
tap the ever-certain, ever-expanding wealth of the nation. In the heyday
of the Great Bull Market, a host of trusts referenced the Share in America
trope pioneered in War Loan imagery and rhetoric. They beckoned investors with myriad invitations to "Invest in the Prosperity of America!" or to
enter into "A Partnership in America's Prosperity." One trust promoter
later identified "the slogan of 'participating in the future growth of American prosperity'" as "the fetish around which the somewhat hectic scram-
ble" to sell trust shares—the "same old stocks, but in a different package"—
took place.[17]

The War Loans had modeled the nation as a financial market in which
citizen-investors acquired their stake in the polity and economy by purchasing war bonds, forging a new financial relationship between themselves
and their debt-issuing state. In contrast, the financial-market nation modeled by the investment trust movement rejected both debt and the state.
This formulation of shareholder democracy instead drew an analogy between the private corporate economy and the polity. Investment trusts
claimed to convey (albeit indirectly) a Share in America in the form of
corporate stock, thereby forging a relationship between individual citizen-
shareholders and the corporate economy at-large through the allegedly
neutral and natural mechanism of the private financial markets. Trusts' use
of the "Share in America" trope suggested that the trust movement would
naturally redistribute the nation's wealth, without resorting to state action.
Distinctions between capital, labor, consumer, and producer—groups con-
ventionally understood as opposed—would dissolve as investment trusts
democratized corporate capitalism, trust marketing promised. A single, unified investing public would emerge. Lastly, promoters contended that investment trusts would resolve both stock market and macroeconomic volatility. All of these buoyant prophecies heralding the advent of shareholder
democracy echoed—indeed, expanded upon—those previously made by
War Loan boosters, New Proprietorship enthusiasts, and architects of corporate employee and customer ownership plans.

Investment trusts promised that by making corporate stock ownership
safe and affordable for the masses, they would preserve individualism in a
political economy dominated by corporations. By investing in one of the
new trusts, Everyman could assume the mantle of individual shareholder,
for, increasingly, he could not claim the status of independent proprietor.

The investment trust movement recast economic individualism as something involving small shareholders rather than property-owning producers. In doing so, trusts turned progressive and populist damnation of the stock market on its head. Far from acting as the money trust's chief instrument for concentrating wealth and crushing entrepreneurialism, the stock market would democratize the corporate economy and preserve individual property-holding, that key attribute of political virtue and citizenship. Corporate concentration would continue, but the burgeoning investing public safeguarded their economic self-determination as they acquired a "Share in America" in the form of investment trust shares.

When trusts made use of Share in America slogans, they emphasized that stocks represented an active claim of ownership and denigrated bonds as passive claims to interest income. When a citizen-shareholder considered American Basic-Business shares, for example, it was as if he had been "approached by the president, or a director, of United States Steel, AT&T, or the great Du Pont Company and asked to go into partnership with him." Stockholders might rightly consider themselves partners, for they actively assumed the risk of enterprise arm-in-arm with the "directing geniuses of our great national enterprises," in contrast to the passive lending relation of bondholding.

Whereas customer- or employee-ownership could only transform one particular corporation into a democracy of shareholders, investment trusts bestowed "the most logical and efficient method of bringing the savings of the public and the business" of the *entire* nation together. Without this innovation, trust marketing warned, Everyman would never gain his share of American enterprise, and plutocrats would retain their iron-fisted hold over nation's wealth. Trust promoters allowed that corporate stocks had once served as the instruments whereby the plutocracy perpetuated— even increased—their fortunes at the expense of average Americans. But investment trusts claimed to wield the same financial weapon to reverse the trend. The "movement" would yield an "industrial democracy . . . a Sovietism far more enlightened and direct than the experiment so freshly originated in Russia," according to one promoter. Individuals who did not achieve their "Share in America" either lacked thrift or had failed to save enough *in the right kind of financial instruments,* according to trust advocates like John J. Raskob, chief financial officer of General Motors. Boosters of the trust movement professed that it would facilitate an equitable, moderate redistribution of wealth without impinging upon private property or private initiative.[18]

American Trustee Share Corp. illustrated just this prospect in its "Share in America" promotional brochure. In the past, the middling Mr. Harrington and his wife might have been alarmed to read that "'200 great corporations reap more than 40 percent of all the net profits.'" Once, populists and progressives might have interpreted this news as evidence of a noxious concentration in wealth. But in the New Era, the fictional Harringtons worried only that they might miss out on "the substantial profits made by others who invested in stocks." The Harringtons determined to join their ranks by acquiring a "Share in America," representing the "greatest and richest corporations" in the forty-eight states and "all forms of industrial activity." Having secured their economic birthright, the Harringtons could expect to "reap the benefit of the entire country's growth and prosperity." Allegedly, investment trusts extended tools of self-improvement to keep, or to make, American society classless. Yet investment trusts exhibited little concern with workers, in marked contrast to War Loans, the New Proprietorship, or corporate stock promoters. Rather, trust marketing defined classlessness as a narrowing gap between the middling and the wealthiest. Readers did not learn where Harrington worked, for his investment portfolio represented his primary economic identity, an instantiation and extension of his role as family breadwinner. By acquiring a Share in America, Harrington purportedly liberated his inner entrepreneur from the dependencies of salaried employment. Corporate stock-ownership— conveyed by the trust share—signaled Harrington's successful familial stewardship.[19]

For those eager to take more aggressive action to narrow the gap between themselves and their economic superiors, some investment trusts *concentrated* their holdings in particular sectors, despite assurances of diversification. These trusts reconstituted the old trusts, those monopolistic archnemeses of Populist theories of political economy. Diversified Standard Securities Limited, for example, purchased shares in all the corporations once included in the Standard Oil trust. United American Electric Companies Bankers Shares invested only in Edison companies. Several trusts focused on the financial sector, invoking the "money trust" exposed by muckrakers before World War I. Goldman Sachs Trading Corporation—one of the most popular and, ultimately, most notorious trusts—invited Everyman inside the money trust. Heretofore, bankers and brokers grew rich with other people's money, sharing their lucre only with "'insiders' and their wealthy associates and clients." Goldman Sachs, in contrast, promised to "share more and more with investors of moderate means" by offering them the same "opportunities to purchase into initial issues" of promising corporations. When it first issued its shares, Goldman Sachs's shortcut piqued the interest of at least 30,000 investors across the country. Whichever monopoly 1920s investment trusts chose to model themselves upon, all forswore control over companies or industries. They promised not to corrupt the political system, pilfer natural resources, or crush small businessmen. But the new trusts would reconcile economic individualism with the awesome power of horizontal and vertical integration, advocates avowed.[20]

In an era in which class distinctions were most conspicuously expressed through consumer goods, the investment trust portrayed itself as a vehicle for sustaining—even enhancing—one's standard of living and class status. Incorporated Investors' "The American Birthright" ad declared:

> Never were man's horizons wider, his opportunity for the finer things of life greater—because never was wealth, upon which these enjoyments depend, so open to attainment . . . the creation of new wealth in fabulous quantities is America's special faculty . . . *And anyone may participate.* Incorporated Investors provides an ideal method.

War Loan boosters had also conceived of investment as a means of reserving and enhancing future purchasing power. But where War Loan propaganda stressed the need to delay immediate gratification, Incorporated Investors denied any incongruity between the pursuit of consumer pleasures and the acquisition of its shares. Indeed, the demand unleashed by unfettered mass consumption seemingly enhanced the value of investment trust shares. Trust investors profited from their own consumption choices as the profits of underlying consumer-goods corporations grew. Thus, the same citizen-shareholder might indulge freely in consumer delights while profiting from his and his fellows' expenditures. Thrift and consumption no longer stood at odds, as they had in the War Loans or in New Proprietorship theory. Universal investment in the stock market—possible only through investment trusts—would augment the nation's capital stock, raising levels of employment and productivity along with the American standard of living, trust boosters further contended. Robust returns to citizen-shareholders—not consumer credit or organized labor's demands for increased wages—would bridge any gap between what corporations produced and what Americans could afford to buy.[21]

Because investment trusts' Share in America formulation conceived of publicly traded corporate enterprise as the entirety of the national economy, trusts could claim that by stabilizing the stock market, they had tamed the business cycle. Some trust sponsors contended that the stock market now stood impervious to panic because it had been buttressed by the participation of an educated shareholding-citizenry. Others attributed market stability to the fact that jumpy small investors now entrusted their funds to judicious, professional trust managers. But whether they believed the best or the worst about amateur investors, all trust enthusiasts argued circularly that small investors might now safely enter the stock market through investment trusts because small investors had entered the stock market through investment trusts. And because trusts eliminated the "waste of capital" that resulted when the small investor was left to his own judgment, they had stabilized the economy at large as well.[22]

Despite the hearty hallelujah chorus venerating the investment trust movement, all the money pouring into Roaring Twenties investment trusts did raise some eyebrows. In 1927, for example, the New York attorney general proposed that the state banking department regulate investment trusts, but Wall Street lobbyists successfully opposed the suggestion. As stock market levels and trust share prices rose, those urging caution—much less regulation—found themselves marginalized. Promises of voluntary disclosure became just another marketing ploy. Neither the state nor the nation's securities exchanges regulated investment trusts to any appreciable degree in the 1920s.[23]

The consequences were disastrous. Incantations of "diversification" masked rather risky investment strategies. Some trusts concentrated their holdings in particular sectors and thereby increased their exposure to industry-specific risks. Indeed, by 1929, several trusts invested exclusively in other investment trusts, swearing that their iron-clad double-diversification guaranteed absolute safety of invested principal. Many years later, trust innovator Paul Cabot admitted that too many Jazz Age investment trusts "never disclosed their portfolio." Investors "didn't know what the hell it was—a pig in the poke." Trusts that were affiliated with brokerages or banks would "load up" on stocks issued by the affiliated bank or brokerage "to the terrible detriment of the investment trust." Cabot recollected that his admittedly mild criticisms at the time angered those trusts with deposits at Shawmut Bank, where he served as a director. To secure Cabot's silence, they threatened to pull their accounts. Ultimately, investment trusts suffered some of the most disastrous losses in the crash of 1929. The $7 billion that nearly 2 million Americans had invested in the shares of the 675 existing trusts in 1929 was worth only $2 billion in 1932.[24]

But in the heyday of the Great Bull Market, perhaps the owner of a trust share did dare to believe that he had liberated his investor-self from his employee- or consumer-self. And yet, could investment trusts truly renew proprietary democracy in any meaningful sense? After all, a trust is Share in America represented only an indirect claim of ownership. Trust managers mediated investors' relationship to the corporate economy as they passed judgment on the companies considered for investment in the common portfolio. Even in a fixed trust, where managers never altered the portfolio contents, the small investor did not decide for himself which securities represented corporate America's best and brightest offerings. By accepting others' selections and the logic of diversification, did a trust investor exercise sufficient independent judgment or assume sufficient risk to achieve virile economic individuality?

NOT AT ALL, answered retail-oriented brokerages, banks, and investment houses. In the second half of the 1920s, their marketing and advertising asserted that American men could best exercise entrepreneurialism and familial stewardship by investing *directly* in the financial securities, especially corporate stocks. The broad-based practice of investment in the stock market would guarantee that the modern, corporatized economy would remain essentially individualistic, competitive, and entrepreneurial, avowed retail-oriented banks and brokerages. Retail brokerage marketing aimed to redefine how securities markets worked, what purposes they served, and who populated them along these lines. In doing so, these financial institutions advanced the notion that the financial securities markets offer a route to economic equity and security for all.

By 1929 perhaps 3.5 million Americans had opened an account for the purpose of acquiring financial securities with a brokerage firm, a bank, a bank's security affiliate, or some other investment firm. First the War Loans, then the corporations' customer- and employee-ownership plans, provided convenient coattails for banks and brokerages to ride. As major corporations attracted shareholders, retail brokerages aimed to capture their interest and to sell them other securities. In Boston, Kidder, Peabody assumed that AT&T and Bell Telephone Securities Co. publicity had piqued the interest of telephone subscribers and the firm solicited them via direct mail. In some cases, corporations outsourced customer-ownership campaigns, offering banks and brokerages a list of customers and a percentage of the capital raised. "WHY NOT BUY STOCK AND BECOME A PARTNER IN THE BUSINESS," Kidder, Peabody demanded of Edison Illuminating Co. customers. "LET YOUR DIVIDENDS PAY YOUR ELECTRIC BILL."[25]

As banks, securities affiliates, investment houses, and brokerages gained clients, they sought to orient "the investor" toward a political agenda of economic conservatism. Retail brokerages and their advertising agents appreciated the way in which customer- and employee-ownership had enhanced public attitudes toward particular corporations, shifted labor relations toward managerial advantage, and refuted calls for regulation and government ownership. Financial industry commentators anticipated that the broad distribution of a *range* of securities would yield "the greatest assurance of law and order yet developed in the nation." When Everyman possessed "something to lose by social upheavals," financial executives and advertising agents contended, social stability would be ensured. Securities investment fortified "the position of the individual, obviating the possibility of his becoming a public charge in his old age, stabilizing his thinking, stimulating his enterprise, and improving his sense of civic responsibility," in the words of an anonymous Kidder, Peabody publicist. Citizen-shareholders would reject deleterious political experiments, whether government takeovers of particular corporations or larger radical agendas, such as state-based social insurance or full-blown socialism.[26]

To realize their vision of mass investment, banks, securities affiliates, brokerages, and investment houses not bound by NYSE censorship policies experimented with new media, especially radio. Halsey, Stuart and Company's "Old Counsellor" radio program made no direct reference to the firm or to particular securities. Instead, Old Counsellor delivered "simple" and "nontechnical" precepts of "investment education" and profiled the executives of corporations whose securities were distributed by Halsey, Stuart. "Inspirational talks given in connection with Labor Day, Decoration Day, Fourth of July" yielded the "heaviest returns" in terms of inquiries. On these occasions, Old Counsellor "linked up investments with the spirit of the times," no doubt referencing Share in America and Back of It All tropes first developed in the War Loan campaigns.[27]

But when retail brokerages aped the Back of It All convention—exposing the vast, complex wonders of modern corporate production—they effaced the visages of labor and the state, once showcased in War Loan imagery. The National City Company (affiliate of National City Bank) inserted the figure of the securities salesman instead. He appeared as gatekeeper for those wishing to seize their direct stake in corporate America.

The shareholder-colossus seemingly mastered, and profited from, corporate enterprise, yet he still required the securities salesman's guidance. How could citizen-shareholders exercise true economic independence in the financial realm if they depended upon others' advice? The National City Company sought to resolve this paradox by portraying their salesmen as dedicated personal advisers or counselors. The financial adviser's expertise lay in his ability to draw out a better, objective understanding of *the client.* Financial advisers allegedly derived their expertise more from their "broad experience in meeting the needs of thousands of other investors" than from the study of thousands of securities issues. To customize a strategy for each distinct investor, staff analyzed corporations, yes, but also clients' "present holdings, personal income, and future plans." The financial adviser recommended securities to match the investor's past and present economic experiences with aspirations for the future.[28]

Thus, the investor and his financial adviser crafted a unique, individual economic self as they assembled a unique, personalized investment portfolio. Just as much as the physical body, this financial self required individualized, regular, direct monitoring by a professional. Kidder, Peabody advertisements, for example, urged readers to consult with "financial advisers just as often" as the "family physician" in order to "make sure . . . that your financial assets are in good order." As an extension of the individual self, the investment portfolio—rather than a farm, a profession, or a small business—could serve as a new locus of masculine economic identity, individuality, and independence. In contrast, the investment trust share offered only a partial, standardized, indirect claim on a shared basket of investments, according to those promoting retail brokerage service.[29]

In the early twentieth century, corporations sought to redefine the meaning of masculine success, for the enduring entrepreneurial ideals viewed corporate employment with suspicion, as Clark Davis has shown. Corporations articulated two defenses for salaried work. First, individual employees could achieve an equally valid form of masculine success by ascending the "corporate ladder." Second, corporate salaries and benefits conveyed economic security far better than did entrepreneurial pursuits. Promotions and pensions served as the new markers of personal economic freedom, according to corporate employers.[30]

In some cases, retail brokerage marketing mirrored this very image of the ambitious corporate ladder-climber. In the hopes of attracting corporate managers as clients, National City Company, for example, celebrated the ways in which "skilled" managers' mental labors—their "brains and experience"—enhanced the value of employers' stock. The investing activities of Halsey, Stuart's "Capable Young Executive" evidenced his diligence, foresight, and fitness for promotion. Yet, this ad also hinted that securities might allow this young man to step off the corporate ladder. He might "capitalize" his "earnings as a preparation for a larger opportunity" outside of the corporation. The content of retail brokerage marketing suggests that white-collar employees in the 1920s continued to look beyond their employing corporation toward other avenues and other definitions of masculine economic success, individuality, and independence.[31]

Yet the New Era's burgeoning consumer delights presented formidable competition for financial securities advertisers. Around mid-decade, they began to follow the lead of War Savings, U.S. Government Savings, and the customer-ownership movement by associating the practice of investment with future consumption. "Save to spend" marketing campaigns hinted that diligent investment permitted greater consumption in the future, consumption that might even transgress class boundaries. "Good bonds," for example, enabled the foresighted father to treat his family to an edifying excursion abroad, depicted in one National City billboard advertisement. And yet, by associating investment with consumption, "save to spend" themes raised the same gender problematics as customer-ownership. Moreover, increasingly obtainable consumer credit offered an easier bridge between current purchasing power and heart's desire.[32]

Retail brokerage marketing sought to reconcile consumers' indulgent impulses with the ideal of masculine abstemiousness by advancing particular idealizations of modern retirement. In doing so, financial marketing at once reflected and influenced evolving attitudes toward—and expectations about—life in old age. Ever since 1880, thanks to rising real incomes and generous Civil War pensions, the number of Americans working after age sixty-five had been diminishing, while the number of elderly living independently of family had been increasing. By the late 1920s, Americans had deliberated over the best means of achieving economic security in old age for at least a generation. The meaning of retirement and ideas about the proper way to achieve that goal remained up for grabs. Increasing use of both corporate and veterans' pensions along with progressive reformers' calls to make economic security a right of the elderly—which pushed many states to introduce old-age pensions in the 1920s—all helped to construct retirement as a social ideal, even expectation.

In the later part of the 1920s, financial marketers drew upon but embellished this new ideal, presenting investment in the stock market as the best route to retirement. Banks and brokerages contended that only through financial securities could men secure the means—and the right—to retire, which they defined as the cessation of labor and indulgence in an extended period of self-betterment and cultured leisure. "In later years," income from investments conveyed "the privilege of leisure and culture," the "time to think and read and ponder and dream," Caldwell and Company explained. If a man steadfastly earned, denied, and invested over the course of his lifetime, he eventually secured both justification and "an income sufficient" to indulge both "needs" *and* "whims." This portrait of retirement reconfigured economic independence as a stream of future investment income distinct from work, rather than individual proprietorship or familial support.[33]

Brokerage marketing suggested that independent men secured their families' well-being less through the work they performed than through the investment portfolio they left behind. Securities markets enabled perpetual stewardship of descendants, brokerage marketing intimated, in contrast to the standard payments that corporations, insurers, or the state might deliver to immediate heirs. Only financial securities could enhance and then fix the social class of future generations. Indeed, as returns compounded "to the end of time," the investor achieved financial immortality, according to brokerage Ames, Emerich and Co. In an investment portfolio, "income coming from sources outside" one's "own efforts" might just "last forever." Pension payments could not compete with such lavish fantasies, even if novice investors rarely achieved old-age extravagance and financial eternity. Allegedly, only the appreciation of stocks held any potential to improve Everyman's standard of living in future years, or at least to maintain future participation in a burgeoning consumer culture. So while brokerage marketing often showcased bonds in order to signal the safety of investment, stockownership implicitly stood at the center of these prescriptions for how to achieve financial immortality and old-age abundance.[34]

Jazz Age banks' and brokerages' depictions of retirement denied the emotional and bodily complications and dependencies of old age. It renounced the responsibility of younger generations for older ones. The notion "that when parents have grown old, it is the duty of children to care for them" undermined "the independence of parents" and deterred "the progress" of children "in the building of their own lives," asserted one financial advertising agent. Each breadwinner must accumulate sufficient capital for "independence in old age." Another agent recommended that banks and brokerages "illustrate the use" of securities by depicting "father and mother busily plan[ning] the future." Their wise investments protected "the smiling baby in his crib." No other kin complicated the happy tableau. Even when *Coast Investor and Industrial Review* recommended "a variety of sound investments" as "a thoughtful Christmas present" for elderly parents "too proud to admit" their "dependence," the stock and bond certificates arrived by mail. Financial instruments replaced physical and emotional attendance in financial firms' conceptualization of retirement.[35]

Alternatively, the recurring theme of retirement sought to stoke anxiety over old-age dependency. While professionals might enjoy a comfortable standard of living in their working years, no corporate employer would provide professionals with a pension, instructed brokerage marketers. "We are impractical, educators not businessmen," lamented "The Teacher" in an ad for "Building-Loan" shares. As a result, teachers rarely retired as comfortably as they deserved. Similarly, "a Nurse" wished she "had also studied finance" so she could retire and "forget sick people." The "Building-Loan" series warned the nurse, the teacher, the doctor, and the architect that only income from financial securities could maintain retired professionals.[36]

Even as the possession of an investment portfolio redefined American manhood, a women-in-the-market trope suggested that the stock market truly mirrored the post-Nineteenth Amendment polity. In the 1920s, retail-oriented banks and brokerages hired female brokers and advisers. They opened special "women's departments," offered "elementary courses in finance" to women's clubs, and purchased ads in ladies' magazines. But perhaps more significantly, the *idea* of ladies' acquiring securities—the trope of women-in-the-market—underscored both the modernity and inclusivity of the Great Bull Market of the late 1920s.[37]

Behind the scenes, financial securities advertisers acknowledged that the demand for securities by women was partly driven by the rising numbers of financially independent women, particularly female professionals. Yet retail brokerage marketing far more often cast women-in-the-market as modern wives and mothers. Their interest in financial markets made them more intelligent and interesting companions for their husbands as they helped to build a better financial future for their progeny. In the 1920s, social scientists charted the emergence of a new marital ideal, one premised on mutual emotional fulfillment and geared toward egalitarian partnership. If modern marriage aimed at "partnership," the *Ladies Home Journal* advised, then it involved a "business" component, along with "emotional" and "child-rearing" dimensions. Thus, the women-in-the-market harnessed shifting marital and gender norms to suggest the modernity of investment without challenging traditional gender roles. Whatever successes women-in-the-market might achieve, they only bolstered the evolving institution of lifelong, heterosexual marriage.[38]

Indeed, banks, securities affiliates, brokerages, and investment houses most often cast the securities salesman-adviser as the widow's trustworthy spousal substitute, offering assistance with the "bewildering burden" of inherited wealth. The stated goal was to maintain the economic shelter that husbands had erected to insulate wives from economic vicissitude, *not* to secure her *own* Share in America. In this articulation of the trope, a woman-in-the-market treaded the financial waters in which she found herself, seeking to avoid the necessity of earning her "own living" after a husband died.

Even when the women-in-the-market trope celebrated female investors, brokers, and advisers, marketers and commentators sought to defuse any radical implications these figures might pose. *Ladies Home Journal* allowed that financial success and independence made female stockbrokers pickier choosers on the marriage market. But they aspired to marriage and nonworking motherhood all the same: "'this idea of a wife's working . . . you can't share babies with bonds.'" In the end, by encouraging the minor transgression of gender conventions in opening a brokerage account, women-in-the-market provided the securities investment with a touch of avant-garde gloss. The trope certainly did not aim to inspire female financial independence apart from father, husband, and marriage. After the Nineteenth Amendment bestowed suffrage upon American women, women-in-the-market imagery could safely signal the democratic inclusiveness of the financial securities markets without raising more problematic issues of race, ethnicity, or class. Indeed, minorities never appeared in financial securities advertising, which always figured women-in-the-market as middle- or upper-class white women, consistent with minorities' general absence in consumer advertising of the period. And after the Great Crash of 1929, women-in-the-market provided a ready explanation for the erratic instability of the stock market.[39]

THE IDEOLOGY of shareholder democracy promulgated by both corporations and financial firms in the 1920s envisioned an economy and politics built around mass investment in the stock market. Shareholder democracy associated the acquisition of corporate stocks with the exercise of economic freedom and individuality. 1920s stock distributors in both the corporate and financial sectors promised that the stock market would universalize property-ownership, democratize corporations, provide security in old age or unemployment, and liberate the innate entrepreneurialism of the American male. These shareholder democrats avowed that universal stock investment would equitably distribute the benefits of corporate capitalism and stabilize the economy. Whether it was espoused by corporations, banks, brokerages, or investment trusts, the ideology of shareholder democracy embedded in Jazz Age stock marketing championed the stock market as a means to achieve key social goals. Ideologists of shareholder democracy all ignored the demands for corporate governance reform, securities market regulation, and labor or consumer activism put forward by William Z. Ripley and other loyal critics of the New Proprietorship. Instead, Jazz Age corporate stock distributors urged Americans to renounce the regulatory or welfare state as an agent for managing economic risk across society.

Still, the ideology of shareholder democracy was not static or monolithic. As voiced by distinct actors in varied contexts, it took on different nuances. At the height of the Jazz Age, financial firms elaborated upon the old-age security theme. Banks and brokerages asserted that private markets offered the best mechanism for individuals to attain security and independence in advanced years, thereby positioning their vision of shareholder democracy against both the welfare state *and* the welfare capitalism of corporate stock distributors. Responsible individuals would never fall back upon, or rest contented with, collective solutions, their marketing contended. The predefined, fixed amounts paid to a retiree by a government or corporate pension, an insurance policy, or even a bond portfolio too strongly associated future standard of living with the contributions made in the working years.

Of course, analysis of marketing images and slogans only reveals so much. We cannot know how investors received these messages, or whether they actually inspired Americans to buy a share or to open an account. Perhaps every single new investor in the 1920s ignored corporate stock distributors' appropriations of War Loan and New Proprietorship conventions. Perhaps novice retail investors simply acquired stock in the hopes of a quick killing, and their decision held no deeper political or cultural significance. However, it is difficult to imagine that the constant repetition of shareholder democracy themes by a broad range of corporate stock distributors played no role in shaping demand, that is, in framing public understanding about what made stocks desirable—what social needs and political problems stock ownership might address. We should not underestimate corporations' and financial firms' efforts to redefine political liberty and economic autonomy in terms of financial securities investment. Nor should we dismiss their promotion of individual, market-based actions over collective, state-based programs as a solution to the uncertainties of modern capitalism.

The ethos of shareholder democracy embedded in Jazz Age stock marketing was attractive—indeed, powerful—because it conceded that corporate capitalism and mass consumer culture might erode democratic political traditions if citizens no longer exercised any claim of ownership over the means of production. The shareholder democracy ideal proved attentive to certain drawbacks of industrial corporate capitalism and mass consumer culture. It frankly acknowledged the tensions that existed between producer and consumer, labor and capital, small proprietor and big business. It offered corporate stock as the antidote to these antagonisms, as the only solution consistent with quintessential American commitments to private property and private initiative. Shareholder democracy ideology highlighted, then promised to resolve, particular shortcomings of the ascendant corporate order: the white-collar worker's loss of a sense of entrepreneurialism, the problem of old-age security, and concern over the viability of political democracy in the face of concentrated wealth and power.

In the 1920s, corporate and financial leaders offered the middle and working classes access to instruments of corporate wealth but withheld the levers of real economic power. Participation in the stock market, after all, warranted no input in corporate policy and required significant disposable income. Despite promises of affordability, democratization, and redistribution, mass investment could only yield a one-share–one-vote polity—and only a metaphorical one, at that. The dream of shareholder democracy, therefore, held little real potential for substantially reshaping the contours of economic power in the United States.

Still, the pervasiveness and the appeal of the shareholder democracy ideology encouraged broad-based corporate stockownership in 1920s. Moreover, corporate stock distributors' efforts supported a political culture that rejected state-based solutions to problems of economic equity and security in favor of broad-based participation in privately administered financial securities markets. By the Crash of 1929, the political outlook of "the investor" had been aligned with a conservative agenda. This could not have been predicted at the close of the Great War.

Even so, if the New York Stock Exchange had never revised its institutional identity, mission, and message to promote a culture of mass investment, the shareholder democracy ideal might have never amounted to anything more than a sales pitch.

CHAPTER NINE

"The People's Market"

WHEN R. T. H. HALSEY retired from the New York Stock Exchange in 1923 to devote himself to the completion of the American Wing at the Metropolitan Museum of Art and the renovation of the White House, he felt confident that the NYSE Committee on Library had navigated the Stock Exchange through its worst crises successfully. Halsey believed that his new role as curator and trustee of the Metropolitan Museum complemented his work as an Exchange governor. Against the "influx of foreign ideas utterly at variance with those held by the men who gave us the Republic" that inundated the nation, the two institutions Halsey held most dear upheld "the traditions so . . . invaluable in the Americanization of many of our people to whom much of our history has been hidden in a fog of unenlightenment."[1]

The Exchange had come a long way during R. T. H. Halsey's stint as the chairman of its Committee on Library. The Committee had met the challenge of the Pujo hearings in 1912–1913, as well as the very serious prospect of federal securities markets regulation immediately following World War I. Then there was the suit filed by opera star Mme. Alda in 1917 against Halsey's close colleague, William C. Van Antwerp, which had embarrassed the Exchange considerably. Alda had alleged that Van Antwerp "represented that his firm had exceptional facilities for advance information as to the impending course of the stock market and would . . . put the plaintiff in upon the ground floor" in a plan to manipulate the stock of International

Nickel. On account of the scandal, Van Antwerp sold his Exchange seat. Jason Westerfield—a paid, nonmember employee—took his place on the COL; he was soon promoted to director of publicity. NYSE members Seymour L. Cromwell, E. H. H. Simmons, and James C. Auchincloss also joined the COL after World War I. Together, Halsey, Westerfield, Simmons, Cromwell, and Auchincloss narrowly steered the Stock Exchange through its worst public relations crisis to date: NYSE member Allan A. Ryan's brazen corner of the stock of Stutz Motor Car Company in the spring of 1920.[2]

Faced with disciplinary action, the charismatic Ryan revived demands for exchange regulation. NYSE commission houses were outraged to watch the governors squander all the goodwill built up in the War Loan drives. Faced with mutiny, the Exchange leaders granted two concessions to their commission house members. First, steps were taken to crush the Consolidated Exchange, the NYSE's greatest competitor for the burgeoning business of retail brokerage. Second, a new Committee on Publicity—which replaced the Committee on Library—revised Exchange public relations to support the commission houses' pursuit of retail investors. After 1921, the New York Stock Exchange presented itself not only as the "free and open market"—as it had since 1913—but as "the people's market" (mimicking Louis Brandeis, "the people's lawyer"). It seized upon universal stock-ownership as its raison d'être.

The crisis provoked by the Stutz affair—not an obvious opportunity for profit—catalyzed a change in institutional course that supported an expansion retail brokerage by NYSE firms. It provided NYSE commission houses with sufficient leverage to convince the governors that corporate stockholders would become political sympathizers and that national networks of NYSE brokerages could offer a conduit for the Exchange's finance-centered variant of laissez-faire. In the 1920s, NYSE members extended brokerage service—and billions of dollars in credit—to retail investors in the hopes of forging political affinities.

As in the prewar period, Stock Exchange public relations engaged issues far beyond its own self-governance. Exchange emissaries promulgated a very specific version of shareholder democracy ideology. In many ways, it resembled the arguments about corporate stock ownership that suffused the stock marketing of corporations and financial firms in the 1920s. Like customer and employee shareownership plan boosters, investment trust sponsors, and nonmember retail-oriented banks and brokerages, the Exchange recast the corporation as a democracy of shareholders, America as a nation of stockowners, and the stock market as both an analog and an instrument of political democracy and economic justice. NYSE publicists also upheld shareholder return as the proper goal of economic policy and corporate governance. The Stock Exchange concurred that Everyman could best preserve his political stature and economic stake in a modern, corporate-dominated political economy as a shareholder. And like so many 1920s corporate stock distributors, the NYSE reworked War Loan conventions and New Proprietorship ideals.

Unlike other shareholder democracy ideologists, however, the New York Stock Exchange placed its own ability to self-govern, free from all government interference, at the center of its vision of shareholder democracy. The NYSE presented the stock market as a means to achieve key social goals— the preservation of economic liberty, the assurance of economic security, the democratization of corporate capitalism—but it rejected any suggestion that citizen-shareholders might benefit from any measure of state oversight. Instead, Exchange envoys urged Everyman to renounce the state as an agent for managing economic risk.

In the 1920s, the Stock Exchange distinguished itself as the most resourceful apostle of shareholder democracy. NYSE public relations made use of its commission house members' branch networks, the national Better Business Bureau system, and new forms of mass media. It took advantage of perennial public fascination with Wall Street, promising to unveil all the mysteries of modern finance. The Exchange also differentiated itself as the most resolutely laissez-faire promulgator of shareholder democracy ideology. After Armistice, the National Association of Owners of Railroad Securities and some advocates of the New Proprietorship had integrated organized labor and a more activist model of the state in their investor-centered theories of political economy. But by the end of the decade, the Stock Exchange anti-regulatory agenda would be heard the loudest. They would also prove the most enduring.

The question at the heart New York Stock Exchange public relations in the 1920s—whether laissez-faire financial markets or the modern liberal state can best promote economic equity and security—has echoed in American politics throughout the twentieth century. Faced with financial calamity and growing inequality, twenty-first-century Americans debate it still.

THE PRICE of Stutz Motor Car Company common stock began a sharp ascent in January 1920. It soon attracted short sellers, who borrowed the stock and sold it, believing the price would drop in the future. If it did, they could repurchase the stock at a lower price, return it to the lender, and pocket the price difference.

However, Stutz shares *rose* to $391 by March 31. The NYSE's Committee on Business Conduct (CBC) summoned member Allan A. Ryan, president of Stutz, to discuss rumors of a corner, a form of stock market manipulation in which one party gains control over the supply of stock. Ryan revealed that he now controlled 80 percent of the shares and had acted as lender to all those now short. Ryan had cornered Stutz! To settle their contracts, the squeezed shorts would need to purchase Stutz shares *from* Ryan to cover the shares they owed *to* Ryan. Ryan dictated his terms: $750 per share. When Stock Exchange governors threatened delisting because Stutz shares no longer enjoyed "a free and open market," Ryan *increased* his "offer" to $1,000. In response, the governors—publicly committed to the impossibility of such manipulation—suspended trading in the common stock of Stutz Motor Car Co. They declared outstanding short contracts void, refused to negotiate settlement, and told Ryan to seek his remedy in the courts. A battle for the hearts and minds of the small investor had begun.[3]

Hoping to build support for the governors' actions, the NYSE reported that only small investors had been caught short. The *New York Times* found "hardly any particular glory to a corner which merely trapped small traders" rather than "some large operator who would have to pay dearly." The *New York Post* approved the governors' decision to suspend Stutz, surmising that Ryan had been playing "with marked cards." The NYSE scored a victory in the first round.[4]

In response, Ryan confessed to manipulating Stutz's stock price but asserted that he acted only to prevent others from driving the price down. He insinuated that certain *NYSE governors* had led this attempted bear raid. Ryan reassigned the stereotype of the small investor as a greedy, skittish lamb to his short adversaries. "They have no sense of genuine values. They're automatic alarmists, like a flock of sheep." Ryan decried the tepid patriotism of his foes: "buy production, build it up, remember you are living in America and go ahead regardless of the fools who sell real values short on passing flurries." Amidst unprecedented levels of union membership and ongoing strike activity, Ryan audaciously mocked Wall Street's bearish attitude toward labor activism. "Start . . . a strike rumor, for instance, and they'll all start short selling, in full expectation that the bottom is dropping out of the country."[5]

Ryan referenced older producer-oriented theories of political economy as he rhetorically aligned himself, shareholders, workers, and managers against elite, parasitic financial raiders. Ryan claimed he "started with nothing" and "made every cent" by building Stutz from scratch, although in truth his father, Thomas Fortune Ryan, had amassed a fortune in insurance and mass transit. Stutz's buoyant share price properly reflected tangible assets, skilled workers, and "what American opportunity combined

with initiative and right management can accomplish." Ryan offered this
managerial philosophy as justification for the costliness of Stutz shares:

> Keep your dividends down and put the surplus back into the business . . . As
> long as fixed dividends and interest changes stand against your earnings your
> President will have to be working partly for the capitalists . . . when he ought
> to be working solely for production . . . Treat everyone square as another,
> whether your workmen, your partners, your managers or your stockhold-
> ers, . . . I won't stand for any destructive raiding, . . . I have twenty thousand
> stockholders and they're going to be protected.

In truth, an indeterminate number held 20,000 *shares* of Stutz.[6]

The controversy over the proper price of Stutz shares reveals the lack of
a shared analytical framework for determining the value of corporate
stocks in 1920. If broad, national, impersonal securities markets required
the development of a shared analytical framework for estimating the value
of securities, as financial historians suggest, then public debates between
Allan Ryan and the NYSE about the proper price of Stutz's shares demonstrate just how tenuous this process remained in 1920.[7]

Thanks to his savvy management of the press, newspapers now turned
in favor of Ryan for protecting Stutz stockholders "from the raids of 'bears' "
who sought to drive the "market price far below its real value." The Stutz
episode became a national sensation when papers across the United States
picked up the story of a loyal Midwestern Stutz customer who had sold her
shares (purchased at $40) to desperate shorts for $701 at auction. Woman-
in-the-market had bested the Wall Street bear raider! Meanwhile, Exchange staff grew anxious about possible political consequences. "You
aren't the only one worried over the Stutz developments," NYSE Director
of Publicity Jason Westerfield wrote to the Exchange's lobbyist in Washington, D.C.[8]

On April 24, those short of Stutz stock settled with Ryan for $550 per
share, fearing the courts might overturn the Exchange governors' voidance
of their contracts. Allan Ryan then resigned his NYSE membership and
called for "the incorporation of the New York Stock Exchange to be governed by law for the good of the investing public." Issuing from the mouth
of a member, Ryan's critique of self-policing—alleging that the CBC refused
to enforce settlement conventions, but applied rules prohibiting corners
selectively—could not have been more noxious. Just as Exchange leaders
feared, papers across the nation began to call for the incorporation of the
NYSE under a state or federal charter, in order to curb the "menace of irresponsible power in high places" and to take "control of the country's investment markets" out of "the hands of a private club."[9]

Refusing his resignation, the Stock Exchange governors expelled Allan A. Ryan. Yet the NYSE remained caught in a public relations corner, trapped by the governors' adamancy regarding self-governance and their assurances about the impossibility of manipulation. NYSE publicists secured little coverage as they protested that the "Stutz Market Wasn't Free" and that the governors had acted judiciously. Some editors, like those of the *Globe,* backed away from Ryan when the COL threatened to order NYSE members to withdraw their advertisements. But the press assault against the Exchange only subsided in the wake of the anarchist bombing at the corner of Broad and Wall in September.[10]

Although Ryan declared bankruptcy in July 1922 and dropped a $1 million defamation suit against the NYSE in 1925, that institution paid dearly in public esteem and internal discipline. Congressmen and state legislators specifically cited the Stutz corner as they introduced bills to regulate the NYSE and even to ban "speculation in stocks and bonds." The Stutz debacle also threw momentum behind veterans' bonus bills, many of which were to be funded in part through a stock and bond transfer tax, intended to simultaneously curtail speculation. Working with the National Association of Manufacturers, Exchange leaders struggled to prove the fiscal folly of the bonus and to rally commission house customers to write legislators in opposition. Nonetheless, thirty-eight states passed bills. In New York, voters approved a referendum in November 1920. When the U.S. Senate Finance Committee finally invited NYSE representatives to testify, Stock Exchange assertions that the bonus would crush its "free and open market" rang hollow in light of the Stutz delisting. Overcoming presidential veto, the bonus bill became federal law in May 1924.[11]

Hoping to save face with the public, who seemed to favor Ryan's account, NYSE commission houses broke with the governors and jumped on the reform bandwagon. The NYSE's largest commission house, J. S. Bache & Co., seconded Ryan's call for incorporation. In truth, commission house dissatisfaction with the governors had been simmering for some time. Since 1913, most of these brokerages had dutifully curtailed business with bucket shops, distributed literature to customers, and interceded with politicians and journalists on behalf of the Exchange. NYSE governors had returned the favor by censoring advertising, then bumbling the Stutz ordeal and bonus bill opposition. Now, the CBC faced both J. S. Bache's mutinous endorsement of exchange incorporation law and rampant noncompliance with advertising restrictions. Moreover, the institutional balance of power had shifted. Since the war, the commission houses had amassed both Exchange seats and public esteem. They had, after all, helped Everyman buy his Liberty bonds.[12]

"'What we must give is service to the public,'" these firms insisted. The NYSE could best dissipate agitation for securities market regulation by enlarging the shareholding class, the commission houses asserted. More was at stake than potential profits or the prospect of regulation, according to these firms and their advertising agents. Their demands for a shift in Exchange policy pitted democracy, private property, and privately administered securities markets against the global scourge of scarlet-tinged statism.

> The modern democratic world comes face to face with extreme radicalism. The age-old right of private property will be challenged by communism. That challenge was heard in the Senate last week from Senator Borah, who raised the question of government ownership of the coal mines . . . between Daniel Willard and William G. McAdoo, as to what really happened in the government operation of the railways . . . The Exchange is the greatest market for private property in the world . . . when the right of private property is universally exercised it will be universally defended . . . [when corporations] are owned by the public, but on a private ownership basis . . . That will be the time of a true democratic state when industry and finance are democratic as well as government.

According to NYSE commission houses and their agents, the business of retail brokerage stood at the frontlines of a global struggle between capitalism and political democracy on one side, and deadening regulation, statist appropriation, and communist oppression on the other.[13]

Accordingly, NYSE commission houses demanded public relations to attract new citizen-investors lured by competitors—especially members of the Consolidated Exchange—with window displays, billboards, electric signage, novelty giveaways, streetcar postings, direct mail, even motion pictures. Exchange spokesmen should position NYSE self-governance as essential for both the efficient operation of financial markets and the advent of shareholder democracy, where Everyman would attain his birthright "Share in America" in the form of corporate stocks.

Competition with the Consolidated Exchange, which proclaimed itself the "the greatest odd lot exchange in the world," further enraged the commission houses. Due to an old contractual loophole, Consolidated brokers enjoyed access to NYSE quotations. Exchange leaders and members considered its archrival nothing more than a den of bucket shops, pricing trades according to NYSE quotations but charging half the commission.[14]

And although NYSE odd-lot trading (in lots of fewer than 100 shares) also grew after the war, it presented a quandary. At the Stock Exchange, all odd-lot trades ultimately executed through four odd-lot houses at prices up to one-quarter away from the last trade. Both NYSE commission houses and the Committee on Business Conduct reported retail customers' dissatisfaction with odd-lot procedures, for odd-lot trades were often executed at less favorable prices than the full-lot quotations published over the ticker. And much like a bucket shop, NYSE odd-lot firms based prices for customers' orders on the results of prior trades, and *not* in the "free and open" regular market. Exchange governors despaired that they would be able to defend odd-lot procedure if investigated under New York's 1921 Martin Act (which later became Eliot Spitzer's favorite weapon as attorney general). Although NYSE lobbyists could not prevent passage of the Martin Act after the Stutz scandal, they ensured it did not create any commissions to license brokers or to approve new securities. Instead, it enhanced the attorney general's ability to investigate securities fraud. Thus, efforts to distinguish legitimate NYSE brokerage from fraudulent bucketing became even more critical.[15]

The time was ripe for reviving campaigns against bucketeers and swindlers. NYSE governors compensated the commission houses for advertising censorship when they donated $100,000 to launch investors' sections of the Better Business Bureau. Bureaus alerted novice investors—and the attorney general—of get-rich-quick swindles in bulletins disseminated "through banks . . . reputable brokerage concerns and factories." Bureau investigations helped Attorney General Albert Ottinger "search out and punish" Consolidated brokers under the Martin Act. The Consolidated closed its doors in 1926. Bureaus declined to investigate NYSE members or listings, however, forwarding complaints to the Committee on Business Conduct for private discipline. As a consequence, the BBB never commented on many of the greatest swindles of the 1920s: the Van Sweringen, Krueger & Toll, and Insull public utility holding companies, National City Bank's South American bonds, or the inflated and fee-soaked shares of investment trusts.[16]

But the Better Business Bureau provided a valuable talking point for the NYSE. Exemplifying voluntary, cooperative self-governance, the BBB illustrated the inane redundancy of state-based regulation. Boosters stoutly maintained that bureaus acted more quickly and thoroughly than inept, even untrustworthy regulators. Moreover, if swindlers' "innumerable victims" found "relief and protection" with the state, NYSE President E. H. H. Simmons warned, the regulation of "all enterprise" would follow. Government interference in the economy would only "cripple" the "private initiative of a people" and hamper the "dynamic and constructive energies" upon which "national achievement" depended. From whence sprang such pernicious proposals? Simmons's answer suited postwar xenophobia. Surely the "influx of foreign-born immigrants" had introduced this "dangerous" and "wholly different conception of government." The foreign-born sought to "regulate" the "lives and activities of all . . . citizens to the greatest extent and in the most minute detail." But the Better Business Bureau demonstrated how American men could "check the evils to which a free society is subject." Voluntary initiative buttressed the nation against "paternalism," against "state socialism," against squandering the "freedom of business." No matter that NYSE firms largely escaped Bureau oversight.[17]

Funding the Better Business Bureau represented only one way in which the NYSE governors changed course to support their commission houses in the wake of the Stutz ordeal. Restrictions on commission house advertising were relaxed to some degree. Commission houses were no longer limited to business card-like "tombstone" ads, although the CBC continued to reject illumination, billboards, outdoor signage, radio, or anything it deemed too dramatic, too clever, or too ornate. Prognostication about price movements in a particular security and macroeconomic economic forecasting were forbidden. Members could not suggest "speculative possibilities" or promise particular returns—at least not in writing.[18]

Most importantly, the governors revised NYSE public relations to support members' retail brokerage. The Exchange's on-site library closed and a new Committee on Publicity (COP) pursued six measures: press relations, publications, hosting, academic relations, speaking tours, and motion pictures. Director of Publicity Jason Westerfield (a salaried nonmember), COP Chairman James C. Auchincloss, and NYSE Presidents Seymour Cromwell and E. H. H. Simmons led the charge, along with R. T. H. Halsey until his retirement in 1923. These publicists amended the sobriquet "people's market" onto the prewar "free and open market" concept. They heralded universal ownership of corporate stock—traded on unregulated securities markets—as the key to an equitable distribution of prosperity, the democratization of corporate power, and the modernization of proprietary democracy. Far from quashing independence and entrepreneurialism, the "people's market" conveyed economic power to citizen-shareholders, NYSE spokespersons averred.

FOR R. T. H. HALSEY and his fellow NYSE governors, the Stutz affair confirmed that Americans lacked adequate knowledge "about Wall Street as it really exists," preferring to accept Allan A. Ryan's "delusion" that "'the insiders' and 'the interests'" engineered "price-swings" at "the cost of the investing and speculating public." Nor could Americans recognize "fraudulent financial operations." The "misguided" financial reformer, the swindler, and the bolshevik all preyed upon rampant economic illiteracy. All three inflamed "passionate hatred" of American "social, political, and economic institutions." After 1921, the NYSE Committee on Publicity devoted itself to *"preventative educational activity"* to counter all "the lies and sophistries" about the American political and financial system. Meanwhile, members also aimed to solicit political sympathy for the Stock Exchange as they extended brokerage service—and billions in credit—to novice investors.[19]

To ferret out pernicious mistruths, COP staff monitored coverage and portrayals of the NYSE, its members, and relevant political issues. The Hearst papers warranted close attention, given their support of the bonus bill and securities market regulation, as well as their charge that Wall Street firms had engineered the First World War to protect their investments in Allied bonds. The COP also tracked rural papers, for leading proponents of exchange regulation hailed from agricultural districts. But Henry Ford's *Dearborn Independent,* distributed through Ford dealerships, drew the most scrutiny. Like Allan Ryan, Henry Ford denied any link between legitimate corporate enterprise and the manipulative machinations of mere stockbrokers. He dismissed the notion that the stock market acted as a "barometer of business." Just as betting on a horse "adds neither strength nor speed," Ford held, stock price fluctuations bore no relation to corporate performance. "Ideas, labor, and management" constituted "the principal ingredients in industry," Ford avowed. These found "natural expression" in "utility, quality, and availability" of product, not in stock price or even dividends. Indeed, Ford had never offered stock to the public. His management model combined closely held ownership, high wages, small profit margins, high sales volume, and expansion funded with retained earnings. One of the most respected men in the United States, Ford identified mass consumption—dependent upon the robust purchasing power of workers—as the best route to corporate profits and national economic vibrancy. For the NYSE, Ford's formulas for corporate governance and political economy placed the wage, price, and retained-earnings cart before the return-to-shareholders horse. According to the Exchange, increasing shareholders' returns constituted the proper goal of both corporate and state policy.[20]

To counter Ford and to improve the tenor of media coverage, COP staff delegated "assignments" to favored journalists, reached out to new financial magazines, and obliged friendly journalists with interviews, tours, and free luncheons. The NYSE greatly increased its publication volume in the 1920s. Its direct distribution list ultimately totaled nearly a million.[21]

The Stock Exchange became far more hospitable in the 1920s. Gallery visits and trading floor tours were offered to groups perceived as potentially hostile: out-of-town bankers, farmers' groups, state securities commissioners, and Democratic National Convention delegates. The Exchange also opened its doors to several thousand individuals each month and to organizations convening in New York City. "After standing in the gallery and looking down into the pit," one Kansas Odd Fellow confessed he "knew just about as much of what was going on" as "before the visit, which was absolutely nil." But he grasped the main point: "bucket shops located everywhere . . . were illegitimate and brought odium upon the Stock Exchange."[22]

More than any other group, the COP sought out educators and students, allegedly misguided purveyors of "fluffy-minded internationalism and camouflaged communism." The average high school or college student knew nothing of "the absolute interdependency of all the elements" of the "economic structure," spokesman Jason Westerfield lamented. The COP distributed literature and films on "the principles of sound investment" and "economic fundamentals," highlighting "the equal opportunities enjoyed by and guaranteed to every citizen under our democratic form of government." It dispatched delegates to high schools, educators' conventions, and religious assemblies to attract young men to work at the NYSE. Recruiters portrayed Exchange employment as a path to a financial career and as a "Moral Force" in "the Building of Proper Manhood," rather than a descent into gambling hell.[23]

Despite all its emphasis on education, the Exchange offered precious little practical instruction in how to analyze or select securities. "How about investigating a stock promotion? How can it be done? This question needs no answer. The man qualified to speculate will not ask it." That arcane art retained its mystery. Novice *investors* ought to seek the guidance of a "reputable" banker or NYSE broker and buy shares in local, "known" enterprises. This advice, of course, failed to address outsiders' lack of information about the men controlling the modern, national, hierarchical corporation.[24]

What guidance could an investor expect from a NYSE broker? "Smith's First Investment," published by the NYSE to dramatize "with sufficient realism" a new investor's "experience" and the process of an "actual" transaction, proved telling. Because Smith wished to invest $10,000, the drama did not involve the more complicated and controversial odd-lot trading process. The play begins when customer Smith enters a NYSE brokerage admitting ignorance and loss in a bucket shop failure. Johnson concurs with Smith's choice of U.S. Steel, but fails to explain whether the ask of 97 represented a good price at which to buy. Instead, the scene shifts abruptly to a conversation between Bill, a messenger delivering Smith's order, and Johnny, a clerk recording the transaction.

Bill: I've been thinkin' about this business, and readin' the newspapers, an' I
    know it's all run by the "insiders" and the "interests" . . .
Johnny: But who are these big interests? Name a few of 'em.
Bill: I don't know who they are. But they run it all, just the same.
Johnny: I suppose that stock you're deliverin' was bought by "the big interests."
Bill: Sure it was.
Johnny: You're going to deliver to Wilkins & Co. They get orders on their
    wires from all over the country . . . If you'd ever worked on the books of
    a wire house, as I have, you'd know that most of the orders in the market
    come from outside New York, and that all this stuff about "the interests"
    and the rest of it is a bunk . . . You'd better do is study the business
    harder, instead of swallowing whole everything that you read or are told.

In the end, the true lesson of "Smith's First Investment" was not investment analysis but the revelation of a shareholder democracy—one dependent upon the self-governed facilities of the New York Stock Exchange—
heretofore invisible to the bumpkin Bill.[25]

ALTHOUGH they characterized their efforts as purely educational, NYSE
representatives sought to preempt regulation, to promote members' brokerages, and to ensure a steady flow of loans to members. After 1921, Exchange spokesmen retraced the routes of many a War Loan speaker. The
institution depicted as a ravenous serpent in the nineteenth century now
ordered its envoys to the heartland, where they sipped from the loving cup
at the local Elks lodge. NYSE Presidents Seymour L. Cromwell and E. H. H.
Simmons addressed trade, finance, industrial, and professional associations in large cities. Director of Publicity Jason Westerfield visited professional and business organizations, high schools, and colleges in small cities
and towns in upstate New York and the Great Plains, Midwest, South, and
West. These regions traditionally favored blue-sky laws and exchange
regulation. In the 1920s, they saw intense competition between NYSE and
nonmember retail brokerages.[26]

As they had since the Pujo investigation of 1913, publicists portrayed
the Exchange as the "free and open market." NYSE speakers continued to
deny the possibility of stock market manipulation, championed the utility
of speculation, and positioned speculators as key economic intermediaries.
They continued to celebrate the Exchange as the nation's central economic
institution, reiterating a synecdoche that conceptualized the stock market
as both the entire national economy and the piloting apparatus of the
NYSE.

But after 1921, Exchange emissaries newly endorsed universal stockownership. They encouraged Everyman to exercise economic self-determination,

to participate in economic modernity, and to claim his stake in corporate prosperity by investing in corporate stocks through the "people's market." In the Exchange's particular version of shareholder democracy ideology, *unregulated* securities markets functioned as both an analog and an instrument of political democracy and economic justice.

In the 1920s, the citizen-shareholder assumed center stage in the NYSE public relations. Spokesmen contended that the Exchange operated a *direct* referendum, a kind of national town hall meeting that determined the value of each listed corporation and delivered a "daily health report" on the "state of modern American capitalism." Spokesmen avowed that only the "people's market"—the privately administered NYSE—could instantiate a shareholders' democracy by enabling Everyman to claim a stake in corporate enterprise in the form of a share. Its ambassadors credited the NYSE with the comfort and abundance of modern consumer culture, with the preservation of entrepreneurial opportunity, with bridging ancient social cleavages, and with the assurance of macroeconomic stability. Time and again, Exchange publicists decried regulation as an elitist plot: "the public has infinitely more to fear from the arbitrary actions of a few men in artificially 'regulating'" the stock market than from "the average judgment and courage of the whole people of the country." Any rationale for state oversight of the financial securities markets was dismissed as an elitist attack on citizen-shareholders. The state could only constrain the market, the true sphere of freedom.[27]

The NYSE avowed the prices pouring from the ticker registered votes in a *direct* economic democracy. No manipulative pool of insiders could "oppose successfully" the "collective judgment" of the "vast investing public," NYSE President Simmons swore (despite the fact that NYSE members continued to orchestrate manipulative pools). However, any "artificial attempt" by the state "to control and regulate" securities prices would "pervert and interfere with" citizen-shareholders' verdicts. When NYSE brokerages lent Everyman funds to open a brokerage account, they did not entice him into dissolute gambling. Rather, these firms nurtured financial self-determination, the Exchange insisted. If Exchange firms denied margin to *any* of "the public," it would stymie the NYSE's mission to promote stockoownership among all Americans.[28]

Stock Exchange spokesmen imagined an analogous "representative form of government" inside each listed corporation. Although the separation of corporate ownership from control drew increasing attention in the 1920s thanks to the work of Harvard economist William Z. Ripley, it did not trouble the NYSE. Indeed, publicists rejected the notion that state oversight could improve corporate disclosure or governance, as Ripley and other loyal critics of the New Proprietorship had argued. "However necessary it may be to restrain the unwise or unfair management of capital," it would "never do for the State to hamper and inhibit" the market's natural process of self-correction. Financial markets rectified corporate mismanagement as dissatisfied citizen-shareholders sold out and invested elsewhere.[29]

Similarly, Exchange emissaries brought the small investor to the fore as they asserted that corporations could never meet their capital needs without NYSE facilities. Through the agency of the Exchange, corporations tapped the "savings of the people," using the masses' funds to secure "the successes of industry and applied science and all the comforts and ameliorations" of modern life. "Do you patronize the 5-and-10 cent store?" asked NYSE Director of Publicity Jason Westerfield.

> Do you use the telephone and the telegraph . . . automobiles, tires and accessories, fertilizers, agricultural machinery, canned goods, chewing gum, drugs, leather goods, shoes, lead, and copper? If you do, you are benefiting from service that would be impossible without accumulated capital; and the greatest agency for efficient, safe and economic accumulation of capital is . . . the New York Stock Exchange.

In an era of mass consumption, "there scarcely a thing you do—there is not a puff of smoke you draw—for which you are not in some degree indebted" to the Exchange, he concluded.[30]

Even as households in the top 1 percent of the national income distribution increased their share of national income from 14.8 to 22.4 percent, as unemployment grew among unskilled workers, and as the agricultural sector languished, Jason Westerfield dismissed the widening gap between rich and poor. The NYSE contrasted the *average* standard of living quite favorably against the dark, hunger, filth, disease, and warfare of the pre-corporate age, which Westerfield equated with the Middle Ages. Referencing Edward Bellamy's classic futuristic utopian novel *Looking Backward* (1888), Westerfield advised "looking backward" to "measure the distance mankind" had *already* traveled "on the road to betterment" under corporate capitalism. A few decried "industrialism," but "the great body of people" embraced corporate capitalism every time they purchased consumer goods or invested in shares of consumer goods companies. Moreover, Westerfield claimed, the NYSE had narrowed the gap in regional living standards by delivering capital to the rail and utility industries. In truth, however, states had contributed a great deal of capital to these sectors historically. And as Exchange agents circulated in the 1920s, railroads and utilities sold shares directly to customers and employees, raising considerable capital and enlarging the American shareholding class *without* the aid of NYSE brokerages.[31]

In the 1920s, many progressive thinkers asserted that the political economy should be organized on behalf of consumers. Like Henry Ford, they viewed robust mass purchasing power as essential for a vibrant national economy. The Stock Exchange concurred that proof of economic efficacy could be found in the pudding of consumer plenty. However, it placed the small investor in the driver's seat of the national economy.

> A textile mill with its hundreds of steel fingers . . . [h]ow many see beyond the machines . . . to the sources of their creation? First is the individual investor who, through work and self-denial, has saved money . . . If the project appeals to an investment banker . . . he and his associate[s] . . . will advance the money.

Jason Westerfield demanded "due recognition" for the "investment agencies," which converted "savings" into the "machines and power" that produced "former luxuries" for Everyman. But instead of accolades, the "Forgotten Factor" of finance (a homage to William Graham Sumner's "Forgotten Man") received only insult from an ever-grasping state.[32]

The NYSE rejected any suggestion that consumption might be sustained or enhanced by Hooverian planning, public works spending to stimulate employment, or a strong labor movement (or Fordist concessions) to bolster wages. Despite cosmetic integration of consumerist language, unregulated capital supply best stimulated consumer demand in the Exchange's fundamentally investor-centered model of political economy. "The machinery of finance" had enabled humanity to "wring" an "abundance" from nature. It would continue to do so if left alone.[33]

In the 1920s, the Exchange disparaged traditional notions of proprietary democracy, the American political ideal that equated possession of the tangible means of production with citizenship and manhood. What red-blooded American man would rest satisfied with a petty proprietorship when, someday, his bright idea might be admitted to the Big Board? Regulatory interference, of course, would "strangle" this avenue of upward mobility and dam generative flows of finance. Without the NYSE, innovation would wither "in obscure and humble workshops." Moreover, workers could expect "starvation" to "solve the problem of excess labor with neatness [and] dispatch" if regulatory constraints discouraged financiers from funding entrepreneurs' employing enterprises. Traditional proprietorship simply proved unviable. Inevitably, modern entrepreneurs recognized the "superior" qualities of incorporation—legal personhood and perpetuity, limited liability—and sought an NYSE listing so that "the public" could "be taken into partnership" in a stock offering. In contrast to the corporate commonwealths listed on the NYSE, partnerships and privately held corporations (like Ford Motor Co.) were, in the Exchange's estimation, atavistic, autocratic forms. Yet every NYSE firm was organized as a partnership, and the unincorporated, associational Stock Exchange flourished alongside the corporations whose shares NYSE members traded.[34]

Stock Exchange spokesmen also erased proprietors and partnerships from their version of the nation's economic history past, as well as its future. They elevated the assumption of risk—rather than the possession of property, skill, or labor—as the essential, most enduring attribute of American citizenship and masculinity. "America has been a pioneer country," NYSE president Simmons declared, "involving heavy risk and constant speculation." Not farmers but the shareholder exhibited that same "old spirit" when he risked his "bank balance" in the stock market, just as his "grandfathers risked their lives." The nation's "essential pioneer spirit" had not passed away, Simmons affirmed, but the "form which the spirit" assumed had changed its shape. The achievement of universal stockownership should palliate Turnerian anxieties about the impact of frontier closure on American character.[35]

Exchange spokespersons contended that large publicly traded corporations and the NYSE itself, in fact, embodied individual economic self-determination, an ethos purported to be endangered by the incipient welfare state. As states added worker's compensation and pensions for impoverished women and elderly in the 1920s, the NYSE devised a gendered critique of the welfare state. Westerfield decried all of them as a "drift toward paternalism," a "delusion that government is the source of all blessings" or "a fairy godmother whose magic wand" could "banish" the necessity of industry and thrift. Only ignorant immigrants felt animosity toward the financial system, "established government," and "the successful," Jason Westerfield sniffed. With lies about "barriers . . . to success," the foreign "demagogue and agitator" destroyed a man's "power to rise by instilling self-pity." Acquisition of stock through private markets could meet every social need, without any redistribution of wealth or socialization of economic risk.[36]

Misguided nostalgia for traditional proprietorship left American farmers particularly susceptible to paternalism, Westerfield warned. They had fattened on wartime contracts and postwar federal relief, the NYSE maintained. In 1920, the Federal Farm Loan Act interjected the federal government into the farm mortgage business, while the 1929 Agricultural Marketing Act authorized $500 million in loans to agricultural marketing cooperatives. Exchange envoys recommended that farmers wean themselves from the state, corporatize their cooperatives, and seek NYSE listing. Privately administered securities markets *alone* best directed the concentration and circulation of capital, they contended. The Exchange found no reasonable cause for farmers to resist corporate consolidation—ironic, given NYSE resistance to its own incorporation and the partnership form taken by its member firms.[37]

With this proposal to corporatize American agriculture, the Exchange revealed its deep suspicion of Herbert Hoover's "associative" model of the state—the notion that if firms, business associations, and government agencies voluntarily shared data and coordinated strategy, then economic stability and growth could be ensured. Hoover supported cooperative marketing to rationalize food markets and preserve independent farms. The NYSE feared he might seek to rationalize other kinds of markets. The Commerce Secretary's vision of state-facilitated (but privately conducted) macroeconomic planning alarmingly implied inefficiency in private, "free and open" markets.[38]

If noncorporate business forms had fallen into the dustbin of history, how could the American male exercise his innate entrepreneurialism? The Exchange recommended he ask his stockbroker. The NYSE claimed a new mission in the 1920s: the advancement of shareholder democracy, a modern form of proprietary democracy distinguished by universal shareownership. Exchange representatives obscured the role of financial institutions and the importance of corporate employee and customer-ownership plans in spreading stockownership in the 1920s, however. Instead, they posited a direct link between the Stock Exchange and the American investing public. By "providing at all times a free and open market where shares can be bought and sold," the Exchange "played a prominent and vital part" in the "tremendous widening" of corporate stockownership.[39]

NYSE orators emphasized that expanded shareholding necessitated no new regulations, contrasting the freedom and openness of the people's market with any alternative "outside market" (that is, purchase from nonmember firms or from the issuing corporation) and, most especially, with state regulation. "To plunge" the NYSE into "politics" with regulation would "destroy it," and "at the same time destroy industrial, financial and economic efficiency" along with any prospect of shareholder democracy. Only Soviets dared "a government under which speculation would not be permitted." Exchange officials offered their self-administered institution as the prime instantiation of both private property and "free government."[40]

Those speaking on behalf of the Stock Exchange during the Roaring Twenties vacillated between pronouncing shareholder democracy a fait accompli and heralding the *imminent* arrival of the financial millennium, "when the average American will be a capitalist and security owner as well as an employee." Aping Allan Ryan, NYSE orators deliberately exaggerated the prevalence of shareholding to imply that the economy had democratized already. They thereby blurred the *potential* for broadened stock ownership to reform capitalism with the *realization* of economic democracy. This left a range of questions unanswered. Was this a one-share–one-vote model of shareholder democracy consistent with a one-citizen–one-vote model of political democracy? Must every American own stock? In how many corporations? How dispersed should the ownership of a corporation be? How could shareholders ensure that corporations were operated according to their interests? Were the best interests of shareholders monolithic? Were they identical to the best interests of the political nation? NYSE ambassadors remained silent on these issues.[41]

Instead, they simply envisioned that as the "real public"—the "real capitalist class"—emerged, any "likelihood of class struggles" withered away. The "perennial quarrels of capital and labor," corporation and proprietor would dissolve without union intermediation, state intervention, or any appreciable alteration in existing relations of power. In this "democratic type of capitalism," shareholders' returns constituted the prime consideration in matters of corporate governance and economic policy.[42]

Historians contend that in the 1920s, the progressive concept of "the public"—a unified polity sharing a common good toward which the state, advised and administered by impartial experts, should devote itself—lost traction in American political culture. Wartime propaganda and vigilantism—along with postwar labor strife, nativism, and consumerism—convinced some, like writer and commentator Walter Lippmann, that Americans were too easily manipulated, too ill informed, and too fractured. As progressive notions of "the public" languished, the NYSE promised it would forge "the public" anew through universal stock ownership. Shareholder democracy would never involve—rather, it would substitute for—class conflict and the emerging system of interest-group politics. Once upon a time, economists like John Bates Clark, Jeremiah Jenks, and Richard Ely, as well as progressive financial reformers like Louis Brandeis and Samuel Untermyer, had imagined that universal stockownership would *require* a strong regulatory state. In the 1920s, as the NYSE urged Americans to identify as actual or potential citizen-shareholders, it specified laissez-faire as the investor's necessary and natural orientation. Although Stock Exchange representatives spoke in populist and progressive idioms, they rejected any and all manner of state intervention into the economy as compromising both efficiency and individual ambition. The NYSE's ideology of shareholder democracy dismissed the state as an agent of risk management, a mechanism for wealth redistribution, and a watchdog for investors.[43]

As EXCHANGE emissaries traversed the nation, the Committee on Publicity distributed celluloid dramatizations of shareholder democracy to NYSE members, their correspondents, and a range of nonprofit exhibitors. Encouraged to screen in their branches, Stock Exchange commission houses thrilled to these clever customer lures. In 1928, the NYSE's most popular film debuted. *The Nation's Market Place* materialized the shop floor and crossroads of industrial capitalism. "By providing a free and open market for securities where all might buy and sell with perfect equality, the New York Stock Exchange has played a tremendous part in the building of America." Smoking factory chimneys, a spewing forge, whirling gears, trains lifted aloft and barreling down the tracks, a massive steamship coasting into harbor, all testified to what the securities markets had wrought. "Back of it all stands the unparalleled industrial and financial America whose progress and prosperity are reflected in the Nation's Market Place." Here, the NYSE referenced the Back of It All imagery of the War Loans, but it removed both labor and the state.[44]

Inside the Exchange, neither brimstone nor farm animals could be found. Instead, a scrum of traders quivered on the trading floor. "There is a slight 'flurry' in [U. S] Steel. At first glance it seems like hopeless confusion, but under the apparent chaos there is order and efficiency." The corporation that Samuel Untermyer had once excoriated as "the greatest enemy to industrial peace in America" was cast as the iconic investment in a shareholders' democracy.[45]

On the floor, traders act as mere agents of average folks. In Tacoma, Washington, James Blair orders shares of "Mountain High" on the phone, conjuring the visible hand of his broker. Another investor in New Orleans places an order to sell in the branch office of a NYSE commission house. "Thus the machinery is started which enables Tacoma and New Orleans to buy and sell in the Nation's Market Place." Widely dispersed yet acting in concert, retail investors summon a series of mechanisms and a host of clerks to do their bidding: from phone to broker to clerk to operator, over wire, to operator to clerk to tube to runner to post to trader, then back again. At last, "the trade is made without witnesses or signed contracts. Each broker's word is sufficient" in accordance with the highest moral standards. Transaction complete, a price is born, writ up on the board, spewed out on the ticker.

Capitalizing upon long-standing popular yearning for revelations about Wall Street's inner secrets and the meaning of its exorbitant confusion, *The*

Nation's Market Place revealed a marvelous, democratic truth. The Stock Exchange's national network of members' offices, brokers, and clerks—linked by tubes, telegraphs, tickers, and telephones rather than by snakes' coils—existed only to execute the will of Everyman, everywhere. True, the NYSE helped to corporatize the U.S. economy, but behind large corporations stood only small shareholders. The financial securities markets appeared as a field of economic activity distinct from the corporations whose shares traded in those markets. The markets administered by the NYSE at once erected the corporate order and stood apart from that order. So, too, did the citizen-shareholder. In the "people's market," Everyman competed on equal footing with all other investors; the NYSE empowered the entrepreneurial individual to exercise initiative and autonomy in the financial realm. Under the aegis of the self-governed New York Stock Exchange, competitive capitalism and proprietary democracy would endure, *The Nation's Market Place* seemed to promise.[46]

Like many corporations in the period, the Stock Exchange used new mass communication technologies in an effort to mold public opinion and to increase sales. Like them, it, too, defined democracy and equality as equal access to identical products (in this case, stocks). Yet the Exchange subtly undermined concurrent corporate public relations initiatives, celebrating financial markets in contrast to corporate hierarchies. Even as it claimed credit for rising standards of living under corporate capitalism, the NYSE ingeniously leveraged criticism of corporations to build a case for its own legitimacy and for the desirability of stockownership. The ideology of shareholder democracy embedded in Exchange public relations implied that corporate capitalism might undermine democracy if citizens lost all connection to property ownership. The distribution of corporate stock by NYSE brokers was presented as the restorative for economic democracy in the industrial age.[47]

IN 1928, NYSE Director of Publicity Jason Westerfield took stock of the Exchange's efforts. Because the NYSE had materialized and humanized "the business of finance," the "public" would never again believe "the old nonsense that the members are assembled in some sinister conspiracy, against the public interest." Citizen-shareholders now understood that any regulatory interruption of "free traffic" over the "invisible highways" of finance would "instantly" produce a "corresponding halt" in all other economic activity. Now educated, the investing public would ever "guard" the "machinery of finance" against "crude interference and demagogic attacks," Westerfield boasted. At the time, he appeared correct.[48]

Federal and New York State blue-sky bills were defeated in 1921 and 1923. Better Business Bureau and Martin Act investigations shuttered bucket shops and Consolidated brokerages. Hundreds of new NYSE commission house branch offices replaced them; the total number nearly tripled between 1920 and 1929. Even the humble inhabitants of Ponca City, Oklahoma, and Paris, Illinois, enjoyed the services of a local branch of a NYSE firm. Several members operated truly national retail brokerage networks. Hundreds of corporations had introduced employee and customer stock ownership plans to address their own particular public relations needs. NYSE brokerages stood well positioned to take advantage of the resulting growth of the investor class. Upon the eve of the Great Crash, 1.5 million Americans held trading accounts with brokers holding membership on the nation's organized exchanges. And, of course, beginning in 1926, the stock market soared. The Dow Jones Industrial Average nearly doubled between March 1928 and September 1929 alone.[49]

Much like recent bubbles in the stock and housing markets, the Great Bull Market of the late 1920s depended upon credit. NYSE brokers borrowed heavily, expending these brokers' loans in their own speculations or lending on to customers who wished to trade "on margin." In 1928, the gargantuan volume of outstanding brokers' loans—$6 billion to NYSE members alone—provoked considerable criticism and prompted the Federal Reserve to raise interest rates in 1928. This action only increased the proportion of funds lent by nonbank entities, especially corporations. From the floor of the U.S. Senate, Robert La Follette Jr. (Republican-Wis.), Hendrick Shipstead (Farmer-Laborite, Minn.), and J. Thomas Helfin (Democrat-Ala.) all condemned loans to brokers. Proposals to restrict brokers' loans appeared in Democratic and progressive Republican platforms in 1928. In February 1929, the Federal Reserve counseled member banks to limit loans to brokers and again raised the discount rate in an attempt to discourage borrowing by brokers by increasing their costs of doing so.[50]

In response, NYSE president Simmons aimed to sustain stock prices by encouraging more lending to brokers. To justify stock market levels and brokers' loan volume, he characterized the Exchange as the "balance wheel of commerce," appropriating a term that Herbert Hoover had used to describe countercyclical public works projects. As the multitudes invested in corporate stocks, Simmons contended, they secured stable prosperity, for their funds fortified NYSE-listed companies against any future "business depressions and money market troubles." The "socialistic fallacies" of wartime economic planning had not secured this victory over the business cycle, nor had the "widespread movement to gather and compile statistics" coordinated by Hoover's Commerce Department. Rather, Simmons explained, American citizen-shareholders achieved economic stability as they acquired shares through the self-governed "people's market." It proved more efficient and more democratic than any scheme that academics, government regulators, or corporate executives might concoct. Although "the business cycle" had "ceased to operate," Simmons warned that "commercial and industrial stability" would collapse if any "artificial restraints" were placed on stock prices or brokers' loans. Why proceed on "purely theoretical or dogmatic grounds to kill a goose that has been laying golden eggs?" he asked.[51]

In speeches delivered in the last late-summer days of the Great Bull Market, Simmons construed the raging stock market as a register of universal confidence in a New Era of economic democracy and prosperity. Even as market commentators, economists, politicians, and the Federal Reserve all expressed concern about stock market levels and the volume of outstanding brokers' loans, Simmons advised both retail investors and the institutions that lent to NYSE brokers to ignore eggheaded prognosticating pencil pushers. "Economic soothsayers or any small group of experts" only sought "autocratic control" over citizen-shareholders.

> The American people are neither mentally nor morally unfit to manage the prosperity they have created. I refuse to believe [they] are less able to exercise the prerogatives of economic and financial freedom than they are to use wisely political freedom . . . We do not need panaceas or artificial legislation. Mere pride of supposedly expert opinion must yield place before the hard facts of a new society. The universal thrift and intelligence which have created the progress and prosperity of American business will continue to manage and administer it.

How could anyone "indict a whole nation" for their collective rush into the stock market?[52]

Throughout the 1920s, NYSE representatives perceived avowedly pro-business Republican administrations as threatening the Exchange's image and autonomy. Despite its status as a self-governing association—that lynchpin institution of Hooverian "managerial government"—the New York Stock Exchange steadfastly refused to ally with the state.[53]

IN THE AFTERMATH of Allan Ryan's corner in the stock of Stutz Motor Company, it seemed almost certain that the New York Stock Exchange would lose its self-governed status. Instead, by 1929 the NYSE had emerged as both the nation's leading securities exchange and an icon of a New Era in American capitalism. Moreover, Stock Exchange members dominated a vastly enlarged market for retail brokerage—a market that NYSE public relations did much to encourage.

The year 1921 was a turning point. Before 1921, NYSE members struggled to develop a shared political orientation. After the Stutz debacle, they propagated that orientation, shaping American political culture as they developed the market for retail brokerage. The governors did *not* change course and begin to promote mass investment because the retail market presented an obviously lucrative business opportunity for NYSE members. Rather, the governors sought to appease disaffected commission house members whose branch networks offered an ideal conduit for the Exchange's specific variant of shareholder democracy ideology.

Although the governors of the New York Stock Exchange altered their attitude toward retail brokerage in the wake of the Stutz affair, in many ways NYSE publicists simply extended initiatives launched nearly a decade before, in the wake of the damning Pujo report. In the several years on either side of the Great War, Exchange authors and orators accomplished a tremendous amount of ideological work. They labored to refigure the stock market as an instrument and instantiation of democracy in response to prewar progressive and corporate liberal proposals to regulate securities exchanges, the wartime state's oversight of capital markets, postwar proposals to retain federal interventions into the economy, Fordist models of corporate governance, and, ultimately, Herbert Hoover's associative state.

The early twentieth-century public relations initiatives of the New York Stock Exchange laid an intellectual foundation for modern economic conservatism. Its spokesmen propagated two precepts that would echo in the twentieth century and early twenty-first century. First, that *if left free of state-based regulation,* financial securities markets best allocate capital and economic risk while facilitating every individual's quest for economic opportunity, prosperity, and security. Second, that return-to-shareholders must be treated as a central objective of economic policy and corporate governance. Stock Exchange antistatism did not *react* to modern liberalism. Rather, it *anticipated* the passage of federal securities market regulation and the expansion of the welfare state under the New Deal.[54]

The Enduring Quest

I N OCTOBER 1929, the ideology of shareholder democracy and the project to enlarge the American shareholder class met a severe crisis in the worst stock market crash in U. S. history. Nonetheless, the incidence of equity-ownership in the United States has consistently exceeded that of other nations, never dropping below 10 percent of households. Ownership of the typical publicly traded corporation in the United States has remained more diffuse than in corporations located in other countries. Belief in the primacy of shareholders has retained its influence in ongoing debates over the proper relationship between the financial markets, the state, and the real economy. The institutions, practices, and ideas examined in this book both shaped modern liberalism *and* sustained those who sought to roll it back. The legacy of mass investment and of shareholder democracy ideology has been at once ambiguous and profound.[1]

I N the 1920s, shareholder democrats allowed that Everyman *should* invest in stocks. Analogies linking market and nation, corporation and polity, trade and vote, shareholder and citizen had implied—often quite unintentionally—that the state might owe the investing public some consideration. Ironically, then, the shareholder democracy ideal offered an entering wedge for the regulatory state. In fact, the most enduring legacy of the New Deal may be the Securities and Exchange Commission (SEC), which aims to safeguard retail investment, not to sustain aggregate demand or to protect producers as in other New Deal–era programs and agencies.

And yet, the New York Stock Exchange managed to shape the parameters of New Deal securities market regulation. Despite post-Crash investigations—including NYSE president Richard Whitney's conviction for larceny—the Stock Exchange retained a significant degree of autonomy by orchestrating the first large-scale mobilization against the New Deal. Initial financial reform bills entertained prohibitions on short selling, brokers' loans, and trading on "margin"; the separation of specialists' broker and dealer functions; the segregation of investment banking from brokerage; even the abolition of specialists and floor traders (that is, all NYSE members *except* commission houses executing the trades of the "investing public"). Some New Dealers, including Rexford Tugwell and Adolf Berle, even proposed that the state influence the volume and circulation of financial capital, along the lines of the wartime Capital Issues Committee.[2] In response, the NYSE Committee on Publicity—the "most vicious and persistent lobby ever known," according to one reform bill sponsor—determined to "rally the conservatives of the country." It persuaded sympathetic press, the National Association of Manufacturers, the Chamber of Commerce, the Investment Banking Association, NYSE commission house customers and employees, executives of NYSE-listed corporations, and regional exchanges to enjoin congressmen against establishing "a form of nationalization of business and industry which has hitherto been alien to the American theory of Federal Government."[3]

As a result, the Stock Exchange became a *self-regulatory organization* under the Securities and Exchange Act of 1934. As a private, not-for-profit association, it continued to select and police members and to fix commissions. The SEC declined to regulate the NYSE directly or to break up its concentrated economic power. The federal government would monitor the playing field for its investor-citizenry only indirectly, simply aiming to ensure that outsider investors enjoyed equal, timely access to truthful corporate data and equal treatment from their brokers. In the words of Commissioner John Landis, the SEC sought only "disclosure in the hope that an informed public have both the ability and independence to guide the direction of national savings . . . [and] investment can most profitably still be a matter of private choice." New Deal agencies and policies acquiesced to Exchange assertions of expertise, indispensability, and democratic access. They accepted as fact the theory that self-governing financial securities markets ensure the optimal distribution of economic resources and risk. They envisioned that shareholders—if informed adequately—could govern the actions of corporate executives. In 1900, these claims would have struck most Americans as ludicrous, as preposterous as the sight of NYSE members dancing the cakewalk on New Year's Eve.[4]

Yet despite New Deal deference to investors and financial institutions, the faithful adherents of shareholder democracy could be counted among the most stalwart holdouts against modern liberalism from the darkest days of the Great Depression through the Reagan revolution and beyond. After 1932, economic conservatives struggled against the notion that the federal government held responsibility for maintaining stable economic growth and ensuring the broad distribution of its benefits, the expectation that the federal fiscal and monetary policy should maintain mass purchasing power and support the demand side of the economy (as recommended by the theories of economist John Maynard Keynes), the creation and expansion of an economic safety net for citizens, and the power of organized labor. In opposition to modern liberalism, a significant cohort continued to promote stockownership and to assert the three tenets of shareholder democracy: first, that mass investment democratizes corporate capitalism and preserves entrepreneurialism and independence; second, that shareholders' interests warrant prioritization by managers and policy makers alike; and third, that economic resources and risk are best distributed when securitized and traded on privately administered markets.[5]

After the theories of John Maynard Keynes came to dominate both the Harvard economics department and national economic policy, Thomas Nixon Carver moved west and veered right. In the 1930s, Los Angeles businessmen flocked to hear Carver proselytize for individual thrift and investment, population control, and immigration restriction as the proper path to national economic salvation. In 1946, Carver helped to establish the nation's first libertarian think tank, the Foundation for Economic Education (FEE). Styling itself as the "spearhead of an active crusade for the return of the principle of freedom of enterprise," FEE sought to incite a "revolt" against modern liberalism, which Carver's colleague Leonard Read characterized as a set of "political devices and ideas incidental to government in the role of *master*." Social Security came under sharp criticism as an "affrontery" to "liberty and responsibility," inimical to the true "sources of security—individual and family responsibility, self-discipline, private enterprise, and voluntary" savings and investment. When the Mont Pelerin Society first convened in 1947, FEE dispatched a delegation second only in size to that of the University of Chicago's economics department. FEE also supported the work of Henry Hazlitt, whose best-selling books and columns in the *Wall Street Journal, Newsweek,* and *New York Times* steadfastly maintained the primacy of investors and investment, deriding Keynes and his adherents for failing to appreciate the ability of securities markets to allocate economic risk and resources correctly and to preserve economic freedom. Hazlitt's writings introduced American readers to Austrian economists Ludwig von Mises and Friedrich von Hayek, who characterized free markets—in contrast to the modern liberal state—as the last best hope against the twin menaces of communism and fascism. And all throughout the 1930s and 1940s, the New York Stock Exchange proudly proclaimed itself the "citadel of Conservatism," excoriating the New Deal for disregarding the "three cardinal instruments of recovery: Provide adequate incentives for private enterprise! Grant management the maximum of freedom! Restore confidence to capital!"[6]

In the years immediately following the Second World War—the high point of organized labor in the United States—American corporations reintroduced employee stockownership plans, especially for employees not covered by collective bargaining arrangements. Much like the Taft-Hartley Act, the "economic education" campaigns of the National Association of Manufacturers and the Chamber of Commerce, and corporate welfare offerings such as pensions and health insurance, ESOPs aimed to check union strength, to limit regulatory incursions, and to contain the welfare state. As early as 1957, 77 percent of the corporations listed on the New York and American stock exchanges offered employee stockownership plans (for executives, at least). In addition, the investor relations department became a standard fixture of the postwar corporation, routinizing communications from management to shareholders in the hopes of fostering political sympathy. Good relations with shareholders, advised Alfred P. Sloan Jr. of General Motors in 1950, cultivated a "fertile field" of "knowledge . . . and consistent support" for a corporation's policies while "promot[ing] and support[ing] the capitalistic system" against the forces of "regimentation, socialization or something worse."[7]

For its part, the New York Stock Exchange contributed to the postwar renaissance of free enterprise ideology and middle-class investment by inviting Everyman to "own your own share." After Merrill Lynch and other NYSE brokerages rediscovered the retail market during the bond drives of World War II, the Exchange revived its efforts to support members in their quest to increase stockownership. In 1954, NYSE president G. Keith Funston stressed the supreme "importance of a broader base of corporate ownership" for "improving the climate for business operation . . . enlighten[ing] the electorate" and "strengthen[ing] our country against the onslaught of foreign ideologies." Even as postwar corporations turned to internal sources and commercial banks for funding, the Stock Exchange continued to assert that "equity capital . . . primarily supplied by individuals" constituted the "foundation of all business activity" because stock prices governed "the overall flow of capital investment" while stockownership preserved the economic "initiative and freedom" of individuals. In materials supporting member firms' marketing, in communications before corporate executives and educators, in literature produced for members' customers and for the shareholders of listed corporations, in radio and television appearances, and in testimony before legislators, NYSE representatives engaged in a "ceaseless effort to impress the fact upon the general public" that the American way of life depended on a "steady and ample flow of private capital" from individuals into the stock market.

As the Exchange promoted "people's capitalism" after World War II, it revivified investor-centered theories that anticipated the supply-side economics of the Reagan revolution.[8] Keynesian economic policies and welfare programs destroyed incentives for savings and investment, the Stock Exchange asserted, while enormous federal budgets crowded out private investment and raised interest rates. Exchange spokesmen promised that slashing the federal budget (especially for social programs), decreasing capital gains and dividend taxes, accelerating depreciation schedules, and reducing both corporate income tax rates and the progressivity of personal tax rates would stimulate investment and improve the allocation of capital. More private-sector investment, in turn, would sustain high levels of employment, yield higher rates of economic growth, enhance Americans' standard of living, and, ultimately, generate more tax revenue.[9]

Echoing the NYSE's postwar "people's capitalism" campaign and harkening back to the New Proprietorship of the Jazz Age, a new generation of writers emerged to validate corporations' and brokerages' attempts to revive mass investment at mid-century. Venture capitalist and economic thinker Louis O. Kelso, philosopher Mortimer Adler, and finance professor Marcus Nadler all upheld the first precept of shareholder democracy ideology: the notion that universal shareownership could regenerate individualism and revitalize democracy. Universal stock ownership would contain the "collectivism" inherent in both communism and unionization, Kelso, Adler, and Nadler alleged. Further, these three predicted, mass investment would alleviate the drudgery and alienation of organizational man. Workerowners would achieve a measure of dignity as individuals in a Fordist political economy otherwise distinguished by hierarchy, bureaucracy, and conformity—something the "creeping socialist revolution" represented by collective bargaining and the modern liberal state could never deliver. Indeed, this critique of modern industrial society shared much with the nascent counterculture and associated stockownership with the economic and existential liberation of the individual once again. Leading management theorist Peter Drucker, for his part, spied in pension funds a potential vehicle for organizing a new constituency of citizen-investors that could confront an increasingly unresponsive, bureaucratic welfare state.[10]

Ultimately, the work of Louis Kelso and Peter Drucker made a tangible and lasting impact on public and corporate policy, encouraging U.S. employers to shift away from defined benefits and toward defined contribution retirement plans for their workers. Kelso worked with Senator Russell Long (son of Louisiana governor Huey Long) in the 1970s and 1980s to revise the tax code to encourage employee stockownership and individual retirement accounts. Kelso also served as an NYSE governor and acted as consultant to languishing corporations, organizing employee buyouts and refinancings.

The primacy of shareholder returns—the second tenet of shareholder democracy ideology—also was reasserted beginning in the 1950s as part of a crusade against the "managerial" model of the corporation. Corporate managerialism sought to balance the financial interests of shareholders with the needs of other corporate stakeholders and society-at-large. High levels of retained earnings, which provided corporations with an internal source of funding that insulated managers from the stock market, made this orientation possible. In opposition, economists Milton Friedman and Friedrich von Hayek, jurist Eugene V. Rostow, and law and economics pioneer Henry Manne all championed the maximization of shareholders' returns. All three celebrated the stock market as a mechanism for imposing discipline on otherwise unaccountable corporate managers. "Few trends" posed as great a threat to "free society as the acceptance of corporate officials of a social responsibility other than to make as much money for their shareholders as possible," Milton Friedman declared. "Self-elected private individuals" must never be allowed to decide "the social interest." Instead, Friedman urged, corporate managers should act as mere agents "of the individuals who own the corporation" and eschew any suggestion that they held any other obligations. Hayek similarly rejected the extension of corporate managers' power "over cultural, political, and moral issues" for which they held neither "special competence" nor legitimate mandate. A proper focus on the interests of shareholders, in contrast, safeguarded "against the acquisition of arbitrary and politically dangerous powers by corporations," Hayek contended. It also prevented the misallocation of corporate capital, Rostow added. Concurring with Kelso and Adler, Hayek and Friedman recommended that corporations be required to pay out a greater proportion of their earnings to shareholders, perhaps even allowing each shareholder to decide what portion of his allotment of corporate earnings he wished the corporation to retain and reinvest. Henry Manne demanded that antitrust laws be relaxed so that the mergers and acquisitions—conducted through the stock market—could dethrone poorly performing executives. Both proposals sought to increase managers' accountability to shareholders.[11]

Many of these writers who resurrected a vision of an economy and a polity grounded in mass investment found happy homes in postwar conservative think tanks, many of which were organized, funded, and directed by prominent individuals in the financial securities industry. After serving as Treasury secretary and chairman of the Economic Policy Board under Presidents Nixon and Ford, William E. Simon of Salomon Brothers helmed the Olin Foundation for twenty-three years, while Walter Wriston of Citibank played a central role at both the Manhattan Institute and the Cato Institute. These institutions brought together businessmen, financiers, academics, journalists, and policy makers to develop and to disseminate a neoconservative agenda centered on the deregulation of the economy and the dismantling or privatization of the welfare state. Writers such as George Gilder, Irving Kristol, J. A. Dorn, and Milton Friedman proclaimed the vitality and centrality of investment. Resurrecting the dream of shareholder democracy, they urged citizens to shed the shackles of the welfare state and turn to the financial markets to amass economic reserves as individuals. For Gilder, the employment-stimulating "financial markets" performed a "crucial alchemy, turning fear into growth, caution into creativity, timidity into entrepreneurship, and the desire to conserve into the drive to build and innovate." Social programs funded by taxes, in contrast, frittered away funds best invested in the private sector, bred dependency, and fueled inflation. Kristol, meanwhile, called upon corporations to organize their shareholders against the regulatory and welfare state. And for his part, Friedman lambasted New Deal securities regulation for increasing the costs of raising capital. He denounced Social Security as a "paternalistic" program that discouraged private saving, misallocated capital, and weakened the family. With the election of President Ronald Reagan, these authors, ideas, and institutions attained considerable influence over economic policy.[12]

The Reagan revolution enjoyed the hearty backing of the financial securities industry. Firms and institutions that once fought to prevent the establishment of the modern liberal state rallied behind the presidential candidate that sought to dismantle it. Frustrated by the unwillingness of Establishment Republicans to rein in a newly activist SEC in the 1970s, the New York Stock Exchange emerged as one of the earliest, most enthusiastic, and most influential supporters of candidate Ronald Reagan. As early as 1964, while campaigning for Barry Goldwater, Reagan had recommended stock investment over Social Security as the best route to retirement. During his failed 1976 bid for the Republican nomination, Reagan reiterated his belief that citizens would be better off if they could invest their otherwise taxed dollars "in the industrial might of America" via the stock market. Attracted to campaign promises of rapid deregulation of industry and tax cuts to favor investment, NYSE leaders and members organized fund-raisers for Reagan, lent the trading floor for speeches, and provided "issue research." By assembling Reagan's Business Advisory Panel, they built an important bridge to the initially skeptical corporate community. Upon Reagan's election, Exchange leaders gushed over the new administration's recognition that "high tax rates are counter-productive . . . federal budgets have to be pared down . . . [and] federal regulations produce a drag on the economy." Reagan's supply-side approach would "help us all," the NYSE predicted, "smoothing the way for more capital investment and higher productivity. The net result then will be more jobs and better-paying jobs."[13]

President Reagan returned their ardor, celebrating the stock market as the heart and soul of American capitalism and democracy. "Open markets, built on the principles of entrepreneurship and stock ownership," enabled all Americans to share "both the risks and rewards" of capitalism and provided "the foundation for the creation of wealth" and the highest standard of living in the world, he told Soviet paper *Izvestiya*. "People's capitalism— free and open markets, robust competition, and broad-based ownership of the means of production" would serve developing nations well, Reagan advised a group of Latin American and Caribbean ambassadors.[14]

Reagan rewarded financial industry insiders and privatization proponents with important positions in his administration. He entertained policies to deregulate financial institutions and markets, to reinvigorate retail investment, to relax antitrust laws, and to raze the welfare state. Before Donald Regan served as Reagan's Treasury secretary and chief of staff, Regan oversaw both an innovative expansion of retail business at Merrill Lynch and the abolition of fixed commissions at the New York Stock Exchange (to encourage mass investment). Immediately upon election, the Reagan administration moved to downsize the SEC in order to eliminate "regulatory barriers to capital formation" and to allow self-regulatory organizations like the NYSE more latitude. "We favor increasing the use of private regulation and decreasing the SEC's authority . . . wherever possible," his transition team declared. Of course, Reagan was the first president to flirt with the privatization of Social Security, appointing influential early proponents of the idea to key posts.[15]

Since the Reagan administration, every major presidential candidate has proposed some degree of Social Security privatization in some form. Even as candidate Barack Obama dismissed George W. Bush's vision of an "ownership society" grounded in widespread securities ownership as "social Darwinism," Obama concurred that individuals *should* "pursue higher-risk, higher-return investment strategies," just with "savings other than those put into Social Security."[16]

Although Social Security has survived these challenges, the dream of a mass investment society came to fruition as increasing numbers of American invested in stocks and stock mutual funds. Tax code changes in the 1970s and 1980s, including the Employee Retirement Income Security Act (ERISA) of 1974, made defined contribution retirement plans (which involve individual investment accounts) tax-advantaged for both employers and employees. At the dawn of the twenty-first century, the majority of U.S. households owned financial securities, and most Americans regarded broad-based investment as legitimate, perhaps even essential, for a vibrant democracy. Given the extent of Americans' participation in the stock market, the Federal Reserve maintained remarkably low interest rates in the hopes that the dot.com downturn could be prevented from deepening a recession in the real economy. This course of action only fueled an asset bubble in housing.[17]

But because so many Americans invested their savings *indirectly* in the stock market, institutional investors like pension and mutual funds emerged as the driving force in the global financial markets in the last third of the twentieth century. By 2000, institutional investors owned nearly 60 percent of corporate equity, with roughly three-quarters of the total stock of the 1,000 largest U. S. corporations held by institutions. Accordingly, institutions wielded increasing ideological and economic leverage over corporate management after about 1970. As institutional investors chased the globe for higher returns, they demanded leaner payrolls. They participated in hostile takeovers that purged corporate boardrooms of management that seemed insufficiently willing to downsize and distribute to shareholders.[18]

These forceful assertions of the primacy of shareholder returns were validated by a new generation of management theorists. In particular, the writings of Michael Jensen encouraged corporate boards to grant an ever increasing proportion of executive pay in the form of stock and stock options, ostensibly to align the interests of executives with those of shareholders. This change in compensation procedures swelled executive pocketbooks relative to workers. By 2004, the ratio of CEO compensation to that of an average U.S. employee stood at 531:1. Stock-based compensation arrangements—along with an active market in corporate control and corporations' increasing practice of buying back their own stock to support its price—all encouraged an orientation toward short-term stock performance that often proved detrimental to the long-term well-being of the corporation, as evidenced in earnings restatements and accounting scandals like Enron, Fannie Mae, and WorldCom.[19]

The third axiom of shareholder democracy ideology was also repackaged in a new academic wrapper in the 1970s when Wall Street traders began to apply the options-pricing model devised by Fisher Black, Myron Scholes, and Thomas Merton to establish prices for derivative contracts. Much like the NYSE's concept of the "free and open market," the Black-Scholes-Merton model assumes that unregulated financial markets serve to aggregate all available economic information into the form of a price. The prices of financial instruments, in turn, offer the best signals for directing economic resources and risk across the national economy. By enabling the originators of complex securities and derivatives (such as those backed by subprime mortgages) to derive prices for those instruments, the Black-Scholes-Merton formula transformed how the financial industry conceptualized and managed risk. Furnished with a price, originating firms could sell a bewildering volume and variety of complicated financial instruments, while acquirers often took on tremendous amounts of debt in the hopes of amplifying their returns on such investments. Ultimately, the circulation of these instruments failed to eliminate, and most likely enhanced, the likelihood of systemic failure in the nation's financial markets. The mathematical sophistication of the Black-Scholes-Merton model lulled policy makers into complacency, even as the unregulated global market for over-the-counter derivatives swelled to $683 trillion by 2008.[20]

As neoliberalism—with its elevation of the investor and finance—replaced Keynesianism as the reigning paradigm of U.S. economic policy after 1980, even economic reformers conceded shareholder value as the benchmark for managerial performance and sought to harness the power of purportedly self-correcting financial markets. "For a market to be truly free and efficient and have the full confidence of its participants, two things are required: integrity and transparency," wrote crusading New York Attorney General Eliot Spitzer as he resurrected the Martin Act to pursue indictments against corporate and financial malfeasants. Similarly, the Sarbanes-Oxley Act of 2002 aimed to improve the quality and quantity of information corporations disclosed in the hopes that adequately informed investors could better oversee executives. But Sarbanes-Oxley failed to provide shareholders with any new methods for disciplining executives. As ever, shareholders could only sell their holdings so that the stock market might signal their lack of confidence in management's course. The restricted nature of economic reform in the neoliberal era is best understood as an enduring legacy of the way in which the early twentieth-century ethos of shareholder democracy has continued to shape basic assumptions about political economy in the United States, rather than a new development dating from the Reagan revolution.[21]

Faith in unfettered finance and the primacy of shareholders' returns—dogma first promulgated by financial securities marketers in the 1920s—inspired the reckless securitization and regulatory laxity of the early twenty-first century. Policy makers and regulators assumed that self-governing financial markets and expert financial actors properly securitize and distribute economic resources and allocate risk to those best able to bear it. Systemic risk, the aggregate amount of leverage, and the possibility of market gridlock or a liquidity crisis were ignored. The results proved catastrophic.[22]

Yet even as the securities and credit markets roiled, policy makers adhered to the axiom that financial markets and institutions constitute the bedrock of American capitalism, and they resolved to preserve them in a privately owned form. The ideology of shareholder democracy continued to condition what could be imagined in the way of bailouts, stimulus, and regulatory reform. In addressing the crisis, both the Bush and Obama administrations privileged the financial sector and deferred to the "expertise of the market," whether using taxpayer money to bail out distressed banks or lending it to private firms in the hopes of jump-starting a market for the unsalable or "toxic" assets on those banks' balance sheets. As of November 2009, over three-quarters of the total amount expended by the federal government to contain the crisis shored up financial institutions and markets; broader stimulus initiatives received less than one-quarter of the total. Proposals for improving the national and international regulatory infrastructure were slow to emerge. Ultimately, the suggestion to bring derivatives onto exchanges to be monitored by self-regulatory organizations stood at the core of the Dodd-Frank Wall Street Reform and Consumer Protection Act of 2010.[23]

While the health of financial institutions drew considerable attention, too few asked why so much faith was placed in finance as the engine of economic growth and stability in the first place. Too few considered the underlying conditions—mounting inequality, households' enhanced exposure to financial markets—that drove so many into so much debt.[24]

The question of whether the liberal state or laissez-faire financial markets best promote economic equity and security has resurfaced as one of the key political questions of the twenty-first century. This book has traced the assertion that self-governing financial markets best promote economic growth, equity, and security to the political and marketing strategies of certain institutions at a specific historical moment. Why should it constrain Americans as they seek solutions to current economic dilemmas? The political orientation and the economic interests of "the investor'" or "capital" are neither timeless nor predetermined. Indeed, the ideal of a mass investment society inspired both demands to expand the regulatory and welfare state *and* challenges to modern liberalism.

Despite the greatest financial catastrophe since 1929, mass participation in the stock market remains a fixture of economic life in the United States. Given their long-standing suspicions toward a robust regulatory and welfare state, as long as Americans struggle to balance equality of opportunity against inequality of outcome, the dream of an investors' democracy will endure.

Yet Americans might reassess broad-based investment as a social, political, and economic goal. Although the dream of investor democracy has supported regulatory reform and managerial restraint at times, it has tended to marginalize questions about the distribution of economic wealth, security, and power. Certainly financial securities have offered millions of individuals a lucrative savings vehicle along with economic fulfillment. But because securities investment requires significant disposable income, the wealthiest segments of society have enjoyed its benefits most. Dispersed shareownership generally renders shareholders impotent to influence corporate behavior. And even when political and corporate leaders have proclaimed investors' interests to be consistent with those of workers, consumers, and communities, initiatives to expand shareholding and claims to speak on behalf of investors most often have aimed to deflect demands made by other parties to the corporation.[25]

Even universal acquisition of financial securities cannot correct inequalities of opportunity in the real economy, or the disparities in social condition and economic power that result. If Americans wish to do so, they must reevaluate not only the policy requirements of a mass investment society, but the very ideal itself. They must engage in a broader debate about what form of political economy is most consistent with their traditions and their values.

Abbreviations

AAAPSS	*Annals of American Academy of Political and Social Science*
ACLRG53	Advertising, Clippings, and Literature Relating to the First, Second, and Third Liberty Loans (Entry NC-120, 624), Records of the Bureau of Public Debt (Record Group 53), National Archives, College Park, Md.
AHR	*American Historical Review*
BBB	Better Business Bureau
BHR	*Business History Review*
CBC	Committee on Business Conduct
COL	Committee on Library
COP	Committee on Publicity
DFH	David F. Houston papers (MS Am 1510), Houghton Library, Harvard University, Cambridge, Mass.
FAA	Financial Advertisers Association
GFRG53	General Files Relating to Liberty Loan and War Savings Bonds, 1917–1925 (Entry NC-120, 622), Records of the Bureau of Public Debt (Record Group 53), National Archives, College Park, Md.
GPO	Government Printing Office
HIT	Edgar Higgins Investment Trust Collection (Mss 783), Baker Library Historical Collections, Harvard Business School, Boston, Mass.
IL	Ivy Lee papers, Seeley Mudd Library, Princeton University, Princeton, N.J.
JAH	*Journal of American History*
KP	Kidder, Peabody and Company collection, Baker Library, Harvard Business School, Boston, Mass.

LOC   Library of Congress, Washington D.C.

LWRG53   Liberty Loan and War Savings Correspondence Files (Entry UD 323), Records of the Bureau of Public Debt (Record Group 53), National Archives, College Park, Md.

NAORS   National Association of the Owners of Railroad Securities

NICB   National Industrial Conference Board

NELA   National Electric Light Association

NP   Walter W. and Lillian F. Norton papers, Manuscripts and Archives, Yale University Library, New Haven, Conn.

NWA   N. W. Ayer Advertising Agency Records, Archives Center, National Museum of American History, Smithsonian Institution, Washington, D.C.

NWLLC   National Woman's Liberty Loan Committee

NYSE   New York Stock Exchange

NYT   *New York Times*

NYW   *New York World*

OK   Otto Kahn papers, Manuscripts and Archives, Firestone Library, Princeton University, Princeton, N.J.

PAPS   *Proceedings of the Academy of Political Science*

PHS   Pennsylvania Historical Society, Philadelphia, Pa.

QJE   *Quarterly Journal of Economics*

ST   *Savannah Tribune*

TWL   Thomas W. Lamont Papers, Baker Library, Harvard University, Cambridge, Mass.

WMQ   *William and Mary Quarterly*

WSJ   *Wall Street Journal*

WW   *World's Work*

Notes

Introduction: The Quest for an Investors' Democracy

1. "Bulls and Bears Frolic," *New York Times (NYT)*, December 30, 1899, 14; *NYT*, "Bulls and Bears in Wild Revel," December 23, 1900, 12.

2. David F. Hawkins, "The Development of Modern Financial Reporting Practices Among American Manufacturing Corporations," *Business History Review (BHR)* 37 (1963), 145.

   By 1929, nearly 1 million employees had acquired employers' stock, at least 1.5 million utility customers had purchased shares in a utility, almost 2 million Americans had acquired shares of investment trusts, and 1.5 million held a brokerage account. An estimated 2 million more acquired stock through bank securities affiliates (National City Company being the most famous). Given that most—but not all—stock ownership would be captured in these five acquisition avenues, 8 million (26.8% of households) seems reasonable (although some replication between categories is possible). National Industrial Conference Board (NICB), *Employee Stock Purchase Plans in the United States* (New York: NICB, 1928), 2, 35–36; Charles Amos Dice, *New Levels in the Stock Market* (New York: McGraw Hill, 1929), 198; National Electric Light Association, *Political Ownership and the Electric Light and Power Industry* (New York: NELA, 1925), 20; U.S. Securities and Exchange Commission, *Investment Trusts and Investment Companies* (Washington, D.C.: Government Printing Office (GPO), 1939–1942), 362, 370; U.S. Congress, U.S. Senate, Committee on Banking and Currency, *Stock Exchange Practices,* 73rd Cong., 2d sess., 1934, 9–10; Thomas F. Huertas and Harold van B. Cleveland, *Citibank: 1812–1970* (Cambridge: Harvard University Press, 1985), 120; Twentieth Century Fund, *The Securities Markets* (New

York: The Fund, 1935), 50, 56–57; Edwin Burk Cox, *Trends in the Distribution of Stock Ownership* (Philadelphia: University of Pennsylvania Press, 1963), 33.

It is assumed that individuals are household heads and that only household heads own stock. As late as 1952, the ratio of households holding stock to individuals holding stock was 0.73 (4.75 million households vs. 6.49 million individuals), so assuming each 1929 household contained *two* stockholders seems unjustified. J. L. Kimmel, *Shareownership in the United States* (Washington, D.C.: Brookings Institution), 89.

The aggregate number of stockowners of record reported by American corporations grew from an estimated 4.4 million in 1900 to 18 million in 1928. These figures do not adjust for individuals owning stock in more than one corporation. Gardiner Means, "The Diffusion of Stock Ownership in the United States," *Quarterly Journal of Economics (QJE)* 44 (1930), 565, 595; H. T. Warshow, "The Distribution of Corporate Ownership in the United States," *QJE* (November 1924), 15–38.

3. The incidence of equity investment (stock ownership either held directly or indirectly, as through a mutual fund, pension, or other retirement plan) peaked at 53 percent of U.S. households in 2001, retreating to 45 percent in 2008. Ownership of any financial securities (either held directly or indirectly) peaked at 57 percent of U.S. households in 2001, falling to 47 percent in 2008. Investment Company Institute and Securities Industry Financial Markets Association, *Equity and Bond Ownership in America* (2008), 6–7.

4. For scholarship that understands efforts to universalize securities investment as a hallmark of neoliberalism, see Adam Harmes, "Institutional Investors and the Reproduction of Neo-liberalism," *Review of International Political Economy* 5 (1998), 92–121; Adam Harmes, "Mass Investment Culture," *New Left Review* 9 (2001), 103–124; Thomas Frank, *One Market Under God: Extreme Capitalism, Market Populism, and the End of Economic Democracy* (New York: Anchor Books, 2000); Randy Martin, *The Financialization of Everyday Life* (Philadelphia: Temple University Press, 2002).

For the dating of the origins of shareholder maximization ideology to the 1970s or after, see William Lazonick and Mary O'Sullivan, "Maximizing Shareholder Value: A New Ideology for Corporate Governance," *Economy and Society* 29 (2000), 13–35; Ernie Englander and Allen Kaufman, "The End of Managerial Ideology: From Corporate Social Responsibility to Corporate Social Indifference," *Enterprise and Society* 5 (2004), 404–450; Dirk Zorn, Frank Dobbin, Julian Dierkes, and Man-Shan Kwok, "Managing Investors: How Financial Markets Reshaped the American Firm," in *The Sociology of Financial Markets,* ed. Karin Knorr-Cetina and Alex Preda (New York: Oxford University Press, 2005); Karen Ho, *Liquidated: An Ethnography of Wall Street* (Durham: Duke University Press, 2009); Gerald F. Davis, *Managed by the Markets: How Finance Re-shaped America* (New York: Oxford University Press, 2009); Neil Fligstein, *The Transformation of Corporate Control* (Cambridge: Harvard University Press, 1990).

5. For the underdevelopment of the U.S. stock market until World War I, see Mary O'Sullivan, "The Expansion of the U.S. Stock Market, 1885–1930: Historical Facts and Theoretical Fashions," *Enterprise and Society* 8 (2007), 489–542;

Leslie Hannah, "The Divorce of Ownership from Control in 1900: Re-calibrating Imagined Global Historical Trends," January 2007, www.e.u-tokyo.ac.jp/cirje/ research/03research02dp.html.

For early twentieth-century anxiety about industrial corporate capitalism, see T. J. Jackson Lears, *No Place of Grace: Anti-Modernism and the Transformation of American Culture, 1880–1920* (New York: Pantheon Books, 1983); Roland Marchand, *Creating the Corporate Soul: The Rise of Public Relations and Corporate Imagery in American Big Business* (Berkeley: University of California Press, 1998); Nell Irwin Painter, *Standing at Armageddon: The United States, 1877–1919* (New York: W. W. Norton, 1987); Robert H. Wiebe, *The Search for Order, 1877–1920* (New York: Hill and Wang, 1967).

On the Seventh Regiment, Sven Beckert, *Monied Metropolis: New York City and the Consolidation of the American Bourgeoisie, 1850–1896* (New York: Cambridge University Press, 2001), 118, 233–34.

6. Noyes quoted in George A. Akerlof and Robert J. Shiller, *Animal Spirits: How Human Psychology Drives the Economy, and Why It Matters for Global Capitalism* (Princeton, N.J.: Princeton University Press, 2009), 66–67; Walter Werner, "Adventure in Social Control of Finance: The National Market System for Securities," *Columbia Law Review* 75 (November 1975), 1233–1290.

7. Jonathan Barron Baskin argues that the key prerequisite for anonymous public markets in common stock was the development of a shared analytical framework "to enable outsider investors better to estimate the value of businesses." However, little evidence suggests that investors' ability to evaluate the "true" value of securities improved much in the first three decades of the twentieth century, or that securities distributors improved the quality of the information they disclosed or made any attempt to assist new investors in developing analytic skills. Baskin, "The Development of Corporate Financial Markets in Britain and the United States," 225; O'Sullivan, "The Expansion of the U.S. Stock Market, 1885–1930."

8. This argument draws upon social and cultural studies of finance that use the theory of performativity to analyze how economic concepts alter economic reality (a performative is a linguistic act that enacts what it names). As agents act in accordance with the dictates of financial or economic theory, markets become more consistent with those theories. Alex Preda, *Framing Finance: The Boundaries of Markets and Modern Capitalism* (Chicago: University of Chicago Press, 2009); Donald Mackenzie, *An Engine, Not a Camera: How Financial Models Shape Markets* (Cambridge: MIT Press, 2006); Donald MacKenzie, Fabian Muniesa, and Lucia Siu, eds., *Do Economists Make Markets?: On the Performativity of Economics* (Princeton, N.J.: Princeton University Press, 2008); Donald MacKenzie, *Material Markets: How Economic Agents are Constructed* (New York: Oxford University Press, 2009); Marieke De Goede, *Virtue, Fortune and Faith: A Genealogy of Finance* (Minneapolis: University of Minnesota Press, 2005); Robert Aitken, *Performing Capital: Toward a Cultural Economy of Popular and Global Finance* (New York: Palgrave Macmillan, 2007); Paul Langley, *The Everyday Life of Global Finance: Saving and Borrowing in Anglo-America* (New York: Oxford University Press, 2008). These sociologists and anthropologists draw from Judith Butler, *Excitable Speech: A Politics of the Performative*

(New York: Routledge, 1997); J. L. Austin, *How to Do Things with Words* (Oxford: Clarendon, 1962).

9. Theda Skocpol, *Protecting Soldiers and Mothers: The Political Origins of Social Policy in the United States* (Cambridge: Harvard University Press, 1995); Brian Balogh, *A Government Out of Sight: The Mystery of National Authority in Nineteenth-Century America* (London: Cambridge University Press, 2009); David A. Zimmerman, *Panic! Markets, Crises, and Crowds in American Fiction* (Chapel Hill: University of North Carolina Press, 2006); Steve Fraser, *Every Man a Speculator: A History of Wall Street in American Life* (New York: HarperCollins, 2005).

10. This argument draws upon the fields of behavioral finance and economic sociology. Behavioral finance rejects the standard neoclassical model of investors as rational economic actors with consistent preferences who formulate investment decisions by first estimating probabilities of future gain and risk, then allocating accordingly. This literature holds that individuals in fact construct their preferences *during* the decision-making processes, heavily influenced by social and cultural contexts. Drawing upon psychology, behavioral finance enumerates many noneconomic factors that influence investors, including the desire to accord with prevailing norms and perceived consensus, the narrative framing of options, and the confidence, intuition, and emotions of individuals. The field establishes the pervasiveness of certain systematic biases or heuristics among agents faced with uncertainty, including overconfidence, anchoring to an initial or default number, the tendency to extrapolate from recent trends or to persist in beliefs even when faced with contradictory evidence, and the compartmentalization of wealth and spending into distinct "mental accounts." Economic sociology analyzes economic decisions and arrangements within their context, which includes cultural norms and beliefs, political systems, institutions, and social relationships of trust, power, and authority.

For an overview of the field of behavioral finance, see Shiller and Akerlof, *Animal Spirits;* Robert J. Shiller, *Irrational Exuberance* (Princeton, N.J.: Princeton University Press, 2000); Nicholas Barberis and Richard Thaler, *A Survey of Behavioral Finance* (Cambridge, Mass.: National Bureau of Economic Research, 2002). Richard Thaler, "From Homo Economicus to Homo Sapiens," *Journal of Economic Perspectives* 14 (Winter 2000), 133–141. For some of the most influential empirical work, see Amos Tversky and Daniel Kahneman, "Judgment under Uncertainty: Heuristics and Biases," *Science* 185 (September 27, 1974), 1124–1131; John Y. Campbell and Robert J. Shiller, "Stock Prices, Earnings, and Expected Dividends," *Journal of Finance* 43 (1988), 661–676; Robert J. Shiller, "Do Stock Prices Move Too Much to Be Justified by Subsequent Changes in Dividends?" *American Economic Review* 73 (1983), 236–237; Randall Morck, Andrew Shleifer, and Robert W. Vishney, "The Stock Market and Investment: Is the Market a Sideshow?" *Brookings Papers on Economic Activity 1990* (1990), 157–215; Robert J. Shiller, "Stock Prices and Social Dynamics," *Cowles Foundation Paper* (New Haven: Yale University, 1984); George A. Akerlof and Rachel E. Kranton, "Economics and Identity," *QJE* 115 (2000), 715–753; Nicholas Barberis, Andrei Shleifer, and Robert

Vishnay, "A Model of Investor Sentiment," *Journal of Financial Economics* 49 (1998), 307–343.

For economic sociology, see Mark Granovetter, "Economic Action and Social Structures: The Problem of Embeddedness," *American Journal of Sociology* 91 (November 1985), 481–520; Michel Abolafia, *Making Markets: Opportunism and Restraint on Wall Street* (Cambridge: Harvard University Press, 2001); Rowena Olegario, *A Culture of Credit: Embedding Trust and Transparency in American Business* (Cambridge: Harvard University Press, 2006); William Roy, *Socializing Capital: The Rise of the Large Industrial Corporation in America* (Princeton, N.J.: Princeton University Press, 1997); Viviana Zelizer, *The Social Meaning of Money* (New York: Oxford University Press, 1994).

11. Existing literature tends to attribute the early twentieth-century increase in securities ownership to corporate demand for capital, rational individuals seeking higher returns for their savings, and/or irrational individuals' greed and naïveté. Histories of the Great Bull Market of the late 1920s and the Crash of 1929 often identify the Jazz Age *zeitgeist* as a factor in stimulating popular participation in the stock market, but they fail to situate this sea change in investment practice in the context of investors' long-standing political concerns or distributors' political goals. A few biographies and institutional histories examine specific innovators in financial securities marketing, while Steve Fraser's *Every Man a Speculator* and some cultural studies monographs largely consider changing *representations* of financial markets. Lawrence Mitchell's *Speculation Economy* charts the legitimization of securities investment prior to World War I but focuses on regulatory debates.

John Kenneth Galbraith, *The Great Crash of 1929* (Boston: Houghton Mifflin, 1997); Maury Klein, *Rainbow's End: The Crash of 1929* (New York: Oxford University Press, 2001); Charles Geisst, *Wall Street: A History* (New York: Oxford University Press, 1997); B. Mark Smith, *Toward Rational Exuberance: The Evolution of the Modern Stock Market* (New York: Farrar, Straus, and Giroux, 2001); B. Mark Smith, *Equity Culture: The Story of the Global Stock Market* (New York: Farrar, Straus, and Giroux, 2003); Kenneth Lipartito, *Investing for Middle America: John Elliott Tappan and the Origins of American Express Financial Advisors* (New York: Palgrave for St. Martin's, 2001); Edwin J. Perkins, *Wall Street to Main Street: Charles Merrill and Middle Class Investors* (New York: Cambridge University Press, 1999); Lawrence Mitchell, *The Speculation Economy: How Finance Triumphed Over Industry* (New York: Barrett-Koehler, 2009); Huertas and Cleveland, *Citibank: 1812–1970*; Fraser, *Every Man a Speculator*; Rob Aitken, *Performing Capital: Toward a Cultural Economy of Popular and Global Finance* (New York: Palgrave Macmillan, 2007); De Goede, *Virtue, Fortune and Faith*; David Hockfelder, "'Where the Common People Could Speculate': The Ticker, Bucket Shops, and the Origins of Popular Participation in Financial Markets, 1800–1920," *Journal of American History (JAH)* 93 (2006), 335–58.

12. Historians of American consumer culture and politics recognize the ways in which commodities and the experience of consumption mediate social relationships

and political identities—an approach applied here to financial securities and the practice of investment. Lizabeth Cohen, *A Consumer's Republic: The Politics of Mass Consumption in Postwar America* (New York: Alfred A. Knopf, 2003); Lizabeth Cohen, *Making a New Deal: Industrial Workers in Chicago, 1919–1939* (New York: Cambridge University Press, 1990); T. H. Breen, *The Marketplace of Revolution: How Consumer Politics Shaped American Independence* (New York: Oxford University Press, 2005); Meg Jacobs, *Pocketbook Politics: Economic Citizenship in Twentieth-Century America* (Princeton, N.J.: Princeton University Press, 2005); Roland Marchand, *Advertising the American Dream: Making Way for Modernity, 1920–1940* (Berkeley: University of California Press, 1986); Charles McGovern, *Sold American: Consumption and Citizenship, 1890–1945* (Chapel Hill: University of North Carolina Press, 2006); Robert Weems, *Desegregating the Dollar: African American Consumerism in the Twentieth Century* (New York: New York University Press, 1998); Kathy Peiss, *Hope in a Jar: The Making of America's Beauty Culture* (New York: Metropolitan Books, 1998); Walter Johnson, *Soul by Soul: Life Inside an Antebellum Slave Market* (Cambridge: Harvard University Press, 1997); Sidney Mintz, *Sweetness and Power: The Place of Sugar in Modern History* (New York: Penguin, 1986).

13. Contests to fix the meaning and implications of inherited political language are critical sites of struggle over power in society. But political rhetoric does not simply express or describe preexisting political interests and affiliations. Rather, language constructs political identities, forges political alliances, and links these to a shared set of concerns and demands that may ultimately produce enduring change in government policy and institutions. Advertising, marketing, and public relations may communicate transformative political discourse as much as traditional texts. For scholarship that views discourse as critical for effecting political change, see Gary Gerstle, *Working Class Americanism: The Politics of Labor in a Textile City, 1914–1960* (Princeton, N.J.: Princeton University Press, 1991); Joseph A. McCartin, *Labor's Great War: The Struggle for Industrial Democracy and the Origins of Modern American Labor Relations, 1912–1921* (Chapel Hill: University of North Carolina Press, 1998); Joseph Lowndes, *From the New Deal to the New Right: Race and the Southern Origins of Modern Conservatism* (New Haven: Yale University Press, 2008); Victoria Hattam and Joseph Lowndes, "The Ground Beneath Our Feet: Language, Culture, and Political Change," in *Formative Acts: Politics in the Making*, ed. Stephen Skowronek and Matthew Glassman (Philadelphia: University of Pennsylvania Press, 2007).

14. For those who date emergence of modern free-market conservatism later, see Elizabeth Fones-Wolf, *Selling Free Enterprise: The Business Assault on Labor and Liberalism, 1945–1960* (Urbana: University of Illinois Press, 1994); Karen S. Miller, *The Voice of Business: Hill and Knowlton and Postwar Public Relations* (Chapel Hill: University of North Carolina Press, 1999); Kim Phillips-Fein, *Invisible Hands: The Making of the Conservative Movement from the New Deal to Reagan* (New York: Norton, 2009); Frank, *One Market Under God.*

Janice Traflet and Robert Aitken consider the NYSE's post–World War II "Own Your Own Share" companion as a component of a resurgent of free enterprise ideology. Rob Aitken, *Performing Capital: Toward a Cultural Economy of Popular and Global Finance* (New York: Palgrave Macmillan, 2007); Janice Traflet, "'Own Your Own Share of American Business': Public Relations at the NYSE During the Cold War" at www.hnet.org/~business/bhcweb/publications/BEHonline/2003/Traflet.pdf.

15. In Gramscian terms, twentieth-century financial and corporate-managerial elites secured hegemony as the legitimacy of the securities markets, and the desirability of mass investment became accepted as "common sense." For other work documenting the role of political-economic ideology and state policy in shaping the development of financial institutions and markets, see Louis Hyman, *Debtor Nation* (Princeton, NJ: Princeton University Press, 2010); Jonathan Ira Levy, "Contemplating Delivery: Futures Trading and the Problem of Commodity Exchange in the United States, 1875–1905," *American Historical Review (AHR)* 111 (2006), 307–335; Daniel Wadhwani, "Citizen Savers: The Family Economy, Financial Institutions, and Social Policy in the Northeastern United States from the Market Revolution to the Great Depression" (Ph.D. diss., University of Pennsylvania, 2002).

16. Raghuram G. Rajan and Luigi Zingales, "The Great Reversals: The Politics of Financial Development in the 20th Century," *Journal of Financial Economics* 69 (2003), 49, 51. For the comparatively dispersed nature of shareholding in American corporations, see Rafael La Porta, Florencio Lopez-de-Silanes, and Andrei Schleifer, "Corporate Ownership Around the World," *Journal of Finance* 54 (April 1999), 471–517; Randall Morck and Bernard Yeung, "Never Waste a Good Crisis: A Historical Perspective on Comparative Corporate Governance," National Bureau of Economic Research no. 15042 (June 2009), 3, 11.

From the 1960s until the 1980s, the percent of households owning corporate shares (either indirectly or indirectly) hovered between 20 and 30 percent. Beginning in the 1980s, indirect holdings through mutual funds increased dramatically, such that the majority of households owned equity in 2000. Between 1970 and 1997, U.S. households held between 10 and 20 percent of their assets in equities. This proportion reached a peak of 32.9 percent in 1999, then ebbed to 22 percent in 2003.

John V. Duca, "The Democratization of America's Capital Markets," *Economic and Financial Review* (2001), 13; Gerald F. Davis, "A New Finance Capitalism? Mutual Funds and Ownership Re-Concentration in the United States," *European Management Review* 5 (2008), 15; Brian K. Bucks, Arthur B. Kennickell, and Kevin B. Moore, "Recent Changes in U.S. Family Finances," *Federal Reserve Bulletin* 92 (2006), a19.

17. Davis, *Managed by the Markets;* Greta Krippner, "Financialization of the American Economy," *Socio-Economic Review* 3 (2005), 173–208.

18. Several cultural critics share my interest in using history to question the inevitability of contemporary financial arrangements. These scholars draw upon the work of Michel Foucault to generate "genealogies" of contemporary finance. The analytic practice of "genealogy" aims to demonstrate that beliefs and

circumstances unquestioned in the present were, in fact, not inevitable and could yet be altered. Aitken, *Performing Capital;* De Goede *Virtue, Fortune and Faith;* Michel Foucault, "Nietzsche, Genealogy, and History," in *The Foucault Reader,* ed. Paul Rabinow (New York: Pantheon, 1984).

1. The Problem with Financial Securities

1. Nell Irwin Painter, *Standing at Armageddon: The United States, 1877–1919* (New York: W. W. Norton, 1987); Roland Marchand, *Creating the Corporate Soul* (Berkeley: University of California Press, 1998); Robert H. Wiebe, *The Search for Order, 1877–1920* (New York: Hill and Wang, 1967).
2. Alfred D. Chandler, *The Visible Hand: The Managerial Revolution in American Business* (Cambridge, Mass.: Belknap, 1977), 145–175, 195–203; Charles Perrow, *Organizing America: Wealth, Power, and the Origins of Corporate Capitalism* (Princeton, N.J.: Princeton University Press, 2002), 200–201; William Roy, *Socializing Capital: The Rise of the Large Industrial Corporation in America* (Princeton, N.J.: Princeton University Press), 18, 107–109; Naomi Lamoreaux, *The Great Merger Movement in American Business, 1895–1904* (New York: Cambridge University Press, 1985); James Livingston, "The Social Analysis of Economic History and Theory: Conjectures on Late Nineteenth Century American Development," *AHR* 92 (1987), 69–95; Walter Licht, *Industrializing America: The Nineteenth Century* (Baltimore: Johns Hopkins University Press, 1995).
3. Marchand, *Creating the Corporate Soul,* 1–5; James Livingston, *Origins of the Federal Reserve System: Money, Class, and Corporate Capitalism, 1890–1913* (Ithaca, N.Y.: Cornell University Press, 1997), 42–46; Kenneth Lipartito and Carol Heher Peters, *Investing for Middle America: John Elliott Tappan and American Express Financial Advisors* (New York: Palgrave, 2001), 98.
4. Lawrence Goodwyn, *The Populist Moment: A Short History of Agrarian Revolt in America* (New York: Oxford, 1976); Michael Kazin, *The Populist Persuasion: An American History* (New York: Basic Books, 1995); Charles Postel, *The Populist Vision* (New York: Oxford, 2007); Elizabeth Sanders, *The Roots of Reform: Farmers, Workers, and the American State, 1877–1917* (Chicago: University of Chicago Press, 1997).
5. "Tom Watson on Wall Street," *New York World (NYW),* October 4, 1896, 1.
6. Lamoreaux, *Great Merger Movement,* 2.
7. J. G. A. Pocock, *The Machiavellian Moment: Florentine Political Thought and the Atlantic Republican Tradition* (Princeton, N.J.: Princeton University Press, 1975); Joyce Appleby, *Liberalism and Republicanism in the Historical Imagination* (Cambridge: Harvard University Press, 1992); Robert E. Shalhope, "Toward a Republican Synthesis: The Emergence of an Understanding of Republicanism in American Historiography," *William and Mary Quarterly (WMQ)* 29 (1972), 49–80; Robert E. Shalhope, "Republicanism and Early American Historiography," *WMQ* 39 (1982), 334–356; Steven J. Ross, "The Transformation of Republican Ideology," *Journal of the Early Republic* 10 (1990), 323–330; Daniel T. Rodgers, "Republicanism: The Career of a Concept," *JAH* 79 (1992), 11–38; Linda K. Kerber, "Making Republicanism Useful," *Yale Law Journal* 97 (1988),

1662–1672; Joyce Appleby, "Republicanism in the History and Historiography of the United States," *American Quarterly* 37 (1985), 461–473.; Joyce Appleby, "Republicanism in Old and New Contexts," *WMQ* 43 (1986), 20–34; C. B. Macpherson, *The Political Theory of Possessive Individualism: From Hobbes to Locke* (Oxford: Claredon Press, 1962); Jeff Sklansky, *Soul's Economy: Market Society and Selfhood in American Thought, 1820–1920* (Chapel Hill, N. C.: University of North Carolina Press, 2001), 1–35; Gregory S. Alexander, *Commodity and Property: Competing Visions of Property in American Legal Thought, 1776–1970* (Chicago: Chicago University Press, 1997); Carol Rose, *Property and Persuasion: Essays on the History, Theory and Rhetoric of Ownership* (Boulder: Westview, 1994); James T. Kloppenberg, "The Virtues of Liberalism: Christianity, Republicanism, and Ethics in Early American Political Discourse," *JAH* 74 (1987): 9–33; Gordon S. Wood, *The Radicalism of the American Revolution* (New York: Knopf, 1992); Alan Taylor, *Liberty Men and Great Proprietors: The Revolutionary Settlement on the Maine Frontier, 1760–1820* (Chapel Hill: University of North Carolina Press, 1990); Daniel Vickers, "Competency and Competition: Economic Culture in Early America," *WMQ* 47 (1990), 3–29; Robert J. Steinfeld, "Property and Suffrage in the Early American Republic," *Stanford Law Review* 41 (1989), 350; Steven J. Ross, "The Transformation of Republican Ideology," *Journal of the Early Republic* 10 (1990), 323–330; Linda K. Kerber, "The Republican Ideology of the Revolutionary Generation," *American Quarterly* 37 (1985), 474–495; Bernard Bailyn, *Ideological Origins of the American Revolution* (Cambridge: Belknap Press of Harvard University Press, 1967); Drew R. McCoy, *Elusive Republic: Political Economy in Revolutionary America* (Chapel Hill, NC: University of North Carolina Press, 1980).

For the male head of household's mastery of dependents' labor as constitutive of political liberty, see Nancy F. Cott, "Marriage and Women's Citizenship in the United States, 1830–1934," *AHR* 103 (1998), 1440–1475; Toby L. Ditz, "Ownership and Obligation: Inheritance and Patriarchal Households in Connecticut, 1750–1820," *WMQ* 47 (April 1990), 235–265; Joan Gunderson, "Independence, Citizenship and the American Revolution," *Signs* 13 (1987), 59–77; Nancy Fraser and Linda Gordon, "Civil Citizenship against Social Citizenship?" in *The Condition of Citizenship*, ed. Bart Van Steenbergen (Thousand Oaks, Calif.: Sage Press, 1994); Stephanie McCurry, *Masters of Small Worlds: Yeoman Households, Gender Relations, and the Political Culture of the Antebellum South Carolina Low Country* (New York: Oxford University Press, 1995); Nancy Fraser and Linda Gordon, "A Genealogy of Dependency: Tracing a Keyword of the U.S. Welfare State," *Signs* 19 (1994), 309–336.

8. Lizabeth Cohen, *Consumer's Republic: The Politics of Mass Consumption in Postwar America* (New York: Knopf, 2003), 21; Stuart Banner, *Anglo-American Securities Regulation: Cultural and Political Roots, 1690–1860* (New York: Cambridge University Press, 1998), 14–36, 48–75, 89–94, 122–160, 198–222; Alex Preda, *Framing Finance: The Boundaries of Markets and Modern Capitalism* (Chicago: University of Chicago Press, 2009), 26–33, 86–87, 82–110, 144–197; Roy, *Socializing Capital*, 118, 122–124.

9. Woody Holton, "'From the Labour of Others': The War Bond Controversy and the Origins of the Constitution in New England," *WMQ* 61 (2004), 271–317; Woody Holton, "Did Democracy Cause the Recession that Led to the Constitution?" *JAH* 92 (2005), 442–649; Victoria Hattam, *Labor Visions and State Power: The Origins of Business Unionism in the United States* (Princeton, N.J.: Princeton University Press, 1993).

10. Holton, "'From the Labour of Others'"; Lance Banning, *The Jeffersonian Persuasion: The Evolution of a Party Ideology* (Ithaca, N.Y.: Cornell University Press, 1978); Taylor, *Liberty Men and Great Proprietors*; T. H. Breen, *Tobacco Culture: The Mentality of the Great Tidewater Planters on the Eve of the Revolution* (Princeton, N.J.: Princeton University Press, 1985); Bruce Mann, *Republic of Debtors: Bankruptcy in the Age of American Independence* (Cambridge: Harvard University Press, 2002), 113–114, 168, 175–6, 190–198; David P. Szatmary, *Shays' Rebellion: The Making of an Agrarian Insurrection* (Amherst: University of Massachusetts Press, 1980); Hattam, *Labor Visions and State Power*; Roy, *Socializing Capital*, 17, 53–55, 72–73; Preda, *Framing Finance*, 86–87, 174–175.

11. Steinfeld, "Property and Suffrage," 352, 375; Sean Wilentz, *Chants Democratic: New York City and the Rise of the American Working Class, 1788–1850* (New York: Oxford University Press, 1984); Bruce Laurie, *Artisans into Workers: Labor in Nineteenth-Century America* (New York: Hill and Wang, 1989); Amy Dru Stanley, *From Bondage to Contract: Wage Labor, Marriage, and the Market in the Age of Slave Emancipation* (New York: Cambridge University Press, 1998); Jonathan Glickstein, *Concepts of Free Labor in Antebellum America* (New Haven: Yale University Press, 1991); Eric Foner, *Free Soil, Free Labor, Free Men: The Ideology of the Republican Party Before the Civil War* (New York: Oxford University Press, 1970); Lawrence Glickman, *A Living Wage: American Workers and the Making of Consumer Society* (Ithaca, N.Y.: Cornell University Press, 1997).

12. Hattam, *Labor Visions and State Power*; Sanders, *Roots of Reform*.

13. William Graham Sumner, "The Forgotten Man" (1883). Sumner later moved away from a theory of society grounded in property ownership; see Sklansky, *Soul's Economy*, 105–136.

14. Carnegie quoted in David Nasaw, "Gilded Age Gospels," in *Ruling America: A History of Wealth and Power in a Democracy*, ed. Steve Fraser and Gary Gerstle (Cambridge: Harvard University Press, 2005), 132. Rockefeller quoted in Vincent P. Carosso, *Investment Banking in America* (Cambridge: Harvard University Press, 1970), 42.

15. Steinfeld, "Property and Suffrage," 369; Sven Beckert, *Monied Metropolis: New York City and the Consolidation of the American Bourgeoisie, 1850–1896* (New York: Cambridge University Press, 2003), 179, 184–236, 277, 281, 321, 324, 325.

16. Rohit Daniel Wadhwani, "Citizen Savers: The Family Economy, Financial Institutions, and Social Policy in the Northeastern United States from the Market Revolution to the Great Depression" (Ph.D. diss., University of Pennsylvania, 2002), 10–15.

A few rare exceptions prove the point. In 1878, John Bates Clark deliberated upon possible means of "securing that union of labor and capital in the same hands" but failed to identify corporate securities. John Bates Clark, "How to Deal with Communism," *Yale and New Englander Review* (1878), 541.

New York City Mayor Abram Hewitt may have been the first to suggest that corporate securities could integrate wage-laborers into the polity and elicit their fealty to corporate capitalism. Hewitt did so following his narrow victory in the contentious 1886 election against the famous anti-monopolist and single taxer Henry George, the candidate of the United Labor Party. Hewitt doubted, however, "that all workmen should thus become shareholders," allowing there "would always be a considerable element of an unstable and unintelligent character whose participation in the ownership is neither desirable or possible." "Under Full Headway Now," *NYT*, October 2, 1890, 9.

17. Melinda Lawson, *Patriot Fires: Forging a New American Nationalism in the Civil War North* (Lawrence: University of Kansas Press, 2002); Preda, *Framing Finance*, 10–14, 22, 54, 88–104, 114–142, 176–194; Banner, *Anglo-American Securities Regulation*, 217–221; Martin J. Sklar, *The Corporate Reconstruction of American Capitalism, 1890–1916: The Market, the Law, and Politics* (New York: Cambridge University Press, 1988), 49–50; Jonathan Ira Levy, "Contemplating Delivery: Futures Trading and the Problem of Commodity Exchange in the United States, 1875–1905," *AHR* 111 (2006), 307–335; Bill Maurer, "Forget Locke?: From Proprietor to Risk-Bearer in the New Logics of Finance," *Public Culture* 11 (1999), 365–385; Morton J. Horwitz, *Transformation of American Law, 1790–1860* (Cambridge, MA: Harvard University Press, 1979), 65–107; Sklansky, *Soul's Economy*, 207–215; David Hockfelder, "'Where the Common People Could Speculate': The Ticker, Bucket Shops, and the Origins of Popular Participation in Financial Markets, 1800–1920," *JAH* 93 (2006), 335–358; Ann Fabian, *Card Sharps, Dream Books, and Bucket Shops: Gambling in Nineteenth Century America* (Ithaca, N.Y.: Cornell University Press, 1990); Cedric Cowing, *Populists, Plungers, and Progressives: A Social History of Stock and Commodity Speculation, 1890–1936* (Princeton, N.J.: Princeton University Press, 1965).

Important cases include *County of San Mateo vs. Southern Pacific Railroad Co.*, 13 F. 722 (1882); *County of Santa Clara vs. Southern Pacific Railroad Co.*, 18 F. 385 (1883); *Santa Clara County vs. Southern Pacific Railroad Co.*, 118 U.S. 396 (1886).

The quote is from Oliver Wendell Holmes in *Christie Grain and Stock Co. vs. Board of Trade of the City of Chicago* (1903), quoted in Hockfelder, "'Where the Common People Could Speculate,'" 351.

18. Steve Fraser, *Every Man a Speculator: A History of Wall Street in American Life* (New York: HarperCollins, 2005); Charles Francis Adams Jr. and Henry Adams, *Chapters of Erie* (Boston: J. R. Osgood and Co., 1871); James Steele Gordon, *The Scarlet Woman of Wall Street: Jay Gould, Jim Fisk, Cornelius Vanderbilt, the Erie Railroad Wars, and the Birth of Wall Street* (New York: Weidenfeld and Nicholson, 1988); Richard White, "Information, Markets, and

Corruption: Transcontinental Railroads in the Gilded Age," *JAH* 90 (June 2003), 19–43; David A. Zimmerman, *Panic!: Markets, Crises, and Crowds in American Fiction* (Chapel Hill: University of North Carolina Press, 2006).

19. Mary O'Sullivan, *Contests for Corporate Control: Corporate Governance and Economic Performance in the United States and Germany* (New York: Oxford University Press, 2000), 75; David F. Hawkins, "The Development of Modern Financial Reporting Practices Among American Manufacturing Corporations," *BHR* 37 (1963), 145; Leslie Hannah, "The 'Divorce' of Ownership from Control from 1900 Onwards: Re-Calibrating Imagined Global Trends," *Business History* 49 (2007), 406.

Gardiner Means counted 4.4 million shareholders of record in all publicly traded corporations in 1900, but Means could not adjust for individuals owning shares in more than one corporation. Gardiner Means, "Diffusion of Stock Ownership in the United States," *QJE* 44 (1930), 561–600.

For postal savings, see Wadhwani, "Citizen Savers," 10–15, 308–317; Richard B. Kielbowicz, "Government Goes into Business: Parcel Post in the Nation's Political Economy, 1880–1915," *Studies in American Political Development* 8 (Spring 1994), 150–172.

For the Spanish-American War bond drive, see Frank A. Vanderlip, *From Farm Boy to Financier* (New York: D. Appleton-Century Co., 1935), 83–92.

For railroad securities, see U.S. Senate Industrial Commission, *Report of the Industrial Commission*, vol. 19 (1902), 403–404; Nathaniel T. Bacon, "American International Indebtedness," *Yale Review* (1900), 265–285.

20. In the late nineteenth century, British investors alone owned half of the capital of the railroad lines traded on the NYSE. Leland Jenks, *The Migration of British Capital to 1875* (New York: A. A. Knopf, 1927); Mira Wilkins, *The History of Foreign Investment in the United States to 1914* (Cambridge: Harvard University Press, 1989); Vincent P. Carosso, *The Morgans: Private International Bankers, 1854–1913* (Cambridge: Harvard University Press, 1987); John C. Coffee, "The Rise of Dispersed Ownership: The Roles of Law and the State in the Separation of Ownership and Control," *Yale Law Journal* 111 (October 2001), 1–82; Roy, *Socializing Capital*, 105–110, 133–137.

During the turn-of-the-century merger wave, all types of financial institutions increased the proportion of their assets invested in corporate securities. Gene Smiley, "The Expansion of the New York Securities Market at the Turn of the Century," *BHR* 55 (Spring 1981), 79–83; Larry Neal, "Trust Companies and Financial Innovation, 1897–1913," *BHR* 45 (1971), 35–51.

Late nineteenth-century retail distributors typically specialized in municipal, utility, and mortgage—rather than corporate or rail—bonds. Carosso, *Investment Banking*, 95–97, 102; Vincent P. Carosso, *More than a Century of Investment Banking: The Kidder, Peabody and Co. Story* (New York: McGraw-Hill, 1979), 32–33, 36; Lipartito, *Investing in Middle America*.

As late as 1917, the mailing list of one of the largest NYSE brokerages, J. S. Bache, held only 7,000 names. Jules Bache to Otto Kahn, May 21, 1917, box 21, folder 3, Otto Kahn papers, Manuscripts and Archives, Firestone Library, Princeton University, Princeton, N.J.

21. At the turn of the century, yearly income for middle-class households ranged between $900 and $3,500 per year. See Painter, *Standing at Armageddon,* xxiii. For typical transaction size, see Hannah, "'Divorce' of Ownership," 406–407. In 1865, the NYSE accepted orders for no less than $500, nearly equal to per capita wealth ($513) in that year. Preda, *Framing Finance,* 74; Livingston, *Origins of the Federal Reserve System,* 179.

22. Banner, *Anglo-American Securities Regulation,* 250–278.

23. John J. Wallis, "American Government Finance in the Long-Run: 1790–1990," *Journal of Economic Perspectives* 14 (Winter 2000), 66; O'Sullivan, *Contests for Corporate Control,* 78–79; William Lazonick and Mary O'Sullivan, "Finance and Industrial Development, Part I: The United States and the United Kingdom," *Financial History Review* 4 (1997), 13–14, 21; Lawrence Mitchell, *The Speculation Economy: How Finance Triumphed Over Industry* (San Francisco, Berrett-Koehler Publishers, 2007); Roy, *Socializing Capital,* 4, 18, 24, 108, 128–129, 192–194; Naomi R. Lamoreaux and Jean-Laurent Rosenthal, "Corporate Governance and the Plight of Minority Shareholders in the United States Before the Great Depression," www.econ.ucla.edu/people/papers/Rosenthal/Rosenthal308.pdf; T. R. Navin and M. V. Sears, "The Rise of a Market for Industrial Securities, 1887–1902," *BHR* 29 (1955), 105–138; Jonathan Barron Baskin, "The Development of Corporate Financial Markets in Britain and the United States, 1600–1914: Overcoming Asymmetric Information," *BHR* 62 (1998), 199–237; Hannah, "'Divorce' of Ownership," 404–408; Jonathan Barron Baskin and Paul Miranti Jr., *A History of Corporate Finance* (Cambridge: Cambridge University Press, 1997), 177–178.

24. Lazonick and O'Sullivan, "Finance and Industrial Development, Part I," 10–11; Edward Sherman Meade, "Financial Aspects of the Trust Problem," *AAAPSS* 16 (1900); Navin and Sears, "Rise of a Market," 134–137; Brian R. Cheffins, "Mergers and Corporate Ownership Structure: The United States and Germany at the Turn of the Twentieth Century," *American Journal of Comparative Law* 51 (Summer 2003), 473–503; O'Sullivan, *Contests for Corporate Control,* 75.

25. Cheffins, "Mergers and Corporate Ownership Structure"; Brian Cheffins and Steven Bank, "Is Berle and Means Really a Myth?" *BHR* 83 (Autumn 2009), 451; Marco Becht and J. Bradford DeLong, "Why Has There Been So Little Blockholding in America?" in *A History of Corporate Governance Around the World: Family Business Groups to Professional Managers,* ed. Randall K. Morck (Chicago: University of Chicago, 2005); Mitchell, *Speculation Economy,* 13.

   For NYSE branches, see New York Stock Exchange member directories, NYSE Archives.

   In 1902, five American corporations counted more than 10,000 shareholders (including foreign and institutional investors): American Sugar Refining Company (10,816), New York Central Railroad (11,781), Pennsylvania Railroad (51,543), Union Pacific Railroad (14,256), and United States Steel (54,016). In 1910, nine American corporations counted more than 10,000 shareholders: American Telephone and Telegraph Co. (40,381), American Sugar Refining

Company (19,551), Great Northern Railroad (16,298), New York, New Haven, and Hartford Railroad (17,573), Swift and Co. (18,000), Pennsylvania Railroad (65,283), Union Pacific Railroad (20,282) United States Steel (94,934), and Western Union (12,731). See Means, "Diffusion"; H. T. Warshow, "The Distribution of Corporate Stock Ownership in the United States," *QJE* 39 (1914), 15–38; Mitchell, *Speculation Economy,* 202–203.

26. Meade, "Financial Aspects of the Trust Problem," 30–32.
27. Ibid., 28; Lazonick and O'Sullivan, "Finance and Industrial Development," 10, 14–15.
28. U.S. Senate Industrial Commission, *Report of the Industrial Commission* 19 (Washington, D.C.: GPO, 1902), 398–413.
29. U.S. Senate Industrial Commission, *Preliminary Report of the Industrial Commission* (Washington, D.C.: GPO, 1900), 34, 967.
30. Ibid., 5, 9, 32, 33.
31. Ibid., 13, 15.
32. Ibid., 5–7; Industrial Commission, *Report of the Industrial Commission* vol. 19, 637, 645; Mitchell, *Speculation Economy,* 124–127.

The Commission also urged the criminalization of price discrimination and price-cutting for the purpose of driving out competition. It recommended that states pass laws outlawing stock-watering, regulating the rates of public-service corporations, and improving disclosure standards for firms incorporated within their boundaries. It further proposed a progressive annual franchise tax on all interstate corporations, with reports filed with a bureau in the Treasury Department to serve as the basis for calculating that tax. This information would be made public for the benefit of investors in corporate securities. Should these remedies prove inadequate, the commission concluded, a federal incorporation law should be considered. The Industrial Commission further recommended that the Interstate Commerce Commission regulate corporate disclosure in the railroad industry.

33. Industrial Commission, *Preliminary Report,* 34, 1164; Industrial Commission, *Report of the Industrial Commission,* vol. 19, 635–637.
34. Jeremiah Jenks, *The Trust Problem* (New York: McClure, Phillips, 1907); John Bates Clark and John Maurice Clark, *Control of the Trusts* (New York: Macmillan, 1912), 79–80.

Both Jenks and Clark worked with the National Civic Federation to draft legislation that ultimately resulted in the Clayton Antitrust Act and the creation of the Federal Trade Commission (FTC) during the Wilson administration. James Weinstein, *The Corporate Ideal and the Liberal State, 1900–1918* (Boston: Beacon Press, 1968).

35. Jenks, Clark, and Ely belonged to a cohort of social theorists who began to reconsider some of the basic tenets of proprietary democracy around 1890. The protracted economic downturn of the late nineteenth century prompted founders of the American economics profession to push consumption and distribution to the forefront of their analyses. They jettisoned both the labor theory of value and Say's Law, a central tenet of classical economics that held that supply always generated its own demand. Marginalists like John Bates Clark

as well as institutionalists like Simon Patten, Richard Ely, and Thorstein Veblen grounded economic value in consumers' demand for a good or service, rather than the amount of labor time expended in production. Meanwhile, social theorists like John Dewey and Henry George set aside long-standing and still vibrant concerns about individual property ownership, arguing that widespread enjoyment of the fruits of industrial progress and an increased sense of social interconnectedness would provide a new basis for liberty, equality, and citizenship. Still these new departures in social and political theory were exceptional for their day, even avant-garde. Sklansky, 161–188; Glickman, *Living Wage;* Livingston, 88; Preda, *Framing Finance,* 147.

36. Jenks, *The Trust Problem,* 39; Richard T. Ely, *Monopolies and Trusts* (New York: Grosset & Dunlap, 1906), 53, 220; Clark, *Control of the Trusts,* 11; John Bates Clark, "Disarming the Trusts," *Atlantic Monthly,* January 1900, 50; Kim Phillips-Fein, "Free Markets, 'Potential Competition,' and Investors' Rights: The Merger Movement and Late Nineteenth Century Economic Thought," unpublished paper in author's possession.

37. Clark, "Disarming the Trusts," 50; Ely, *Control of the Trusts,* 269; Jenks, *Trust Problem,* 97, 223.

38. Mitchell, *Speculation Economy,* 98; Peter S. Grosscup, "The Beef Trust Enjoined," *Outlook,* February 28, 1903; Peter S. Grosscup, "How to Save the Corporation," *McClure's Magazine,* February 1905; Peter S. Grosscup, "The Corporation and the People: Are We on the Right Track?" *Outlook,* January 12, 1907.

39. Grosscup, "Beef Trust Enjoined"; Peter S. Grosscup, "Anti-Trust Laws," *Proceedings of the National Conference on Trusts and Combinations Under the Auspices of the NCF* (Chicago, 1907), 226; Peter S. Grosscup, "The Corporation Problem and the Lawyer's Part in Its Solution," *American Law Review* 39 (1905), 835–852.

40. Grosscup, "The Corporation Problem," 840, 848–850; Grosscup, "Anti-Trust Laws," 228; Mitchell, *Speculation Economy,* 116, 121, 143; Melvin Urofsky, "Proposed Federal Incorporation in the Progressive Era," *American Journal of Legal History* 26 (1982), 160–183.

41. Grosscup, "Rebirth of the Corporation," 192, 196.

42. Ibid., 188, 192; Grosscup, "Anti-Trust Laws," 226.

43. By corporate governance, I mean the relationship between parties to the corporation (particularly corporate managers, directors, and shareholders) as defined by the corporate charter, bylaws, public policy, and law.

44. Mitchell, *Speculation Economy,* 136, 137–165, 180–91, 209–219.

45. Theodore Roosevelt, "First Annual Address to Congress," December 3, 1901, in *Major Problems in American Business History,* ed. Regina Lee Blaszczyk and Philip B. Scranton (New York: Houghton Mifflin, 2006), 251–253; Melvin Urofsky, "Proposed Federal Incorporation in the Progressive Era," *American Journal of Legal History* 26 (1982), 160–183; Sklar, *Corporate Reconstruction,* 201–217, 252, 285; Mitchell, *Speculation Economy,* 183–185; Lamoreaux, *Great Merger Movement,* 169–170; Carosso, *Investment Banking,* 178–179.

46. Urofsky, "Proposed Federal Incorporation," 167, 176–183; Mitchell, *Speculation Economy*, 137–143, 158, 170–174, 180–182; Lamoreaux, *Great Merger Movement*, 169–170.

47. Marchand, *Creating the Corporate Soul*, 22–24; Stuart Brandes, *American Welfare Capitalism, 1880–1940* (Chicago: University of Chicago Press, 1976), 86; Robert F. Foerster and Else H. Dietel, *Employee Stock Ownership in the United States* (Princeton, N.J.: Princeton University Industrial Relations Section, 1926), 6–8.

48. "Workmen as Investors," *New York Times*, May 8, 1903, 8; "A Nation of Investors," *Wall Street Journal*, October 26, 1904, 1; "Workingmen as Capitalists," *NYT*, February 17, 1903, 8; Industrial Commission, *Report of the Industrial Commission* vol. 19, 804–805; Mitchell, *Speculation Economy*, 100.

49. Thomas Lawson, *Frenzied Finance: The Crime of the Amalgamated* (Boston: 1905); Louis Brandeis, *The Financial Condition of the New York, New Haven, and Hartford Railroad Company and of the Boston and Maine Railroad* (Boston: 1907); Louis Brandeis, *Other People's Money and How the Bankers Use It* (New York: Augustus M. Kelley, 1971), 8, 46–47; Carosso, *Investment Banking*, 113–132; Ron Chernow, *The House of Morgan: An American Banking Dynasty and the Rise of Modern Finance* (New York: Atlantic Monthly Press, 1990), 149.

50. Robert F. Bruner and Sean D. Carr, *The Panic of 1907: Lessons Learned from the Market's Perfect Storm* (Hoboken, N.J.: John Wiley and Sons, 2007); Chernow, *House of Morgan*, 122–29; Livingston, *Origins of the Federal Reserve*, 138–142, 178.

51. Mitchell, *Speculation Economy*, 166–177, 192, 204; Lamoreaux, *Great Merger Movement*, 170; Livingston, *Origins of the Federal Reserve*, 178–179.

52. Cowing, *Populists, Plungers, and Progressives*, 39–41, 67–69; Carosso, *Investment Banking*, 129–135, 156–187; Mitchell, *Speculation Economy*, 178–180.

53. "Two Million Partners Own the Corporations," *NYT*, October 4, 1908, SM1; "What 'Small Buyers' Mean to Wall Street," *NYT*, May 9, 1909, SM2; Mitchell, *Speculation Economy*, 200–205.

54. Hannah, "'Divorce' of Ownership," 419; "Report of Special Committee on Odd Lots," 1907, NYSE Archives, New York; "Report of Special Committee on Ways and Means: Subcommittee on Odd Lots," box 3, folder 7, 43, and folder 8, 237, NYSE Archives.

As late as 1916, only an estimated 80 NYSE firms accepted trades in less than 100 shares. Hockfelder, "'Where the Common People,'" 357.

New publications included Richard Wyckoff's *Ticker* (1907), later renamed *The Magazine of Wall Street*, along with Louis Guenther's *Financial World* (1902), *Commerce and Finance* (1912), and John Moody's *Moody's Magazine* (1905). Limited circulation periodicals as well as market news and analysis services catering to the financial industry appeared earlier, including the *Wall Street Journal* (1889), the *Commercial and Financial Chronicle* (1865), *Financier* (1884), *Poor's Handbook of Investment Securities* (1890), *Financial Age* (1900), and *Investment World and Banking Weekly* (1899). Wall Street Jour-

nal editor Charles Dow inaugurated the Dow Jones Industrial Average in 1884 and the Dow Jones Industrial Average in 1896. Preda, *Framing Finance*, 89, 155–171; Marieke De Goede, *Virtue, Fortune and Faith: A Genealogy of Finance* (Minneapolis: University of Minnesota Press, 2005), 87–120; Lloyd Wendt, *The Wall Street Journal: The Story of Dow Jones and the Nation's Business Newspaper* (Chicago: Rand McNally, 1982).

55. Woodrow Wilson, *The New Freedom: A Call for the Emancipation of the Generous Energies of a People* (Englewood, N.J.: Prentice-Hall, 1961), 26.

56. Wilson, *New Freedom*, 28, 76, 85, 105–106.

57. Quoted in Chernow, *House of Morgan*, 153.

58. Mitchell, *Speculation Economy*, 222–227; "Policy Holders Control," *NYT*, April 27, 1906, 6; U.S. Congress, House of Representatives, *Report of the Committee Pursuant to House Resolutions 429 and 504 to Investigate the Concentration of Control of Money and Credit* [hereafter known as *Pujo Report*], 62nd Cong., 3rd sess., 1913, H. Rep. 1593, 37, 116, 133–134; Carosso, *Investment Banking*, 113, 151.

59. *Pujo Report*, 46; "Offers to Debate on Stock Exchange," *NYT*, January 3, 1915.

60. Ibid., 34–45, 47, 116.

61. Ibid., 114–115.

62. Ibid., 115–119, 122–122, 162–163, 170–173; Carosso, *Investment Banking*, 151; Mitchell, *Speculation Economy*, 219–223.

  Untermyer preferred federal incorporation but feared constitutional challenges. "'Ends Free Press'—Hitchcock," *Washington Post*, February 5, 1914, 1.

63. Samuel Untermyer assisted in drafting this legislation. "Untermyer Dead in His 82nd Year; Long Had Been Ill," *NYT*, March 17, 1940, 1.

64. Carosso, *Investment Banking*, 178. The brokerage industry carried out exemptions for exchange-listed securities and members.

65. William G. McAdoo, *Crowded Years: The Reminiscences of William G. McAdoo* (Boston: Houghton Mifflin, 1931), 343; Louis Brandeis, *Other People's Money*, 13–27; Samuel Untermyer, "A Legislative Program to Restore Business Freedom and Confidence," January 5, 1914. Samuel Untermyer, "Argument before U.S. Senate Committee on Banking and Currency in Support of Senate Bill no. 3895," 19. Samuel Untermyer, "Speculation on the Stock Exchange and Public Regulation of the Exchanges, *American Economic Review* 5 (March 1915), 28, 50.

2. The "Free and Open Market" Responds

1. "Independents Win," *NYT*, May 1, 1912, 16; "'Insurgents' Win the Day" *New York American*, May 15, 1912, 1; "The Stock Exchange," *NYT*, February 23, 1913, 61; "Reforms Are Due," *New York American*, April 14, 1912, 1.

2. NYSE representatives found it difficult to establish that NYSE governors took swift action against manipulation while simultaneously denying the existence of manipulation. U.S. Congress, House of Representatives, Subcommittee of

the Committee on Banking and Currency, *Money Trust Investigation: Investigation of Financial and Monetary Conditions in the United States* [*Money Trust Investigation*], 62nd Cong., 3rd sess., 1913, 332–333, 369–372, 394–399, 483, 1120–1185, 1796–1797; U.S. Congress, House of Representatives, *Report of the Committee Pursuant to House Resolutions 429 and 504 to Investigate the Concentration of Control of Money and Credit* [*Pujo report*], 62nd Cong., 3rd sess., 1913, H. Rep. 1593, 33, 40–42, 114; "Offers to Debate on Stock Exchange," *NYT,* January 3, 1915, x3.

3. Peter M. Kenny, "R. T. H. Halsey: American Wing Founder and Champion of Duncan Phyfe," *Magazine Antiques,* January 2000; "Mayor Gives Murphy First Patronage," *NYT,* January 8, 1910, 3.

4. Wendy Kaplan, "R. T. H. Halsey: An Ideology of Collecting American Decorative Arts," *Winterthur Portfolio* 17 (Spring 1982), 43–53; "In Memoriam: Richard Townley Haines Halsey, 1865–1942," *Metropolitan Museum of Art Bulletin* 37 (March 1942), 50.

5. For Halsey's examinations of makers' marks on early American silver and his quests to establish the provenance of early American furniture, see R. T. H. Halsey letter book, vol. 1, NYSE Archives.

   "Untermyer Dead in His 82d Year; Long Had Been Ill," *NYT,* March 17, 1940, 1; "Samuel Untermyer Sounds a Warning," *NYT,* June 11, 1905; Thomas W. Lawson, "The Remedy," *Everybody's Magazine,* January 1913, 404–415; "Lawson Will Sue National City Bank," *NYT,* May 7, 1904, 1; "Committee Visit Wabash Terminal," *NYT,* September 17, 1910, 13; "Greystone as Restored," *NYT,* June 17, 1900, 15; "Dog Show Opens Today in Garden," *NYT,* February 11, 1908, 8; "Dogs of Class Please Society," *NYT,* May 24, 1908, S4; "High Class Dogs in Garden Show," *NYT,* February 10, 1907, 7; "Women Win Prizes at Flower Show," *NYT,* March 17, 1910, 9; "Vase and Picture Auction," *NYT,* April 18, 1913, 11. Lawrence Mitchell, *The Speculation Economy: How Finance Triumphed Over Industry* (San Francisco: Berrett-Koehler, 2007), 220–221.

6. "Untermyer Again Attacks Exchange," *NYT,* April 4, 1913; "Asks Untermyer for His Evidence," *NYT,* January 2, 1915, 10; Samuel Untermyer, "The Lawyer-Citizen: His Enlarging Responsibilities" (address before the Commercial Law League, Atlantic City, N.J., July 27, 1916), 12; Mitchell, *Speculation Economy,* 219, 227–230; "'Ends Free Press'—Hitchcock," *Washington Post,* February 5, 1914, 1; "Asks Untermyer for His Evidence," *NYT,* January 2, 1915, 10; Vincent P. Carosso, *Investment Banking in America* (Cambridge, MA: Harvard University Press, 1970), 178.

7. Proposed incorporation charters would subject governors' actions to judicial review and force exchanges to put vacant seats up for sale at a public auction. "Danger in Stock Tax Bill," *Washington Post,* February 24, 1913, 6; "Exchange a Power when Incorporated," *NYT,* February 24, 1913, 15; Cedric Cowing, *Populists, Plungers, and Progressives: A Social History of Stock and Commodity Speculation, 1890–1936* (Princeton, N.J.: Princeton University Press, 1965), 64–69; Carosso, *Investment Banking,* 156–87; R. C. Mitchie, *The London and*

New York Stock Exchanges, 1850–1914 (New York: HarperCollins, 1987), 200; Mitchell, *Speculation Economy,* 229–230.

8. R. T. H. Halsey to Lawrence Abbott, June 25, 1914, Halsey letter book, vol. 1, NYSE Archives; Elizabeth Sanders, *Roots of Reform: Farmers, Workers, and the American State, 1877–1917* (Chicago: University of Chicago Press, 1999); Elizabeth Clemens, *The People's Lobby: Organizational Innovation and the Rise of Interest Group Politics in the United States, 1890–1925* (Chicago: University of Chicago Press, 1997).

9. Kim McQuaid, "Corporate Liberalism in the American Business Community, 1920–1940," 52 (Autumn 1978), 341–368; Martin J. Sklar, *The Corporate Reconstruction of American Capitalism* (New York: Cambridge University Press, 1988); Robert Wiebe, *Businessmen and Reform: A Study of the Progressive Movement* (New York: Cambridge University Press, 1962); James Weinstein, *The Corporate Ideal in the Liberal State* (Boston: Beacon Press, 1968); James Livingston, *Origins of the Federal Reserve System: Money, Class, and Corporate Capitalism, 1890–1913* (Ithaca, N.Y.: Cornell University Press, 1986); R. Jeffrey Lustig, *Corporate Liberalism: The Origins of Modern American Political Theory, 1890–1920* (Berkeley: University of California Press, 1982); Louis Galambos, "The Emerging Organizational Synthesis in Modern American History," *BHR* 44 (1970): 279–90; Brian Balogh, *Government Out of Sight: The Mystery of National Authority in Nineteenth Century America* (New York: Cambridge University Press, 2009), 352–378; Ellis W. Hawley, "The New Deal State and the Anti-Bureaucratic Tradition," in *The New Deal and Its Legacy,* ed. Robert Eden (New York: Greenwood Press, 1989), 77–92; Samuel Untermyer, "A Legislative Program to Restore Business Freedom and Confidence" (address before the Illinois Manufacturers' Association, Chicago, January 5, 1914), 28; Mitchell, *The Speculation Economy,* 227.

The NYSE did not publicly oppose the Federal Reserve Act, hoping it would "relieve . . . such criticism as that which grew out of the Panic of 1907" and thereby remove the threat of securities market regulation. "Money Bill Suits Exchange," *NYT,* December 22, 1913, 12; Livingston, *Origins of the Federal Reserve,* 178–180, 199.

10. "General Scrapbook, September 1911–October 1917," NYSE Archives; Special Committee of Five on Publicity, "Report," folder "December 30, 1912 to February 13, 1913," NYSE Archives; R. T. H. Halsey to W. R. Houston, February 6, 1914, R. T. H. Halsey letter book vol. 1, NYSE Archives; R. T. H. Halsey to John W. Prentiss, April 2, 1917, R. T. H. Halsey letter book, vol. 2, NYSE Archives.

11. William C. Van Antwerp, *The Stock Exchange from Within* (Garden City, N.Y.: Doubleday, Page, 1913), 5–7, 14, 16–18, 22, 42, 60–61, 230; William C. Van Antwerp, "Digest of the Preliminary Work of the Special Committee on Bucket Shop Operations," June 25, 1913, NYSE Archives, 10–15.

For regulation by regulatory bodies, see Thomas K. McCraw, *Prophets of Regulation* (Cambridge: Harvard University Press, 1984); Morton Keller, *Regulating a New Economy: Public Policy and Economic Change in America,*

1900–1930 (Cambridge: Harvard University Press, 1990); Gerald Berk, "Whose Hubris? Brandeis, Scientific Management, and the Railroads," in *Constructing Corporate America*, ed. Kenneth Lipartito and David Sicilia (New York: Oxford, 2004); Gerald Berk, *Alternative Tracks: The Constitution of the American Industrial Order, 1865–1917* (Baltimore: Johns Hopkins University Press, 1994), 157–174.

For the move from a property-based to risk-based definition of value and ownership, see Bill Maurer, "Forget Locke? From Proprietor to Risk-Bearer in the New Logics of Finance," *Public Culture*, 11, no. 2 (1999), 365–385; Jonathan Ira Levy, "Contemplating Delivery: Futures Trading and the Problem of Commodity Exchange in the United States, 1875–1905," *AHR* 111 (April 2006), 307–335.

12. Mitchel Y. Abolafia, *Making Markets: Opportunism and Restraint on Wall Street* (Cambridge: Harvard University Press, 1996), 109. N. Wolfson and T. A. Russo, "Stock Exchange Specialists: An Economic and Legal Analysis," *Duke Law Journal* 1970 (August 1970), 707–746; Joel Seligman, *The Transformation of Wall Street: A History of the Securities and Exchange Commission and Modern Corporate Finance* (Boston: Houghton Mifflin, 1982); J. E. Meeker, *The Work of the Stock Exchange* (New York, 1922), 40–48, 174, 209–211.

13. Van Antwerp, *The Stock Exchange from Within*, 91, 124, 205.

14. Ibid., 38, 42, 48 60, 75–77, 88–93.

15. John G. Milburn, *Money Trust Investigation: Brief on Behalf of the New York Stock Exchange* (New York: C. G. Burgoyne, 1913), 42; Henry C. Emery, "Speculation on the Stock Exchanges and Public Regulation of the Exchanges," *American Economic Review* 5 (March 1915), 74–80; Henry Crosby Emery, "Speculations on the Stock and Produce Exchange of the United States," *Studies in History, Economics, and Public Law* 7 (1896), 179, 181; Henry Crosby Emery, "Results of the German Exchange Act of 1896," *Political Science Quarterly* 13 (June 1898), 287, 318; Charles A. Conant, *Wall Street and the Country* (New York: G. P. Putnam, 1904), 89–91, 116; Livingston, 109–110, 136–139, 192–193.

16. Alfred D. Chandler, *The Visible Hand: The Managerial Revolution in American Business* (Cambridge: Harvard University Press, 1977), 158–175, 195–203; William Roy, *Socializing Capital: The Rise of the Large Industrial Corporation in America* (Princeton, N.J.: Princeton University Press, 1997), 108; Vincent P. Carosso, *Investment Banking*, 95–97, 102; T. R. Navin and M. V. Sears, "The Rise of a Market for Industrial Securities, 1887–1902," *BHR* 29 (1955), 105–138; Mary O'Sullivan, *Contests for Corporate Control: Corporate Governance and Economic Performance in the United States and Germany* (New York: Oxford University Press, 2000).

For noncorporate varieties of capitalism, see Berk, *Alternative Tracks;* Philip Scranton, *Proprietary Capitalism: The Textile Manufacture at Philadelphia, 1800–1885* (New York: Cambridge University Press, 1983); Charles Sabel and Jonathan Zeitlin, eds., *World of Possibility: Flexibility and Mass Production in Western Industrialization* (New York: Cambridge University Press, 1997); Gerald Berk and Marc Schneiberg, "Varieties *in* Capitalism, Varieties *of* Association: Collaborative Learning in American Industry, 1900–1925," *Politics and Society* 33 (2005), 46–87; Louis Galambos, "Recasting the Organizational Synthesis: Structure and Process in the Twentieth and Twenty-First Centuries," *BHR* 79 (2005), 1–38.

17. Van Antwerp, *Stock Exchange from Within*, 13, 26–27. Rockefeller quoted in Carosso, *Investment Banking*, 42. Wanamaker quoted in William Leach, *Land of Desire: Merchants, Power, and the Rise of a New American Culture* (New York: Vintage, 1993), 35.

18. Meeker, *Work of the Stock Exchange* 87–90; Van Antwerp, *Stock Exchange from Within*, 44–45.

19. Van Antwerp, *Stock Exchange from Within*, 13, 26–27.

20. Ibid., 52, 55, 57, 67, 164, 230; R. T. H. Halsey to Charles H. Ludington, October 4, 1913, Halsey letter book, vol. 1.

21. "Asks Untermyer for His Evidence," *NYT*, January 2, 1915, 10.

22. Van Antwerp, *Stock Exchange from Within*, 22, 179–180.

23. R. T. H. Halsey to H. J. Howlands, June 15 and 21, 1913; R. T. H. Halsey to Robert H. Dodd, June 18, 1913; R. T. H. Halsey to Charles M. Newcombe, June 28, 1913; R. T. H. Halsey to K. V. S. Howland, June 5 and 9, 1913; R. T. H. Halsey to Hank C. Hoyt, July 9, 1913; R. T. H. Halsey to Albert W. Atwood, September 30, October 2 and 25, 1913; R. T. H. Halsey to Charles H. Ludington, February 21, 1914, all in Halsey letter book vol. 1; R. T. H. Halsey to Albert Atwood, February 1, 1918, Halsey letter book, vol. 2 NYSE Archives; William C. Van Antwerp to C. I. Hudson, August 14, 1913, Van Antwerp letter book, NYSE Archives; R. T. H. Halsey to National Board of Censorship, May 15, 1914, Committee on Library (COL) letter book vol. 1, NYSE Archives; COL to Albert Atwood, February 1, 1918, COL letter book, vol. 4, NYSE Archives; Minutes, October 14, November 11, 14, and 18, December 30, 1920, and April 13, 1921, Committee on Publicity (COP) minute book vol. 2, NYSE Archives.

   For Gilded Age and Progressive Era representations of financial trading and stock market panics, see David A. Zimmerman, *Panic! Markets, Crises, and Crowds in American Fiction* (Chapel Hill: University of North Carolina Press, 2006); Steve Fraser, *Every Man a Speculator: A History of Wall Street in American Life* (New York: HarperCollins, 2005).

24. For commodities exchanges' earlier efforts to distinguish themselves from bucket shops and to deny access to commodity exchange tickers, see Cowing, *Populists, Plungers, and Progressives*; David Hochfelder, "'Where Common People Could Speculate': "The Ticker, Bucket Shops, and the Origins of Popular Participation in Financial Markets, 1880–1920," *JAH* 93 (2006), 335–58; Ann Fabian, *Card Sharps, Dream Books & Bucket Shops: Gambling in Nineteenth Century America* (Ithaca, N.Y.: Cornell University Press, 1990).

25. Van Antwerp, "Digest," 7, 10–15, 22, 31, 36–37, 42–43, 67–71, 77–94, 116–152. Van Antwerp drew upon the work of Henry C. Emery and the Supreme Court's Christie decision of 1905. William C. Van Antwerp to Walter Taylor, July 16, 1913, COL letter book, vol. 1, NYSE Archives; "Bucket Shops Open Here and Outside," *NYT*, May 16, 1913; Albert Atwood, "The Bucket Shop Curse," *Harper's Weekly*, Dec. 20, 1913.

26. William C. Van Antwerp to Joseph J. Manning, June 17, 1913, Van Antwerp letter book, vol. 1, NYSE Archives; R. T. H. Halsey to J. H. Howland, August 13, 1913, Halsey letter book, vol. 1; Untermyer, "Legislative Program," 3; Mitchell, *Speculation Economy,* 217, 239–241.

27. R. T. H. Halsey to Henry L. Higginson, August 13, 1913, R. T. H. Halsey to J. H. Howland August 13, 1913, R. T. H. Halsey letter book, vol. 1.

28. R. T. H. Halsey to James B. Mabon, July 25, 1913, and R. T. H. Halsey to Chairman Heaton, Halsey letter book, vol. 1; William C. Van Antwerp to R. T. H. Halsey, August 8, 1913, Van Antwerp letter book, vol. 1; Minutes, March 24, 1913, September 28 and October 15, 1914, March 1, 1916, and March 26, 1917, CBC minute book, vol. 1, NYSE Archives.

29. April 12, 1916, June 21, 1916, April 30, 1917, February 18, 1918, CBC minute book, vol. 1, NYSE Archives.

30. *Proceedings of the First Annual Convention of the FAA* (Chicago, 1916), 59–63, 71, 75.

31. William C. Van Antwerp to Ivy Lee, November 10 and 17, 1914, December 1, 1914, in Van Antwerp letter book. COL to Otto Kahn, February 2 and 28, 1917; COL to Ivy Lee, April 24, 1917; COL to Ivy Lee, April 30, 1917, all in COL letter book, vol. 4, NYSE Archives.

32. Carosso, *Investment Banking in America,* 221.

33. Otto Kahn, "Strangling the Railroads" (n.p., 1914), 84. McCraw, *Prophets of Regulation,* 91; Clyde Spillinger, "Elusive Advocate: Reconsidering Brandeis as People's Lawyer," *Yale Law Journal,* 105 (April 1996), 86.

34. "Says Roads Are Strangling," *NYT,* December 16, 1914; Otto Kahn, "Strangling the Railroads" (n.p., 1914); Otto Kahn, "The Government and the Railroads," *World's Work (WW),* February 1916; Otto Kahn, "High Finance" (address before the American Newspaper Publishers Association, New York, 1916); Ivy Lee, "Publicity": A Cure for Railroad Evils" (address before Calvary Presbyterian Church, Buffalo, N.Y., January 17, 1915); Ivy Lee, "Telling the Railroad Story" (address before the Chamber of Commerce, Wilmington, Del., April 14, 1914).

35. Ivy Lee, "Telling the Railroad Story," 62–63; R. T. H. Halsey to Rev. Charles A. Richmond, September 29, 1914, and October 1, 1914, Halsey letter book, vol. 1; Ivy L. Lee, "Human Nature and the Railroads" (address before the American Railway Guild, n.p., 1915), 19; Ivy Lee to W. W. Atterbury, August 9, 1913, folder 10, box 1, Ivy Lee papers, Seeley Mudd Library, Princeton University, Princeton, New Jersey (IL); Ivy L. Lee, "Publicity for Public Service Corporations" (address before the American Electric Railway Association, Atlantic City, N.J., October 10, 1916); Ivy L. Lee, "The American Railway Problem" (address before the London School of Economics, London, UK, February 7, 1910); Ivy L. Lee, "The Crux of the Railroad Difficulty" (address before the Traffic Club of New England, Boston, 1916); Ivy L. Lee, "Is Railroad Regulation Becoming Strangulation?" (address before Men's League of Highland Park Church, New Brunswick, N.J., November 20, 1914); Ivy L. Lee, "The Outlook for the Railroads" (address before the Boston City Club, Bos-

ton, 1916); Roland Marchand, *Creating the Corporate Soul* (Berkeley: University of California Press, 1998); 80.

36. Lee, "Publicity, A Cure for Railroad Evils," 87.

37. Ibid., 84, 92; "Proposes Federal Railroad Charters," *NYT,* November 15, 1913, c2; "Says Railroads are Strangling," *NYT,* December 16, 1914, 17; "Strike Cure Worse than Strike," *NYT,* September 3, 1916, 2.

NYSE brokerages distributed pamphlets penned by Ivy Lee's public relations firm to oppose the Adamson Act. Van Antwerp and Kahn floated the idea of establishing a "League of American Investors" to oppose the bill. See folder 8, box 271, (OK); folder 5, box 115, IL.

38. "Untermyer Dead in His 82d Year; Long Had Been Ill," *NYT,* March 17, 1940, 1.

39. "Hearing Before Interstate Commerce Commission on Behalf of the NAORS, June 6, 1917" (Baltimore, June 6, 1917), 11, 17, 21; Walter Naughton, "Organizing the Railroad Investor," *Magazine of Wall Street,* 1917, 307–309.

40. S. Davies Warfield, "Report . . . to the Committee of NAORS in Respect to the Legislation Incident to the Return and Regulation of the Railroads (Transportation Act of 1920)," (Baltimore, 1920), 9, 10.

41. "Hearing before Interstate Commerce Commission," 42.

42. John J. Pulleyn, "The Institutional Investors' Part in the Rehabilitation of the Railroad" (an address before the National Conference of Mutual Savings Banks, Philadelphia, 1921), 7; Executive Committee of Associated Railroads of Pennsylvania and New Jersey, "For Better Service" (1917), N. W. Ayer Advertising Agency Records, Archives Center, National Museum ofAmerican History, Smithsonian Institution, Washington, D.C. (NWA); David Kennedy, *Over Here: The First World War and American Society* (New York: Oxford University Press, 1980), 254–255.

43. Kathleen Donohue, *Freedom from Want: American Liberalism and the Idea of the Consumer* (Baltimore: Johns Hopkins University Press, 2003), 8, 73; Meg Jacobs, *Pocketbook Politics: Economic Citizenship in Twentieth-Century America* (Princeton, N.J.: Princeton University Press, 2005); Lizabeth Cohen, *A Consumer's Republic: The Politics of Mass Consumption in Postwar America* (New York: Knopf, 2003); Lawrence Glickman, *A Living Wage: American Workers and the Making of a Consumer Society* (Ithaca, N.Y.: Cornell University Press, 1997); James Huston, *Securing the Fruits of Labor: The American Concept of Wealth Distribution, 1765–1900* (Baton Rouge: Louisiana State University Press, 1998); William Leach, *Land of Desire: Merchants, Power, and the Rise of a New American Culture* (New York: Pantheon Books, 1993).

44. William L. Silber, *When Washington Shut Down Wall Street* (Princeton, N.J.: Princeton University Press, 2007); "Mr. Untermyer Replies," *NYT,* October 22, 1914, 13; H. G. S. Noble, *The Stock Exchange in the Crisis of 1914* (New York, 1914); "Liberty Loan of 1917," *NYT,* May 28, 1917, 4; "Hurry to Convert Liberty $3\frac{1}{2}$s to 4," *Washington Post,* October 21, 1917; "Speed Bond Sales on Wilson's Plea," *NYT,* October 12, 1918; "See Need for New York to Rush Its Loan Work," *NYT,* October 3, 1918; "Victory Notes," *NYT,* May 5, 1919, 14;

"Thousands Cheer as McAdoo Pleads for Liberty Loan," *NYT,* June 7, 1917; "Taft Talks to Wall Street," *Washington Post,* October 23, 1917; "Says We Must Save Heritage of Liberty," *NYT,* April 16, 1918; "Hearst Denounced as Fountain Head of Sedition," *NYT,* November 3, 1917; "Serbian Mission at Stock Exchange," *NYT,* February 9, 1918.

45. R. T. H. Halsey to Winthrop Daniels, May 9, 1917, October 10 and 15, Halsey letter book, vol. 2, NYSE Archives.

46. Cowing, *Populists, Plungers, and Progressives,* 80–86.

3. "Be a Stockholder in Victory!"

1. "To Show Phases of War for Loan, *NYT* April 27, 1919, 25; "Spectacular Campaign for the Victory Loan," *NYT,* April 20, 1919, x5; John K. Allen, "Captured German Helmets as Liberty Loan Prizes," folder 5, box 1, Walter W. and Lillian F. Norton papers, Manuscripts and Archives, Yale University Library, New Haven, Connecticut (NP); U.S. Department of the Treasury, *Annual Report* (Washington, D.C.: Government Printing Office (GPO), 1919), 71; U.S. Department of the Treasury, *Report of the NWLLC for the Victory Loan Campaign,* 9; Hugh Rockoff, "Until It's Over, Over There: The US Economy in World War I," in *The Economics of World War I,* ed. Stephen Broadberry and Mark Harrison (New York: Cambridge University Press, 2005), 316.

2. "Triumph's Symbols Adorn Victory Way," *NYT,* April 22, 1919, 4; "Mrs. McAdoo to Speak," *NYT,* April 23, 1919, 4; "Mrs. M'Adoo Lauds Women," *NYT,* April 24, 1919, 4; "Women in Charge Today," *NYT,* April 26, 1919, 6; untitled clippings, *New York Herald,* April 22, 23, and 27, 1919, Guy Emerson scrapbook, vol. 7, Library of Congress (LOC) Washington D.C.

3. Charles Taylor, *Modern Social Imaginaries* (Durham, N.C.: Duke University Press, 2004).

4. William Gibbs McAdoo, *Crowded Years: The Reminiscences of William G. McAdoo* (New York: Houghton Mifflin, 1931), 382–383, 391, 408.

During the war, Treasury Department officials offered estimates of 300,000 to 350,000 individual bondholders resident in the United States, which they derived from consultations with leading bankers. They did not formulate any estimate of the number of stockholders, but it may be assumed to have been less, with significant overlap between bondholding and stockholding. A figure of 500,000 seems reasonable. U.S. Department of the Treasury, *Second Liberty Loan of 1917: A Source Book* (Washington, D.C.: GPO, 1917), iv; untitled clipping, *New York Tribune,* April 8, 1918, in Guy Emerson scrapbook, vol. 1, 120, LOC; U.S. Department of the Treasury, *Annual Report* (Washington, D.C.: GPO, 1917), 6; "Before the War There Were Only 310,000," *NYT,* June 8, 1917, vol. 1, page 4; Advertising, Clippings, and Literature Relating to the First, Second and Third Liberty Loans (Entry NC-120, 624), Records of the Bureau of Public Debt (Record Group 53), National Archives, College Park, Maryland (ACLRG53); "Minutes of a Conference Among Members of Treasury Department Savings Division and Representatives from the Federal Reserve

Districts," June 12, 1919, vol. 1, 15, 81–82, box 26, General Files Relating to Liberty Loan and War Savings Bonds, 1917–1925 (Entry NC-120, 622), Records of the Bureau of Public Debt (Record Group 53), National Archives, College Park, Maryland (GFRG53).

Estimates for the total amount of War Savings ranged from $907 million to $1.6 billion. See "Report of Discussion at Dinner Given by Mr. Vanderlip to Magazine Publishers and Editors," July 17, 1918, 4, box 44, GFRG53; National War Savings Committee, "Report of August 5, 1918," 15, appendix 2–6, 15, folder "National War Savings Committee," box 25, GFRG53; U.S. Treasury, *Annual Report* (1919), 61.

Because local War Loan committees reported the number of subscriptions, and not the number of subscribers, it is impossible to determine exactly how many Americans acquired federal war debt in any one drive, much less across all the War Loan campaigns. At the end of the war, Treasury Department officials offered 20 million as their best estimate. See McAdoo, *Crowded Years*, 409; Transcript, War Loan Organization Conference, vol. 2, 13, June 1919, folder "General Files Related to Liberty Loan and War Savings Bonds, 1917–25–1917–1920 Conferences," box 26, GFRG53; U.S. Department of the Treasury, *Weekly Press Matter*, August 7, 1918; "Minutes of Conference Among Members of the Treasury Department Savings Division and Representatives from the Federal Reserve Districts," vol. 1, June 12, 1919, 103–104, 246, 351, box 26, GFRG53.

The dates of issue and amounts raised in the various War Loan campaigns were as follows: First Liberty Loan, June 1917, $2 billion; Second Liberty Loan, November 1918, $3.8 billion; Third Liberty Loan, May 1918, $4.2 billion; Fourth Liberty Loan, October 1918, $7 billion; Victory Loan, April 1919, $4.5 billion. Charles Gilbert, *American Financing of World War I* (Westport, Conn.: Greenwood Press, 1970), 122–141.

5. For debates about the optimal mix of war financing options, see Ajay K. Mehrotra, "Lawyers, Guns and Public Moneys: The U. S. Treasury, World War I and the Administration of the Modern Fiscal State," *Law and History Review* 28 (2010), 173–225.

6. Gary Gerstle, "The Protean Character of American Liberalism," *AHR* 99 (October 1994), 1044, 1051; Gary Gerstle, *American Crucible: Race and Nation in Twentieth Century America* (Princeton, N.J.: Princeton University Press, 2002); James R. Barrett, "Americanization from the Bottom, Up: Immigration and the Remaking of the American Working Class, 1880–1930," *JAH* 79 (December 1992), 996–1020; Russell A. Kazal, "Revisiting Assimilation: the Rise, Fall, and Reappraisal of a Concept in American Ethnic History," *AHR* 100 (April 1995), 437–471; Gary Gerstle, *Working Class Americanism: The Politics of Labor in a Textile City, 1914–1960* (New York: Cambridge University Press, 1989); Jonathan Hansen, "True Americanism: Progressive Era Intellectuals and the Problem of Liberal Nationalism," in *Americanism: New Perspectives on the History of an Ideal,* ed. Michael Kazin and Joseph McCartin (Chapel Hill, N.C.: University of North Carolina Press, 2006), 73–89; William J. Novak, "The Legal Transformation of Citizenship in Nineteenth-Century America," in *The Democratic*

Experiment: New Directions in American Political History, ed. Meg Jacobs, William J. Novak, and Julian E. Zelizer (Princeton, N.J.: Princeton University Press, 2003), 85–119; Nancy F. Cott, "Marriage and Women's Citizenship in the United States, 1830–1934," *AHR* 103 (December 1998), 1440–1474; Linda K. Kerber, "The Meanings of Citizenship," *JAH* 84 (December 1997), 833–854; Jonathan Zimmerman, "Ethnics Against Ethnicity: European Immigrants and Foreign-Language Instruction, 1890–1940," *JAH* 88 (March 2002), 1383–1404; Lucy E. Salyer, "Baptism and Fire: Race, Military Service, and U.S. Citizenship Policy, 1918–1935," *JAH* 91 (December 2004), 847–876.

7. Christopher Capozzola, *Uncle Sam Wants You: World War I and the Making of the Modern American Citizen* (New York: Oxford University Press, 2008); Christopher Capozzola, "The Only Badge Needed Is Your Patriotic Fervor: Vigilance, Coercion, and the Law in World War I America," *JAH* 88 (March 2002), 1354–1382.

8. Thomas Nixon Carver, *Recollections of an Unplanned Life* (Los Angeles: Ward Ritchie Press, 1949), 225; Stephen Vaughn, *Holding Fast the Inner Lines: Democracy, Nationalism, and the Committee on Public Information* (Chapel Hill, N.C.: University of North Carolina Press, 1980); John E. Gardin, "Liberty Bonds and Civilization" (Buffalo, N.Y., October 1, 1917), 6.

9. U.S. Department of the Treasury, *The Liberty Loan of 1917: Campaign Textbook* (Washington, D.C.: GPO, 1917), 29; U.S. Department of the Treasury, *Annual Report* (Washington, D.C.: GPO, 1918), 1; William G. McAdoo, "The Second Liberty Loan" (Atlantic City, N.J., September 28, 1917), 17–18; U.S. Department of the Treasury, *The Liberty Loan of 1917*, 11–29; U.S. Treasury, *Annual Report* (1918), 1; Frank A. Vanderlip, "The Liberty Loan and Its Economic Status and Effects," 10; James M. Beck, "The Fateful Hour," (New York, 1917); Thomas Nixon Carver, "The Meaning and Function of Thrift" (1918), reprinted in Carnegie Endowment for International Peace, *Preliminary Economic Studies of the War* 10 (1919): 38, 40; U.S. Department of the Treasury, "Strengthening Business Foundations," folder 6, box 125, GFRG53.

The American War Loan campaigns followed mass bond drives in Britain, France, Germany, and Japan. Memorandum, folder "British Savings Certification Plan," box 30, GFRG53; "Montague Report" January 26, 1916, 1, folder "Report on the Committee on War Loans for the Small Investor," box 30, GFRG53; "Report of Discussions at Dinner Given by Mr. Vanderlip," July 17, 1918, 1, folder "Miscellaneous letters A," box 44, GFRG53; "Report of Discussion at Dinner," October 12, 1917, folder "Conference War Savings Certificates," box 25, GFRG53.

10. War Savings Committee of Massachusetts, *Bay State Bulletin*, November 7, 1918, folder "Bulletins," box 13, GFRG53.

On nations as constituted, in part, by the shared beliefs, commitments, and cultural practices of its inhabitants (and their recognition of each another as distinctively sharing those beliefs, commitments, and practices), see David Miller, *On Nationality* (Oxford: Oxford University Press, 1995); Lowell Barrington, *After Independence: Making and Protecting the Nation in Postcolonial and Postcommunist States* (Ann Arbor: University of Michigan Press,

2006); Ernst B. Haas, *Nationalism, Liberalism, and Progress* (Ithaca, N.Y.: Cornell University Press, 1997); Yael Tamir, *Liberal Nationalism* (Princeton, N.J.: Princeton University Press, 1993); Anthony D. Smith, *Cultural Foundations of Nations: Hierarchy, Covenant, and Republic* (Malden, Mass.: Blackwell Publishing, 2008); Benedict Anderson, *Imagined Communities: Reflections on the Origins and Spread of Nationalism* (London: Verso, 1983).

For the precedence of national consciousness over the nation-state, see Ernest Gellner, *Nations and Nationalism* (Ithaca, N.Y.: Cornell University Press, 1983); Eric J. Hobsbawm, *Nations and Nationalism since 1780: Programme, Myth, Reality* (New York: Cambridge University Press, 1990).

11. Macy Campbell, "Thrift Talk No. 5," 1918, folder "War Savings leaflets 7th District," box 16, GFRG53; "War Savings Societies—A Home Defense," *War Savings Society Bulletin,* no. 4; Memorandum, "Outline for an Address on the Liberty Bond Situation," folder 1, box 124, GFRG53; Robert F. Herrick to B. Nason Hamlin, March 30, 1918, folder "War Savings Leaflets 7th District," box 13, GFRG53; "The Country and the Loan," *NYT,* October 15, 1917; untitled clipping, *New York Tribune,* April 4, 1918, Guy Emerson scrapbook, vol. 1, LOC.

War Savings was specifically designed for the propertyless immigrant. Transcript, Conference on War Savings Certificates, October 12, 1917, box 25, GFRG53.

12. "War Savings Societies—A Home Defense," *War Savings Society Bulletin,* 1918, no. 4.

13. U.S. Department of the Treasury, *The Second Liberty Loan of 1917,* 25; John Muir and Co., "How to Raise the Money: The Third Liberty Loan Drive" (New York, 1918), 7; "Message of the Secretary of the Treasury to all Liberty Loan workers," June 6, 1918, folder "Directors' Correspondence—4," box 34, GFRG53.

14. "Exhibitor's Press Book" in folder 1, box 125, GFRG53; William Gibbs McAdoo, "Enlist Your Dollars for the Period of the War," [n.d.], folder "Secretary McAdoo itinerary/speeches 2/2," box 20, GFRG53; William G. McAdoo, "Address at the Liberty Loan Luncheon" (St. Paul, Minn., May 19, 1919), 3, folder "Secretary McAdoo itinerary/speeches 2/2," box 20, GFRG53; National War Savings Committee, "War Savings Societies," Box 35, GFRG53; War Savings Society of Massachusetts, "War Saving Stamps—War Saving Societies," folder "War," box 13, GFRG53; "Activities of the National Committee in Connection with the 6/28 National War Savings Day," folder "WS—General," box 39, GFRG53.

15. For wartime inflation, see Rockoff, "Until It's Over, Over There;" Meg Jacobs, *Pocketbook Politics: Economic Citizenship in Twentieth-Century America* (Princeton, N.J.: Princeton University Press, 2004), 53–54; Dana Frank, "Housewives, Socialists and the Politics of Food: The 1917 New York Cost-of-Living Protests," *Feminist Studies* 11 (Summer 1985), 255–285.

For War Loans as a means of absorbing wages and propagandizing against extravagance, see McAdoo, *Crowded Years,* 384; Transcript, Conference on War Savings Certificates, October 12, 1917.

The Federal Reserve decision to maintain easy money policies throughout the war—so that financial institutions, corporations, and voluntary associations might finance acquisitions of Liberty bonds by customers, employees, or members on partial payment plans—exacerbated inflation.

16. Transcript, Conference on War Savings Certificates, October 12, 1917, 8; Report of the National War Savings Committee, August 5, 1918, 5, William G. McAdoo papers, LOC; Report of the National War Savings Committee, August 5, 1918, 9–10, folder "National War Savings Committee," box 25, GFRG53; William G. McAdoo, "The Second Liberty Loan" (address delivered at the Annual Convention of the ABA, Atlantic City, N.J., September 28, 1917), 16; Frank A. Vanderlip, "How to Win the War" (New York: National City Bank, 1917), 7, 19; Frank A. Vanderlip, "One Hundred Million Soldiers" (sound recording, 1918), LOC; Federal Reserve Bank of Richmond, "The Hope of the World," folder "Directors' Correspondence 4," box 34, GFRG53; War Savings Committee of Massachusetts, *Bay State Bulletin,* November 7, 1918, folder "bulletins," box 13, GFRG53.

17. National War Savings Committee, "War Savings Societies," Box 35, GFRG53; National War Savings Committee, "War Savings Societies;" Jerome Thralls and R. F. Ayers to Frank A. Vanderlip, December 26, 1917; National War Savings Committee Report, August 5, 1918, 9, William G. McAdoo papers, LOC; Paper bank, folder "Forms, Blanks, Christmas savings," box 13, GFRG53; Federal Reserve Bank of Richmond, "The Seed of Success: The Third Liberty Loan," April 27, 1918, box 13, GFRG53; Marvin M. Parks, "Thrift: An Appeal to Parents and Teachers" (1918), 2, folder "Georgia War Savings Committee—6th District," box 16, GFRG53; Macy Campbell, "On to Berlin! Children's Talk No. 1," folder "War Savings Leaflets 7th District," box 16, GFRG53; "Exhibitor's Press Book," folder 1, box 125, GFRG53; "Buy a Liberty Bond and Kill Two Birds" and "Want in Old Age," Guy Emerson scrapbook, vol. 2, LOC.

18. McAdoo, *Crowded Years,* 378–380.

For a discussion of the significance of "symbolic" dimensions of citizenship, as distinct from its formal legal aspects, see Cott, "Marriage and Women's Citizenship"; Anderson, *Imagined Communities.*

19. McAdoo, *Crowded Years,* 381; Carter Glass to Senator Wm. Calder, March 31, 1919, folder "Misc. Letters A-3," box 44, GFRG53; John Muir and Co., "Your Liberty Bond" (New York: 1919), 17; Second Federal Reserve District Liberty Loan Committee, *Handbook for Speakers: Third Liberty Loan,* (Washington D.C.: GPO, 1918), 7.

20. U.S. Treasury, *Annual Report* (1918), 6; "Libertys and Their Market Price," *WW,* March 1919, 499.

Hundred-dollar Liberty bonds traded as low as $82 in 1920. Lawrence E. Mitchell, *The Speculation Economy: How Finance Triumphed Over Industry* (San Francisco: Berrett-Koehler Publishers, 2007), 256, 340.

21. Nathaniel Whitney, *The Sale of War Bonds in Iowa* (Iowa City: State Historical Society of Iowa, 1923), 87; Richard L. Metcalf to Brice Clagett, May 23, 1918, file 10, LWRG53; Committee on Library to William McAdoo, April 22,

1920, COL letterbook, vol. 4, NYSE Archives; R. T. Ayers to Frederick A. Delano, January 10, 1918, file 42, LWRG53; U.S. Department of the Treasury, "Exchange of Bonds," December 29, 1917, file 42, LWRG53.

22. McAdoo, "Enlist Your Dollars"; "Memorandum of Conference of Liberty Loan Executive and Publicity Directors," June 17–18, 1918, 2–7, folder "NWLLC," box 124, GFRG53; "Outline for an Address on the Liberty Bond Situation," folder 1, box 124, GFRG53; "McAdoo Urges War Loans," *NYT,* December 18, 1917, 10; Hon. Geo R. Seay to Clarkson Potter, September 23, 1918, folder "Directors' Correspondence—1," box 34, GFRG53; Federal Reserve Bank of Richmond, "Hold Fast to the Best Investment in the World: Important Statement by the Secretary of the Treasury," February 1, 1918, folder "Directors' Correspondence—3," box 34, GFRG53; U.S. Treasury, *Annual Report* (1917), 3–4.

23. John Muir and Co., "Your Liberty Bond," 18 (New York 1918), 18; Theodore Hardee, "You and Your Bonds: An Exclusively Suggested Editorial," folder "Press Twelfth District," box 17, GFRG53.

24. "Would End Short Selling," *NYT,* October 14, 1918, 18; Gilbert, *American Financing,* 130.

25. Gilbert, *American Financing,* 130, 133, 181; William J. Shultz, *Financial Development of the United States* (New York: Prentice Hall, 1937), 535; Russell C. Leffingwell, untitled address before the American Economic Association, December 29, 1920, box 3, DFH; Elmus R. Wicker, *Federal Reserve Monetary Policy, 1917–1933* (New York: Random House, 1966), 16–17, 35, 44; Allan H. Meltzer, *A History of the Federal Reserve, Volume I: 1913–1951* (Chicago: University of Chicago Press, 2003), 88; U.S. Treasury, *Annual Report* (1917), 4, 14, 60; Charles Hamlin to David F. Houston, August 1920, box 1, DFH; U.S. Treasury, *Annual Report* (1919), 107; Vincent P. Carosso, *Investment Banking in America* (Cambridge, Mass.: Harvard University Press, 1970), 231–234.

26. Marc Allen Eisner, *From Warfare State to Welfare State: World War I, Compensatory State Building, and the Limits of the Modern Order* (University Park, Pa.: Pennsylvania State University Press, 2000), 222–230, 245–247; Donald R. Wells, *The Federal Reserve System: A History* (Jefferson, N.C.: McFarland Publishing Company, 2004), 35–37; Meltzer, *History of the Federal Reserve,* 127–132, 152–153; Mitchell, *Speculation Economy,* 256–261; Gilbert, *American Financing,* 218.

27. Available at http://eh.net/encyclopedia/article/Rockoff.WWI; Rockoff, "Until It's Over, Over There;" "Report of Discussions at Dinner Given By Mr. Vanderlip," July 17, 1918, 1, folder "Miscellaneous Letters A," box 44, GFRG53; Carver, "Meaning and Function of Thrift," 53–58.

28. Carver, *Recollections,* 230; U.S. Treasury, *Annual Report* (1917); Thomas Nixon Carver, "War Thrift: Conservation of Food and Man Power" (address at the Milton Public Library, Milton, Mass., January 13, 1918), 6; Carver, "Meaning and Function of Thrift," 26–32, 52–58, 61.

For consumer-based theories of political economy, see Jacobs, *Pocketbook Politics;* Kathleen Donohue, *Freedom from Want: American Liberalism and the Idea of the Consumer* (Baltimore: Johns Hopkins Press, 2005); Lizabeth Cohen, *A Consumer's Republic: The Politics of Mass Consumption in Postwar America* (New York: Knopf, 2003); Lawrence B. Glickman, *A Living Wage: American Workers and the Making of Consumer Society* (Ithaca, N.Y.: Cornell University Press, 1997); William Leach, *Land of Desire: Merchants, Power, and the Rise of a New American Culture* (New York: Pantheon Books, 1993).

29. National War Savings Committee, "(Confidential) Composite Questionnaire," August 17, 1918, 179, box 51, GFRG53; "10 Original Ads for Liberty Bonds," vol. 32, RG 53, NA; "Report of Discussions at Dinner Given by Mr. Vanderlip," July 17, 1918, 1, folder "Report of a Discussion at Dinner," box 44, GFRG53; "Sketches for Liberty Loan Window Trims," folder "2nd District," box 1, GFRG53; Folder "2nd Federal Reserve District," box 126, GFRG53; "A Few Specimen Window Trims" and "Merchants and the Fighting Fourth Liberty Loan," folder 5, box 1, NP; Vanderlip, "How to Win the War," 15; "McAdoo in St. Paul," n.d., folder "Secretary McAdoo Itinerary/Speeches 2/2," box 20, GFRG53.

30. "'Business as Usual' a Delusion," *Bay State Bulletin*, April 4, 1918, folder "Bulletins 1st Federal Reserve District," box 13, GFRG53; James W. Gerard, "Why We Should Buy Liberty Bonds?" *(WW)*, December 1918, 597.

   For McAdoo's speeches against "business as usual," see folder "McAdoo Speeches 2/2," box 20, GFRG53.

31. *The Sticker* (Portland, Ore.), November 1, 1918, folder "Publicity 12th District," box 17, GFRG53.

32. Thomas Nixon Carver, "Conservation of Human Resources," in *The Foundations of National Prosperity: Studies in the Conservation of Permanent National Resources,* ed. Richard T. Ely, Thomas Nixon Carver, C. K. Leith, and Ralph Henry Hess (New York: Macmillan, 1917), 336; Carver, *Recollections,* 230; Carver, "War Thrift," 6–7.

33. Vanderlip, "How to Win the War," 8; Ellis Parker Butler, "Robinson Crusoe and Thrift Stamps," *War Thrift* (War Savings Committee for New Jersey, 1918), 6; "Exhibitor's Press Book," folder 1, box 125, GFRG53; Carver, "War Thrift"; *The War Saver,* April 1918, folder "The War Saver," box 36, GFRG53.

34. "War Saving Stamps—War Saving Societies," folder "War," box 13, GFRG53; Carver, "War Thrift," 6–7.

35. Daniel Rodgers, *Contested Truths: Keywords in American Politics Since Independence* (Cambridge, Mass.: Harvard University Press, 1998), 184; Shelton Stromquist, *Reinventing 'The People': The Progressive Movement, the Class Problem, and the Origins of Modern Liberalism* (Chicago: University of Illinois Press, 2006).

4. Mobilizing the Financial Nation

1. Ann Hagedorn, *Savage Peace: Hope and Fear in America* (New York: Simon and Schuster, 2007), 13; Adriane Lentz-Smith, *Freedom Struggles: African Americans and World War I* (Cambridge, Mass.: Harvard University Press,

2009), 9, 34–38, 43–44; Carole Marks, *Farewell—We're Good and Gone: The Great Migration* (Bloomington: Indiana University Press, 1989).

2. "Campaign Suggestions and Outline of Work," folder 2, box 125, GFRG53; "News of the Nation's Capital," *Savannah Tribune (ST)*, October 20, 1917, 6.

3. William Gibbs McAdoo, *Crowded Years: The Reminiscences of William G. McAdoo* (New York: Houghton Mifflin, 1931), 378, 385; Martha L. Olney, *Saving and Dissaving by 12,817 American Households: 1917–1919* (Ann Arbor, Mich.: Inter-University Consortium for Political and Social Research, 1995).

4. Christopher Capozzola, *Uncle Sam Wants You: World War I and the Making of the Modern American Citizen* (New York: Oxford University Press, 2008), 7–10, 86–87.

5. Transcript, Conference on War Savings Certificates, October 12, 1917, folder "Conference War Savings Certificates 10/12/17," box 25, GFRG53; "Some Notes Taken at Conference of Members of the Savings Division," April 19, 1919, 23, folder "1917–1920 Conferences," box 25, GFRG53; National War Savings Committee, Report, August 5, 1918, 1, folder "National War Savings Committee," box 25, GFRG53; "Frank Vanderlip, Banker, Dies at 72," *NYT*, June 30, 1937, 23; Frank A. Vanderlip, *From Farm Boy to Financier* (New York: D. Appleton-Century, 1935), 83–92; Rhode Island Savings Association, form letter, April 30, 1918, folder "form letters—general," box 13, GFRG53; U.S. Department of the Treasury, *Annual Report* (Washington, D.C.: GPO, 1918), 32; Minutes, War Savings Society Conference, September 23–25, 1918," folder "War Savings Society Conference," box 25, GFRG53; H. R. Bonner, *Teaching of Thrift* (n.p., 1917), 43.

6. National War Savings Committee, Report, August 5, 1918, 5; Folder "Cartoons 1918 Treasury Department," box 27, GFRG53; State Director of Maine, "Notes on War Savings Stamp Advertising," folder "Advertising," box 13, GFRG53; Second Federal Reserve District Liberty Loan Committee, "Feature Publicity (Stunts) Others Have Used Successfully," folder 9, box 1, NP.

    For emphasis on the importance of technologies of mass communication and daily practices in national consciousness, see Eric Hobsbawm, *Nations and Nationalism Since 1780: Programme, Myth, Reality* (New York: Cambridge University Press, 1990); Benedict Anderson, *Imagined Communities: Reflections on the Origins and Spread of Nationalism* (London: Verso, 1983); Etienne Balibar, "The Nation Form: History and Ideology," *Review: A Journal of the Fernand Braudel Center* 13 (Summer 1990), 329–361; Carroll Smith Rosenberg, "Discovering the Subject of the 'Great Constitutional Discussion,' 1786–1789," *JAH* 79, no. 3 (December 1992), 841–873.

7. Nathaniel Whitney, *The Sale of War Bonds in Iowa* (Iowa City: State Historical Society of Iowa, 1923), 53–54; American Bankers Association, *The Liberty Loan of 1917* (n.p., 1917), 10; Liberty Loan Organization of the Eighth Federal Reserve District to Frank R. Wilson, October 21, 1918, file 40, Liberty Loan and War Savings Correspondence Files (Entry UD 323), Records of the Bureau of Public Debt (Record Group 53), National Archives, College Park, Maryland (LWRG53); Antoinette Funk, Report, May 15, 1918, 1, folder 6, box 125,

GFRG53; "Advertising Campaigns: Second Liberty Loan" scrapbook, vol. 9, GFRG53; "Exhibitors' Press Book," folder 1, box 125, GFRG53.

8. U.S. Department of the Treasury, *The Second Liberty Loan of 1917: A Source Book* (Washington, D.C.: GPO, 1917), 1; Transcript, Conference on War Savings Under the Auspices of the Savings Bank Section, 43, box 30, GFRG53; National Education Association, "Program of the 49th Annual Meeting of the Department of Superintendence" (1919), folder "National Education Association," box 30, GFRG53.

9. Bonner, *Teaching of Thrift*, 1; Josephine Bacon, "Members of One Family" and "A Liberty Loan That's a Victory Loan," *The Rally* (June 1918), folder "Miscellaneous War Savings Materials," box 35, GFRG53; National War Savings Committee, Report, August 5, 1918, 1–4.

10. William H. Richardson, *Half an Hour with 'Over the Top' Empey* (Jersey City, N.J.: Press of Gaddis, 1917), 15, 21, 27; R. W. Woolley, "Report of the Foreign Language Division," folder 6, box 125, GFRG53, 19; Charles F. Heartman, "The Liberty Loan: Why Americans of German and Austrian Origin Should Buy Bonds" (New York: n.p., 1918), 4; Hon. Joseph Buffington to American people of Slavic Blood, November 1918, folder "Miscellaneous Letters A-3," box 44, GFRG53.

11. Woolley, "Report of the Foreign Language Division," 17; "Patriotic Chinese Invests," *NYT*, October 24, 1917, 3.

12. "Triumph's Symbols Adorn Victory Way," *NYT*, April 22, 1919, 4; Liberty Loan Committee of Buffalo, N.Y., *Report of the Director of Publicity* (Buffalo, N.Y.: 1918), 10; U.S. Department of the Treasury, *Report of the NWLLC for the Third Liberty Loan Campaign* (Washington, D.C.: GPO, 1918), 21; Horace M. Kallen, *Culture and Democracy in the United States* (New York: Boni and Liveright, 1924).

For the historiography on ideas about pluralism, see David A. Hollinger, *Postethnic America: Beyond Multiculturalism* (New York: Basic Books, 1995); Leslie J. Vaughan, *Randolph Bourne and the Politics of Cultural Radicalism* (Lawrence, Kans: University Press of Kansas, 1997); Jonathan Zimmerman, "'Each "Race" Could Have Its Heroes Sung,': Ethnicity and the History Wars in the 1920s," *JAH* 87 (June 2000), 92–111.

13. "June 28th Set Aside as Thrift Stamp Day," *ST*, June 15, 1918, 1; "Wage Earners Bank Takes $5,000 Bonds," *ST*, April 20, 1918, 1; "Negroes Urged to Give $1 to War Work," *ST*, November 23, 1918, 1; Lentz-Smith, *Freedom Struggles*, 4; "They Say," *Advocate* [Kansas City, Kansas], October 4, 1918, 1; "Our Part in the Liberty Loan Parade," *Advocate* [Kansas City, Kansas], October 4, 1918, 1.

14. "Emancipation Address at Auditorium," *ST*, January 12, 1918, 6; "An Appeal to Every Negro to Help Win the War," *ST*, 33, 6; "20,000 Cheering Marchers Turn Out in Biggest Civic Parade Held in This Country by Negroes," *ST*, May 11, 1918, 1; "Patriotism and Work," *ST*, May 18, 1918, 4; "What Savings May Mean," *ST*, May 4, 1918, 4.

15. Glenda Elizabeth Gilmore, *Gender and Jim Crow: Women and the Politics of White Supremacy in North Carolina, 1896–1920* (Chapel Hill: University of

North Carolina Press, 1996); "Conference of War Savings Stamp Workers," *ST,* April 27, 1918, 4; "Negroes in Big Patriotic Parade," *ST,* June 8, 1918, 1; "Col. Roscoe Simmons Draws Thousands" *Advocate* [Kansas City, Kansas], April 19, 1918, 1; "War Savings Drive at Dale by Negroes," *ST,* June 29, 1918, 4.

16. "6000 Negro Children in Parade," *ST,* October 27, 1917. 1; "Conference of War Savings Stamp Workers," *ST,* April 27, 1918, 4; "NAACP Objects to Forcing Negroes," *ST,* June 29, 1918, 1; "June 28th Set Aside as Thrift Stamp Day," *ST,* June 15, 1918, 1; "Negroes Urged to Give $1 to War Work," *ST,* November 23, 1918, 1.

17. Boxes 16 and 34, GFRG53; Matthew Frye Jacobson, *Whiteness of a Different Color: European Immigrants and the Alchemy of Race* (Cambridge, Mass.: Harvard University Press, 1998); Gail Bederman, *Manliness and Civilization: A Cultural History of Gender and Race in the United States, 1880–1917* (Chicago: University of Chicago Press, 1998).

18. U.S. Department of the Interior, Office of the Commissioner of Indian Affairs, "The Indian's War Activities," December 1, 1918, 1, 22, box 35, GFRG53.

19. Joseph McCartin, *Labor's Great War: The Struggle for Industrial Democracy and the Origins of Modern Labor Relations* (Chapel Hill: University of North Carolina Press, 1997); Transcript, Conference on War Savings Certificates, October 12, 1917, 23, 30, 91–128, 180.

20. Minutes, Conference Among Members of Treasury Department Savings Division and Representatives from the Federal Reserve Districts, vol. 1, June 12, 1919, 183–4, box 26, GFRG53; U.S. Department of the Treasury, "War Savings Stamps: Thrift by the Week" (Washington, D.C.: GPO, n.d.).

21. U.S. Treasury, *The Second Liberty Loan of 1917,* 13–14; Section on Labor Organizations to Dear Sir, n.d., folder "Miscellaneous War Savings Material," box 36, GFRG53; "Suggestion for the Promoting the Sales of Liberty Bonds Among the Trade Unions," folder 4, box 125, GFRG53; National War Savings Committee, Report, August 5, 1918, 1–4; Dana Frank, *Purchasing Power: Consumer Organizing, Gender, and the Seattle Labor Movement, 1919–1929* (New York: Cambridge University Press, 1994), 67; "Thousands Cheer as McAdoo Pleads for Liberty Loan," *NYT,* June 5, 1917, 1; "To Seize Germany's $200 Million Here and Put It into Our Liberty Loan," *NYT,* October 23, 1917, 1; vol. 32, ACLRG53; Quoted in David Montgomery, *Fall in the House of Labor: The Workplace, the State, and American Labor Activism, 1865–1924* (New York: Cambridge University Press, 1987), 384–385.

22. "For Mr. Clagett," March 2, 1918, folder "Secretary McAdoo's itinerary/copies of speeches 2.2," box 20, GFRG53.

23. National War Savings Committee, Report, August 5, 1918, 1–4.

24. Boxes 4 and 20, GFRG53.

25. "Data on Columbia, SC," folder "Secretary McAdoo's itinerary/copies of speeches," box 20, GFRG53; Jonathan W. Simpson to Frank R. Wilson, March 25, 1918, folder "Secretary McAdoo's itinerary/copies of speeches," box 20, GFRG53.

26. Box 20, GFRG53; "Data on Mobile, AL," folder "Secretary McAdoo's itinerary/copies of speeches," box 20, GFRG53; Thomas H. West Jr. to Frank R.

Wilson, April 1, 1918, folder "Secretary McAdoo's itinerary/copies of speeches," box 20, GFRG53; Minutes of a Conference on War Savings Certificates, October 12, 1917, 177.

27. McAdoo, *Crowded Years*, 406.

28. U.S. Department of the Treasury, *Report of the NWLLC for the Victory Loan Campaign* (Washington, D.C.: GPO, 1919), 1; Sara Evans, *Born for Liberty: A History of Women in America* (New York: Free Press, 1987); Paula Baker, "The Domestication of Politics: Women and American Political Society, 1780–1920," in *Women, the State, and Welfare*, ed. Linda Gordon (Madison: University of Wisconsin Press, 1990), 55–77.

29. U.S. Treasury, *Annual Report* (1918), 66; McAdoo, *Crowded* Years, 406; U.S. Treasury, *Report of the NWLLC for the Victory Loan Campaign*, 3; Minutes, Meeting of the NWLLC, December 10, 1917, 5, folder "NWLLC," box 125, RG 53, NA; Minutes, Meeting of State Chairmen and Members of NWLLC, May 16, 1918, 1, folder 5, box 125, GFRG53; Minutes, Meeting of the Washington Club, April 12, 1918, folder 5, GFRG53, NA; Minutes, Meeting of State Chairmen and Members of NWLLC, May 15, 1918, 2–4, folder 5, box 125, GFRG53; Report, February 28, 1918, folder 3, box 1, NP; U.S. Department of the Treasury, *Report of the NWLLC for the Third Liberty Loan Campaign* (Washington, D.C.: GPO, 1918), 4.

30. Mrs. William G. McAdoo to County Chairman, May 18, 1918, folder 3, box 1, NP.

31. Whitney, *The Sale of War Bonds*, 99; Herman Philipson to State Publicity Directors, n.d., box 36, GFRG53; U.S. Department of the Treasury, *Report of the NWLLC for the First and Second Liberty Loan Campaigns* (Washington, D.C.: GPO, 1918), 33–35; untitled clipping, *NYT*, April 27, 1918, Guy Emerson scrapbook, vol. 2, LOC; Liberty Loan Committee of Buffalo, *Report of the Director of Publicity*, 5; U.S. Department of the Treasury, "U.S. Government Bonds of the Second Liberty Loan" (Washington, D.C.: GPO, 1917), 8.

32. Minutes, Meeting of State Chairmen and Members of NWLLC, May 16, 1918, 2; Minutes, Meeting of the NWLLC, December 14, 1917, 5–6, folder 5, box 125, GFRG53; U.S. Treasury, *Report of the NWLLC for the Victory Loan Campaign*, 18–19.

33. U.S. Treasury, *Report of the NWLLC for the Victory Loan Campaign*, 19, 25–26; Memorandum, n.d., folder 1, box 552, William G. McAdoo Papers, LOC.

34. "An Outline for Country Directors," n.d., folder "Campaign," box 13, GFRG53; Margaret Finnegan, *Selling Suffrage: Consumer Culture and Votes for Women* (New York: Columbia University Press, 1999); Capozzola, *Uncle Sam Wants You*, 10.

35. "Instructions for District Chairmen," n.d., folder 5, box 123, GFRG53; Frank Wilson to Hon. Joseph P. Tumulty, January 15, 1919, folder 5, box 123, GFRG53; U.S. Department of the Treasury, *Victory Loan: Handbook for Speakers* (Washington, D.C.: GPO, 1919), 55, 72; Paul M. Warburg, "How Can the Clergy Help the Victory Liberty Loan?" (Washington, D.C.: GPO, 1919), 10, 12.

36. U.S. Department of the Treasury, *Report of the NWLLC for the Fourth Liberty Loan Campaign* (Washington, D.C.: GPO, 1918), 2; "Women Are Citizens," Detroit and Wayne County Liberty Bond Sales Organization (1918); John E. Gardin, "Liberty Bonds for the Business Woman" (address before the Contemporary Club, Newark, N.J., June 8, 1917), 10.

37. Connecticut Woman's Suffrage Association, form letter dated September 15, 1918, folder 3, box 1, NP; David Kennedy, *Over Here: The First World War and American Society* (New York: Oxford University Press, 2004), 30; Capozzola, *Uncle Sam Wants You*, 111–112; "Suffragist Opposes Loan," *NYT,* October 3, 1917, 13 ; "Anti's Pledge Aid to Loan," *NYT,* October 5, 1917, 8; "Denies Criticism of the Loan," *NYT,* October 4, 1917, 13.

38. U.S. Treasury, *Report of the NWLLC for the Third Liberty Loan Campaign,* 14–15; Minutes, Meeting of State Chairmen and Members NWLLC, May 16, 1918, 2; Minutes, Meeting of the NWLLC, December 14, 1917, 6; "Rain of Iron Crosses Booms Liberty Loan," *NYT,* October 21, 1917, 9; U.S. Department of the Treasury, *Report of the NWLLC for the First and Second Liberty Loan Campaigns,* 20.

   For a broader discussion of the role of suffrage organizations in home-front mobilization, see Julianne Unsel, "Women's Hour: Suffrage and American Citizenship in War and Reconstruction, 1914–1924" (Ph.D. diss., Columbia University, 2005).

39. Louise Michele Newman, *White Women's Rights: The Racial Origins of Feminism in the United States* (New York: Oxford University Press 1999); Francesca Morgan, *Women and Patriotism in Jim Crow America* (Chapel Hill: University of North Carolina Press, 2005); Ms. Bukeley to "Madam Chairman," September 28, 1918, folder 3, box 1, NP; Liberty Loan Committee of Buffalo, *Report of the Director of Publicity,* 14, 16; "Campaign Suggestions and Outline of Work"; U.S. Treasury, *Report of the NWLLC for the Third Liberty Loan Campaign,* 18; NWLLC, "Recommendations to County Chairman," 3, box 124, box 20, GFRG53; U.S. Treasury, *Report of the NWLLC for the Fourth Liberty Loan Campaign,* 5.

40. "Fourth Liberty Loan," folder "Promotional Photos," box 126, GFRG53; Rhode Island War Savings Committee, "War Savings Societies," folder "Form Letters—General—2- First District," box 13, GFRG53; William McAdoo, "Enlist Your Dollars," folder "Secretary McAdoo itinerary/speeches 2/2," box 20, GFRG53; "Get the Licker Habit," folder "Mr. Emerson's materials," box 10, GFRG53; Second Federal Reserve District Liberty Loan Committee, "Feature Publicity (Stunts)," 3.

41. Frank B. Coates (Lima, Ohio) to War Loan Organization, May 8, 1918, folder "Promotional Photos," box 126, GFRG53; "Van Cortlandt Park to be a 'Front' Today," *NYT,* April 29, 1919, 4; untitled clipping, *New York Herald,* April 30, 1919, Guy Emerson scrapbook, vol. 7, LOC; "Trenches at Van Cortlandt Park," *New York Tribune,* May 2, 1918, Guy Emerson scrapbook, vol. 8; "To Show Phases of War for Loan, *NYT,* April 27, 1919, 25; U.S. Treasury, *Annual Report* (1918), 63; "Captured U-boat to Aid War Loan," *NYT,* October 19, 1917, 3;

Reminiscences of Guy Emerson (1951), 148, 152–153, Oral History Collection, Butler Library, Columbia University.

42. "Memorandum of Conference of Liberty Loan Executive and Publicity Directors," June 17–18, 1918, 2 in folder "NWLLC," box 124, GFRG53; Newell Dwight Davis, "The Atrocities of Germany," folder "1st and 2nd Districts," box 1, GFRG53; "Exhibitor's Press Book;" "Marie Van Gastel," in folder "Marie Van Gastel," box 35, GFRG53.

43. Second Federal Reserve District Liberty Loan Committee, "Feature Publicity (Stunts)," 3; Daniel T. Rodgers, *Contested Truths: Keywords in American Politics Since Independence* (Cambridge, Mass.: Harvard University Press, 1998), 15, 177–206; Mary P. Follett, *The New State: Group Organization the Solution of Popular Government* (New York: Longmans, Green, 1918).

44. Folder "Mr. Emerson's Materials," box 10, GFRG53.

45. "Nebraska Plan Adopted by Every State in the Union," folder "War Savings— General—Sixth District," box 16, GFRG53; U.S. Department of the Treasury, postcard, n.d., folder "Proclamation," box 17, GFRG53; National War Savings Committee, Report, August 5, 1918, a.2–a.6.

46. Guy Emerson scrapbook, vol. 5, LOC; Second Federal Reserve District Liberty Loan Committee, "Feature Publicity (Stunts)," 2–4; U.S. Treasury, *Report of the NWLLC for the Victory Loan Campaign,* 21, 56. Whitney, *Sale of War Bonds,* 104; untitled clipping, *New York Tribune,* May 2, 1918, Guy Emerson scrapbook vol. 3, LOC.

47. "Puts Full Steam into Loan Drive for Final Week," *NYT,* October 22, 1917, 1; "Summary of Votes Taken at the Conference," June 12–13, 1919, folder "Conference: War Savings Certificates, October 12, 1917," box 25, GFRG53; Carter Glass to the Clergymen of America, March 28, 1919, folder "Miscellaneous Letters A3," box 44, GFRG53; vol. 1, ACLRG53.

48. Transcript, War Savings Society Conference, September 23, 1918, 2, folder "War Savings Conference 9/23/18," box 25, GFRG53.

49. Minutes of District of Columbia Division of NWLLC, April 19, 1918, 1, folder 5, box 125, GFRG53; Massachusetts War Savings Committee, "Happy Jack Tells Children What to Do," *War Savings Bulletin* (May 23, 1918), folder "Bulletin," box 13, GFRG53; Liberty Loan Committee of Buffalo, *Report of the Director of Publicity,* 43; John K. Allen, "Distribution of Treasury Department Medals," folder 5, box 1, NP.

50. Second Federal Reserve District Liberty Loan Committee, "Feature Publicity (Stunts)," 3; Whitney, *Sale of War Bonds,* 140.

51. "Loan Sales Mount to $175 Million," *NYT,* October 5, 1917, 1; Woolley, "Report of the Foreign Language Division," 14; "Some Difference in Patriotism," *ST,* May 24, 1918, p. 1; U.S. Treasury Department to Loundon, September 28, 1918, file 40, LWRG53; Liberty Loan Committee of Washington, D.C., Bulletin no. 2 (April 11, 1918), folder "NWLLC," box 124, GFRG53; Liberty Loan Committee of Buffalo, *Report of the Director of Publicity,* 38.

52. Second Federal Reserve District Liberty Loan Committee, "Feature Publicity (Stunts)," 4; National War Savings Committee, Form Letter [n.d.], folder "Form Letters," box 36, GFRG53.

53. Capozzola, *Uncle Sam Wants You,* 18–19, 21–54, 117–143, 173–205; "Report on the Activities of the State Councils of Defense in the Second Liberty Loan," December 10, 1917, box 35, GFRG53, 12, 17.

54. State Director of Maine, "Notes on War Savings Advertising," n.d., folder "Advertising," box 13, GFRG53; "Instructions to Canvassers," n.d., folder "Committees," box 13, GFRG53; Whitney, *Sale of War Bonds,* 140–141; National War Savings Committee, Confidential Composite Questionnaire, August 17, 1918, 171, box 51, GFRG53.

55. National War Savings Committee, Confidential Composite Questionnaire, August 17, 1918, 163; Whitney, *Sale of War Bonds,* 33–34.

56. U.S. Treasury, *Report of the NWLLC for the Third Liberty Loan Campaign,* 22.

57. Whitney, *Sale of War Bonds,* 135–138.

58. Ibid., 112, 129–132; Charles D. Stewart, "Prussianizing Wisconsin," *Atlantic Monthly,* January 1919, 99–105.

59. "To Intern Austrian During the War," *NYT,* December 28, 1917, 6; Capozzola, *Uncle Sam Wants You,* 10–13, 117–143; "Suspect Brothers as German Spies," *NYT,* October 28, 1917, 16; untitled clipping, *Evening Sun,* April 20, 1918, Guy Emerson scrapbook, vol. 2, LOC; "Exhibitor's Press Book"; Whitney, *Sale of War Bonds,* 116–117, 142.

60. McAdoo, *Crowded Years,* 386; Indiana War Savings Committee, "Basic Principles for the 1919 War Savings Campaign," folder "Committee Seventh District," box 16, GFRG53; Minutes, Meeting of the Liberty Loan Committee of New York, October 8, 1918, folder 49–8, box 49, TWL; Austin P. Haines, "Borrowing with a Club," *New Republic,* March 29, 1919, 273; Whitney, *Sale of War Bonds,* 126; Stewart, "Prussianizing Wisconsin," 99–105.

61. Capozzola, *Uncle Sam Wants You,* 10–12; Brian Balogh, *A Government Out of Sight: The Mystery of National Authority in Nineteenth-Century America* (New York: Cambridge University Press, 2009).

62. Theodore Hardee, "You and Your Bonds," folder "Press 12th District," box 17, GFRG53.

5. The Postwar Struggle for the Financial Nation

1. "Aerogram," folder "Aerogram Twelfth District," box 17, GFRG53; Trench cap brigade hat, folder "War Savings General," box 13, GFRG53; "This is a hand grenade," folder "Miscellaneous War Savings Materials," box 39, GFRG53; "Some Notes Concerning the 1919 Savings Movement," 29, folder "Miscellaneous War Savings Materials," box 40, GFRG53.

2. For convenience, I will refer to the Treasury's postwar marketing efforts as "U.S. Government Savings," although the Treasury continued to use the "War Savings" designation through 1922.

3. Lippmann quoted in Anthony Read, *The World on Fire: 1919 and the Battle with Bolshevism* (New York: W. W. Norton, 2008), 187; "Ole Hanson Here," *NYT,* May 10, 1919, 13.

4. "1 Killed, 40 Injured in Riots," "Casualties in Downtown Riot," "Mounted Police, War Tank and Army Truck Crash Through Maddened Crowds," and

"Socialist Offices Are Stormed and Wrecked," *Cleveland Plain Dealer*, May 2, 1919, 1.

5. David Montgomery, *The Fall of the House of Labor: The Workplace, the State, and American Labor Activism, 1865–1925* (New York: Cambridge University Press, 1989); Leo Wolman, *Growth of the American Trades Unions, 1880–1923* (New York: National Bureau of Economic Research, 1924); Allan H. Meltzer, *A History of the Federal Reserve*, vol. 1 (Chicago: University of Chicago Press, 2003), 90, 109; Beverly Gage, *The Day Wall Street Exploded: A Story of America in Its First Age of Terror* (New York: Oxford, 2009); Adriane Lentz-Smith, *Freedom Struggles: African Americans and World War I* (Cambridge, Mass.: Harvard University Press, 2009); Ann Hagedorn, *Savage Peace: Hope and Fear in America, 1919* (New York: Simon and Schuster, 2007); Dana Frank, *Purchasing Power: Consumer Organizing, Gender, and the Seattle Labor Movement, 1919–1929* (New York: Cambridge University Press, 1994); Read, *The World on Fire*; Robert Whitaker, *On the Laps of Gods: The Red Summer of 1919 and the Struggle for Justice That Remade a Nation* (New York: Crown, 2008); Francis Russell, *A City in Terror: 1919, The Boston Police Strike* (New York: Viking Press, 1975).

6. World War I served as "a testing ground for the principle of government involvement in the economic life of the nation." David Kennedy, *Over Here: The First World War and American Society* (New York: Oxford University Press), 98; Gary Gerstle, *American Crucible: Race and Nation in Twentieth Century America* (Princeton, N.J.: Princeton University Press, 2001), 123.

7. "The War Savings Society," *Bay State Bulletin*, November 7, 1918, folder "Bulletins 1st Federal Reserve District," box 13, GFRG53; U.S. Department of the Treasury, *Annual Report* (Washington, D.C.: GPO, 1919), 1, 60; U.S. Department of the Treasury, *Annual Report* (Washington, D.C.: GPO, 1920), 145–146

8. William Mather Lewis to Ohio Superintendents, February 2, 1920, folder "Form Letters (Jan–Dec 1920)," box 36, GFRG53; U.S. Department of the Treasury, "Thrift Is Good Business for Business," folder "First and Second Federal Reserve District," box 1, GFRG53; Second Federal Reserve District, "War Savings in 1919," January 1919, 8–9, 16–19; "Some Notes on Visit from James K. Lynch," March 24, 1919, 2, folder "Reports 12th District," box 17, GFRG53.

9. Government Loan and Savings Organization of the Tenth Federal Reserve District, "The War Savings Society," folder "leaflets—10th Federal Reserve District," box 17, GFRG53; U.S. Department of the Treasury, "War Savings Societies: The Backbone of the 1919 Thrift Campaign" (Washington, D.C.: GPO, 1919), 3, folder "War Savings—Societies Seventh District," box 16, GFRG53; War Savings Organization of the Seventh Federal Reserve District, "The War Savings Society," folder "War Savings Society—Seventh Federal Reserve District," box 16, GFRG53.

10. U.S. Treasury, *Annual Report* (1919), 62; "Help to Reduce High Prices," folder "War Savings General," box 13, GFRG53.

11. War Loan Organization Savings Division of the Sixth Federal Reserve District, "The Home Circle Thrift Club," folder "Home Circle Thrift Club—Sixth District," box 16, GFRG53; Thomas Nixon Carver, "The Meaning and Function of Thrift" (1918), reprinted in Carnegie Endowment for International Peace, *Preliminary Economic Studies of the War,* 10 (1919), 13.

12. U.S. Department of the Treasury, "The Part of War Savings in Preserving Civilization," February 6, 1919, folder "War Savings Great Britain," box 30, GFRG53; Minutes of a Conference Among Members of the Treasury Department Savings Division and Representatives from the Federal Reserve Districts, vol. 1, June 12, 1919, 172; "Save for a Purpose," folder "How to Invest Your Money," box 18, GFRG53; Carver, "The Meaning and Function of Thrift," 18, 23, 41, 43, 45, 60.

13. "Strengthening Business Foundations," March 21, 1919, 6, folder "NWLLC," box 125, GFRG53; Thomas Nixon Carver, "Economic Theory to Be Made Practical in Our Work" (address before the Bureau of Education, Boston, Mass., January 16, 1919), 5–6, folder "form letters—general—First Federal Reserve District," box 13, GFRG53.

14. William Mather Lewis to Lyceum Lecturers, January 2, 1920, folder "Form Letters (Jan–Dec 1920)," box 36, GFRG53.

15. Otto T. Mallery, "The Long-Range Planning of Public Works" in *Business Cycles and Unemployment: A Report and Recommendations of a Committee of the President's Conference on Unemployment* (New York: McGraw Hill, 1923), 241–242; Minutes, Conference Among Members of the Treasury Department Savings Division and Representatives from the Federal Reserve Districts, vol. 1, June 12, 1919, 39; "Report and Recommendations for the Committee on Unemployment and Business Cycles," in *Business Cycles and Unemployment;* Marc Allen Eisner, *From Warfare State to Welfare State: World War I, Compensatory State Building, and the Limits of the Modern Order* (University Park, Pa.: Pennsylvania State University Press, 2000), 235–240; U.S. Treasury, *Annual Report* (1920), 102; U.S. Treasury, *Annual Report* (1919), 102; Francis H. Sisson, "Capital Needs for American Industrial Development," *Annals of American Academy of Political and Social Science (AAAPSS),* 87 (January 1920), 95; Anne L. Alstott and Ben Novick, "War, Taxes, and Income Redistribution in the Twenties: The 1924 Veterans' Bonus and the Defeat of the Mellon Plan," *Tax Law Review* 59 (Summer 2006), 373–438.

16. Alvin Johnson, "The Promotion of Thrift in America," *AAAPSS,* 87 (January 1920), 233–238.

17. Minutes, Conference Among Members of the Treasury Department Savings Division and Representatives from the Federal Reserve Districts, vol. 1, June 12, 1919, 15–17, 31–32, 49–50, 237.

18. Minutes, Meeting of State Chairmen and Members of NWLLC, May 15, 1918, 4, folder 5, box 125, GFRG53; Antoinette Funk to "Dear Madam Chairman," July 3, 1919, folder 7, box 123, GFRG53.

19. William G. McAdoo to F. A. Delano, December 28, 1918, folder "Misc. Letters A-3," box 44, GFRG53; U.S. Treasury, *Annual Report* (1919), 1; George Zook, "Thrift in the United States," *AAAPSS,* 87 (January 1920): 205–211;

Alstott and Novick, "War, Taxes, and Income Redistribution in the Twenties"; Ajay Mehrotra, "Lawyers, Guns, and Public Moneys: The U. S. Treasury, World War I, and the Administration of the Modern Fiscal State," *Law and History Review* 28 (February 2010), 173–225.

20. Minutes, Conference Among Members of Treasury Department Savings Division and Representatives from the Federal Reserve Districts, vol. 1, June 12, 1919, 12, 16–19, 21, 24–26, 32, 38–42, 44, 55, 69, 248–249, 336, 345.

21. U.S. Treasury, *Annual Report* (1919), 68; U.S. Treasury, *Annual Report* (1920), 77.

22. Minutes, Conference among Members of Treasury Department Savings Division and Representatives from the Federal Reserve Districts, vol. 1, June 12, 1919, 89, 152–154, 164–165, 309–318.

23. Mary Synon to Lewis Franklin, April 1, 1919, folder "Letter to Mr. Franklin," box 124, GFRG53.

24. U.S. Treasury, *Annual Report* (1920), 72–74; "War Savings: Conference of School Authorities," January 15, 1919, 1, folder "Thrift Programs—School 4," box 11, GFRG53.

25. Minutes, Conference on War Savings Under the Auspices of the Savings Bank Section of the American Banking Association, May 15, 1919, 10–11, 14, folder "Conference on War Savings May 19, 1919," box 25, GFRG53.

26. Ibid., 24, 28, 37–39.

27. Minutes, Conference Among Members of Treasury Department Savings Division and Representatives from the Federal Reserve Districts, vol. 1, June 12, 1919, 55, 248–249, 336, 345.

28. James J. Hamilton to "The Officers and Members of Your Local Union," folder "Form Letters—General—1—First Federal Reserve District," box 13, GFRG53; "Some Notes Concerning the 1919 Savings Movement," 5, 21; "Some Notes Taken at Conference of Members of the Savings Division," April 19, 1919, 5, folder "Conference Notes April 19, 1919," box 25, GFRG53; "Resolution No. 96," June 23, 1921, file 97, LWRG53; "Resolution . . . Adopted Unanimously by the American Federation of Labor," June 19, 1920, folder "Form Letters January–December 1920," box 37, GFRG53; Johnson, "Promotion of Thrift," 233–238; Frank, *Purchasing Power,* 68.

29. Frank, *Purchasing Power,* 66–75; Judith Stein, *The World of Marcus Garvey: Race and Class in Modern Society* (Baton Rouge: Louisiana State University Press, 1986); Otis B. Grant, "Social Justice Versus Social Equality: The Capitalistic Jurisprudence of Marcus Garvey," *Journal of Black Studies* 33 (March 2003), 490–498; Jeffrey D. Howison, "'Let Us Guide Our Own Destiny': Rethinking the History of the Black Star Line," *Journal of the Ferdinand Braudel Center* 28 (2005), 29–49; Ramla Bandele, *Black Star: African American Activism in the International Political Economy* (Urbana: University of Illinois Press, 2008).

30. "Summary of Votes Taken at the Conference," June 12, 1919, folder "Conference: War Savings Certificates October 12, 1919," box 25, GFRG53; Minutes, U.S. Government Savings Conference, vol. 2, June 13, 1919, 255, box 26, GFRG53.

31. "Uncle Sam Can Help Your Employees Save Money" (1922), folder "Suggestions for Advertising," box 39, GFRG53; "Thrift as an American Ideal" (1919), folder "First and Second Federal Reserve District," box 1, GFRG53; U.S. Department of the Treasury, U.S. Government Savings Division, "Steady Workers!", folder "Miscellaneous War Savings Material," 7, box 39, GFRG53.

32. U.S. Department of the Treasury, *Annual Report* (Washington, D.C.: GPO, 1924), 83–84, U.S. Treasury, *Annual Report* (1922).

33. Files no. 140–166, LWRG53; E. C. Kibbee to Andrew Mellon, July 2, 1924, file 144, LWRG53; Hugh B. Werver to Andrew Mellon, July 7, 1924, file 144, LWRG53; Lew Wallace to Andrew Mellon, October 15 and November 15, 1924, file 147, LWRG53; Signe A. Berve to Andrew Mellon, August 1, 1924, file 146, LWRG53.

34. Minutes, Conference Among Members of Treasury Department Savings Division and Representatives from the Federal Reserve Districts, vol. 1, June 12, 1919, 15–17, 31–32, 49–50, 237; National Education Association, "Report on Thrift Education," July 1920, 1, folder "Thrift Programs in Schools No. 1," box 11, GFRG53; "Some Notes Taken at Conference of Members of the Savings Division," 19 April 1919, 7.

35. Louis Guenther, "Pirates of Promotion . . . The Wreckage," *WW*, March 1919, 510. Also Guenther, "Pirates of Promotion, Who Are After Your Liberty Bonds," *WW*, October 1918, 584–591. "Pirates of Promotion . . . George Graham Rice" *WW*, November 1918, 29–33; "Pirates of Promotion . . . In the Partial Payment Plan," *WW*, November 1918, 16–17; "Pirates of Promotion . . . The Oil Flotation Game," *WW*, December 1918, 149, 153; "Pirates of Promotion . . . Methods," *WW*, January 1919; "Pirates of Promotion . . . Market Manipulation," *WW*, February 1919, 393–398; "Pirates of Promotion . . . The Wreckage," *WW*, March 1919, 509–515; "Paul W. Warburg Says 'Immigrants Are Potential Capitalists,' " *Magazine of Wall Street*, 226; George W. Perkins, "It Is the Function of Law to Define and Punish Wrongdoing and Not to Throttle Business" (address before the Detroit Board of Commerce, Detroit, Mich., October 1, 1923), 18; Vincent P. Carosso, *Investment Banking in America: A History* (Cambridge, Mass.: Harvard University Press, 1970), 231–234; Charles S. Hamlin to Jason Westerfield, January 1, 1920, "Stock Frauds Better Business Bureau (BBB)" scrapbook, NYSE Archives, New York.

36. $100 bonds traded as low as $82 in 1920. Lawrence E. Mitchell, *The Speculation Economy: How Finance Triumphed Over Industry* (San Francisco: Berrett-Koehler, 2007), 256, 340; U.S. Treasury, *Annual Report* (1919), 48, 62; Guenther, "Pirates of Promotion . . . The Wreckage," 509, 512–513.

37. For other examples, see Guenther's series and "Stock Frauds BBB" scrapbook. Also Edward J. Balleisen, "Private Cops on the Fraud Beat: The Limits of American Business Self-Regulation, 1895–1932," *BHR* 83 (Spring 2009), 113–160; John Richardson, "Business Policing Itself Through Better Business Bureaus," *Harvard Business Review* (October 1930), 69–77.

38. Mitchell, *Speculation Economy*, 264–267.

39. Charles S. Hamlin to Jason Westerfield, January 1, 1920, and Carter Glass to Jason Westerfield, February 12, 1919, "Stock Frauds BBB" scrapbook; "War on Stock Swindling," *NYT*, January 10, 1919, 16.

40. "Stock Frauds BBB" scrapbook, 3; Committee on Library (COL) to Charles S. Hamlin, January 18, 1919, COL letterbook, vol. 4, NYSE Archives; "Committee to Unite Business Associations of the Second Federal Reserve Against Stock Swindling," March 3, 1919, "Stock Frauds BBB" scrapbook; "Committee to Unite Business Associations of the Second Federal Reserve Against Stock Swindling," March 3, 1919, "Stock Frauds BBB" scrapbook; "Unrest Due to Fakers," *Washington Post*, February 22, 1919, and "Stock Frauds Seen as a Spur to Bolshevism," *New York Tribune*, February 22, 1919, in "Stock Frauds BBB" scrapbook; Untitled report, "Stock Frauds BBB" scrapbook.

41. "Business, Labor, and Peace," *W. J. Wollman & Co. Review: Financial, Industrial and Economic Conditions*, January 18, 1919, "Stock Frauds BBB" scrapbook.

42. Myron T. Herrick to Jason Westerfield, November 28 and December 9, 1919, "Stock Frauds BBB" scrapbook.

After December 1919, the Associated Advertising Clubs integrated the work into its National Vigilance Committee working toward truth in advertising. The Exchange continued to advise, to provide funds, and to solicit members for donations. Myron T. Herrick to E. T. Meredith, December 22 and 29, 1919, E. T. Meredith to William Remick, December 29, 1919, William Remick to E. T. Meredith, January 2, 1920, "Stock Frauds BBB" scrapbook.

43. "Stock Frauds BBB" scrapbook; COL to Henry Ford, May 12, 1919, COL letter book, vol. 4, NYSE Archives.

44. Carosso, *Investment Banking in America*, 254; Ralph F. DeBedts, *The New Deal's SEC: The Formative Years* (New York: Columbia University Press, 1964); "Blue Sky Law Won't Fit in New York," *New York Sun*, December 26, 1919, "Stock Frauds BBB" scrapbook.

45. Kenneth Campbell Mackay, *The Progressive Movement of 1924* (New York: Octagon Books, 1972), 30–31; U.S. Treasury Department, *Annual Report* (1920), 102; Charles Kettleborough, "Soldiers' Bonus," *American Political Science Review* 16 (August 1922), 455. B. U. Ratchford, "American Government and Politics: Constitutional Provisions Governing State Borrowing," *American Political Science Review* 32 (August 1938), 705; Alstott and Novick, 431–432; U.S. Bureau of the Census, *Historical Statistics of the United States*, 4th ed. (New York: Cambridge University Press, 2000), accessed online at http://hsus .cambridge.org.proxy.wexler.hunter.cuny.edu/HSUSWeb/toc/tableToc.do?id= Ea61–124.

46. James B. Morman, "Cooperative Credit Institutions in the United States," *AAAPSS* 87 (January 1920), 182; Carosso, *Investment Banking in America*, 229; Edward H. Thomson, "American Farmers' Need for Capital," *AAAPSS* 87 (January 1920), 89–94; Johnson, "Promotion of Thrift," 233–238.

47. John A. Lapp, "The Insurance of Thrift," *AAAPSS* 87 (January 1920), 21–26.

48. William G. McAdoo, "Extending the Period of Government Control of the Railroads," 5, 11–17, 28, 30, 31; Glenn E. Plumb, *Labor's Plan for Govern-*

ment Ownership and Democracy in the Operation of the Railroads (Washington, D.C.: Plumb Plan League, 1919); Richard Waterman, "Proposed Plans for Railroad Legislation," *AAAPSS* (1919), 92.

49. Warfield, *Report of S. Davies Warfield . . . to the Committees NAORS in Respect to the Legislation Incident to the Return and Regulation of the Railroads* (Baltimore: NAORS, 1920), 18; Warfield, "Address . . . on the Occasion of Organization of the National Conference of Mutual Savings Banks," 3.

50. Warfield, *Report,* 12.

51. S. Davis Warfield, "The Return and Regulation of the Railroads," 1–6; Warfield, *Report,* 15.

52. Frank H. Sisson, "The Crux of the Railroad Problem" (address before the Society of Railroad Financial Officers, n.p., October 1919), 6; Warfield, "The Return and Regulation of the Railroads," 1.

53. S. Davies Warfield, "Address of S. Davies Warfield on the Occasion of the Dinner Given in His Honor," Baltimore, 1920, 8; Warfield, "The Return and Regulation of the Railroads," 4; S. Davies Warfield, *Statement Presented to the Chairman of the Committee on Interstate Commerce, U.S. Senate, March 21, 1921* (Baltimore: NAORS, 1921), 13.

54. Waterman, 100; Warfield, "Address . . . on the Occasion of the Organization of the National Conference of Mutual Savings Banks," 1, 2, 10–11; Warfield, *Report,* 24.

55. John J. Pulleyn, "The Institutional Investors' Part in the Rehabilitation of the Railroad" (address before the National Conference of Mutual Savings Banks, Philadelphia, Pa., 1921), 5; Warfield, *Report,* 24; Warfield, *Statement . . . Before the Committee on Interstate Commerce,* 1.

56. Francis H. Sisson, "Russianizing the Railroads" (New York: Guaranty Trust Co. of NY, 1919).

57. Warfield, "The Return and Regulation of the Railroads" 4; Warfield, "The Return of the Railroads to Private Ownership," 2–4, 6.

58. Guaranty Trust Co., press release, October 7, 1920, 3; A. J. County, "Where the Railroad Dollars Come and Go" (n.p., 1923), 7; Warfield, *Report,* 14; Sisson, "Russianizing the Railroads," 4–5, 14; Otto Kahn, "Suggestions Concerning the Railroad Problem," in Kahn, *Our Economic and Other Problems: A Financier's Point of View* (New York: George Doran, 1920), 110–112.

59. Warfield, *Report,* 4, 22; S. Davies Warfield, "Address before the 39th Annual Meeting of the Academy of Political Science," 1, 5, 10–11; Pulleyn, "The Institutional Investors' Part," 13; Warfield, "Address . . . on the Occasion of the Organization of the National Conference of Mutual Savings Banks," 14; Warfield, *Statement,* 4.

60. Eisner, *From Warfare State to Welfare State,* 134–136; Morton Keller, *Regulating a New Economy,* 45, 54; John T. Stover, *American Railroads* (Chicago: University of Chicago Press, 1997), 130, 179–180; Carosso, *Investment Banking In America,* 179; Warfield, "Address . . . on the Occasion of the Organization of the National Conference of Mutual Savings Banks," 3, 9.

61. Pulleyn, "The Institutional Investors' Part," 14–15; Warfield, "Address . . . on the Occasion of the Organization of the National Conference of Mutual Sav-

ings Banks," 2, 14; Warfield, *Statement*, 1, 2, 4, 5, 8, 11, 13, 17; Warfield, "The Return and Regulation of the Railroads," 4; Warfield, "Address . . . on the Occasion of the Dinner Given in His Honor," 21.

62. "Report of Committee of the American Railway Association Analyzing NAORS's Car Pooling Plan" (n.p., 1923); Warfield, *Statement*, 16; Frank H. Sisson, "Laying the Rails for Future Business" (New York: Guaranty Trust Co. of NY, 1918), 24–25.

63. Warfield, "Address . . . on the Occasion of the Organization of the National Conference of Mutual Savings Banks," 6.

6. Swords into Shares

1. Thomas Nixon Carver, *Recollections of an Unplanned Life* (New York: Ward Ritchie Press, 1949), 172, 205, 209–210, 230.

2. Carver, *Recollections of an Unplanned Life*, 83, 111, 141–142. For Ripley's impact on early twentieth-century racial thinking and immigration restriction, see Harwell Wells, "The Birth of Corporate Governance," *Seattle University Law Review* 33 (2010), 17; Eric L. Goldstein, *The Price of Whiteness: Jews, Race and American Identity* (Princeton, N.J.: Princeton University Press, 2006); John Higham, *Strangers in the Land: Patterns of American Nativism 1860–1925* (New York: Atheneum, 1963); Jonathan Spiro, *Defending the Master Race: Conservation, Eugenics and the Legacy of Madison Grant* (Burlington: University of Vermont Press, 2009).

3. Carver quoted in Harold Callender, "America May Soon Become an Economic Utopia," *NYT*, September 13, 1925, BR5; Thomas Nixon Carver, "Conservation of Human Resources," in *Foundations of National Prosperity*, ed. Richard T. Ely, Ralph H. Hess, Charles K. Leith, and Thomas Nixon Carver (New York: Macmillan Company,1917), 332, 353–355; Thomas Nixon Carver, *This Economic World and How It May Be Improved* (Chicago: A. W. Shaw., 1928), 355–356; Wells, "The Birth of Corporate Governance," 28, 37; William Z. Ripley, "From Wall Street to Main Street," *Atlantic Monthly*, January–June 1926, 105; "Professor Ripley and the Facts," *NYT*, November 14, 1925, 14; William Z. Ripley, *Wall Street and Main Street* (New York: Little Brown, 1926), 131.

4. Thomas Nixon Carver, "The Relation of Thrift to Nation Building," *AAAPSS*, 87 (January 1920), 5.

5. Thomas Nixon Carver quoted in "Preface," *Proceedings of the Academy of Political Science* (PAPS), 11 (1925), vi.

6. Thomas Nixon Carver, *Essays in Social Justice* (Cambridge, Mass: Harvard University Press, 1915), 280, 358; Thomas Nixon Carver, *Elementary Economics* (Boston: Ginn, 1920), 101; Thomas Nixon Carver, "The Changing Economic Status of Labor," *American Management Association, General Management Series* 34 (New York: American Management Association,1926, reprint 1967), 6; Thomas Nixon Carver, *The Present Economic Revolution in the United States* (Boston: Little Brown, 1925), 11; Theodore M. Knappen, "Creating Good-will Between Capital and Labor," *Magazine of Wall Street*, December 20, 1924, 262–263.

7. For Carver's opposition to old-age pensions and his skepticism toward labor unions, see Carver, *Essays in Social Justice*, 360–361; Carver, "Conservation of Human Resources," 300, 331.

8. Carver, *Elementary Economics*, 102; Carver, "The Changing Economic Status of Labor," 4–5; Carver, *The Present Economic Revolution*, 94, 123–124.

9. Carver, "Conservation of Human Resources," 327, 345–346, 355; Carver, *Elementary Economics*, 392; Carver, *The Present Economic Revolution*, 6, 7, 114–116, 160, 178; Thomas Nixon Carver, "Four Labor Programs," *Quarterly Journal of Economics* 33 (February 1919), 355; Carver, "The Changing Economic Status of Labor," 7, 11.

10. Carver, *This Economic World*, 356–357.

11. Charles Amos Dice, *New Levels in the Stock Market* (New York: McGraw Hill, 1929), 191, 195; Roy G. Blakely, "Thrift and Readjustment," *AAAPSS* 87 (January 1920), 30–38; Edward L. Thorndike, "Psychological Notes on the Motives for Thrift," *AAAPSS* 87 (January 1920), 30–38; A. C. Miller, "Thrift and the Financial Situation," *AAAPSS* 87 (January 1920), 57–64.

12. William L. Ransom, "Property Ownership as a Social Force," *PAPS* 11 (April 1925), 524.

13. Charles Amos Dice, *New Levels*, 2, 242

14. William A. Prendergast, "Public Regulation and the New Proprietorship," *PAPS* 11 (April 1925), 510; NICB, *Employee Stock Purchase Plans in the United States* (New York: NICB, 1928).

15. Arthur Williams, "Labor's Share in Ownership," *PAPS* 11 (April 1925), 362; Pierrepont B. Noyes, "Cooperation Through Stock Ownership," *PAPS* 11 (April 1925), 459; Carver, *The Present Economic Revolution*, 137–138; Thomas B. McAdams, "The Salable Bank," *Proceedings of the FAA Annual Convention* (Chicago: FAA, 1920), 34; Robert W. Dunn, *The Americanization of Labor: The Employers' Offensive Against Trade Unions* (New York: International Publishers, 1927), 159–160.

16. Charles Amos Dice, *New Levels*, 24, 255, 260.

17. Barnard Powers, "Who Are the Real Owners of Wall Street?" *Magazine of Wall Street*, December 26, 1924, 1104.

18. Arthur Williams, "Labor's Share in Ownership," *PAPS* 11 (April 1925), 360, 362.

19. Carver, *The Present Economic Revolution*, 118; Warren S. Stone, "Labor's Chain of Banks," *WW*, November 1924.

20. William Trufant Foster, "A Wider Distribution of Securities in Relation to Sustained Prosperity," *PAPS* 11 (April 1925), 403, 407.

21. Foster, "A Wider Distribution," 401; William Trufant Foster and Waddill Catchings, "The Dilemma of Thrift," *Atlantic Monthly* (February 1926), 19.

22. Alan Brinkley, *The End of Reform: New Deal Liberalism in Recession and War* (New York: Vintage Books, 1995), 42–46; Donald R. Richberg, "Cooperating with Competitors," *PAPS* 11 (April 1925), 501, 506; Prendergast, "Public Regulation and the New Proprietorship," 510.

23. George H. Soule, "Discussion: Illusions Regarding the Diffusion of Stock Ownership," *PAPS* 11 (April 1925), 482–483; Lewis Corey, "Employee Stock

Ownership," *New Republic,* May 11, 1927, 348; Lewis Corey, "Who Owns the Nation's Wealth?" *New Republic,* August 10, 1927, 300–303.

24. Sidney Hillman, "The Labor Banking Movement in the United States," *PAPS* 11 (April 1925), 469–472; Gorton James, Henry S. Dennison, Edwin F. Gay, Henry P. Kendall, and Arthur W. Burritt, *Profit Sharing and Stock Ownership for Employees* (New York: Harper, 1926), 13; Leland Rex Robinson, *Investment Trust Organization and Management* (New York: Ronald Press, 1926), 497.

25. Ransom, "Property Ownership as a Social Force," 525; Lindsay, "The Economic Revolution in the Ownership of Property in the United States," 356; Herbert Hoover, "Diffusion of Property Ownership," *PAPS* 11 (April 1925), 491.

26. Ransom, "Property Ownership as a Social Force," 528, 534.

27. Herbert C. Pell, "Consequences of Impersonal Ownership," *PAPS* 11 (April 1925), 428.

28. G. A. Bowers, "Employee Investments in Company Securities," *American Management Annual Convention Series* 25 (1926), 9; Richberg, "Cooperating with Competitors," 507; Pell, "Consequences of Impersonal Ownership," 425–428.

29. Ransom, "Property Ownership as a Social Force," 528, 530.

30. Ripley, *Main Street and Wall Street,* 77, 79.

31. Wells, "The Birth of Corporate Governance"; Mark S. Mizruchi, "Berle and Means Revisited: The Governance and Power of Large U.S. Corporations," *Theory and Society* 33 (October 2004), 579–617.

32. Ripley, *Main Street and Wall Street,* 28, 33, 52, 77. Most historians of corporate governance practices tend to agree with Ripley's assessment. John Coffee is the most pronounced exception. John Coffee, "The Rise of Dispersed Ownership: The Role of Law in the Separation of Ownership and Control" (Columbia Center for Law and Economic Studies, Working Paper no. 182, December 2000).

33. Ripley, *Main Street and Wall Street,* 92–96.

34. Ibid., ix, 83, 86.

35. Ibid., 99, 127, 129.

36. Ibid., ix, 109.

37. William Z. Ripley, "Stop, Look, Listen! The Shareholder's Right to Adequate Information," *Atlantic Monthly,* July 1926, 397, 385; Ripley, *Main Street and Wall Street,* 76, 136–137; William Z. Ripley, "From Wall Street to Main Street," *Atlantic Monthly,* January 1926, 103–104.

38. Ripley, *Main Street and Wall Street,* 111, 114, 121–122, 208–210; William Z. Ripley, "Wanted: A Guardian for the Small Stockholder," *Literary Digest,* December 12, 1925, 86; Ripley, "Stop, Look, Listen!" 394–395.

39. Ripley, *Main Street and Wall Street,* 111; John R. Dunlop to Mr. John Blank of Blankville, NY, June 30, 1927, folder 149–18, box 149, Thomas W. Lamont Papers, Baker Library, Harvard University, Cambridge, Massachusetts (TWL); Thomas W. Lamont, "Publicity for Industrial Corporations," *Industrial Management* 74 (July 1927), 2, 4, 6; John R. Dunlop to Thomas W. Lamont, September 13, 1926, folder 149–18, box 149, TWL.

40. Prendergast, "Public Regulation and the New Proprietorship," 516–517; Samuel Untermyer, "Looking Backward and Forward at Finance and Industry" (address before Constitutional Law Class, New York, June 30, 1928), 16; Arundel Cotter, "Discussion: Social Consequences of Employee Ownership," *PAPS* 11 (April 1925), 485.
41. Ripley, "From Wall Street to Main Street," 100; Ripley, "Stop, Look, Listen!" 385.

7. The Corporate Quest for Shareholder Democracy

1. Lawrence L. Murray, "Bureaucracy and Bipartisanship in Taxation: The Mellon Plan Revisited," *Business History Review (BHR)* vol 52 no. 2 (Summer 1978), 200–225; "Estimated Expenditures," June 11, 1920, folder "Estimated Expenditures," (GFRG53); David F. Houston, "Every Worker a Capitalist," *World's Work (WW)* January 1925; David F. Houston, "The City of AT&T," *The Outlook*, January 20, 1926; David F. Houston, untitled address before the Investment Bankers' Association Conference (New York, 1923); David F. Houston, "Speech on the Bell System" (address before the Bond Club of New York, New York, NY, October 22, 1925); David F. Houston, "Mr. Houston's Talk: Bell System Education Conference" (n.p., July 24, 1926); David F. Houston, "The Telephone as a Factor in Modern Business" (n. p., 1926); David F. Houston, "The Meaning and Strength of America" (address before the Commercial Club, Chicago, Ill., January 1, 1927); David F. Houston (address before the Convention of National Edison Light Association, Atlantic City, N.J., June 8, 1927), all in box 3, David F. Houston papers (MS Am 1510), Houghton Library, Harvard University, Cambridge, Mass. (DFH); David F. Houston, "Financing the War" (Washington, D.C., 1921), 3, box 2, DFH; David F. Houston, "What You Need to Know About Federal Taxation," *WW*, October 1922; U.S. Department of the Treasury, *Annual Report* (Washington, D.C.: GPO, 1920).
2. Ajay K. Mehrotra, "Lawyers, Guns, and Public Moneys: The U. S. Treasury, World War I, and the Administration of the Modern Fiscal State," *Law and History Review* 28 (February 2010), 180.
3. Carver had worked under Houston at the Department of Agriculture before World War I. Thomas Nixon Carver, *Recollections of an Unplanned Life* (New York: Ward Ritchie Press, 1949), 176.
4. William Lazonick, "Financial Commitment and Economic Performance: Ownership and Control in the American Industrial Corporation," *Business and Economic History* 17 (1988), 121.
5. David F. Houston, "Every Worker a Capitalist"; Roland Marchand, *Creating the Corporate Soul: The Rise of Public Relations and Corporate Imagery in American Big Business* (Berkeley: University of California Press, 1998), 164–166; Louis Galambos, *The Public Image of Big Business in America*, 193–195, 213, 220–221; Claude S. Fischer and Michael Hout, *Century of Difference*, 156; U.S. Census, Historical Statistics of the United States Millennial Edition Online, Table Db234–241, "Electrical Energy—Retail Prices, Residential Use, and Service Coverage: 1902–2000," at http://hsus.cambridge.org.proxy.wexler.

hunter.cuny.edu/HSUSWeb/essay/showtableessay.do?id=Db234–241&swidth=
1024; U.S. Census, Historical Statistics of the United States Millennial Edition
On-line, Table Df339–342, "Motor Vehicle Registrations, by Vehicle Type:
1900–1995" at http://hsus.cambridge.org.proxy.wexler.hunter.cuny.edu/HSUS-
Web/essay/showtableessay.do?id=Df339–342&swidth=1024; Beverly Gage, *The
Day Wall Street Exploded*, 314–355; O'Sullivan, *Contests for Corporate Con-
trol* 80–81, 84; Martha Olney, *Buy Now, Pay Later: Advertising, Credit, and
Consumer Durables in the 1920s* (Chapel Hill: University of North Carolina
Press, 1991), 6–85, 88, 89; Mary O'Sullivan and William Lazonick, "Finance
and Industrial Development, Part I: The United States and United Kingdom,"
Financial History Review 4 (1997), 16.

6. David F. Houston, "Every Worker a Capitalist": David F. Houston, "Address
of Hon. David W. Houston" (address before the Twelfth Annual Convention
of the Investment Banking Association, Washington, D.C., October 29, 1923),
2–3, box 3, DFH.

7. Marchand, *Creating the Corporate Soul*, 43–85; Stephen H. Norwood, *Labor's Flaming Youth: Telephone Operators and Worker Militancy, 1878–1923*
(Urbana: University of Illinois Press, 1990).

While AT&T institutional advertising dated from 1908, shareholders were
not featured until 1919. See folders 1–3, box 21, N. W. Ayer Advertising Agency
Records, Archives Center, National Museum of American History, Smithsonian
Institution, Washington, D.C. (NWA); Robert MacDougall, "Long Lines: AT&T,
Long Distance Telephony, and Corporate Control," at www.thebhc.org/publica
tions/BEHonline/2005/macdougall.pdf.

8. American Telephone and Telegraph [AT&T], "A Community of Owners
Nation-wide" (1923); AT&T, "Democracy—of the People, by the People, for
the People" (1921); AT&T, "In the Service of All the People" (1929); AT&T,
"Owned by Those It Serves" (1922), folder 3, box 21, NWA.

9. AT&T, "Our Triple Responsibility" (1920); AT&T, "Our Stockholders"
(1919); AT&T, "A Community of Owners Nation-wide;" AT&T, "Democracy," all in folder 2, box 21, NWA.

10. Houston, "Every Worker a Capitalist"; David F. Houston, "Creating Good
Will Between Capital and Labor," *Magazine of Wall Street*, December 30,
1924.

11. Houston, "Mr. Houston's Talk," 345; Houston, "Every Worker a Capitalist,"
24–26. For corporations' ideal of service in the 1920s, see Marchand, *Creating
the Corporate Soul*, 45, 164–166, 201.

12. Houston, "Every Worker a Capitalist," 24–26; David F. Houston, "The City of
A&T," *The Outlook*, January 20, 1926, 5–9.

13. William Z. Ripley, *Wall Street and Main Street* (Boston: Little Brown, Little,
1925); AT&T, "Owned by Those It Serves"; Houston, "Mr. Houston's Talk,"
348–349; Houston, "The City of AT&T," 8–10; David F. Houston, "Some
Aspects of the Telephone Business and Its Financing" (address before the
Massachusetts Bankers' Association, Boston, January 7, 1925), 11.

14. It grew at rate of over 20 percent per year throughout the decade. Folders 1–3,
box 21, NWA.

15. Leslie Hannah, "The 'Divorce' of Ownership from Control from 1900 Onwards: Re-calibrating Imagined Global Trends," *BHR*, 49 (July 2007), 425; Marchand, *Creating the Corporate Soul*, 201.

16. William Mather Lewis, "Freedom Through Thrift," *AAAPSS*, 87 (January 1920), 225–232.

17. "Summary of Votes Taken at the Conference," June 12, 1919, folder "Conference: War Savings Certificates," box 25, GFRG53; "Minutes of Conference Among Members of Treasury Department Savings Division and Representatives from the Federal Reserve Districts," vol. 1, June 12, 1919, 55, 248–249, 336, 345, box 26, GFRG53; Jacoby, *Modern Manors*, 3; Robert F. Foerster and Else H. Dietel, *Employee Stock Ownership in the United States* (Princeton, N.J.: Princeton University Industrial Relations Section, 1926), 6–8; NICB, *Employee Stock Purchase Plans in the United States*; Brandes, *American Welfare Capitalism*, 83.

    The year 1919 marked a high point in union membership (4.08 million in 1920) and a strike wave. See Stuart D. Brandes, *American Welfare Capitalism, 1880–1940* (Chicago: University of Chicago Press, 1976), 29; Lizabeth Cohen, *Making a New Deal: Industrial Workers in Chicago, 1919–1939* (New York: Cambridge University Press, 1990), 161–165; Sanford Jacoby, *Modern Manors: Welfare Capitalism Since the New Deal* (Princeton, N.J.: Princeton University Press, 1997); Nikki Mandell, *The Corporation as Family: The Gendering of Corporate Welfare, 1890–1930* (Chapel Hill: University of North Carolina Press, 2002); Andrea Tone, *Business of Benevolence*, 243; Gerald Zahavi, *Workers, Managers, and Welfare Capitalism: The Shoeworkers and Tanners of Endicott Johnson, 1890–1950* (Urbana: University of Illinois Press, 1988).

18. Robert W. Dunn, *The Americanization of Labor: The Employers' Offensive Against Trade Unions* (New York: International Publishers, 1927); Gorton James, Henry S. Dennison, Edwin F. Gay, Henry P. Kendall, and Arthur W. Burritt, *Profit Sharing and Stock Ownership for Employees* (New York: Harper Bros., 1926), 1; Metropolitan Life Policyholders' Service Bureau, "A Report on Employee Stock-Ownership Plans" (New York: Metropolitan Life, 1923), 8.

19. Jacoby, *Modern Manors*, 13, 24; James, Dennison, et al., *Profit Sharing*, vii, 23; Brandes, *American Welfare Capitalism*, 85.

20. NICB, *Employee Stock Purchase Plans in the United States*, 41–43; Gary quoted in Brandes, *American Welfare Capitalism*, 86.

21. Thomas E. Mitten, "Dividing Up the Profits of Industry," *Main Topics* (Philadelphia), October 1929, 3, in folder 25, box 46, Albert Greenfield papers (Mss 1959), Pennsylvania Historical Society, Philadelphia, Pa. (PHS); Thomas E. Mitten, "Excerpt," 2; Cotter, 486.

22. Thomas E. Mitten, "Employee Ownership," *WW*, March 1929, 18; Foerster and Dietel, *Employee Stock Ownership*, 14, 18–19, 30; Metropolitan Policyholders' Service Bureau, 1; NICB, *Employee Stock Purchase Plans in the United States*, 152, 155, 161.

23. NICB, *Employee Stock Purchase Plans in the United States*, 169; James, Dennison, et al., *Profit Sharing*, 26.

Proposals included state-level campaigns for old-age insurance legislation conducted by the Fraternal Order of Eagles and state labor federations, as well as continued calls for a compulsory national program by the American Association of Labor Legislation and the American Association of Old Age Security. States continued to add mothers' pensions and worker's compensation programs and increase their levels of funding throughout the 1920s.

Jennifer Klein, *For All These Rights,* 17, 20, 66, 80; Theda Skocpol, *Protecting Soldiers and Mothers: The Political Origins of Social Policy in the United States* (Cambridge, Mass: Belknap Press of the Harvard University Press, 1992), 194–202, 234–237, 424–480; Barbara J. Nelson, "The Origins of the Two-Channel Welfare State: Workmen's Compensation and Mothers' Aid," in *Women, The State, and Welfare,* ed. Linda Gordon (Madison: University of Wisconsin Press, 1990), 123–145; Lorraine Gates Schuyler, *The Weight of Their Votes: Southern Women and Political Leverage in the 1920s* (Chapel Hill, N.C.: University of North Carolina Press, 2006), 208–210; Alice Kessler-Harris, *In Pursuit of Equity: Women, Men, and the Quest for Economic Citizenship in Twentieth-Century America* (New York: Oxford University Press, 2001).

24. William L. Ransom, "Property Ownership as a Social Force," *PAPS* 11 (April 1925), 521; G. A. Bowers, "Employee Investments in Company Securities," *American Management Association Annual Convention Series* 25 (1926), 7–8; Foerster and Dietel, *Employee Stock Ownership,* 9, 67; James, Dennison, et al., *Profit Sharing,* 53–55; Alfred P. Sloan, "How Members of the General Motors Family Are Made Partners," 2.

25. Dunn, *Americanization of Labor,* 155–156, 160, 166; Jacoby, *Modern Manors,* 17; NICB, *Employee Stock Purchase Plans in the United States,* 132; George H. Soule, "Discussion: Illusions Regarding the Diffusion of Stock Ownership," *PAPS* 11 (April 1925), 483; Foerster and Dietel, *Profit Sharing,* 93, 95.

A 1926 study by the Industrial Relations Section of Princeton University found that employees owned only 4.26 percent of the stock of the twenty leading corporations studied. NICB, *Employee Stock Purchase Plans in the United States,* 39; Lewis Corey, "Employee Stock Ownership," *New Republic,* May 11, 1927, 348.

26. Dunn, *Americanization of Labor,* 163. James, Dennison, et al., *Profit Sharing,* 95; "Resolution Adopted Unanimously by the Fortieth Convention of the American Federation of Labor," June 19, 1920 (Washington, D.C.: GPO, 1920), folder "Form Letters Jan–Dec. 1920," box 36, GFRG53; Bill Lloyd quoted in Dunn, *Americanization of Labor,* 147.

27. Cohen, *Making a New Deal,* 184.

28. NICB, *Employee Stock Purchase Plans and the Stock Market Crisis of 1929* (New York: NICB, 1930), 29, 33, 56.

29. AT&T, Eastman Kodak, and GE all admitted that more than half "of the stock purchased by employees at a liberal concession from the market price" was sold soon thereafter. NICB, *Employee Stock Purchase Plans in the United States,* 59, 142; Foerster and Dietel, *Profit Sharing,* 14, 54, 56, 66; Arthur Williams, "Labor's Share in Ownership," *PAPS* 11 (April 1925), 364.

30. Knappen, 262; Charles Amos Dice, *New Levels in the Stock Market* (New York: McGraw-Hill, 1929), 198.

31. John D. Long and John Eden Farwell, *Fundamentals of Financial Advertising* (New York: Harper Bros, 1927), 256, 262; Frank LeRoy Blanchard, "Radio for Financial Advertising," *Proceedings of the FAA Annual Convention* (Chicago: FAA, 1928), 263–264.

32. NICB, *Employee Stock Purchase Plans in the United States,* 135–138; F. L. Devereux, "The Development of the Ownership of the Bell System," *PAPS* 11 (April 1925), 420; A. Emory Wishon, "Now and Tomorrow with Customer Ownership," *PAPS* 11 (April 1925), 415; Philadelphia Rapid Transit Co., "Invest with Us," folder 12, box 38, Albert Greenfield papers (Mss 1959), PHS; Mitten, "Employee Ownership," 9–11.

33. Long and Farwell, *Fundamentals,* 262; Wishon, "Now and Tomorrow," 414.

34. Carver, *Recollections,* 140; Kessler-Harris, *In Pursuit of Equity,* 380.

35. Wishon, "Now and Tomorrow," 409, 411, 416.

36. AT&T, "Owned by Those It Serves;" Howard T. Sands, "Consumer Ownership and Corporate Management," *PAPS* 11 (April 1925), 496; Houston, "Some Aspects," 8–9; Wishon, "Now and Tomorrow," 410; Frederick H. Wood, "The Small Investor and Railroad Ownership and Management," *PAPS* 11 (April 1925), 440.

37. NELA, *Political Ownership and the Electric Light and Power Industry* (New York: NELA, 1925), 20; John T. Broderick, *A Small Stockholder* (Schenectady, NY: Robson & Adee, 1926), 26; Sands, "Consumer Ownership and Corporate Management," 499; NICB, *Employee Stock Purchase Plans in the United States,* 44, 135–138.

38. Bowers, "Employee Investments in Company Securities," 9; NICB, *Employee Stock Purchase Plans in the United States,* 139; "Vying for Wider Markets with Stock Split-Ups," *Coast Investor and Industrial Review,* November 1929.

39. Sloan, "How Members of the General Motors Family Are Made Partners," 1, 6; Marchand, *Creating the Corporate Soul,* 130; Samuel Crowther, "Everybody Ought to Be Rich," *Ladies Home Journal,* August 1929, 9; Wishon, "Now and Tomorrow," 410.

40. Broderick, *A Small Stockholder,* 9–11, 29.

8. Finance Joins in the Quest for Shareholder Democracy

1. Calvin Coolidge, "The Press Under a Free Government" (address before the American Society of Newspaper Editors, Washington, D.C., January 17, 1925); Richard G. Holcombe, "The Growth of the Federal Government in the 1920s," *Cato Journal* 16 (Fall 1996), 6, 10; Ajay K. Mehrotra, "Lawyers, Guns, and Public Moneys: The U. S. Treasury, World War I, and the Administration of the Modern Fiscal State," *Law and History Review* 28 (February 2010), 173, 177, 180, 186, 223; Anne L. Alstott and Ben Novick, "War, Taxes, and Income Redistribution in the Twenties: The 1924 Veterans' Bonus and the Defeat of the Mellon Plan," *Tax Law Review* 59 (Summer 2006), 373, 376, 380, 431, 433; Dora L. Costa, *The Evolution of Retirement: An American Economic History,*

1880–1990 (Chicago: University of Chicago Press, 1998), 17, 166–167; Price Fishback, Samuel Allen, Jonathan Fox, and Brendan Livingston, "A Patchwork Social Safety Net," NBER Working Paper 15696 (2010), 37–39; Theda Skocpol, *Protecting Soldiers and Mothers: The Political Origins of Social Policy in the United States* (Cambridge, Mass.: Belknap Press of Harvard University Press, 1992), 446, 457; William Chafe, "Women's History and Political History: Some Thoughts on Progressivism and the New Deal," in *Visible Women: New Essays on American Activism,* ed. Nancy A. Hewitt and Suzanne Lebsock (Urbana: University of Illinois Press, 1993); Seth Koven and Sonya Michel, "Womanly Duties: Maternalist Politics and the Origins of Welfare States in France, Germany, Great Britain, and the United States, 1880–1920," *AHR* 95 (1990), 1080–81; Patrick Wilkinson, "The Selfless and the Helpless: Maternalist Origins of the U.S. Welfare State," *Feminist Studies* 25 (1999), 571–597; U.S. Bureau of the Census, *Historical Statistics of the United States,* 4th ed. (New York: Cambridge University Press, 2000), accessed online at http://hsus.cambridge.org .proxy.wexler.hunter.cuny.edu/HSUSWeb/toc/tableToc.do?id=Ea61-124.

2. For the importance of stories about the economy in shaping investors' preferences and bolstering or destroying confidence, see George Akerlof and Robert Schiller, *Animal Spirits* (Princeton, N.J.: Princeton University Press, 2009), 3–4, 12, 51–55, 66, 119–122; Robert Schiller, *Irrational Exuberance* (Princeton, N.J.: Princeton University Press, 2000), 21–27, 96–98, 138–140, 148–151, 162.

   For the susceptibility of savings decisions to narrative framing, see Richard Thaler and Shlomo Benartzi, "Save More Tomorrow," *Journal of Political Economy* 112 (February 2004), S164–S187; Brigitte C. Madrian and Dennis F. Shea, "The Power of Suggestion: Inertia in 401(k) Participation and Savings Behavior," NBER Working Paper 7682 (2000); Sendhil Mullainathan and Andrei Schleifer, "Persuasion in Finance," NBER Working Paper W11838 (2005); Richard Thaler and Nicholas Barberis, *Survey of Behavioral Finance* (Cambridge: NBER, 2002), 1073–1081. For the significance of norms in economic decision making, see George Akerlof, "The Missing Motivation in Macroeconomics," *American Economic Review* 97 (1), 5–36.

3. For the significance of culture in shaping frameworks of political belief, see Joseph Lowndes, *From the New Deal to the New Right* (New Haven: Yale University Press, 2008), 140.

   The 3.5 million estimate includes the 1.5 million Americans who held an account with an exchange-affiliated brokerage plus an estimated 2 million more who acquired stock through a bank or bank securities affiliate (replication between categories is possible). U.S. Congress, U.S. Senate, *Stock Exchange Practices* (Washington, D.C.: GPO, 1933), 9; Thomas F. Huertas and Harold van B. Cleveland, *Citibank: 1812–1970* (Cambridge: Harvard University Press, 1985); Steven L. Osterweis, "Securities Affiliates and Security Operations of Commercial Banks," *Harvard Business Review* 11 (October 1932), 124–132; Vincent P. Carosso, *Investment Banking in America: A History* (Cambridge: Harvard University Press, 1970), 271–281.

4. James M. Beck, "The Fateful Hour" (address delivered before the Stock Exchange Liberty Loan Committee, New York, October 3, 1917), 1; "Loan Sales

Near a Hundred Million," *NYT,* October 3, 1917; untitled clipping, *New York Tribune,* April 12, 1917, Guy Emerson scrapbook, vol. 1, LOC; "Sure City Will Give Full Loan Quota," *NYT,* October 22, 1917; Liberty Loan Committee of the Second Federal Reserve District, "Report of the Publicity Committee" (New York, 1917), 2; untitled clipping, *Evening Post,* May 11, 1917, vol. 4, ACLRG53.

5. Kidder, Peabody to "The Holders of United States Second Liberty Loan 4% and 4¼% Bonds," May 9, 1927, Kidder, Peabody circulars, vol. 24, KP. See also Kidder Peabody circulars, vols. 20 and 24, KP; U.S. Department of the Treasury to the Banks of Connecticut, December 17, 1917, folder "Banks," box 13, GFRG53; Director to State Directors, n.d., folder "Form Letters" (Jan–Dec 1920), box 36, GFRG53; William Mather Lewis to Editors, December 8, 1920, folder "Form Letters" (Jan–Dec 1920), box 36, GFRG53.

6. *Proceedings of the* FAA *Annual Convention* (Chicago: FAA, 1922), 10; Francis H. Sisson, "Financial Advertising and the Public," *Proceedings of the FAA Annual Convention* (Chicago: FAA, 1917), 3, 8.

7. Sisson, "Financial Advertising and the Public," 8, 12, 14–15; Francis H. Sisson, "Public Relations and the Advertising Man," (New York: Guaranty Trust Co., 1920), 31; Herbert H. Houston, "The Man in the Street and Financial Advertising," *Proceedings of the FAA Annual Convention* (Chicago: FAA, 1920), 18–20; *Proceedings of the FAA Annual Convention* (Chicago: FAA, 1922), 41.

In the 1920s, the FAA and the American Bankers Association [ABA] teamed up for an economic education campaign, spending $100,000. See *Proceedings of the FAA Annual Convention* (Chicago: FAA, 1922), 17–18.

8. John Muir and Co., "The Birth of Thrift" (New York, 1917), 15; John Muir and Co., "Your Liberty Bond" (New York: 1919), 24–25; Margaret H. Shoenfield, *Trend of Wage Earners' Savings in Philadelphia* (Philadelphia: Wharton Business School Industrial Research Department, 1925), 55.

During the war, roughly 800 mercantile and manufacturing organizations sponsored partial payment plans for over half a million employees, while some 8,000 banks serviced roughly 1.7 million citizen-investors in this manner. Liberty Loan Committee of the Second Federal Reserve District, "Report of the Publicity Committee," 20; Shoenfield, *Trend of Wage Earners' Savings in Philadelphia,* 55.

9. Transcript, November 6, 1921, folder 4, CBC Hearings, NYSE Archives, New York.

10. *Proceedings of the FAA Annual Convention* (Chicago: FAA, 1923), 164; NICB, *Employee Thrift and Investment Plans* (New York: NICB, 1929), 71.

11. Paul Cabot, interview by Andrew Tosiello, October 22, 1971, transcript, 1–2, 4, 13, 14, Baker Library, Harvard Business School, Boston, Mass.; William Howard Steiner, *Investment Trusts and the American Experience* (New York: Adelphi Co., 1929), 59, 61; H. Burton and D.C. Corner, *Investment and Unit Trusts in Britain and America* (London: Elek, 1968); Carosso, *Investment Banking,* 281–295; Leland Rex Robinson, *Investment Trust Organization and Management* (New York: Ronald Press, 1926), 548; Harold E. Wood, "Investment Banking in the Next Ten Years," *Proceedings of the FAA Annual Convention* (Chicago: FAA, 1930), 268.

12. Earl Newsom, "Market Study and Merchandise Developments," *Proceedings of the FAA Annual Convention* (Chicago: FAA, 1930); W. W. Townshend, "Advertising and Merchandising Activities of the Fixed Investment Trusts," *Proceedings of the FAA Annual Convention* (Chicago: FAA, 1930), 273, 276–278; Entry dated September 9, 1929, CBC minute book, vol. 7, NYSE.

13. American Trustee Share Corporation, "Shares in America," 6, folder 3, box 1, Edgar Higgins Investment Trust Collection (Mss 783), Baker Library Historical Collections, Harvard Business School, Boston, Mass (HIT); William Howard Steiner, *Investment Trusts: American Experience* (New York: Adelphi, 1929), 1, 2, 11; United American Electric Companies, "United American Electric Companies Bankers' Shares: 20 Questions Answered," 20, folder "Bankers S," box 1, HIT; American Basic Business Shares Corporation, "A Partnership in America's Prosperity," 12–13, folder 3, box 1, HIT.

14. American Founders' Group, "The Alexander Fund: 81st Quarterly Distribution," December 2, 1926, folder "American A to American F," box 1; International Consolidated Investments, untitled circular, folder "I," box 2; United Investment Assurance System, "Through the Archway of a Bygone Century," folder "Founders to FU," box 1, HIT; Dillon, Read Statistical Department, "The Investment Trust," folder "D," box 1, HIT; Allied International Investing Corporation, "An American Investing Company Based upon the Principles of English and Scottish Investment Trusts," folder "American G to American Z," box 1, HIT.

15. Steiner, *Investment Trusts,* 3, 6, 10; American Founders' Group, "The Alexander Fund: 81st Quarterly Distribution," 25.

16. Cabot interview, 6; F. J. Lisman, "The Ideal Investment," 5; American Basic Business Shares Corporation, "A Partnership in America's Basic Industries," 1, folder 3, box 1, HIT.

17. Investors Trustee Shares, "Investment Trust Guide," folder "Investors Trustee Shares," box 2, HIT; American Basic Business Shares Corporation, "A Partnership in America's Prosperity," 12, folder 3, box 1, HIT; F. J. Lisman, "The Handicap Removed," folder "E," box 1, HIT; W. W. Townshend, "Advertising and Merchandising Activities," 271–272.

18. Lemon L. Smith, "Present and Future of Investment Trusts," *Investment Trusts: Issued Monthly by Bankers' Investment Trust of America* (March 1928), folder "B—Bankers R," box 1, HIT; Diversified Investment Trusts Inc., "A Broader and More Flexible Trust," folder "D," box 1, HIT; Steiner, *Investment Trusts,* 11; Newsom, "Market Study and Merchandise Developments," 255; Samuel Crowther, "Everybody Ought to Be Rich," *Ladies Home Journal* August 1929, 9.

19. American Trustee Share Corp., "Share in America," folder 3, box 1, HIT.

20. United American Electric Companies, "United American Electric Companies Bankers' Shares: 20 Questions Answered," and United American Railways Companies, "United American Railways Companies Bankers' Shares: 20 Questions Answered," folder "Bankers S," box 1, HIT; Bankers Security Trust Company, "Bankers Security Trust Company: Specially Chartered by General

Assembly of Connecticut," folder "Bankers S," box 1, HIT. Robinson, *Investment Trust Organization and Management,* 465; folder "Goldman Sachs Trading Corp.," box 1, HIT; John Kenneth Galbraith, *The Great Crash, 1929* (Boston: Houghton Mifflin, 1955); Steiner, *Investment Trusts,* 1.

21. Incorporated Investors, "The American Birthright," August 14, 1929, folder "Incorporated Investors," box 2, HIT.

   For the expansion of consumer credit, see Lizabeth Cohen, *A Consumer's Republic: The Politics of Mass Consumption in Postwar America* (New York: Alfred A. Knopf, 2003); Lendol Calder, *Financing the American Dream: A Cultural History of Consumer Credit* (Princeton, N.J.: Princeton University Press, 1999); Louis Hyman, *Debtor Nation* (Princeton, N.J.: Princeton University Press, 2010).

   For "Living Wage" demands of organized labor, see Lawrence Glickman, *A Living Wage: American Workers and the Making of Consumer Society* (Ithaca, N.Y.: Cornell University Press, 1997).

22. Steiner, *Investment Trusts,* 10–11; "Address of the President [American Founders Corp.] to the Annual Meeting of Stockholders" (April 8, 1929), folder "America A to America F," box 1, HIT.

23. Steiner, *Investment Trusts,* 64; untitled clipping from *Evening Post,* September 28, 1927, folder "Newspaper clippings—Misc. (1927)," box 3, HIT; Albert W. Atwood, "Changing Fashions of Finance: The Investment Trust," *Saturday Evening Post,* April 28, 1928, 12; Harry Krohne, "An Investment Trust That Shares in New York Bank Profits," *Financial Digest* (July 1927), 24–25; "What Does the New York Attorney General Say about Rigid Investment Trusts?," *Diversified Dealer,* January 23, 1928, folder "D," box 1, HIT.

24. Krohne, "An Investment Trust," 25; Diversified Investment Trusts, "A Broader and More Flexible Trust," folder "D," box 1, HIT; Cabot interview, 5; Jonathan Barron Baskin and Paul J. Miranti, *A History of Corporate Finance* (New York: Cambridge University Press, 1997); Burton and Corner, *Investment and Unit Trusts,* 205; U.S. Securities and Exchange Commission, *Investment Trusts and Investment Companies* (Washington, D.C.: GPO, 1939–1942); Kevin Phillips, *Wealth and Democracy: A Political History of the American Rich* (New York: Broadway Books), 62.

25. Kidder, Peabody and Co. Circulars, vol. 20, 33–34, KP; Charles L. Edgar to Messrs Stone Webster, January 26, 1925, Kidder, Peabody and Co. Circulars, vol. 23, 39, KP; Kidder, Peabody and Co. to "Customers and Partners," Kidder Peabody and Co. Circulars, vol. 23, KP.

26. Investment Research Committee of the FAA, *Advertising Investment Securities* (New York: Prentice-Hall, 1928), 52.

27. A. E. Bryson, "The Radio as an Investment Advertising Medium," *Proceedings of the FAA Annual Convention* (Chicago: FAA, 1927), 304, 312–313; A. E. Bryson, "How to Shape Up a Radio Campaign," *Proceedings of the FAA Annual Convention* (Chicago: FAA, 1928), 60–67; Frank Blanchard, "Radio for Financial Advertising," *Proceedings of the FAA Annual Convention* (Chicago: FAA, 1928), 263, 268–269.

28. National City Bank, "I Shouldn't Decide It Alone" and "What Is a Logical Investment for Me?," in *Kundenwerbung Amerikanischer Banken,* ed. Carl Hundhausen (Berlin: L.Weiss, 1929), Appendix.

29. Kidder, Peabody and Co. circular, December 29, 1926, Kidder Peabody Circulars, vol. 24, 71, KP.

30. Clark Davis, *Company Men: White Collar Life and Corporate Culture in Los Angeles, 1892–1941* (Baltimore: Johns Hopkins University Press, 2000).

31. National City Bank, "Taking the Broader View," in Hundhausen, *Kunderwerbung,* Appendix; Halsey Stuart, "The Capable Young Investor," *Harper's Magazine* (March 1921).

32. *Proceedings of the FAA Annual Convention* (Chicago: FAA, 1923), 27; C. C. Childs, "The Work and Save Bond as a Supplement to Savings," *Proceedings of the FAA Annual Convention* (Chicago: FAA, 1926), 189.

33. Dora L. Costa, "Displacing the Family: Union Army Pensions and Elderly Living Arrangements," *Journal of Political Economy* 105 (December 1997): 1269–1292; Costa, *Evolution of Retirement;* Ethel R. Scully, "Appealing to the Accumulators Rather than the Conservators," *Proceedings of the FAA Annual Convention* (Chicago: FAA, 1924), 120.

34. Edmond Boushelle, "The Place of Direct Mail in the Distribution of Investment Securities," *Proceedings of the FAA Annual Convention* (Chicago: FAA, 1924), 112.

35. Milton Harrison, "Development of Thrift Facilities," *AAAPSS* 87 (January 1920), 169–170; H. B. Matthews, "Investment Advertising," *Proceedings of the FAA Annual Convention* (Chicago: FAA, 1922), 61; "A Thoughtful Christmas Present," *Coast Investor and Industrial Review* (November 1929), 59.

36. A. B. Leach and Co., "A Doctor," *Barron's,* July 7, 1924, 16.

37. Earle H. Harrah, "Organizing and Operating a New Business Department," *Proceedings of the FAA Annual Convention* (Chicago: FAA, 1929); Bessie M. Seely, "Do Women Read and Respond to Trust Advertising?" *Proceedings of the FAA Annual Convention* (Chicago: FAA, 1927), 198; Frances S. Rosenblatt, "How to Interest Women of Means in Financial Matters," *Proceedings of the FAA Annual Convention* (Chicago: FAA, 1928), 81.
    A 1928 study credited women with purchasing roughly 20 percent of the total value of new securities issues. Investment Research Committee of the FAA, *Advertising Investment Securities,* 80.

38. *Advertising Investment Securities,* Investment Research Committee of the FAA, 80; Rebecca L. Davis, "'Not Marriage at All, but Simple Harlotry': The Companionate Marriage Controversy," *JAH* 94 (March 2008), 1137–1162; Alice Ames Winter, "The Family Purse," *Ladies Home Journal* 42 (May 1925), 35; Christine Frederick, "Getting 100% Out of Your Income," *Ladies Home Journal* 36 (September 1919), 59.

39. Ernest Poole, "Women in Wall Street," *Ladies Home Journal* 45 (August 1928), 9, 130; Roland Marchand, *Advertising the American Dream: Making Way for Modernity, 1920–1940* (Berkeley: University of California Press, 1985), 192.

9. "The People's Market"

1. "Halsey Sells Seat on Stock Exchange," *NYT*, November 29, 1923, 12; "Leader in Fight Over White House to Arrive Today," *NYT*, July 7, 1925, 20; Halsey quoted in Wendy Kaplan, "R. T. H. Halsey: An Ideology of Collecting American Decorative Arts," *Winterthur Portfolio* 17 (Spring 1982), 49–50.
2. "Mme. Alda Sues for Stock Profits," *NYT*, October 28, 1917, 21; "Mme. Alda Settles Suit," *NYT*, June 8, 1921, 16; "Westerfield to Quit Exchange," *NYT*, August 30, 1938, 27; "Jason Westerfield, a Retired Publicist," *NYT*, August 31, 1959, 29.
3. Untitled column in *New York Post*, April 1, 1920, "Stutz Corner" scrapbook, NYSE Archives, New York; John Brooks, *Once in Golconda: A True Story of Wall Street* (New York: W.W. Norton and Co., 1969), 21–40; March 25 and 31, 1920, CBC minute book, vol. 1, NYSE Archives; "Statement of the New York Stock Exchange," April 15, 1920, "Stutz Corner" scrapbook, NYSE Archives.
4. "Rumor Again Traps Big Man in Stutz," *NYT*, April 3, 1920, 22; untitled column in *New York Post*, April 8, 1920, "Stutz Corner" scrapbook.
5. "Rumor Again Traps Big Man in Stutz"; "Allan Ryan on Wall Street," *NYW*, April 18, 1920, "Stutz Corner" scrapbook.
6. Untitled column in *New York Mail*, April 13, 1920, "'The Street' and Industry," *Globe*, April 9, 1920, "Stutz Corner" scrapbook.
7. Jonathan Baskin and Paul Miranti Jr., *History of Corporate Finance* (New York: Cambridge University Press, 1997), 206, 210, 225.
8. Untitled column in *New York Mail*, April 13, 1920, "$701 Stutz Result of Woman's Whim," *NYW*, April 9, 1920, "Stutz Corner" scrapbook; Jason Westerfield to John P. Ryan, April 19, 1920, COL letter book, vol. 4, NYSE Archives.
9. Brooks, *Once in Golconda*, 31; "Allan Ryan on Wall Street," *NYW*, April 18, 1920, "Allan Ryan's Statement," *Evening Mail*, April 24, 1920, "Stutz Corner" scrapbook; "Ryan Quits Seat on Stock Exchange," *NYT*, April 24, 1920, 1.

   For the media's favoring of Ryan, see a wide variety of clippings from papers across the nation collected by Henry Romeike Inc. in "Stutz Corner" scrapbook.
10. "Diary of Friday, Oct. 10, 1920," COP minute book, vol. 2, NYSE Archives.
11. Untitled clipping, *New York Mail*, April 15, 1920, "Stutz Corner" scrapbook; "Asks Investigation of Stock Exchange," *NYT*, April 21, 1920, 17; "H.R. 13874, World War Veterans' Adjusted Compensation Act," William Remick to Hon. Jos. W. Fordney, April 26, 1920, press release dated May 4 and 8, 1920, insert card dated May 17, 1920, C. I. Hudson and Co., "Week-end Letter," May 22, 1920, Porter J. McCumber to William Remick, December 21, 1920, all in "Bonus Bill" scrapbook, NYSE Archives; "Financiers Fight Stock Sales Tax," *NYT*, May 8, 1920, 27; Porter J. McCumber to William Remick, December 22 and 30, 1920, January 5, 8, 20, 1921, COP minute book, vol. 2.
12. Minutes, Jan. 10, 1921 and Oct. 28, 1920, COP minute book, vol. 2.
13. Transcript, Special Committee on Ways and Means: Subcommittee on Odd Lots, folder 7, box 3, NYSE Archives; CBC minute books, vols. 1–7, NYSE

Archives; "Report of the Special Committee on Odd Lots" (1921), 413, folder 9, box 3, NYSE Archives; Herbert S. Houston, "How to Maintain the Confidence of the Public" (address before the members of the New York Stock Exchange and their partners, New York, April 7, 1922), 4, 5, 11–13.

14. William B. Nash quoted in Transcript, Special Committee on Ways and Means: Subcommittee on Odd Lots, 26, folder 7, box 3, NYSE Archives. For rampant noncompliance, see CBC minute books, vols. 1–7, NYSE Archives; "Report of the Special Committee on Odd Lots" (1921), 413, folder 9, box 3, NYSE Archives; "Report of the Special Committee . . . Odd Lots" (1921), folder 7 and 11, box 3, NYSE Archives.

  The Consolidated launched a mass advertising campaign in 1918. Transcript, Special Committee on Ways and Means: Subcommittee on Odd Lots, 120, folder 7, box 3, NYSE Archives.

  For the significant degree of competition posed by the Consolidated, see William O. Brown Jr., J. Harold Mulherin, and Marc D. Weidenmier, "Competing with the NYSE," working paper, May 2006, in the author's possession.

15. By 1921, odd lot trades constituted up to 40 percent of commission house business. On active days, odd lot trading might account for as much as 40 percent of all NYSE volume. "Report of the Special Committee on Odd Lots" (1921), box 2, folder 9 and box 3, folder 7, NYSE Archives.

  Nicholas Thompson, "The Sword of Spitzer," *Legal Affairs* May/June 2004, www.legalaffairs.org/issues/May-June-2004/feature_thompson_mayjun04. html; "To Ask Congress for Bucket Shop Curb," *NYT,* July 23, 1923, 1; March 8, 1921, COP minute book, vol. 2; Memorandum, Special Committee on Ways and Means, box 1, folder 12, NYSE Archives; "Seymour L. Cromwell Personal Scrapbook" (Jan. 1922 to Dec. 1923), NYSE Archives.

16. May 15, 1922, Governing Committee minute book, vol. 8, NYSE Archives.

  The COP organized BBB funding drives among Exchange members; the BBB distributed NYSE films and literature. The Exchange used bureaus to investigate potential new listings and institutional customers to ensure that they did not operate bucket shops. The BBB of New York's Advisory Committee and officers included several NYSE members. COP Chairman James C. Auchincloss served as executive director of the BBB from 1927 to 1933. January 19, 1923, March 9 and 24, 1923, January 29, 1926, February 5, 1926, COP minute book, vol. 3. NYSE Archives; Report, January 1 and 15, 1922, July 1, 1922, January 17, 1923, "Stock Frauds BBB" scrapbook, NYSE Archives; "Gets New Position: James C. Auchincloss," *NYT,* May 13, 1937, 46.

  "Better Business Bureau Reports on Frauds . . . 60 Court Orders Obtained," *NYT,* March 9, 1926, 32; "Injunction Curbs the Consolidated's Trading Practices," *NYT,* February 5, 1926, 1; "Sues to End Tickers of Consolidated," *NYT,* October 8, 1926, 33; "Consolidated Quits," *NYT,* February 12, 1926, 1; "Exchange Can Stop Stock Quotations," *NYT,* May 27, 1927, 36.

  Edward J. Balleisen, "Private Cops on the Fraud Beat: The Limits of American Business Self-Regulation, 1895–1932," *BHR* 83 (Spring 2009), 113–160; Maury Klein, *Rainbow's End: The Crash of 1929* (New York: Oxford University Press,

2001); John Kenneth Galbraith, *The Great Crash: 1929* (Boston: Houghton Mifflin, 1955); Ferdinand Pecora, *Wall Street Under Oath: The Story of Our Modern Money Changers* (New York: Simon and Schuster, 1939).

17. E. H. H. Simmons, "Suppressing Financial Frauds" (address delivered to the Chicago Association of Commerce, Chicago, Ill., February 25, 1925), 6–9.

18. "Stock Exchange Meeting," *NYT*, March 28, 1922; Governing Committee resolution, March 9, 1921, Special Committee on Ways and Means, folder 1, box 1, NYSE Archives.

19. Jason Westerfield, "Wall Street in Its Relation to the Public" (New York: NYSE, 1924), 10; "Talks on the 'Real Wall St.,'" *NYT*, May 26, 1927, 34; Jason Westerfield, "Dangerous Delusions" (address before the New York Stock Exchange Institute, New York, January 17, 1924), 20; January 1 and 15, 1922, January 17, 1923, loose report, "Stock Frauds BBB" scrapbook.

20. February 19, 1926, COP minute book, vol. 3; October 14, 1930, COP minute book, vol. 4, NYSE Archives; "Mr. Ford's Page," *Dearborn Independent,* January 9, 1926, in "Unfavorable Coverage" scrapbook, NYSE Archives.

21. October 28, 1931, COP minute book, vol. 4.

22. Untitled clipping, *Western Odd Fellow* (Topeka, Kan.), January 1924, Cromwell scrapbook; Visits recorded in COP minute book, vols. 2–4.

23. Jason Westerfield, "Wall Street of Fact and Fiction" (New York: NYSE, n.d.), 6; Jason Westerfield, "The Stock Exchange in Relation to the Public" (New York: NYSE, 1924), 12; Jason Westerfield, "Speculation" (New York: NYSE, n.d.), 10; COP minute books, vols. 2–4; R. T. H. Halsey to "Presidents of Universities and Colleges," October 18, 1920, "Forms, Form Letters, Etc." scrapbook, NYSE Archives; "Some Comments on the Addresses of Jason Westerfield" (New York: NYSE, n.d.).

24. H. S. Martin, *The New York Stock Exchange* (New York: F. E. Fitch, 1918), 102, 115–116; Westerfield, "Speculation," 7–8.

25. J. Edward Meeker, "Smith's First Investment" (New York: NYSE, 1923), 1, 6–8, 23–24.

26. COP minute book, vols. 2, 3, and 4; "Some Comments on the Addresses of Jason Westerfield," 4.

27. E. H. H. Simmons, "Modern Capitalism" (New York: NYSE, 1926), 15; E. H. H. Simmons, "The Stock Exchange and the People" (New York: NYSE, 1924), 15.

28. Simmons, "Stock Market Loans" (New York: NYSE, 1929), 10, 11, 16; E. H. H. Simmons, "Financing Industrial Development" (New York: NYSE, 1929), 162–165; Simmons, "New Aspects of American Corporate Finance" (New York: NYSE, 1929), 14; E. H. H. Simmons, "The Stock Exchange and American Agriculture" (New York: NYSE, 1928), 10, 12; Simmons, "Stock Market Loans," 9; W. S. Cousins, "The Stock Exchange and the People" (New York: NYSE, 1924), 6–7.

29. Simmons, "Modern Capitalism," 11–12, 14–15; Simmons, "Listing Securities on the New York Stock Exchange" (New York: NYSE, 1927), 15; "Simmons Advanced Views Like Ripley's," *NYT*, August 26, 1926; "Bids Corporations Tell

Income Often," *NYT,* June 5, 1926; Simmons, "Listing Securities," 6, 14, 20, 21; Simmons, "Modern Capitalism," 12.

30. Jason Westerfield, "The Stock Exchange in Its Relation to the Public" (New York: NYSE, 1924), 6; Westerfield, "Dangerous Delusions," 10; Westerfield, "The Stock Exchange in Its Relation to the Public," 6.

31. For income inequality statistics: http://elsa.berkeley.edu/~saez/

J. Edward Meeker, *The Work of the Stock Exchange* (New York: Ronald Press, 1922), 494–497; Westerfield, "The Good Old Days," 21–22; Westerfield, "Dangerous Delusions," 15; Simmons, "The Stock Exchange and American Agriculture," 6–8; Westerfield, "Wall Street Is Main Street," in *Four Talks on Wall Street,* 9.

32. Meg Jacobs, *Pocketbook Politics: Economic Citizenship in Twentieth-Century America* (Princeton, N.J.: Princeton University Press, 2005), 74–83.

Jason R. Westerfield, "The Forgotten Factor," *Four Talks on Wall Street* (New York: NYSE, n.d.), 16, 20; Jason Westerfield, "The Good Old Days," *Four Talks on Wall Street,* 27.

33. Westerfield, "The Forgotten Factor," 15.

34. Westerfield, "The Forgotten Factor," 27; Simmons, "Financing American Industry," 8–10; Westerfield, "The Good Old Days," 27; E. H. H. Simmons, "Financing American Industry" (New York: NYSE, 1928), 8–10; Simmons, "New Aspects," 5.

For noncorporate varieties of capitalism, see Gerald Berk, *Alternative Tracks;* Philip Scranton, *Proprietary Capitalism: The Textile Manufacture at Philadelphia, 1800–1885* (New York: Cambridge University Press, 1983); Charles Sabel and Jonathan Zeitlin, eds., *World of Possibility: Flexibility and Mass Production in Western Industrialization* (New York: Cambridge University Press, 1997); Louis Galambos, "Recasting the Organizational Synthesis: Structure and Process in the Twentieth and Twenty-First Centuries," *BHR* 79 (2005), 1–38; Gary Herrigel, "Corporate Governance: History Without Historians" in ed. Geoffrey Jones and Jonathan Zeitlin, *Handbook of Business History* (Oxford: Oxford University Press, 2006).

35. Simmons, "Free Markets and Popular Ownership," 74–75; Simmons, "Frontiers of American Finance" (New York: NYSE, 1926), 8, 12–15.

36. Westerfield, "Dangerous Delusions," 3–4; Westerfield, "Wall Street of Fact and Fiction," 4; Westerfield, "Synthetic Ghosts" (New York: NYSE, n.d.,), 8.

For the American welfare state, Jennifer Klein, *For All These Rights: Business, Labor, and the Shaping of America's Public-Private Welfare State* (Princeton, N.J.: Princeton University Press, 2006); Theda Skocpol, *Protecting Soldiers and Mothers: The Political Origins of Social Policy in the United States* (Cambridge, Mass.: Harvard University Press, 1992); Barbara J. Nelson, "The Origins of the Two-Channel Welfare State: Workmen's Compensation and Mothers' Aid," in *Women, The State, and Welfare,* ed. Linda Gordon (Madison: University of Wisconsin Press, 1990), 123–145.

37. William J. Shultz, *Financial Development of the United States* (New York: Prentice Hall, 1937), 535, 593; Victoria Woeste, *The Farmer's Benevolent Trust: Law and Agricultural Cooperation in Industrial America* (Chapel Hill,

N.C.: University of North Carolina Press, 1998); "Incorporated Farm Studied," *Los Angeles Times,* March 14, 1929, 3.

38. Ellis Hawley, *The Great War and the Search for a Modern Order: A History of
the American People and Their Institutions, 1917–1933* (New York: Waveland
Press, 1997), 78–96; Ellis W. Hawley, "Herbert Hoover, the Commerce Secre-
tariat, and the Vision of an 'Associative State,' 1921–1928," *JAH* 61 (1974),
116–40; Guy Alchon, *The Invisible Hand of Planning: Capitalism, Social Science, and the State in the 1920s* (Princeton, N.J.: Princeton University Press,
1985); William Leach, *Land of Desire: Merchants, Power, and the Rise of a
New American Culture* (New York: Vintage Press, 1993).

39. Seymour L. Cromwell, "The Stock Exchange and the Nation's Credit" (New
York: NYSE, 1923), 8–9.

40. Seymour L. Cromwell, "Private Initiative" (New York: NYSE, 1922), 3, 5, 16;
Simmons, "The Stock Exchange and American Agriculture," 7; Cromwell,
"Problems and Policies" (New York: NYSE, 1923), 4–5.

41. Simmons, "Modern Capitalism," 2, 5; Simmons, "Free Markets and Popular
Ownership," 68.

    The Exchange's economist, J. Edward Meeker, admitted to Harvard professor
William Z. Ripley that Stock Exchange presidents and publicists exaggerated the
number of investors in their speeches. J. E. Meeker to William Z. Ripley, April 16
1931, folder "1931," box 3, William Z. Ripley Papers (HUG 4745.5), Harvard
University Archives, Pusey Library, Harvard University, Cambridge, MA.

42. Simmons, "Modern Capitalism," 8, 11, 18; Cromwell, "The Stock Exchange
and the Nation's Credit," 8–9; Cromwell, "Private Initiative," 5, 15; Westerfield,
"Good Old Days"; Simmons, "Free Markets and Popular Ownership"; Simmons, "New Aspects," 17; Simmons, "Stabilizing American Business" (New
York: NYSE, 1929), 13.

43. Daniel Rodgers, *Contested Truths: Keywords in American Politics Since Independence* (Cambridge, Mass.: Harvard University Press, 1987); David Kennedy,
Over Here: The First World War and American Society (New York: Oxford
University Press, 2004); Jonathan Hansen, *The Lost Promise of Patriotism: De-
bating American Identity, 1890–1920* (Chicago: University of Chicago Press,
1993); Shelton Stromquist, *Reinventing "The People": The Progressive Movement, the Class Problem, and the Origins of Modern Liberalism* (Chicago: Uni-
versity of Chicago Press, 2006); Michael McGerr, *The Decline of Popular
Politics: The North, 1860–1928* (New York: Oxford University Press, 1988);
Walter Lippmann, *Phantom Public* (New York: Macmillan Co, 1925); Brian
Balogh, "'Mirror of Desires': Interest Groups, Elections, and the Targeted Style
in Twentieth-Century America," in *Democratic Experiment: New Directions in
American Political History,* ed. Meg Jacobs and Julian Zelizer (Princeton, N.J.:
Princeton University Press, 2003), 240.

44. The COP also experimented with Chautauqua circuits, expositions, and radio
addresses. See COP minute books, vols. 2–4; "Radio Story of Stock Exchange,"
NYT, February 7, 1924.

    The NYSE released its first film, *A Trip to Wall Street,* in the fall of 1923 and
Under the Spreading Buttonwood Tree in 1925. July 10, 1923, October 2,

1923, November 2, 1923, COP minute book, vol. 2; March 8, 1925, COP minute book, vol. 3, NYSE Archives; insert card, "Forms, Form letters, etc." scrapbook, NYSE Archives.

45. Untermyer quoted in Thomas Nixon Carver, *The Present Economic Revolution in the United States* (Boston: Little, Brown, 1925), 101.

46. *The Nation's Market Place* (1928), DVD, NYSE Archives.

47. For concurrent corporate public relations, see Roland Marchand, *Creating the Corporate Soul: The Rise of Public Relations and Corporate Imagery in American Big Business* (Berkeley: University of California Press, 1998); Louis Galambos, *The Public Image of Big Business in America, 1880–1940* (Baltimore: Johns Hopkins University Press, 1975); Richard Tedlow, *Keeping the Corporate Image: Public Relations and Business, 1900–1950* (Greenwich, Conn.: JAI Press, 1979); Robert MacDougall, "Long Lines: AT&T's Long-Distance Network as an Organizational and Political Strategy," *BHR* 80 (2006), 297–329.

48. Westerfield, "How the NYSE Utilizes Motion Pictures," 78.

49. New York Stock Exchange membership directories, NYSE Archives.

50. Corporate loans placed in the stock market reached $3.885 billion in 1928, which was 60 percent of total value of all loans to brokers. In 1929 the NYSE reported that its membership alone held over $6 billion in brokers' loans. Jeremy Atack and Peter Passell, *A New Economic View of American History* (New York: W. W. Norton and Co., 1994), 606; Cedric Cowing, *Populists, Plungers, and Progressives: A Social History of Stock and Commodity Speculation* (Princeton, N.J.: Princeton University Press, 1970), 133–134, 143–149, 188; Eugene White, "Banking and Finance in the Twentieth Century," in *The Cambridge Economic History of the United States,* vol. 3, ed. Stanley L. Engerman and Robert E. Gallman (New York: Cambridge University Press), 757–758.

51. Simmons, "Stabilizing American Business," 5, 13; Simmons, "New Aspects," 3, 11; Simmons, "Stock Market Loans," 17.

52. Simmons, "New Aspects," 9–10; Simmons, "Stabilizing American Business," 7–9, 11–12, 19.

53. William Leach, *Land of Desire,* 349–378.

54. Those who date emergence of modern free-market conservatism later include: Elizabeth Fones-Wolf, *Selling Free Enterprise: The Business Assault on Labor and Liberalism, 1945–1960* (Urbana, Ill.: University of Illinois Press, 1994); Karen S. Miller, *The Voice of Business: Hill and Knowlton and Postwar Public Relations* (Chapel Hill, N.C.: University of North Carolina Press, 1999); Kim Phillips-Fein, *Invisible Hands: The Businessmen's Crusade Against the New Deal* (New York: W. W. Norton and Co., 2009); Thomas Frank, *One Market Under God: Extreme Capitalism, Market Populism, and the End of Economic Democracy* (New York: Anchor Press, 2001); Alan Brinkley, *The End of Reform: New Deal Liberalism in Recession and in War* (New York: Vintage, 1996).

Epilogue: The Enduring Quest

1. Rafael La Porta, Florencio Lopez-de-Silanes Andrei Schleifer, "Corporate Ownership Around the World," *Journal of Finance* 54 (April 1999), 471–517; Randall

Morck and Bernard Yeung, "Never Waste a Good Crisis: A Historical Perspective on Comparative Corporate Governance," NBER no. 15042 (June 2009), 3, 11; John W. Cioffi and Martin Hopner, "The Political Paradox of Finance Capitalism," *Politics and Society* 24 (2006), 463–502; Neil Fligstein, *Architecture of Markets* (Princeton, N.J.: Princeton University Press, 2001), 123–169.

2. U.S. Congress, U.S. Senate, Committee on Banking and Currency, *Stock Exchange Practices*, 73 Cong., 2d sess., 1934; Ralph F. de Bedts, *The New Deal's SEC: The Formative Years* (New York: Columbia University Press, 1964), 57–63, 73, 78, 80; J. Seligman, *The Transformation of Wall Street: A History of the Securities and Exchange Commission and Modern Corporate Finance* (Boston: Houghton Mifflin, 1982, 144–148, 177–178; Alan Brinkley, *The End of Reform: New Deal Liberalism in Recession and War* (New York: Vintage, 1996), 34–47; Securities and Exchange Commission, *Report on the Feasibility and Advisability of the Complete Segregation of the Functions of Dealer and Broker* (Washington, D.C.: GPO, 1936); William O. Douglas, "Protecting the Investor," *Yale Review* (March 1934).

3. Sam Rayburn quoted in Seligman, *Transformation of Wall Street*, 89–93, 100. June 6, 1933, COP minute book, vol. 4, NYSE Archives. NYSE President Richard Whitney quoted in Seligman, *Transformation of Wall Street*, 90; Sarah Agrillo to President F.D. Roosevelt, March 25, 1934, at http://co403731.cdn .cloudfiles.rackspacecloud.com/collection/papers/1930/1934_03_25_Agrillo_ to_FDR_t.pdf; Milton Dammann (president, American Safety Razor Corporation) to Honorable Sam Rayburn, April 24, 1934, at http://co403731.cdn .cloudfiles.rackspacecloud.com/collection/papers/1930/1934_04_24_ Dammann_t.pdf; Lemuel Benedict to FDR, January 1, 1934 at http://co403731 .cdn.cloudfiles.rackspacecloud.com/collection/papers/1930/1934_Benedict_to_ FDR_t.pdf.

4. Thomas K. McCraw, "With Consent of the Governed: SEC's Formative Years," *Journal of Policy Analysis and Management* 1 (1982), 346–370; Lawrence Mitchell, "The Innocent Shareholder" at http:ssrn.com/abstract=1118471; Thomas McGraw, *Prophets of Regulation* (Cambridge: Belknap Press of Harvard University Press, 1984), 153–209.

Although the SEC induced the NYSE to accept a paid president and non-member board representation, it did so not by reorganizing the NYSE but by encouraging a commission house reform faction. The SEC ordered the abolition of fixed commissions over NYSE objections in 1975. The NYSE finally incorporated and offered shares publicly in 2005. It spun off its regulatory function as the Financial Industry Regulatory Authority in 2007. Seligman, *Transformation of Wall Street*, xii, 118, 160–178, 205–210; De Bedts, New Deal's SEC, 144–167; McCraw, *Prophets of Regulation*, 92–199.

For a somewhat different assessment, see Phil Nicholas Jr., "The Agency That Kept Going: The Late New Deal and Shareholder Democracy," *Journal of Policy History* 16 (2004), 212–238.

Landis quoted in Jessica Wang, "Imagining the Administrative State: Legal Pragmatism, Securities Regulation, and New Deal Liberalism," *Journal of Policy History* 17 (2005), 265.

5. Robert M. Collins, *More: The Politics of Economic Growth in Postwar America* (New York: Oxford University Press, 2000), 43–104; Julian E. Zelizer, *Taxing America: Wilbur D. Mills, Congress, and the State, 1945–1975* (New York: Cambridge University Press, 1998).

6. Upton Sinclair, "Unfair Harvard," *Common Sense* 5 (February 1936), 14–17; Thomas Nixon Carver, *Recollections of an Unplanned Life* (Los Angeles: W. Ritchie Press, 1949), 239–241, 258–261; Thomas Nixon Carver, "How Can There Be Full Employment After The War?" *Economic Sentinel* (1945), 15; Thomas Nixon Carver, *What Must We Do to Save Our Economic System?* (Los Angeles: Los Angeles Chamber of Commerce, 1935), 14; Leonard Read, *Pattern for Revolt* (New York: Press of Joseph D. McGuire, 1948), 7, 33, 43, 46: Henry Hazlitt, *Economics in One Lesson* (New York: Harper, 1946), 28, 194; Henry Hazlitt, *Failure of the "New Economics"* (1959), 131, 179–184, 388; Kim Phillips-Fein, *Invisible Hands: The Businessmen's Crusade Against the New Deal* (New York: W.W. Norton, 2009), 39–40; Charles Gay, "Conservatism" (address before the Mid-Day Luncheon Club, Springfield, Ill., October 18, 1935), 2, Record Group 2-2, box 3, NYSE; Richard Whitney, "Elements of Recovery" (address at the 53rd Annual Dinner of the Engineers' Society of Western Pennsylvania, Pittsburgh, Pa., February 26, 1935), 285, Record Group 2-2, box 3, NYSE.

7. James P. Logan, "Everyone a Stockholder?: Problems in Broadening Shareownership" (Hanover, N.H.: Amos Tuck School of Business Administration, 1956); Elizabeth Fones-Wolf, *Selling Free Enterprise: The Business Assault on Labor and Liberalism, 1945–1960* (Champaign-Urbana: University of Illinois Press, 1995), 1, 84, 89; Sanford Jacoby, *Modern Manors* (Princeton, N.J.: Princeton University Press, 1998); Lawrence Mitchell, *Speculation Economy: How Finance Triumphed Over Industry* (New York: Berrett-Koehler Publishers 2007), 273; Alfred P. Sloan Jr., "Every American a Stockholder" (address of acceptance for the Best 1949 Annual Report, Hotel Statler, New York, October 30, 1950), 7, 9–10.

For examples of corporate managers and conservative organizations issuing political communications to shareholders, see Phillips-Fein, *Invisible Hands,* 10, 12, 53, 105, 110, 127, 163, 190, 194, 249.

8. Rob Aitken, *Performing Capital: Toward a Cultural Economy of Popular and Global Finance* (New York: Palgrave Macmillan, 2007), 16, 113–140; Janice Traflet, "'Own Your Own Share of American Business': Public Relations at the NYSE During the Cold War" at: www.thebhc.org/publications/BEHonline/2003/Traflet.pdf; G. Keith Funston, "Wanted: More Shareholders" (address at Harvard Business School, April 4, 1954), 39–40, box 7, Record Group 2-2, NYSE; NYSE, *Taxes, Equity Capital and Our Economic Challenges* (New York: New York Stock Exchange, 1953), 5, 20–21, 35.

9. New York Stock Exchange, *Jobs and Taxes* (New York: New York Stock Exchange, 1949), 1; Charles Gay, "The Woman Investor in a Changing World" (address before the Junior League of New York, New York, November 17, 1936), 1, box 4, Record Group 2-2 NYSE; New York Stock Exchange, *U.S. Economic Performance in a Global Perspective* (New York: NYSE, 1981), 5, 8; Charles Gay, "Broader Horizons" (address before the Buffalo Chamber of Commerce, Buffalo, N.Y., November 30, 1936), 3, box 4, Record Group 2-2, NYSE;

NYSE, *Taxes, Equity Capital and Our Economic Challenges*, 31; NYSE, *The Capital Needs and Savings Potential of the U.S. Economy* (New York: NYSE, 1974); NYSE, *Jobs and Taxes*, 9, 11, 25, 30–33, 38, 41–43, 50, 54; Emil Schram, "The Capital Gains Tax and the Postwar Economy" (address before the Bond Club of Philadelphia, Philadelphia, Pa., June 6, 1945), box 6, Record Group 2-2, NYSE; Emil Schram, "Informal Remarks" (at a dinner of the Chicago Association of Stock Exchange Firms, Chicago, Ill., January 12, 1942), 1–3, box 6, Record Group 2-2, NYSE; Emil Schram, "Testimony Before Ways and Means Committee" (Washington, D.C., March 20, 1942), 3–5, box 6, Record Group 2-2, NYSE; G. Keith Funston, "Paging Joe Public" (address before the St. Louis Chamber of Commerce, St. Louis, Mo., May 11, 1953), box 7, Record Group 2-2, NYSE; Emil Schram, untitled speech before the D.C. Bankers' Association, July 7, 1947, 7, box 6, Record Group 2-2, NYSE; Emil Schram, "Statement of Emil Schram before the U.S. Senate Finance Committee," August 7, 1942, 2, box 6, Record Group 2-2, NYSE; G. Keith Funston to the president, January 23, 1964, at http://c0403731.cdn.cloudfiles.rackspacecloud.com/collection/papers/1960/1964_0123_FunstonJohnsonT.pdf; NYSE, *The Dividend Tax Credit: Its Importance for Economic Growth* (New York: NYSE, 1956).

10. Marcus Nadler, *People's Capitalism* (New York: Hanover Bank, 1956); Louis O. Kelso and Mortimer Adler, *Capitalist Manifesto* (New York: Random House, 1958), 121; Peter Drucker, *The Unseen Revolution: How Pension Fund Socialism Came to America* (New York: Harper and Row, 1976), 199–204.

11. Adolf A. Berle Jr. and Gardiner C. Means, *The Modern Corporation and Private Property* (New York: 1932), 6–9, 352–357; E. Merrick Dodd, "For Whom Are Corporate Managers Trustees?" *Harvard Law Review* 35 (1932), 1145–1163; John Kenneth Galbraith, *The New Industrial State* (Boston: Houghton Mifflin Co., 1969); Gerald Davis, *Managed by the Markets: How Finance Reshaped America* (New York: Oxford University Press, 2009), 8–10; Bert Spector, "Business Responsibilities in a Divided World: The Cold War Roots of the Corporate Social Responsibility Movement," *Enterprise and Society* 9 (June 2008), 314–336; Karen Ho, *Liquidated: An Ethnography of Wall Street* (Durham, N.C.: Duke University Press, 2009), 3, 189–203; Milton Friedman, "The Social Responsibility of Business Is to Increase Profits," *New York Times Magazine*, September 13, 1970; Milton Friedman, *Capitalism and Freedom* (Chicago: University of Chicago Press, 1962), 132, 399; Friedrich A. von Hayek, "The Corporation in a Democratic Society: In Whose Interest Ought It and Will It Be Run?" in *Management and Corporations 1985*, ed. Melvin Ashen and George Leland Bach (New York: McGraw-Hill, 1960), 101–116; Eugene V. Rostow, "To Whom and for What Ends Are Corporate Managements Responsible?" in *The Corporation in Modern Society*, ed. Edward Mason (Cambridge: Harvard University Press, 1959), 65; Henry G. Manne, "Mergers and the Market for Corporate Control," *Journal of Political Economy* 73 (April 1965), 118.

12. Alice O'Connor, "Financing the Counterrevolution," in *Rightward Bound: Making America Conservative in the 1970s*, ed. Bruce Schulman and Julian Zelizer (Cambridge, Mass.: Harvard University Press, 2008); William E. Simon, *A Time for Reflection* (Washington, D.C.: Regnery, Latham, 2004); William E.

Simon, *Time for Action* (New York: Readers' Digest, 1980); J.A. Dorn, "Social Security: Continuing Crisis or Real Reform?" *Cato Journal* (Fall 1983), 337; George Gilder, *Wealth and Poverty* (New York: Basic Books, 1981), 106, 113; Irving Kristol, *Two Cheers for Capitalism* (New York: New American Library, 1978), 23, 146–150; Irving Kristol, "Why Big Business Is Good for America," in *Neoconservatism: The Autobiography of an Idea* (New York: 1999), 211–229; Milton Friedman, *Free to Choose* (San Diego: Harcourt Brace Javonovich, 1990), 66, 96, 104–106, 123–127.

13. William M. Batten, "The United States in a Competitive World" (address at the Conference on U.S. Competitiveness, Harvard University, Cambridge, Mass., April 25, 1980) at http://co403731.cdn.cloudfiles.rackspacecloud.com/collection/papers/1980/1980_0425_BattenCompetitiveT.pdf; William M. Batten, "The U.S. National Market System" (remarks at a EEC Symposium, Brussels, Belgium, November 13, 1980) at http://co403731.cdn.cloudfiles.rackspacecloud.com/collection/papers/1980/1980_1113_BattenEEC.pdf; George C. Dinsmore to George L. Hinman, undated, at http://co403731.cdn.cloudfiles.rackspacecloud.com/collection/papers/1970/1975_1101_DinsmoreHinman.pdf; Walter W. Stokes to George Hinman, November 7, 1975, at http://co403731.cdn.cloudfiles.rackspacecloud.com/collection/papers/1970/1975_1107_StokesHinman.pdf; Kim Phillips-Fein, *Invisible Hands*, 43, 243; John J. Phelan, "The Eighties May Be the Good New Days" (address at the Yale Club, New York, March 11, 1981), 1, 6–7, at http://co403731.cdn.cloudfiles.rackspacecloud.com/collection/papers/1980/1981_0311_PhelanEighties.pdf.

14. Ronald Reagan, "Written Response to Questions Submitted by the Soviet Newspaper *Izvestiya*" (December 3, 1987) at www.reagan.utexas.edu/archives/speeches/1987/120387e.htm; Ronald Reagan, "Remarks on Receiving the Report of the Presidential Task Force on Project Economic Justice" (August 3, 1987) at http://www.reagan.utexas.edu/archives/speeches/1987/080387a.htm.

15. Apart from Regan, key appointees included Michael Boskin, Martin Feldstein, and David Stockman. J. Craig Jenkins and Craig M. Eckert, "The Right Turn in Economic Policy: Business Elites and the New Conservative Economics," *Sociological Forum* 15 (2000), 321; Donald Regan, *For the Record* (San Diego: Harcourt Brace Jovanovich, 1988), 132–136; Donald Regan, *A View from the Street* (New York: New American Library, 1972), 115–120; Michael Boskin, *Crisis in Social Security* (San Francisco: Institute for Contemporary Studies, 1978); Martin Feldstein and Robert Barro, "The Impact of Social Security on Private Saving" (Washington, D.C.: American Enterprise Institute, 1978); David Stockman, *The Triumph of Politics: How the Reagan Revolution Failed* (New York: Harper and Row, 1986), 181–192; SEC Transition Team, "Final Report" (December 22, 1980), I-2-I-7 at http://co403731.cdn.cloudfiles.rackspacecloud.com/collection/papers/1980/1980_1222_SECTransition_1.pdf.

16. Sylvester J. Schieber and John B. Shoven, *The Real Deal: The History and Future of Social Security* (New Haven: Yale University Press), 11, 70, 127, 266–267, 272–273, 280–288, 310, 318, 323–326, 346–354, 360–365, 379–380, Robin Blackburn, *Banking on Death or Investing in Life: The History and*

Future of Pensions (London: Verso, 2004), 229–361, 379–410; "Remarks of U.S. Senator Barack Obama at the Knox College Commencement" (Saturday, June 4, 2005) at obama.senate.gov/speech/050604-remarks_of_us_senator_barack_o/print.php.

Candidate Obama favored policies to increase the incidence of investment, including automatic IRA and 401(k) enrollment in workplaces and matching incentives for individual retirement accounts. In 2007, Obama looked to shareholders to purify corporate culture when he introduced legislation that would grant them advisory votes on executive pay packages.

17. Davis, *Managed by the Market*, 132.
18. Mary O'Sullivan, *Contests for Corporate Control: Corporate Governance and Economic Performance in the United States and Germany* (New York: Oxford University Press, 2000), 155–161; William Lazonick and Mary O'Sullivan, "American Corporate Finance" in *Competitiveness Matters: Industry and Economic Performance in the U.S.*, ed. Candace Howes and Ajit Singh (Ann Arbor: University of Michigan Press, 2000), 118; Dirk Zorn, Frank Dobbin, Julian Dierkes, and Man-Shan Kwok, "Managing Investors: How Financial Markets Reshaped the American Firm," in *Sociology of Financial Markets*, ed. Karin Knorr-Cetina and Alex Preda (New York: Oxford University Press, 2005), 274; Gerald F. Davis, "A New Finance Capitalism? Mutual Funds and Ownership Re-Concentration in the United States," *European Management Review* 5 (2008), 12, 15; Davis, *Managed by the Market*, 213.
19. Michael Jensen, "Agency Costs of Free Cash Flow, Corporate Finance and Take-overs," *American Economic Review* 76 (1986), 323–329; Michael C. Jensen and William H. Meckling, "Theory of the Firm: Managerial Behavior, Agency Costs and Ownership Structure," *Journal of Financial Economics* 3 (1976), 305–360; William Lazonick, *Sustainable Prosperity in the New Economy?: Business Organization and High-Tech Employment in the United States* (Kalamazoo, Mich.: W. E. Upjohn Institute for Employment Research, 2009); John C. Coffee, "A Theory of Corporate Scandals: Why the USA and Europe Differ," *Oxford Review of Economic Policy* 21, no. 2 (2005), 202–203; Lazonick and O'Sullivan, "American Corporate Finance," 117–118; O'Sullivan, *Contests for Corporate Control*, 161–188; Neil Fligstein, *The Architecture of Markets*, 147–166; Adam Harmes, "Institutional Investors and the Reproduction of Neoliberalism," *Review of International Political Economy* 5 (1998): 92–121; Davis, *Managed by the Market*, 22, 44–52, 181–199; John C. Coffee, "A Theory of Corporate Scandals," *Oxford Review of Economic Policy* 21 (2005), 198–212.

Tax code changes in the 1990s accelerated the trend toward stock-based compensation. Mitchell, *Speculation Economy*, 277.

20. Donald MacKenzie, "An Equation and Its Worlds: Bricolage, Exemplars, Disunity and Performativity," *Social Studies of Science* 33 (December 2003), 831–868; Thomas Ferguson and Robert Johnson, "Too Big to Bail Part I," *International Journal of Political Economy* 38 (Spring 2009), 16; Michael Greenberger, "Out of the Black Hole: Regulatory Reform of the Over-the-Counter Derivatives Markets" at http://www.rooseveltinstitute.org/sites/all/files/OTC%20Derivatives.pdf; www.bis.org/publ/qtrpdf/r_qa0809.pdf#page=103.

21. Holly Brubach, "Spitzer's Justice," *Vanity Fair*, January 2005; Mary O'Sullivan, "What Opportunity Is Knocking? Regulating Corporate Governance in the United States," in *Government and Markets: Towards a New Theory of Regulation*, ed. Edward Balleisen and David Moss (New York: Cambridge University Press, 2009), 335–362; Cioffi and Hopner, "The Political Paradox of Finance Capitalism."

22. Lawrence Summers, Alan Greenspan, Arthur Levitt, William Ranier, *Over-the-Counter Derivatives Markets and the Commodity Exchange Act: Report of the President's Working Group on Financial Markets* (November 1999) at http://www.ustreas.gov/press/releases/reports/otcact.pdf; Peter S. Goodman, "Taking a Hard New Look at the Greenspan Legacy," *NYT* October 9, 2008, B9; James K. Galbraith, "The Great Crisis and the American Response," *Levy Economic Institute, Public Policy Brief* 112 (2010); Andrew Glyn, *Capitalism Unleashed: Finance, Globalization, and Welfare* (New York: Oxford University Press, 2006), 54–65; Robin Blackburn, "The Subprime Crisis," *New Left Review* 50 (2008); Roger Lowenstein, "Triple A Failure," *New York Times Magazine*, April 27, 2008, 36–41; Ferguson and Johnson, "Too Big to Bail Part I," 8, 12–13, 18–20.

23. Galbraith, "The Great Crisis and the American Response"; Ferguson and Johnson, "Too Big to Bail Part I," 7; Thomas Ferguson and Robert Johnson, "Too Big to Bail Part II," *International Journal of Political Economy* 38 (Summer 2009), 28; Timothy Geithner, "Remarks by Treasury Secretary Timothy Geithner Introducing the Financial Stability Plan" (February 10, 2009) at http://www.ustreas.gov/press/releases/tg18.htm; Geithner quoted in Paul Krugman, "Financial Policy Despair," *NYT* March 22, 2009; http://money.cnn.com/news/storysupplement/economy/bailouttracker/.

24. Neil Fligstein, "Politics, the Reorganization of the Economy, and Income Inequality, 1980–2009," *Politics & Society* 38 (May 2010), 233–242; Glyn, *Capitalism Unleashed*, 138, 170.

25. In 1916, the top 100,000 earners who filed tax returns in the United States (0.4% of households) received 78.0% of all declared corporate dividends. In 1928, the top 100,000 earners (0.3% of households) received 54.2% of declared corporate dividends. Gardiner Means, "Diffusion of Stock Ownership in the United States," *QJE* 44 (1930), 561–600.

The percentage of dividends received by the top 1% of earners fell over the first half of the twentieth century, but has always remained above 50% (high of 74.1% in 1919, low of 50.9% in 1946). Edwin Burk Cox, *Trends in the Distribution of Stock Ownership* (Philadelphia: University of Pennsylvania Press, 1963), 118–120; Twentieth Century Fund, *The Securities Markets* (New York: The Fund, 1935), 60, 736–737.

In 2005, the median household income of equity investors was $65,000, with median household financial assets of $125,000 (with $65,000 or 55% of household financial assets held in equities). This compares to a nationwide median household income of $43,200, median family net worth of $93,100, and median financial assets of $29,800 in 2004. Investment Company Institute and Securities Industry Association, *Equity Ownership in America, 2005*

(New York: Investment Company Institute and Securities Industry Association, 2005), 5; Brian K. Bucks, Arthur B. Kennickell, Kevin B. Moore, "Recent Changes in U.S. Family Finances: Evidence from the 2001 and 2004 Survey of Consumer Finances," *Federal Reserve Bulletin* (Washington, D.C.: GPO, 2006), A5, A8, A12.

In 2008, the median household income for mutual fund investors was $80,000, with median household financial assets of $200,000. Investment Company Institute, *Factbook* (New York: Investment Company Institute, 2009), 73.

Institutional investors only very rarely attempt to influence corporate executives, preferring to liquidate investments rather than to attempt activism. Davis, "A New Finance Capitalism?" 12, 14, 15.

Acknowledgments

These acknowledgments can only begin to express my gratitude to all those who contributed to this book in so many ways. It is as much a product of their generosity as it is an assemblage of evidence that I collected from musty manuscripts and rescued from recalcitrant microfilm.

This book received much-needed, much-appreciated financial support from many sources. Major awards included a Whitebox Advisors Doctoral Fellowship in Behavioral Finance from Yale School of Management's International Center for Finance, the John E. Rovensky Dissertation Fellowship in American Economic and Business History, a Miller Center Fellowship in Contemporary History, Politics, and Policy at the University of Virginia, and a Gilder Lehrman Institute Doctoral Fellowship. This project could not have been completed without a Visiting Scholar Fellowship awarded by the Russell Sage Foundation. Other funding included travel grants from the Business History Conference and the Social Science History Association, as well as short-term research grants from the Hagley Museum and Library, the New-York Historical Society, the Program in Early American Economics and Society at the Library Company of Philadelphia, an Andrew W. Mellon fellowship at the Massachusetts Historical Society, an Alfred D. Chandler grant from Harvard Business School, and the Mellon Seminar in Gender Studies at the Radcliffe Institute (under the direction of Nancy F. Cott).

I relied tremendously upon the assistance and institutional knowledge of archivists and librarians at Yale, Columbia, the New York Stock Exchange, Harvard, Princeton, the National Archives, the Library of Congress, the Smithsonian's National Museum of American History, the Library Company of Philadelphia, the Historical Society of Pennsylvania, and the New York Public Library. I especially thank Laura Linard and her efficient, knowledgeable staff at Baker Library (Harvard Business School), Franklin Noll at the Treasury Department's Bureau of Engraving and Printing, and Steven Wheeler, Janet Linde, and their excellent staff at the NYSE Archives (who lent plenty of cheer, time, and space). NYSE Group, Inc. reserves all rights to all the materials cited in this book from the NYSE Archives. Please see http://www.nyse.com/about/history/1089312755484.html for up-to-date information about the history of the New York Stock Exchange.

I extend my deep gratitude to Leoni Dalmau, Evan Daniel, Jordan Somers, Geoff Traugh, Amanda Zadorian, and Daniel Kressel for their excellent research assistance and their tremendous organizational skills. Claire Gabriel, Katie Winograd, Alexsa Rosa, and Galo Falchettore at the Russell Sage Foundation provided precious assistance during my tenure as a Visiting Scholar. Truly, I could not have completed this project without their aid.

During my many research excursions, friends old and new offered couches, meals, and good company: Kara and Kevin Smith, Rachel Baden, Michael Finegold, Mark Herman, Anna Horner, Claire and Joshua Nelson, Tina LaRoche, John Ott, Rachel Seher, Marissa Greif, and, most of all, Brad and Kate Abruzzi. One of the greatest joys of this intellectual journey has been all the new friends and intellectual partners-in-crime that I discovered along the way. I thank especially Michael Jo, Rebecca Rix, Rebecca Davis, Serena Mayeri, Bethany Moreton, Dan Levinson-Wilk, Louis Hyman, Brian Luskey, Kim Phillips-Fein, the 2005–2006 Miller Center fellows, and the 2009–2010 cohort of Visiting Scholars at the Russell Sage Foundation. Their contributions and camaraderie sustained me. For selfless assistance extended over so many years, I thank Jennifer Klein, William Goetzmann, and Beverly Gage. To Jean-Christophe Agnew I extend my deep gratitude for his wise counsel, unflagging support, brilliant interjections, and, most of all, his example.

As I struggled to reshape a research project into a book, I accrued substantial intellectual debts to those who provided invaluable criticism, especially members of the Business History Conference, the Initiative for Historical Social Sciences at the State University of New York at Stony Brook, the Committee on Historical Studies and Economics Department at the New School, the Financial History Seminar at New York University's Stern School of Business, the Market Cultures NYC work-in-progress group, the Tobin Project, the Political Economy of Modern Capitalism Seminar at Harvard University, and the Miller Center for Public Affairs at the University of Virginia. Meg Jacobs, Barbara Welke, Sven Beckert, Paul Gootenberg, Richard Sylla, Mark Rose, Ajay Mehrotra, and Brian Balogh all deserve particular acknowledgment for their generosity and their insight. So, too, do the reviewers and editorial staff at the *Journal of American History*, where portions of this book appeared in article form (Julia Cathleen Ott, "The Free and Open People's Market: Political Ideology and Retail Brokerage at the New York Stock Exchange, 1913–1933," *Journal of American History* 96 (June 2009), 44–71).

I chose Harvard University Press because of Joyce Seltzer's reputation for improving her authors' writing and subjecting them to the most rigorous scholarly criticism. She has thoroughly exceeded my expectations. Jeannette Estruth and the anonymous readers for Harvard University Press (including Kenneth Lipartito and Edward Balleisen, who revealed themselves) also deserve credit for making the publication process so exceedingly fruitful for me. Many thanks to each of them.

My beloved family surely tired of the indeterminacy of this project, but they never failed to convey enthusiasm, lend good cheer, and muster every possible means of support. Thank you, Cathie, Bill, Dick, Kathy, Thomas, Mary Catherine, Maggie, Rob, Tina, John, and Bibi. Lydia Catherine, Cecily Burrow, and Cora Belle provided focus, joy, love, meaning, and perspective in ways I never imagined possible.

Richard Vermillion has earned my deepest gratitude, far beyond what words could ever express. Because he sustained me every time I lost faith. Because he endured an endless succession of deadlines and shouldered more than his fair share of late nights and early mornings—and he still brought me my coffee. Because he respects me too much to agree with me all the time. Because he loves our life and makes sure that I enjoy it. Because he makes my dreams our dreams.

I dedicate this book to Richard and to our daughters. I love them dearly.

Index